C0-DKL-898

18

TALIBANISATION OF PAKISTAN
From 9/11 to 26/11 and Beyond

TALIBANISATION OF PAKISTAN

From 9/11 to 26/11 and Beyond

Amir Mir

Foreword by
Khaled Ahmed
Writer and Political Analyst

PENTAGON SECURITY
INTERNATIONAL
AN IMPRINT OF PENTAGON PRESS

Talibanisation of Pakistan: From 9/11 to 26/11 and Beyond / Amir Mir

ISBN 978-81-8274-470-7

First Edition 2009
Second Revised Edition 2010

Published by

PENTAGON SECURITY INTERNATIONAL
An Imprint of
PENTAGON PRESS
206, Peacock Lane, Shahpur Jat, New Delhi-110049
Phones: 011-64706243, 26491568
Telefax: 011-26490600
email: rajan@pentagon-press.in
website: www.pentagon-press.in

Printed at
Syndicate Binders, A-20, Hosiery Complex, Phase II, Noida-201305.

I dedicate this book to
former Pakistani Prime Minister Ms Benazir Bhutto who
laid down her life while struggling against the forces of
extremism and dictatorship in her pursuit to make
Pakistan a modern and secular state, as envisioned
by the founder of the nation,
Mohammad Ali Jinnah

Foreword

Amir Mir's book "*Talibanisation of Pakistan: From 9/11 to 26/11 and Beyond*" is actually a story of Pakistan's "non-state actors" inducted into state-organised jehad that predated the process of *Talibanisation* under the *Tehrik-e-Taliban Pakistan* (TTP). It also makes clear the fact that *Talibanisation* was not something imported from abroad through *Al-Qaeda*, but a sequel of the process of Islamisation of Pakistan starting from the 1980s under President General Zia ul Haq, the third military dictator who ruled Pakistan for ten long years [September 1978 – 17 August 1988].

Pakistan has become what it has because of the consequences of two covert wars it took part in. The first war, under General Zia ul Haq, was against the Soviet Union in Afghanistan from 1980 to 1988; and the second was the civil war in Afghanistan and jehad in the Indian-administered Kashmir from 1990 to approximately 2001. The first blowback from the Afghan war brought about internal change in the shape of the creation of new centres of power. Certain sections of the Pakistan Army that handled the Afghan 'jehad' became more influential by reason of the spread of their power within civilian institutions[1]. Because of the instrumentalisation of Islam, the state began to lose a larger measure of internal sovereignty than was justified by the prosecution of Afghan jehad through non-state actors. The political process suffered the consequences of this blowback when it returned after the death of General Zia ul Haq on 17 August 1988 in a mysterious plane crash.

The chaos that characterised the 1990s can only be understood in the context of the first blowback. The disorder of the post-2001 period can be understood in the context of the second blowback of the Afghan civil war and the jehad in Kashmir. The decade of the 1990s saw the weakening of the political process because of the internal sovereignty waived in favour of the non-state actors training in Afghanistan and fighting in Kashmir. Ironically, the decade also saw the weakening of the military leadership in Pakistan because army chiefs began to be selected on the basis of promotions meant to sideline officers fired with the passion of holy war. Although the Pakistan army was not directly involved in fighting a war, a large number of its officers were 'contaminated' by the 'Islamic warrior' image of the Afghan *mujahideen*. At least two former director generals of the Pakistani Inter Services Intelligence (ISI) were reverse-indoctrinated into the paranoid worldview of, first, Gulbaddin Hekmatyar, the chief of *Hizb-e-Islami Afghanistan* and then the *ameer* of the Afghan Taliban Mullah Mohammad Omar.

The jehad in Afghanistan and the Indian-administered Jammu & Kashmir was covert warfare. Most of its effect on Pakistani civil society went unrecorded. Due to the weakness of the political process in the face of jehad, massive public indoctrination in favour of private warriors was allowed to go unchallenged. Impunity from prosecution under the Pakistan Penal Code (PPC) offered to the jehadi organisations by the ISI added fear to indoctrination to achieve a massive brainwash that merged with the mission statement of Pakistani nationalism as it evolved after 1947. Surrender of internal sovereignty to the private warriors led to a steep fall in the quality of law and order in the country even as Islam was used as a de-legitimising force in national politics. Youth from all strata of society joined the jehad, took guerrilla training in the camps run by the jehadi organisations funded with Arab money, and swelled the ranks of those that challenged the state's credentials. Society fell back to the tribalism it had partially grown out of in the years when the state still enjoyed internal sovereignty and was able to enforce the municipal law uniformly.

Pakistan's fourth military dictator General Pervez Musharraf was elevated to his rank as the Chief of Army Staff Prime Minister Nawaz Sharif, who had in the past supported the Islamist officers in the army, but who had grown to fear the de-legitimising nature of their faith. General Musharraf was like the past chiefs who had suffered because of the mismatch between their worldview and the Islamist mind nurtured in the Pakistan army, especially under General Zia ul Haq. When time came to change the jehad (read foreign policy) paradigm, his job of 'the great repudiator' was rendered difficult by the Islamist army officers who flanked him and by a society, which was by now deeply influenced by the rhetoric of jehad.

The rule of General Pervez Musharraf was the era of Pakistan's second blowback. The most lethal aspect of the second blowback is the public mind. The state of denial about what actually transpired in the decade of the 1990s has become a part of the new trans-national feeling among the Pakistanis. Deep alienation, with the West in general and the United States in particular, has made the task of disabusing the collective consciousness of the fantasy of jehad difficult and dangerous.

Therefore, Pakistan is today facing the consequences of what it did in the 1990s. As Pakistan moves into the turbulence of a global economic downturn, three invasive discourses cause diversions and distortions. The world outside thinks Pakistan has become a centre of international terrorism. It is ground zero for the West in the hunt for *Al-Qaeda* and its fugitive leader, Osama bin Laden. Inside Pakistan, there is an opposed people's narrative, starting with a protest against the definition of terrorism and ending with a pledge of confrontation with the West. The third narrative is an India-driven narrative which serves to delay any reconciliation between the other two clashing narratives.

The External Narrative is typically information-based. Its knowledge of *Al-Qaeda* is comprehensive enough to enlist the support of the masses of America and the European Union. Information gathered from the Arab secret services, journalistic inquiry and confessional material from *Al-Qaeda* agents caught by America, enables the West to know more about the penetration of Pakistan by *Al-Qaeda* than Pakistanis do. Western observers at times find it quite shocking that Pakistanis don't even know the names of their own jehadi organisations active in the region.

The second narrative of Pakistan is the Civil Society Narrative based on people's perception of *Al-Qaeda* and America. It is typically based on ideology rather than facts. It denies the way the non-Muslim world has defined terrorism and activities of *Al-Qaeda*. It is a counter-version of what transpired on 9/11 and has no knowledge about the origins and development of *Al-Qaeda* as an organisation.

The third narrative is the Nationalist Narrative that is purely India-driven and is supported by the Pakistan army. It diverts the West-induced threat to the security of Pakistan from *Al-Qaeda* to the traditional threat from India. It is here that a meeting of the minds between at least one institution of the state and civil society at large comes into being. It sees the presence of India and its intelligence services in Afghanistan as a threat to the security of Pakistan. It points to India's interference in Baluchistan as an example. The moment the state of Pakistan puts abroad this new angle of threat, it unconsciously destroys the justification for looking at *Al-Qaeda* as a threat. The state institutions under this narrative seem to become divided in their approach.

The three clashing and merging narratives, therefore, cause upheaval in Pakistan today. They are like the end-of-the-world theorems, and Pakistan must choose one of them to perform the act of dying as a state. There are secondary diversionary sources of disorder too, like the lawyers' movement, which simply tend to exacerbate the conflict. Hurt by the steep economic downturn, the people of Pakistan are hardly able to accept the state as a benign entity. The state and *Al-Qaeda* rival each other for the status of enemy. And the state seems to be losing out all the time.

The account given by Amir Mir in this book is about the split nature of the state of Pakistan as it lives under the sway of these three narratives. Did the state in Islamabad kill Benazir Bhutto or did the *Al-Qaeda* warlord Baitullah Mehsud located in South Waziristan? If the answer is "both" then we are on to a very uncertain base of inquiry. Increasingly, this is what people point to when they ask: Was Baitullah a genuine rebel from the state or was he functioning fully or partially in concert with the state? There is so much past jurisprudence which points to a possible area of collaboration that it is possible to talk persuasively about it.

Amir Mir has brought together a lot of material in his book which points mysteriously and not so mysteriously – "if I am killed, hold General Musharraf responsible" – to the possibility of a "split" state acting under a schizoid pathology. This kind of work was needed in Pakistan, although the common reader might be offended by this book because he too, like the Pakistani press, has internalised the surrender of internal sovereignty to the jehadi militias during the 1990s.

By restricting itself to the study of the jehadi organisations located inside Pakistan – and all of them non-Pushtun with the exception of the *Tehrik-e-Taliban Pakistan* – the book correctly focuses on the role played by Pakistan in organising the rudiments of the process called *Talibanisation* before it was transferred into the hands of the TTP *ameer* Commander Baitullah Mehsud and his patron, *Al-Qaeda*.

When the state decided in 2009 to separate itself from the process, the non-state actors it had raised decided to go over to the Taliban. With them went – as if uprooted by the momentum of change – some elements of the state establishment, too.[2] Some left the establishment and raised the standard of revolt from behind their NGO covers, some took to crime on behalf of the Taliban and their warlords, and some, more dangerously, remain embedded inside the guts of the state.[3]

Talibanisation is usually linked to the Taliban and the Taliban are somehow linked to Afghanistan as if they had caught the disease of hard Islam from there. The Afghans have complained in vain that Afghanistan had actually caught the disease from the religious seminaries of Pakistan where their Taliban leaders were trained. This complaint is credible because during the jehad against the Soviet Union, the *mujahideen* did not practice precisely the Islam that was later imposed in Afghanistan and Pakistan.

The seminaries of Pakistan began absorbing Saudi funds and *Wahabi* creed during the 1980s when a kind of Arab-Iran war was relocated into Pakistan through state institutions and through the seminaries.[4] A complete dominance of hard Islam in Pakistan was postponed till after the withdrawal of the Soviet forces from Afghanistan. The decade of the 1990s is therefore the period in which the process of *Talibanisation* was begun with a full consciousness of what it would entail by those who allowed it.

I hope an ISI officer who used to call on me in my consultant editor's room in Lahore in those days will recall how he praised the work the *Lashkar-e-Toiba* (LeT) was doing in the Pakistani-administered Azad Kashmir. He was an innocent young brigadier whose gratitude for the *Lashkar's* incursions into the Indian-administered Jammu & Kashmir was genuine. If that ISI officer is still around, he will be bemused by what turn the policy to field the LeT as Pakistan's non-state actor proxy has taken in 2009 [in the wake of the Indian allegations that it was accused of masterminding the 26/11 terrorist attacks in Mumbai. But the *Lashkar-e-Toiba* is a *Wahabi* or, less offensively, an *Ahl-e-Hadith* outfit. Its rise and dominance are owed to the unwavering patronage of the state, which is why it can't be proceeded against in any credible way now that it is banned even in its second incarnation as *Jamaatul Daawa* (JuD).

The mother of all jehadi organisations in Pakistan, however, is the *Sipah-e-Sahaba Pakistan,* (SSP or the Corps of Prophet Mohammad's Companions) the central nerve of *Talibanisation* that joins all *Deobandis* in the overt support to acts of terrorism and covert support to acts of *Shia*-killing on the side. I had thought that *Sipah-e-Sahaba* was an organisation the Pakistani state no longer stomached by the end of the 1990s because it killed the *Shia* and offended Iran. But I was shocked as late as 2006 when the ISI facilitated a grand congregation of the SSP in Islamabad under the very nose of a "liberal" General Pervez Musharraf. He was to be brought down the very next year by his hubris vis-à-vis the Supreme Court of Pakistan but, more poignantly, by his assault on the very *Lal Masjid* in Islamabad from where the *Sipah-e-Sahaba Pakistan* had organised the grand rally[5] on 7 April 2006.

To tell the truth, the temperament of the state of Pakistan has been determined by its extremely inflexible "mission statement" of making India cough up Kashmir. It cannot live in peace with India unless it can force a many-times-stronger India to surrender Kashmir to it. It wrote up textbooks that made permanent the "painful birth" narrative of Partition and the ethnic cleansing that accompanied it. The *homo pakistanicus* has grown up hating India as part of his nationalism and looked at regional peace as a ruse to yield hegemony to India. After fighting wars with India with predictable results, Pakistan has developed a negative nationalism akin to the Serbs of the Balkans who sang songs of their defeat at the hands of the Turks. And Pakistan yielded paramountcy to the army as an adjunct of its nationalism.

The recent defeat - in the shape of loss of internal sovereignty and territory to the very non-state actors it nurtured against India – may have lessons that can no longer be ignored. Perhaps Pakistan is finally ready to learn from its defeats. Victory teaches nothing; but Pakistan also rebuffs self-knowledge that comes from defeat. It can learn from how India suddenly gave up projecting its power into Sri Lanka riding on the Tamil minority that Sri Lanka shared with India. It can stop repeating the fiasco of riding the Pushtuns into Kabul when the NATO-US forces quit Afghanistan, leaving a power vacuum behind.

Pakistan can learn from Sri Lanka too. It can normalise its relations with India in order to face up more realistically to the terrorist threat from the very non-state actors it once prepared for a low-intensity epochal conflict with India. Sri Lanka is finally rid of the Liberation Tigers of Tamil Eelam [following the May 2009 defeat of the separatist organization by the Sri Lankan Army] because of its careful nurturing of relations with India.

Pakistan has a geopolitical dividend it can realise if it goes back to being a tolerant terrain for international trade routes. Unless it changes it identity – and it doesn't have to do that by renouncing Islam – of a revisionist state, it has probably run out its course as a state. As a nuclear power it has more chances than any other small state of South Asia of having the peaceful conditions it needs to rise as an economic power. And once its economy gets going, it can easily get rid of its non-state actors.

March 2010 **Khaled Ahmed**

ENDNOTES

1. Although the Inter-Services Intelligence (ISI) officers were drawn from the army, their role at the battlefront and their financial autonomy delinked them from the army. Their ability to 'get things done' in the enemy territory as well as within Pakistan changed their view of the army. Under General Zia, the ISI virtually ran the country internally as well as its foreign policy. In 1990, the ISI officers were caught trying to overthrow their own prime minister. After being sacked from the army, they were inducted into the civilian Intelligence Bureau (IB). COAS General Asif Nawaz had to confront the IB as his rival. He complained to the President that he was being threatened by the IB. Similar confrontation was at one time reported between the Military Intelligence (MI) and the ISI. It was in fact a confrontation between the 'warrior' officers in the ISI and the 'professional' COAS. The IB was able to induct a 'religious warrior' general into the ISI as its chief. A retired ISI chief, who had missed becoming COAS, dared the army chief to take action against him for making statements against the 'secularisation' of the army. The most symbolic incident was the sabotage of a decision taken during the Afghan war by the COAS, together with the president and the PM, by a retired ISI chief.

2. *Daily Times*, 4 August 2009, Army majors arrested for collaborating with terrorists: Elements in the intelligence agencies who were sympathetic towards terrorists had resigned and had been arrested, a private TV channel quoted Interior Minister Rehman Malik, adding they were officers of the rank of major and wanted to target army generals.

3. It is common knowledge in Pakistan that some operatives found guilty of doubtful acts of omission and commission, have been allowed to function on contracts after retirement. Some retired intelligence officers have started speaking out in public too.

4. Qasim Zaman, *The Ulema in Contemporary Islam: Custodians of Change*, Princeton University Press, 2002. p.176. Author Zaman mentions the efforts made by the *Deobandi* scholars in Pakistan to attract Saudi patronage in the form of money and training. He makes reference to a *Deobandi* seminary in Kohat in the NWFP which actually publicised the fact that it had "formulated its goals in accordance with not only those of the other *Deobandi madrassas* of Pakistan and India but also with those of the Islamic University of Madina and the Islamic Institute of Doha, Qatar.

5. Human Rights Commission of Pakistan (HRCP) handout of 10 April 2006: the banned *Sipah Sahaba* held its rally in Islamabad presumably with the approval of the administration. The Friday rally preached jehad and sectarianism. Its activists distributed anti-*Shia* literature and VCDs showing the killing of American soldiers in Iraq. The police stood aside and watched, despite the fact that literature being distributed was against the law, as the *Sipah Sahaba* speakers thanked the Islamabad administration for letting them stage the rally.

Preface

"Talibanisation of Pakistan: From 9/11 to 26/11 and Beyond" – is a blend of information and analyses of the post-9/11 state of militant Islam and the jehadi organisations in Pakistan, particularly in the aftermath of the 26/11 Mumbai terrorist attacks. It takes stock of present-day Pakistan, eight years after the 9/11 attacks in the US that shook the entire world. It notes that Pakistan, despite being a key American ally in the war against terror for years, continues to be plagued with the peril of the growing *Talibanisation*.

The book states that the dilemma Pakistan faces today is the blowback of the mighty military and intelligence establishment's policy of using the jehadi mafia to advance its geo-strategic agenda in the region. Yet, with the so-called strategic depth no longer in sight, Pakistan's own social fabric is at risk since *Al-Qaeda* and Taliban elements currently pose an existential threat to Pakistan itself. As the menace of the Islamic militancy spreads like a jungle fire across the country, the Taliban militia and the *Al-Qaeda* network keeps thriving by evolving a modus operandi that exploits its local affiliates - the Pakistani militant groups active in neighbouring India and Afghanistan - to pursue their global jehadi agenda.

I have tried my best to put together the published and unpublished facts about the Pakistani militant groups and their leaders, as well as their links with *Al-Qaeda* and Taliban and the role of the Pakistani intelligence agencies. I have attempted to produce a variety of information on the past and present of the jehadi groups, their historical roots, and a background of their leaders, in such a way that it creates a narrative to help the reader analyse the situation in present-day Pakistan.

Eight years after 9/11 and the subsequent launching of the war against terror, the swelling forces of extremism along the troubled Pak-Afghan border not only pose a grave threat to the US-led Allied Forces in Afghanistan but also to India and Pakistan. Despite the deployment of 80,000 Pakistani troops along the Pak-Afghan border to counter terrorism, the situation remains unstable in the rugged tribal region which is crucial to four key world capitals - Islamabad, New Delhi, Washington and Kabul. The extent of the threat can be gauged from the spreading influence of the militancy from the Federally Administered Tribal Areas (FATA) to the settled urban areas of Pakistan like Peshawar, Quetta, Lahore, Karachi, Rawalpindi and Islamabad.

With militancy and the extremist jehadi groups literally marching on the state; the Taliban forces are nowhere near defeated either in Pakistan or in Afghanistan. Senior Obama administration officials and the commanders of the NATO and the ISAF troops stationed in Afghanistan have accused the Pakistani military and intelligence establishment of pursuing a policy of running with the hare and hunting with the hound.

With the assumption of the White House by the Democrats, the Obama administration has stepped up drone attacks in the tribal areas of Pakistan besides intensifying pressure on Islamabad to do more in the war on terror, saying if there is one country that matters most to the future of *Al-Qaeda*, it is none other than Pakistan.

Amidst all these developments, Pakistan today faces a complex security situation which can have adverse spill-over effects for its neighbouring India and Afghanistan as well. The book takes off with the 26/11 Mumbai terror attacks, stating that the Indo-Pak relations, which appeared to be on course towards normalisation after return of civilian rule in Islamabad in the wake of the 2008 general elections, have touched rock bottom after the Mumbai mayhem, carried out by a group of ten *Lashkar-e-Toiba* operatives. The gory incident, which killed 175 people, came as a devastating blow to hard won Indo-Pak peace process. This attack drew international frenzy against the pro-Kashmir jehadi groups operating from Pakistani.

Besides profiling the lethal *Lashkar-e-Toiba* (LeT) and its founding *ameer* Hafiz Mohammad Saeed, the book brings to life the sketches of Zakiur Rehman Lakhvi, the chief operational commander of the LeT and the prime suspect in the 26/11 attacks and Mohammad Ajmal Kasab, the sole surviving Mumbai attacker. The motto jehad against India has been a defining feature in the life of Lakhvi, who is being tried by a Pakistani anti-terrorism court inside the high security Adiala Jail in Rawalpindi. While profiling Hafiz Saeed, the book states that for the LeT founder, 'killing infidels is a pious man's obligation and it is his duty to destroy the forces of evil and disbelief.' The book claims that the infrastructure and the leadership of the LeT continue to survive and morph into something that threatens both India and Pakistan.

The book then moves ahead to profile almost all the important militant groups in Pakistan which are either active in *Jammu & Kashmir* or in Afghanistan, besides exploring their clandestine links with the Pakistani intelligence agencies and the fugitive leadership of Taliban and *Al-Qaeda*. It states that long before the 9/11, which had prompted the US to launch its war on terror; India had been the only country accusing the ISI of fomenting terror in its neighbourhood. When the Pakistani establishment would dismiss these allegations, the global community would mostly accept this logic with the problem being confined to the Indo-Pak subcontinent. This perception, however, has changed drastically, considering the flood of charges from around the world against the ISI since the 26/11 attacks, in which several Americans and Jews were also killed.

The book states that while the Pakistani establishment under General (retd) Pervez Musharraf had been making overt noises about clamping down on the terrorist outfits, they had implemented only half-hearted measures against them a these outfits were considered by many in the Pakistani establishment as the civilian face of the Army.

The book then dwells upon why the decision-makers in the White House keep questioning Pakistan's role in the war against terror, adding that eights years after the 9/11 attacks, Islamabad's cooperation on terrorism continues to be under suspicion by the international community. The root of the problem seems to be the ambivalence of the Pakistani military and intelligence establishment vis-à-vis Islamic militants, and its failure to stop using terrorism as an instrument of state policy.

The book states that the religious and sectarian wars are not only being exported to other countries from the Pakistani soil, but they are being fought on the local turf as well, thereby threatening the very society that sustains them. Consequentially, highly-disciplined and motivated jehadi organisations continue to operate in almost every neighbourhood of Pakistan, creating new models of terror such as suicide bombers. With the aim of purging 'the land of the pure' of all those elements which are siding with the forces of the infidel, this new breed of human bombs strike not only Western and American targets, but also the civil and military society of Pakistan.

Consequently, in the aftermath of the bloody Operation Silence carried out against the fanatic clerics of *Lal Masjid* in the heart of Islamabad, Pakistan seems to have been turned into the suicide bombing capital of the world, with the security forces, especially the Army and the Police, frequently being targeted by lethal human bombs. Look at the casualty figures for the Pakistani security forces since then: over 1000 members of the armed forces, Frontier Constabulary and police had been killed by human bombs across Pakistan between 3 July 2007 [the day the Operation Silence was launched] and 31 December 2009. The operation, which ended up in the killing of hundreds of hundreds of people, including the commandos, terrorists, students and civilians, also dealt a serious blow to the decades-long mullah-military-militant nexus.

The book also takes stock of the tragic assassination of Pakistan's twice-elected former Pakistani Prime Minister Benazir Bhutto and raises the pertinent question as to 'who' actually orchestrated her murder and 'why.' Benazir herself was convinced that the most recent attempt on her life (carried out on 18 October 2007 on her welcome rally in Karachi) could not have been possible without the consent of General Musharraf. On 13 November 2007, hardly a few weeks before her murder, she told me in a one-on-one meeting in Lahore that General Pervez Musharraf should be named for her murder if she is assassinated.

The book states that despite having been tagged by the Musharraf regime as the mastermind of Benazir's assassination in Rawalpindi, the involvement of the slain *Tehrik-e-Taliban Pakistan* (TTP) *ameer* Commander Baitullah Mehsud in the murder seems dubious, keeping in view the TTP chief's own denials as well as Benazir Bhutto's declaration shortly before her death.

While Benazir had named in her posthumous book - *"Reconciliation: Islam, Democracy, and the West"* the *Harkatul Jehadul Islami* (HUJI) chief Qari Saifullah Akhtar as a key suspect in the bid to kill her in Karachi, upon her return home from exile, she had desired in her 20 October 2007 email to Wolf Blitzer of the *CNN* that General Musharraf should be named as her assassin in the event of her murder.

The book further states that the hijacking of an Indian airliner in 1999 that led to the release of Sheikh Ahmed Omar Saeed and Maulana Masood Azhar from an Indian jail was linked to the ISI because its Quetta-based officers talked to the hijackers on the wireless set at Kandahar. Masood Azhar then went on to attack the Parliament in New Delhi in 2001, three months after 9/11. A former ISI chief Lt Gen (retd) Javed Ashraf Qazi admitted on 6 March 2004 that the *Jaish-e-Mohammad* (JeM) was involved in the Indian Parliament assault.

The book states that for long considered a nursery for the global jehad, the *madrassa* system in Pakistan is closely linked to the country's so-called foreign policy objectives in Jammu & Kashmir and Afghanistan. The Pakistani religious seminaries or *madrassas* have been at the centre of the debate on extremism and radicalisation of society, which has intensified after Musharraf, had joined the US-led war on terror following the 9/11. However, it was only seven years later that the Operation Silence reinforced the Western notion about the Pakistani religious schools still being used as breeding grounds for Islamic militants and suicide bombers.

An interesting chapter on the infiltration of the Pakistani cricket team by the *Tableeghi Jamaat* (TJ) has been included. As a result, the team under captain, Inzamam ul Haq lost its playing ability to its obsession with preaching of Islam. The Pakistan Cricket team that was once known as a hot band of happy-go-lucky stars seems to have undergone a total transformation in the last decade, slowly turning into a coterie of preachers more interested in preaching Islam than concentrating on the game. The book states that concerns are being raised by the international media about how much the Islamic missionary organisation has been infiltrated by the jehadi elements which might be using the platform of the *Tableeghi Jamaat* (the party of preachers) as a cover to promote their violent jehadi agenda across the globe.

The last part of the book deals with the Pakistan government's ongoing efforts to nip the evil of *Talibanisation* through a massive military operation in the picturesque Swat valley of the NWFP. The book describes Pakistan as the new battleground for the US-led war on *Al-Qaeda* and Taliban-linked terrorists, a majority of whom are still hiding in the Pak-Afghan tribal belt, thus making the Waziristan region a prime target of the US-drone attacks. The book states that the country's Army Chief General Ashfaq Kayani has already declared that the tide in Swat had decisively been turned against the Taliban and his forces were now turning their attention towards the South Waziristan region where yet another military operation has already been launched. However, many security experts argue that counter-insurgency operations cannot be a one-time action, and it would be premature to conclude that the Swat militants will give up their fight altogether.

While Pakistani public opinion has largely turned against the *Al-Qaeda* and Taliban-linked militant organisations active in the NWFP and FATA regions, there are still large pockets of support in the country's military and intelligence establishment for the pro-Kashmir jehadi organisations. Although the Pakistani authorities had initiated military action against the *Tehrik-e-Taliban Pakistan* (TTP) and the *Tehrik-e-Nifaz-e-Shariat-e-Mohammadi* (TNSM), which had dared to target the security and intelligence agencies, some key Pakistani militant outfits which are active in Jammu & Kashmir simply escaped a concrete state action.

Despite the involvement of the *Lashkar-e-Toiba* in the 26/11 Mumbai attacks and the subsequent international pressure on Islamabad to act against the Pakistani jehadi elements behind the plot, barely a few cosmetic steps were taken to satisfy India. Despite repeated demands by New Delhi and frequent assurances by Islamabad to uproot the terrorist infrastructure from the Pakistani soil, no tangible action has so far been taken to dismantle the same. This is mainly due to the fact that the Pakistani military and intelligence establishment remains deeply embroiled with most of these jehadi proxies and continues to treat them as the civilian face of the Army. Therefore, neither Islamabad nor the wider region can hope for peace and stability unless the Pakistani establishment decides to abandon applying terrorism as an instrument of state policy to advance its so-called geo-strategic agenda in the region.

March 2010 **Amir Mir**

Gratitude

I extend my gratitude to my former editor and eminent writer and analyst, Mr. Khaled Ahmed, for having spared precious time to write the foreword of this book. At the same time, I am thankful to Pentagon Press, for taking interest in the project and ensuring quick publication of the book.

Contents

CHAPTER 1

Pakistan on the Verge of *Talibanisation*

Eight years after the 9/11 terror attacks in the United States that shook the entire world, Pakistan, despite being a key American ally in the so-called war against terror during all those years, is imperiled by growing *Talibanisation*. The Taliban are claiming new grounds and the *Al-Qaeda* network keeps thriving by evolving a *modus operandi* which exploits its local affiliates – the Pakistani militant groups active in Jammu & Kashmir and Afghanistan – to pursue their global jehadi agenda.

The meteoric rise of the Taliban militia in Pakistan since the 11 September 2001 attacks has literally pushed the Pakistani state to the brink of civil war. Since the US-led Allied Forces launched their offensive against *Al-Qaeda* and the Taliban in Afghanistan in the aftermath of the 9/11 episode, the leadership of the two non-state actors in the war-torn Afghanistan has been systematically moving fighters across their eastern border into Pakistan where they have taken over the rugged mountainous regions of the North West Frontier Province (NWFP) and the Federally Administered Tribal Areas (FATA) after joining hands with the local Taliban militia. The militants' choice of using the NWFP and the FATA regions as their hideout enabled them to build a new power base, separate from Afghanistan.

As the George Bush era [20 January 2001 to 20 January 2009] has already ended amidst an unending war against terror, the threat of Islamic militancy largely emanating from the Pak-Afghan tribal belt is spreading its tentacles across the globe. The swelling forces of extremism along the troubled Pak-Afghan border not only pose a grave threat to the US-led Allied Forces in Afghanistan but also to the people of Pakistan. Like their Afghan counterparts, Taliban militia in Pakistan, especially in the country's Federally Administered Tribal Areas, is doing whatever it can – from target killings to suicide bombings – to pressurising the government in Islamabad into conceding to their demands, especially the enforcement of their extremist version of Islamic *Shariah* (Islamic laws) in the country.

Despite the deployment of more than 80,000 Pakistani troops along the rugged Pak-Afghan border to counter *Al-Qaeda* and Taliban-linked militancy, the situation is far from stable in the trouble-stricken tribal region which is crucial to three world capitals – Islamabad, Washington and Kabul. Though the Musharraf regime [20 June 2001 to 18 August 2008] had aligned itself with the United States soon after the 9/11 attacks, only half-hearted steps were taken by the Pakistani establishment to dismantle the infrastructure of Islamic terrorism that was built up during the last two decades. This happened mainly because a commando president was ruling the roost in Pakistan during all those years. He deemed it fit like a typical South Asian military dictator to employ terrorism as an instrument of state policy both in Afghanistan and the Indian-administered Jammu & Kashmir, to advance the so-called geo-strategic agenda of the military establishment. So, with Islamic militancy gaining new grounds in the country and fanatic jehadis literally marching on the state, the Taliban nowhere near defeated either in Afghanistan or Pakistan; and the *Al-Qaeda* network still unbroken on both sides of the Pak-Afghan border, senior Obama administration officials and the commanders of the NATO and the ISAF troops stationed in Afghanistan are openly accusing the Pakistani establishment of pursuing a policy of running with the hare and hunting with the hounds.

Despite an eight-year long war against terror being fought by Washington with the help of Islamabad, a Pakistan-based Taliban movement, inspired by the former fanatic Taliban rulers of Afghanistan, keeps spreading in the Waziristan tribal region along the Pak-Afghan border, challenging the efforts of the Allied Forces to stamp out insurgents in Afghanistan and hunt down the Most Wanted FBI fugitives like Osama bin Laden and Mullah Mohammad Omar.

The trouble-ridden Waziristan is divided into two tribal agencies, North Waziristan and South Waziristan, with estimated populations of 361,246 and 429,841 respectively. The Waziristan region is historically known as the land that cannot easily be conquered or subjugated. It was an independent tribal territory since 1893, remaining outside of British-ruled Empire and Afghanistan. Even at that time, tribal raiding into British-ruled terrain was a constant problem for the Britons, requiring frequent punitive expeditions between 1860 and 1945. The region eventually became part of Pakistan in August 1947, at the time of its independence.

Making headlines in the international media since 2002 due to frequent clashes between the Pakistani security forces and the *Al-Qaeda* and Taliban-linked militants, South Waziristan Agency is largely under the control of the local Taliban, who are using it as a base to wage their resistance against the US-led Allied Forces stationed in Afghanistan. South Waziristan is the southern part of Waziristan, a mountainous region of Pakistan, bordering Afghanistan and covering some 11,585 square kilometers. South Waziristan is the most volatile tribal agency which has its district headquarters at Wana, and has three tribes – Wazir, Mahsud and Burki. North Waziristan's district capital is Miran Shah a.k.a Miramshah (or Mirumshah in the local dialect). The area is mostly inhabited by the Darwesh Khel (better known as Utmanzai Waziris, a majority of whom are related to Ahmedzai Waziris of South Waziristan), a sub-clan of the Wazir tribe (from which the region derives its name), who live in fortified mountain villages, including Razmak, Datta Khel, Spin wam, Dosali, Shawal and the Dawars (also known as Daurr or Daur).

The extent to which the danger of Islamic militancy has swelled in the country after the 9/11 attacks can be well gauged from its spread from the border to the urban areas of Pakistan – be it Peshawar, Quetta, Lahore, Karachi, Rawalpindi or Islamabad. After capturing much of the North West Frontier Province and the Federally Administered Tribal Areas, the Taliban and *Al-Qaeda*-linked jehadis have now clearly brought their war to Pakistani cities. The steady erosion of the state control in the regions that the Taliban militia has taken over is ominous. Having established their stronghold in the FATA and NWFP through violent means, the Taliban–*Al-Qaeda* blend has already activated its sleeper cells in the largest province – Punjab. Similarly, the country's urban heartland – the federal capital, Islamabad – and the garrison town of Rawalpindi, is under repeated terrorist attacks, mostly being carried out by human bombs. Searching new havens amid continuous US drone attacks on their strongholds in the Pakistani tribal belt, the Taliban militants are teaming up with local militant groups in the Punjab and Sindh provinces to push deeper into the country, in a bid to reduce Pakistan to the status of being a captive territory from where they can launch and sustain their worldwide jehadi agenda.

The intentions of the Pakistani jehadi mafia are evident from the 8 April 2009 statement of a senior Pakistani Taliban commander in Waziristan, Mullah Nazeer Ahmed. In an interview with *Al-Qaeda's* media arm, *Al-Sahab*, he had expressed the hope that the Taliban militia would soon capture Islamabad. "The day is not far when Islamabad will be in the hands of the *mujahideen*". Therefore, analysts believe the risk of *Talibanisation* is escalating rapidly primarily because of a new generation of highly charged and equally committed jehadis. As things stand, new militant leaders, new cadres and new groups are emerging while the jehadi old guard of the 1980 Afghan war vintage no longer enjoys the kind of hold and sway which they used to command, especially before the 9/11 terror attacks.

While these extremist elements might represent a minority view, their threat is real. Generally referred to as the Pakistani Taliban, the new militant leadership is a recent phenomenon. The original Taliban led by their *ameerul momineen* Mullah Mohammad Omar, who had ruled Afghanistan till 2001, were mostly the Afghan fighters and a product of the Soviet occupation of their homeland. They were fundamentally created and cultivated by the Pakistani Inter Services Intelligence (ISI). However, the newfangled generation of Islamic militants is all Pakistani which emerged after the US invasion of Afghanistan and represents a rebellion against the Pakistani military establishment's decision in 2001 to join hands with the United States in its war against terror.

The current leadership of the Pakistani Taliban militia is mostly led by young militants who, unlike the original Taliban, are technology- and media-savvy, and are influenced by various indigenous tribal nationalisms honouring the tribal codes that govern social life in Pakistani rural areas. The capacity of the Taliban militants to cause enormous deaths and destruction cannot be underestimated. The Taliban militia is virtually destroying anything that does not fall in line with their way of thinking. Although they share the same ideology as the Afghan Taliban, they are essentially Pakistani and aim at nothing less than cleansing Pakistan of all liberal and secular elements to turn it into a pure Islamic state by enforcing Islamic *Shariah* (Islamic Laws) there though the founding father of Pakistan Mohammad Ali Jinnah, had envisioned a secular and liberal Pakistan.

A common trait of the new Pakistani Taliban leadership is getting inspiration from the Afghan Taliban and openly calling them local Taliban. According to a 20 April 2009 research report prepared by a Washington-based US think tank – Council on Foreign Relations (CFR), – "*Talibanisation* of the Pakistani Pashtun belt is gradually moving eastward into settled districts, creating new terrorist safe havens in once-tranquil locales. If rapid *Talibanisation* of Pakistan continues, the next generation of the world's most sophisticated terrorists will be born, indoctrinated, and trained in that nuclear-armed nation. Today, *Al-Qaeda's* top leadership is most likely based in Pakistan, along with top Taliban leaders, both Afghan and Pakistani", said the 17-page CFR report "From Af-Pak to Pak-Af: A Response to the New US Strategy for South Asia".

In the post-9/11 period, the Bush administration kept describing the Pakistani military ruler President General Pervez Musharraf as the most trusted US ally in the war on terror. However, the seriousness with which the *khaki* dictator might have taken part in the terror war remained a debatable issue from day one. Most of the leading militant commanders now ruling the roost in FATA and NWFP regions are the products of the Musharraf period and had mushroomed after the 9/11 terror attacks with the blessings of the military and intelligence establishment working under Musharraf.

President Asif Zardari was the first civilian Pakistani leader to have admitted that these militants and extremists were created and nurtured by the military establishment to achieve some short-term tactical objectives in the neighbouring states of India and Afghanistan. "Let's be truthful to ourselves and make a candid admission of the realities. The terrorists of today were the heroes of yesteryears. But they began haunting Pakistan in the post-9/11 era", so said President Zardari on 7 July 2009 during an interactive meeting with senior civil servants at the presidency in Islamabad while discussing ways and means to contain the growing phenomenon of *Talibanisation* in the country.

Analysts say President Zardari might have good intentions but he hardly has the power and authority to do what he thinks or says what should be done about Jammu & Kashmir or terrorist groups. Take for instance, they say, the case of *Lashkar-e-Toiba* (LeT), the Pakistan-based jehadi group which had carried out the 26/11 Mumbai attacks. The Pakistan government had enough evidence to proceed against the group, unravel its infrastructure and put its leadership on trial. But the country's mighty military establishment opposed any such action.

President Asif Zardari's remarks came amid a massive military operation in the Swat district of the NWFP against the fanatic Taliban militants who used to project themselves in radio broadcasts and sermons as Islamic Robin Hoods, defending the rural poor from the Pakistani ruling elite which they used to describe as corrupt and oppressive and dancing to the American tune. Who are these Islamic Robin Hoods? The opening sentence of a 30 June 2008 *TIME* magazine report by Aryn Baker titled "Pakistan: Negligent on Terror", stated: "It's almost like a bad joke. A bus driver, a ski lift operator and a gym rat have turned the Islamic world's only nuclear-armed nation upside down".

Commander Baitullah Mehsud, a former trainer at a small time fitness centre in South Waziristan and the founding *ameer* of the *Tehrik-e-Taliban Pakistan* (TTP), Maulana Fazlullah, a former ski lift operator in Swat and the fugitive *ameer* of the *Tehrik-e-Nifaz-e-Shariat-e-Mohammadi* (TNSM) and Mangal Bagh, a former truck conductor and the absconding *ameer* of the *Lashkar-e-Islami* (LI), were regarded by their followers as the uncrowned kings of South Waziristan, the Swat Valley and the Khyber Agency, respectively before the Pakistan army was made to proceed against them in 2009. Aged between 30 and 35, the three Taliban and *Al-Qaeda*-linked jehadi commanders were young and had created ripples not only on the Pakistani side of the Afghan border due to their militant power and substantially large following but also rung alarm bells across the border in Afghanistan which was gradually coming under their growing influence.

Despite having been declared most wanted criminals for their involvement in deadly acts of terrorism, including suicide bombings targeting the security forces, neither the Musharraf regime nor the incumbent government in Islamabad had the guts to challenge them until April 2009 when the much-awaited military operation in Swat was launched. Both the governments had first resorted to army operations against the private armies of Baitullah, Fazlullah and Mangal, but had eventually decided to hold talks with them as a last resort with a view to strike peace deals in the trouble-stricken Waziristan, Swat and Khyber areas.

Before 9/11, the age span for these jehadi leaders would not have been beyond 23-27 years. Hardly five years ago, no one had even heard of these jehadi commanders. What actually happened then? It is largely believed they were groomed by the Pakistani military establishment to secure the Pakistani border with Afghanistan which it thought had become vulnerable following the fall of the Taliban regime in Kabul and the subsequent assumption of power by the pro-India and anti-Pakistan Northern Alliance. After 9/11, it had also become harder for the Pakistani establishment to use the already established and known jehadi groups in Afghanistan to advance its geo-strategic agenda in the region, and thus the Musharraf regime deemed it fit to create and nurture a new breed of jehadis.

Troubled by the astonishing resurgence of the Taliban militia in Afghanistan, relations between three strategic partners – Pakistan, US and Afghanistan – are already going through a critical phase. The international community and the Western media continue to portray Pakistan as a breeding ground for the Taliban militia and a sanctuary for the fugitive *Al-Qaeda* leaders. Despite repeated denials by the Pakistan government, the international media keeps reporting them having established significant bases in Peshawar and Quetta, the provincial capitals of the NWFP and *Baluchistan*, and carrying out cross-border ambushes against their targets in Afghanistan, while the *Al-Qaeda* suicide bombing teams target the US-led Allied Forces from their camps in the mountainous region.

According to Aryn Baker's 30 June 2008 *TIME* magazine report, the Taliban in Afghanistan had regrouped after their fall from power and coalesced into tough rebellion outfits finding sanctuary in the largely lawless tribal areas of Pakistan along the border. Hardly 24 hours before the report was published, former American Defence Secretary Robert Gates said that Pakistan was contributing to Afghanistan's instability by failing to prevent militants from crossing into the neighbouring Afghanistan to carry out attacks on the coalition forces. Earlier, on 10 June 2008, the US Joint Chiefs of Staff Chairman Admiral Michael Mullen had declared that any future terrorist attack against American interests would most likely be carried out by militants based in the Federally Administered Tribal Areas of Pakistan. "The tribal groups in FATA with ties to *Al-Qaeda* and Taliban represent the worst security threat to the US," he had observed.

Pakistan has received $10 billion in financial support as a key US ally in the war on terror since 9/11, mainly to hunt down the Most Wanted fugitive *Al-Qaeda* and Taliban operatives. However, the US military assistance to the Pakistan Army in combating terrorism has remained largely indirect. As the militant activity by the Taliban–*Al-Qaeda* combine continues to multiply, the decision makers in the Washington are becoming skeptical about the ability of the Pakistan Army and the will of its political leadership to fight out the Taliban and *Al-Qaeda* linked jehadi groups operating in the Pak-Afghan tribal region. But the Americans are not the only disappointed lot. The officials of the coalition force stationed in Afghanistan, too, have noticed a distinct pattern with cross-border strikes, saying the point of origin of the attacks [from Pakistan into Afghanistan] is routinely next to border posts of Pakistani Frontier Corps (FC).

"Either they are ignoring the fact that the Taliban are fighting within their areas or they are complicit," said a senior NATO commander in Kabul on 10 June 2008 while defending the death of 11 Pakistani soldiers in an American drone attack on a Pakistani military post in Mohmand Agency. The Pakistani soldiers were apparently fighting alongside the Taliban forces against the Northern Alliance troops and the American army units in the Pak-Afghan border area. "People are kidding themselves in Pakistan if they think they can solve their insurgency problem by sending it across the border," the NATO commander had observed.

Going by international media reports, talk in Washington after the installation of the Obama government indicates a rising concern with the ever-growing *Talibanisation* of Pakistan. These reports suggest that the American military might soon decide to assume a more direct role in the counter-terrorism campaign by allowing its commandos to stage 'hot pursuit' raids into the Pakistani tribal areas to stem mounting Taliban attacks against the US-led troops in Afghanistan and to disrupt the efforts of the resurgent *Al-Qaeda* operatives to map strikes against the United States. Some senior US intelligence officials had even stated that the threat of yet another 9/11-like terror attack on the American soil had been significantly enhanced by the growing cooperation between the local Taliban militants and international elements of *Al-Qaeda* which had taken root there.

Indeed, history seems to be repeating itself. The United States is experiencing exactly what the Soviet Union had in the 1980s while fighting against the Islamic *mujahideen* of those times. Today's 'Islamic terrorists' on both sides of the Pak-Afghan border, now giving sleepless nights to President Obama, are the '*mujahideen*' of the past who had been raised by the decision-makers in the White House to smoke out the Russian forces from Afghanistan. They are the very rebels who had been sustained by the same intelligence network that served as paymaster, quartermaster and taskmaster to the *mujahideen* during the so-called Afghan jehad – a conduit largely supervised by the Pakistani military and intelligence establishment during the General Zia-ul Haq era [16 September 1978 – 17 August 1988].

Following the Russian occupation of Afghanistan, the American Central Intelligence Agency (CIA) had decided to use the Pakistani Inter Services Intelligence (ISI) to organize, finance and train Islamic resistance groups against the Soviet troops. Thousands of Muslim volunteers from various parts of the world were trained in Pakistan under the supervision of the American CIA and sent across the Afghan border to fight the Soviet troops. Besides the United States, China, Saudi Arabia and many other Muslim countries poured in huge resources in men, material and money to organize resistance to the Soviet occupation forces. Thousands of Afghan refugees who had taken shelter in the border areas of Pakistan were then converted into well-trained and equally motivated Afghan *mujahideen*.

With the advent of the 1980s, a sophisticated, well-equipped infrastructure to train militant Islamists was fully available in Pakistan to the military regime of Zia-ul Haq. The American CIA then tasked the ISI to regulate the *mujahideen* operations and provide advice and support to them. The Zia regime was so much committed to the Afghan jehad that it even used commandos from the Special Services Group (SSG) of the Pakistan Army to guide the guerrilla operations in Afghanistan. International media reports say the ISI trained about 85,000 Afghan *mujahideen* during the Afghan jehad, which also resulted in the enhancement of the Pakistani secret agency's covert action capabilities. Officers from the Covert Action Division (CAD) of the ISI received training in the US and many covert action experts of the CIA were attached to the ISI to guide guerrilla operations against the Soviet troops in Afghanistan. Militants from all over the Muslim world descended on Afghanistan, turning it into the largest ever training ground for Islamic fighters.

However, following the withdrawal of the Soviet Occupation forces from Kabul in 1989, the CIA also withdrew from the scene, leaving it to Pakistan to deal with the menace of militancy. What remained now was a huge force of highly motivated, militarily trained Islamic militants looking for new pastures. Since there was no dearth of funds coming from domestic as well as foreign sources, Pakistan had at its disposal all the means required for the pursuit of promoting and sustaining Islamic militancy and utilising the same to become one of the leading lights of the Islamic world. The veterans of the Afghan jehad, thus, moved on to other embattled lands and dispersed to the Indian-administered Jammu & Kashmir, Chechnya, Bosnia, Tajikistan, Egypt and Algeria, to name a few.

During the Afghan jehad, the Pakistani military and intelligence establishment had openly sided with the *Hizb-e-Islami* (HI) led by

Pushtun leader Gulbaddin Hekmatyar, hoping that once in power, the Afghan guerilla leader commander would protect and promote the strategic interests of Islamabad. But Hekmatyar could not attain power in Kabul after the withdrawal of the Soviet troops. The ISI subsequently devised a plan to raise a new band of soldiers – Taliban (a Pashto word meaning "students", the plural of Talib) – as an alternative to Hekmatyar's *Hizb-e-Islami*. The vast majority of the Taliban militia was ethnic Pushtuns from southern Afghanistan and western Pakistan, along with a smaller number of volunteers from Islamic countries.

Initially, most of the Afghan and Pakistani youth constituting the Taliban militia were the products of Maulana Fazlur Rahman's *Jamiat Ulema-e-Islam*-run religious *madrasas* in the NWFP and the *Baluchistan* Provinces of Pakistan bordering Afghanistan. The major chunk of the former Taliban regime and soldiers actually came from two religious schools – *Darul Uloom* at Akora Khattak in Peshawar and the chain of Binori *madrasas*, the centre of which is situated in Binori Town, Karachi. Six months before the Taliban militia were sent to fight against the Afghan warlords, military training camps were set-up by the Pakistani Frontier Corps to train them in guerilla warfare. *Sunni* fundamentalists to the core and highly motivated, many of these Taliban had returned to their *deeni madrasas* after the withdrawal of the Soviet forces. It was from among these that the ISI had eventually recruited and raised the Taliban militia in the Spin Baldak area of the Kandahar city inside Afghanistan

In 1994, the Taliban forces eventually captured Kandahar and Herat regions of Afghanistan, culminating in the September 1996 occupation of Kabul and bringing two-thirds of Afghanistan under their control. Thus was catapulted to power in Afghanistan the infamous Taliban militia of hardliner *Sunni* Muslims of the *Deobandi* sect and highly motivated Afghan young fighters, trained, armed, funded, equipped and guided by the ISI. In the process, however, Pakistan became the base and transit point for many extremist Islamic militant groups active in various parts of the world.

The fallout of Pakistani military and intelligence establishment's ill-conceived policy of nursing, promoting and sponsoring Islamic militancy is there for everyone to see. Even after a lapse of almost two decades since the end of the Afghan war, the world's only super power is struggling hard to subdue the jehadi monster that its intelligence establishment had created with the help of its Pakistani counterpart and which was held responsible for the 9/11 attacks. Outraged by the US invasion of Afghanistan, it now seems that the monster of jehad on both sides of the Pak-Afghan border has taken to wreaking reprisal against its creators. The American civilian and military leadership is, therefore, keen on evolving some kind of safeguards against the growing threat of Islamic terrorism emanating from Pakistan and Afghanistan.

With the exit of the Republicans and the assumption of the White House by the Democrats, the new Obama administration intensified pressure on Islamabad to do more in the ongoing war against terror, saying if there was one country that mattered most to the future of *Al-Qaeda*, it was Pakistan. While unveiling a new war strategy for Afghanistan on 28 March 2009 in Washington, President Obama said that its key goal was to crush *Al-Qaeda* militants there and in Pakistan, who are plotting new attacks on the United States. Obama, flanked by the Secretary of State Hillary Clinton and the Secretary Defence Robert Gates, said the US military in Afghanistan would shift the emphasis of its mission to training and expanding the Afghan National Army so that it could take the lead in counter-insurgency operations and allow the US troops to leave Afghanistan.

On 29 March 2009, hardly four hours after President Obama announced his new strategy for Afghanistan, two top US generals accused the Pakistani intelligence establishment of helping *Al-Qaeda* and Taliban extremists hiding in Pakistan, saying that the Washington had evidence that elements within the ISI continued to provide support for the Taliban and *Al-Qaeda*. Admiral Mike Mullen, chairman of US Joint Chiefs of Staff and General David Petraeus, the head of US Central Command, said that the ISI continues to have links with some of the militant groups it had established.

Some senior American officials, speaking anonymously to the *New York Times*, gave more details which were published by the newspaper on 30 March 2009. They said the strengthening of the Taliban campaign in southern Afghanistan was being made possible by continued military supplies from Pakistan. The newspaper said electronic surveillance and informants had shown that the level of the Pakistani cooperation was deeper and more extensive than earlier thought. Consequently, as the military option remains key to the Obama administration's strategy to deal with the growing Taliban insurgency in Afghanistan and Pakistan, the Allied Forces stationed in Afghanistan intensified their cross border predator attacks on the Pakistani tribal areas, saying they wanted to target the *Al-Qaeda* and Taliban hideouts.

During his presidential election campaign, President Obama had repeatedly warned that his administration would take out 'high-value terrorist targets' if Pakistan did not act first. Soon after assuming the presidency, Obama chaired the first meeting of the National Security Council on Afghanistan and Pakistan in January 2009 and endorsed a decision to step up drone strikes inside the Pakistani territory. The decision made it obvious that Obama would like to continue the policies of his predecessor Bush to combat the Taliban in Afghanistan and Pakistan. Resultantly, almost 700 Pakistani civilians were killed in 45 drone deadly attacks carried out by the American predators in the tribal areas of Pakistan in the 12 months of 2009 (between January and December 2009).

Of the 45 drone attacks, only five were able to hit their actual targets, killing five key *Al-Qaeda* leaders. But for each *Al-Qaeda* terrorist killed by the American drones, 140 Pakistanis also had to die on average. Compared with the 45 drone attacks carried out during the first year of Obama's presidency [in 2009], there were 34 predator strikes inside the Pakistani territory during the last year of Bush's presidency [in 2008], which left 385 people dead. The Obama administration has already described these attacks as a part of the war against terror, meant to defeat *Al-Qaeda* and Taliban militants hiding in the Pakistani tribal areas.

The American drone attacks targeting the Pakistani tribal areas have already intensified with the beginning of the 2010, especially in the aftermath of the 31 December 2009 suicide attack on the Central Intelligence Agency (CIA) Forward Operating Base in the Khost province of Afghanistan bordering the North Waziristan area, which had killed seven CIA officers. The CIA base was at the heart of a covert program overseeing drone strikes by the American intelligence agency's remote-controlled aircrafts along the Pak-Afghan border.

A subsequent video tape aired by *Al-Jazeera* television on 9 January 2010, showed the suicide bomber, Humam Khalil Abu-Mulal Al Balawi, sitting next to the fugitive *ameer* of the *Tehrik-e-Taliban Pakistan* (TTP) Baitullah Mehsud, and recording his last message, saying: "We tell our deceased *ameer* Baitullah Mehsud that we will never forget his blood. It is up to us to avenge him in and outside the United States of America. This is a message to the enemies of the Muslim nation, especially the American CIA".

Therefore, with the dawn of the year 2010, the Afghanistan-based US predators carried out a record number of 12 deadly missile strikes in the tribal areas of Pakistan in January 2010, killing 123 civilians, compared with only two such attacks which were conducted in January 2009 and killed 36 people.

Many analysts believe this is also a critical stage for the future of Islamabad's troubled relationship with Washington. The dilemma Islamabad is confronted with in these difficult times is quite hard to explain. On one hand, it is critical of continuing US drone strikes on its soil, but on the other, it is unable to go beyond some mild protests over the violation of its airspace by the Americans. The problem is that Islamabad doesn't want to risk American wrath by trying to shoot down the CIA-operated drones. Although Islamabad has the capability to bring down the intruding drones, such an act would be considered hostile and unpardonable by the US. The problem is that Pakistan has been designated the closest non-NATO ally by the US and members of the western military alliance, and is expected to remain a steadfast partner in the war on terror.

As the new Obama administration intensified pressure on Islamabad to "do more" in the war against terror, the Pakistani military establishment has already abandoned all peace deals with the Taliban and *Al-Qaeda*-linked militants in the Swat and South Waziristan regions besides resorting to a massive crackdown against the Pakistan-based network of *Quetta Shura,* led by the fugitive *ameer* of the Afghan Taliban, Mullah Mohammad Omar. In a major policy shift, the Pakistani establishment seems to have abandoned the former rulers of Afghanistan by launching a massive crackdown against their command-and-control structure which has already led to the arrest of nine of the 18 key members of the *Quetta Shura* from different parts of Pakistan, and that too within a short span of two months, beginning 2010.

The decision-makers in the powerful Pakistani establishment seem to have concluded in view of the ever-growing nexus between the Pakistani and the Afghan Taliban that they are now one and the same and the *Tehrik-e-Taliban Pakistan* (TTP) and the *Quetta Shura Taliban* (QST) could no more be treated as two separate jehadi entities. Therefore, the establishment is believed to have revised its previous strategic assessment of the two Taliban groups which have a common mentor (Mullah Mohammad Omar) and decided to proceed against the Afghan Taliban as well, considering them a greater threat for Pakistan now than in the past.

The arrests of the Afghan Taliban leaders have come at a crucial juncture when the US-led Allied Forces are busy launching a massive military offensive against the Afghan Taliban forces in the Marjah town of Afghanistan's southern province Helmand, after President Obama's new-year public declaration to kill or capture the top fugitive leaders of Taliban and *Al-Qaeda*, both in Afghanistan and Pakistan. Since the beginning of 2010, the Pakistan authorities have captured seven senior members of the *Quetta Shura Taliban*, including Mullah Abdul Ghani Baradar, the deputy of Mullah Omar and four Taliban shadow governors of the Afghan provinces.

While Pakistani public opinion has largely turned against the *Al-Qaeda*-linked Taliban groups active in NWFP and FATA regions, there are still large pockets of support in Pakistani military and intelligence establishment for the pro-Kashmir jehadi organisations. Although the Pakistan army has already launched military action against the *Tehrik-e-Taliban Pakistan* (TTP) and the *Tehrik-e-Nifaz-e-Shariat-e-Mohammadi* (TNSM), after they targeted the security and intelligence agencies, some leading Pakistani jehadi groups active in the Indian-administered *Jammu & Kashmir* continue to escape a concrete state action. Indeed, the failure of the Pakistani establishment to act against the *Lashkar-e-Toiba/Jamaatul Daawa* and some other pro-Kashmir jehadi groups even after the 26/11 attacks, is a big question mark on Islamabad's willingness to treat as terrorists all the jehadi groups active in India and Pakistan.

This is mainly because of the fact that the Pakistani establishment still wants to play its old double game, while ignoring with impunity repeated calls by the international community to take a decisive action against the Pakistani jehadi organisations active in India and Afghanistan. Such an action is a prerequisite to rehabilitate the writ of the state and restore the confidence of the masses in the capability and determination of their elected government to seize the fast growing *Talibanisation* of Pakistan.

REFERENCES

1. Interview: Mullah Nazeer Ahmed, *Al Sahab*, 8 April 2009.
2. Council on Foreign Relations (CFR) Report titled "From Af-Pak to Pak-Af: A Response to the New US Strategy for South Asia", 20 April 2009.
3. Aryn Baker, Pakistan: Negligent on Terror, *TIME* Magazine, 30 June 2008.
4. *New York Times* report, 30 March 2009.
5. Statement, President Asif Ali Zardari, 7 July 2009.
6. Statement, President Barrack Obama, 28 March 2009.
7. Videotape, *Al-Jazeera*, 9 January 2010.

CHAPTER 2

The 26/11 Mumbai Terror Attacks and their Fallout

Indo-Pak relations, which appeared to be on course towards normalisation after the return of civilian rule in Islamabad in the wake of the 2008 general elections, touched rock bottom after the 26/11 Mumbai terrorist attacks, carried out by a group of ten *Lashkar-e-Toiba* (LeT) operatives who traveled by sea all the way from the port city of Karachi, across the Arabian Sea, hijacked an Indian fishing trawler, killed its crew and entered the Indian commercial capital Mumbai on a rubber dinghy to carry out the deadly assault.

The bloody episode in Mumbai, which killed over 175 people, came as a devastating blow to the Indo-Pak peace process that was initiated by the South Asian nuclear armed neighbours in a bid to bring some form of normalcy in their bilateral ties. The Mumbai episode cast a long shadow over a spate of confidence building steps being taken by the Pakistan Peoples Party and the Congress governments to thaw a long freeze in bilateral ties between the two nuclear armed neighbours.

The attacks drew international ire against Pakistan-based Islamist jehadi groups and damaged beyond repair India's already strained relationship with Pakistan. The gravity of the stress in the Indo-Pak relations in the aftermath of the Mumbai terror attacks could be gauged from the Indian External Affairs Minister Pranab Mukherjee's open declaration that India may indulge in military strikes against the *Lashkar-e-Toiba* terrorist training camps in Pakistan to protect its territorial integrity.

The Mumbai attackers possibly wanted to cripple the economic hub of India by targeting the country's commercial capital. But those behind the deadly attacks may have miscalculated the impact of their action, thinking that like other acts of terrorism which India had experienced in the past, the Mumbai episode, too, would evoke nothing more than expressions of sympathy from the outside world and a sense of impotent rage in India. Only once before, following the 2001 terrorist attack on its Parliament building in New Delhi, did India move its troops to the border with Pakistan, eliciting renewed promises of good behaviour from the Musharraf regime.

However, the 26/11 carnage turned out to be entirely different because of its 60-hour duration and commando-style operation which prompted the Indian establishment to equate it with an act of war, largely because of the fact that the attackers had targeted prominent Indian landmarks. Unlike the previous terrorist assaults, the Mumbai episode was not a hit-and-run affair. A series of coordinated terrorist attacks on Mumbai, which drew over 1,000 men from the Indian Army, Marine Commandos, the National Security Guard besides the local police to neutralise the well-armed and highly-trained Islamist terrorists, was one of the most daring assaults on India. The deadly incident consisted of 11 synchronised shooting and bombing attacks across Mumbai which started on 26 November and lasted until 29 November, 2008.

Eight of the attacks occurred in South Mumbai: at Chhatrapati Shivaji Terminus, the Oberoi Trident, the Taj Mahal Palace & Tower, Leopold Cafe, Cama Hospital, the Orthodox Jewish-owned Nariman House, Metro Cinema and a lane behind the Times of India building and St. Xavier's College. There was also an explosion at the Mazagaon docks, in Mumbai's port area, and in a taxi at Ville Parle. By the early morning of 28 November, all sites except the Taj Mahal Palace had been secured by Mumbai Police and security forces. A commando action by India's National Security Guards on 29 November resulted in the elimination of the last remaining attackers at the Taj Mahal Palace.

Although the *Lashkar-e-Toiba* strongly refuted its involvement and an Indian jehadi group calling itself the Deccan *Mujahideen* claimed responsibility for the carnage, the Indian authorities claimed that Mohammad Ajmal Amir Kasab, the sole Mumbai attacker captured alive has confessed to being a member of the LeT. Kasab disclosed during interrogations that all the ten attackers were members of the *Lashkar-e-Toiba* and were sent on the mission by Zakiur Rehman Lakhvi, the chief operational commander of the LeT, stationed in Pakistani administered Azad Kashmir.

The revelation was followed by New Delhi's open declaration that the country may resort to military strikes against the LeT terrorist training camps in Pakistan to protect its territorial integrity. Some Indian and Pakistani media reports even hinted at the possibility of the Indian Air Force (IAF) contemplating an attack on the Muridke Headquarters of the *Jamaatul Daawa* to avenge the Mumbai attacks. The Indian threat was followed by the US ambassador to India, David Mulford's statement that the Mumbai probe into the ruthless killing of American and Israeli citizens would be taken to its logical conclusion.

The Mumbai assault acquired an international dimension given the fact that 25 of those killed were foreigners including 17 men and eight women. The deceased included four Israeli, three American, three German, two French, two Canadian, two Australian nationals and one national each from Britain, Japan, Italy, Malaysia, Mexico, Netherlands, Singapore, Thailand and Mauritius. The game plan of the attackers was believed to be a simple one. Judging from the Indian response to the attack on Parliament in 2001, they may have expected India once again to move its troops to the border, thereby making Pakistan, too, divert its troops from the northwest to the eastern borders, which would relieve pressure on the Taliban and *Al-Qaeda* elements active on the restive Pak-Afghan border besides creating a warlike atmosphere which would scuttle any prospect of an Indo-Pak peace pact.

But a timely intervention by Western powers helped avoid outbreak of a major conflict between India and Pakistan as the ruling political elite in New Delhi and Islamabad agreed to act maturely and responsibly to foil the nefarious designs of the war mongers. Yet, the attacks did undermine the credibility of the civilian government in Islamabad whose installation had raised hopes of improvement in the already tense Indo-Pak relations. The 26/11 led to widespread international criticism of the Pakistani establishment for its failure to dismantle the jehadi infrastructure from its soil despite being a US ally in the war on terror. Amidst mounting evidence to prove that the perpetrators of the Mumbai attacks were trained in Pakistan, the noose was further tightened around Islamabad, literally isolating the Zardari-led PPP government.

On 4 December 2008, an investigative report carried by a Hong Kong-based web newspaper – Asia Times Online (AToL) – claimed that the militants who carried out the Mumbai terrorist attacks were originally meant to head for the Indian administered Kashmir as part of a low-profile campaign of Pakistani-sponsored militancy there. However, it added that key reshuffles within the Inter Services Intelligence at that time as well as Islamabad's refocus on unrest in the trouble-stricken Pak-Afghan tribal belt resulted in *Al-Qaeda* hijacking the operation. Subsequently, a low profile terrorist attack in Jammu & Kashmir, orchestrated by the ISI that had been in the pipeline for a few months, eventually turned into the massive 26/11 attacks.

The AToL report filed by a Pakistani journalist Syed Saleem Shehzad claimed the original plan was highjacked by the *Lashkar-e-Toiba* that generally focused on the Kashmir struggle, and *Al-Qaeda*, resulting in the death of nearly 200 people in Mumbai. The report claimed the PNS Iqbal (a Pakistani naval commando unit) was the main outlet for the militants to be given training and through deserted points they were launched onto the Arabian Sea and on into the Indian region of Gujarat.

"Under directives from Lieutenant General Ashfaq Pervez Kayani, who was then director general of the ISI, a low-profile operation was prepared to support the Kashmir militancy,, the report claimed. Although Pakistan had closed down its major operations, it still provided some support to Kashmiri militants to ensure that the freedom movement did not die down completely there. After General Kayani was promoted to the rank of the country's army chief, Lieutenant General Nadeem Taj was placed as Director General of the ISI. The external section under him routinely executed the plan of Kayani and trained a few dozen *Lashkar-e-Toiba* militants near Mangla Dam, close to the federal capitals Islamabad. They were sent by sea to Guajrat, from where they had to travel to Kashmir to carry out operations".

In the meantime, the report said, a major reshuffle in the ISI officially shelved this low-key operation as the country's whole focus had shifted towards the restive Pakistani tribal areas. The director of the ISI's external wing was also changed, placing the game in the hands of a low-level ISI forward section head (a major) and the LeT's chief operational commander Zakiur Rehman Lakhvi. The AToL report claimed that Zakiur Rehman Lakhvi was in Karachi for two months to personally oversee the plan.

"However, the militant networks in India and Bangladesh comprising the *Harkatul Jehadul Islami*, which were now in *Al-Qaeda's* hands, tailored some changes. Instead of Jammu & Kashmir, they planned to attack the port city of Mumbai, using their existent local networks, with Westerners and the Jewish community centre as targets. Lakhvi and the forward section of the ISI in Karachi, completely disconnected from the top brass, somehow approved the plan under which ten LeT militants took Mumbai hostage for nearly three days and successfully established a reign of terror", the report concluded.

In a related development, *New York Times*, while quoting a senior Pentagon official, reported on 5 December 2008 that some former Pakistan Army officers and those from the Inter Services Intelligence helped train the 26/11 attackers. The allegation came as US Secretary of State Condoleezza Rice held meetings with Indian leaders in New Delhi and Admiral Mike Mullen, chairman of the Joint Chiefs of Staff, met their Pakistani counterparts in Islamabad, in a two-pronged effort to pressure Islamabad to cooperate fully in tracking down the perpetrators of the bloody attacks. However, the Pakistan government kept refuting Indian allegations that militants operating from its soil were responsible for the deadly attacks, with President Asif Zardari describing them as "non-state actors".

Nevertheless, he was probably ignoring a crucial difference between all previous terrorist strikes in India and the one in Mumbai, following which a wealth of information became quickly available to the Indian investigation agencies. Key to this was none other than Ajmal Kasab, the lone surviving Pakistani terrorist caught by the Mumbai police on the night of the attack. What emerged from his interrogation, collated with other strands of investigation and mobile intercepts, clearly established the involvement of the *Lashkar-e-Toiba*. Ajmal Kasab's revelations to a joint team that includes officers of the Mumbai police's crime branch, the Intelligence Bureau (IB) and the Research and Analysis Wing (RAW), helped the Indian investigators piece together several key elements of the Mumbai plot.

The investigators came to know that Amir Kasab was part of a 24-member team of *Lashkar-e-Toiba* terrorists who underwent two years of commando training. While most of it was of a general nature, involving basic training in firearms, explosives and physical toughening, it became focused and more mission-oriented six months before the Mumbai attacks. According to Ajmal Kasab, they had been through not just *daura aam* (general training) but also *daura khaas* (special training). While Kasab was unable to identify some of his trainers, he confirmed that much of it was designed and conducted by Commander Zakiur Rehman Lakhvi.

In a crucial development on 12 December 2008, Pakistan's leading English daily *Dawn* confirmed for the first time the findings of the Indian authorities that the lone Mumbai attacker arrested alive after the carnage happens to be a Pakistani national. A front page story by the newspaper reported that during the course of *Dawn's* own investigations, a team of reporters that was dispatched to Faridkot was finally able to locate a family which claimed to be the kin of Ajmal Kasab – the sole survivor among the 10 Mumbai attackers. The special team of reporters was dispatched to ascertain the veracity of Indian government claims that the attacker was a Pakistani national from the Faridkot area near Dipalpur district of Punjab.

According to the *Dawn* story, its reporters met one Amir Kasab in the courtyard of his house in Faridkot, a village of about 2,500 people just a few kilometers from Dipalpur on the way to Kasur, who confirmed that Ajmal Amir Kasab whose face had been beamed over the media was his son. "For the next few minutes, the fifty – something man of medium build agonized over the reality that took time sinking in, amid sobs complaining about the raw deal that fate had given him and his family", the story stated while quoting him as saying: "I was in denial for the first couple of days, saying to myself it could not have been my son. But now I have accepted it. This is the truth. I have seen the picture in the newspaper. This is my son Ajmal who had disappeared from home four years ago after I failed to provide him with new clothes on Eid festival, making him angry".

The newspaper report stated: "While Amir was talking, Ajmal's two sisters and a younger brother were lurking about. To Amir's right [on a nearby charpoy] sat their mother, wrapped in a chador and in a world of her own. Her trance was broken as the small picture of Ajmal Kasab lying in a Mumbai hospital was shown around. They appeared to have identified their son. The mother shrunk back in her chador but the father said he had no problem in talking about the subject. Amir Kasab said he had settled in Faridkot after arriving from the nearby Haveli Lakha many years ago. He owned the house and used to make his earnings by selling *pakoras* in the streets of the village.

On 23 December 2008, the Indian authorities provided to Pakistan a letter written by Ajmal Amir Kasab as well as his confessional statement, wherein he claimed to be a Pakistani national from Faridkot and a *Lashkar-e-Toiba* operative, besides seeking legal assistance from Islamabad. On 5 January 2009, India provided a 70-page dossier to Pakistan as evidence of the *Lashkar-e-Toiba's* role in the Mumbai terror attacks, besides urging Islamabad to hand over the conspirators to face justice in India, dismantle the infrastructure of terrorism in Pakistan, prevent further terrorist attacks from Pakistan soil and to adhere to all bilateral, multilateral and international obligations to take the 26/11 Mumbai attackers to task.

The Indian dossier titled "Mumbai Terrorist Attacks (Nov.26-29, 2008)", stated: "The evidence gathered so far unmistakably point to the territory of Pakistan as a source of the terrorist attacks in Mumbai between November 26 and 29, 2008. It is abundantly clear that senior functionaries of the *Lashkar-e-Toiba* were the controllers and handlers of the ten terrorists. The evidence clearly establishes that all the ten terrorists were chosen, trained, dispatched, controlled and guided by *Lashkar-e-Toiba* which is the organisation responsible for the terrorist attacks in Mumbai".

The dossier said that the lone surviving attacker Ajmal Kasab had disclosed the names and identities of the other nine Mumbai attackers who were killed by Indian security forces in the gun battle. It described all the nine dead terrorists as Pakistani nationals – Ismail Khan (25) from Dera Ismail Khan, Babar Imran alias Abu Akasha (25) from Multan, Naser alias Abu Umar (23) from Faisalabad, Shoaib alias Abu Saheb (21) from Sialkot, Nazir alias Abu Umer (28) from Faisalabad, Hafiz Arshad alias Abu Abdar Rehman Bara (23) from Multan, Javed alias Abu Ali (22) from Okara, Abdur Rehman alias Abu Abdar Rehman Chhota (21), and Fahadullah (23) from Okara.

However, it is important to mention that all the ten terrorists addressed each other by code names. In fact, none of them knew the real names of the others and each of these code names was handpicked by their boss. These young men were made to believe that they were "God's messengers" out to "bring justice to the world". The code names were in Arabic, describing either their personalities or their roles in the 26/11 attacks. The Indian investigators came to know six of the code names during sustained interrogation of Ajmal Kasab. Two people – Zaim and Nasir Al Deen – were in charge of the 10-member squad. Investigators say Zaim means General – a person in-charge of an operation while Nasir Al Deen means one who protects Islam. These two barged into the Taj Mahal Hotel.

According to Ajmal Kasab, one of the militants who unleashed terror at Oberoi Hotel was named Al-Hamas which means happy and enthusiastic in Arabic. He was a jovial person and thus he was given that name. Another terrorist, for being an excellent orator, very well-versed in the Koran, was given the name Fakih. He used to give the group religious discourses. Two more had the code names of Abdul Melham and Al-Abbas which meant fearless in Arabic. The terrorist known by the name motivated others to believe in the need to protect Islam, Kasab told his interrogators. According to Kasab, all ten of them were taught spoken Arabic and Hindi during their training sessions. He further told the Indian cops that they had also planned to ram explosive-laden vehicles at the Taj and Oberoi, just the way it was done at the Marriott Hotel in Islamabad a few months earlier.

The dossier India had provided to Pakistan contained photographs of materials found on the hijacked fishing trawler, from a bottle of Mountain Dew packaged in Karachi to Diamond-brand pistols, bearing markings of a gun manufacturer in Peshawar to a Pakistani-made matchbox, dried Nestle milk powder packet, sogo spray paint, detergent powder and tubes of Medicam tooth paste and Touch Me shaving cream. The dossier included pictures of a Yamaha outboard motor that was used by the terrorists during the sea journey and was allegedly sold by a Pakistan distributor. "An attempt was made by the terrorists to erase the engine number but it has been retrieved by the Indian investigators. The outboard motor number is 67CL-1020015, manufactured by Yamaha Motor Corporation Japan and imported into Pakistan and distributed by a company 'Business & Engineering Trends', located at No 24, Habibullah Road, Davis Road Lahore".

The Indian dossier narrated a journey of passion by the Mumbai attackers whose blow-by-blow media coverage was being followed by their handlers, who were apprising the gunmen on the ground about the movement of the Indian security forces besides motivating them to keep fighting. The dossier said the *Lashkar-e-Toiba* initially trained 32 terrorists for the Mumbai terror attacks. "Of these, 13 were short listed following a rigorous selection procedure. Six were then sent away to a still unknown destination and three new members joined, taking the group's membership to 10. Among the new faces was Ismail Khan, who led the assault".

Zakiur Rehman Lakhvi, aka Chachaji (uncle), the supreme commander of LeT, was repeatedly named in the dossier as the chief planner of the Mumbai attacks. "His role in the Mumbai attacks was confirmed by Ajmal Kasab during interrogation. It was Commander Zakiur Rehman Lakhvi who planned and executed the plot with his operations chief, Yusuf Muzammil", the dossier said, adding that the 10 men boarded a small boat in the port city of Karachi at 8 a.m. on 22 November 2008, sailed a short distance before boarding a bigger carrier called Al-Huseini.

"The following day, the 10 men took over an Indian fishing trawler, called the MV Kuber, killed four of its crew members, spared its captain, Amar Singh Solanki, and sailed 550 nautical miles across the Arabian Sea. Between November 22 and November 26, the Kuber maintained a distance of 60-80 NM from the Indian coast. The terrorists then plotted their way using four reference points referred to as JALA 1, 2, 3 and 4. Of these, the last two – JALA 3 was 4 NM off the Mumbai coast while the last reference point, JALA 4, was Budhwar Park where they landed. En route, the terrorists were in touch with their handlers via a Thuraya satellite phone (+8821655526412) using a code language".

The dossier added: "Each man had two-hour watch duties on board and each carried individual weapon packs: ammunition, a Kalashnikov, a 9-millimetre pistol, hand grenades and a bomb, weighing 8 kilograms and containing a military-grade explosive called RDX, steel ball bearings as well as a timer with instructions inscribed in Urdu. By 4 p.m. on 26 November 2008, the trawler approached the shores of Mumbai. The last four nautical miles to the Mumbai shore were covered in a dinghy after the Kuber was abandoned and its captain killed".

"They finally reached Mumbai at about 8:30 p.m., and in five teams of two, set upon their targets: the busiest railway station of the port city of Mumbai known as Victoria Terminus, a tourist haunt called Café Leopold, the Jewish centre in Nariman House, and two luxury hotels, the Taj and Oberoi". However, going by the dossier, they made one mistake, which they told their handlers later on the phone – they left behind Ismail Khan's satellite phone which was recovered by the Indian investigators and its photograph included in the dossier. "Once in Mumbai, they (LeT) militants went on a killing spree, all the while receiving detailed instructions and pep talks from their handlers".

According to the Mumbai police's chief investigator Rakesh Maria, the attackers had examined the layout and landscape of Mumbai city by using images from Google Earth, which provides satellite photos for much of the planet over the Internet. "The gunmen also had studied detailed photographs of their targets on laptop computers. When they traveled by boat from Karachi to Mumbai, they used four GPS systems to navigate. The sets could also be used as walkie-talkies. They were equipped with a satellite phone and nine cell phones. Throughout the Mumbai attacks, they used to call their handlers in

Pakistan who had eschewed conventional phones for voice-over-Internet telephone services", the Mumbai police's chief investigator had stated.

According to the Indian dossier, the Mumbai attackers were being contacted from a virtual phone number – 12012531824, which was actually generated by a Voice over Internet Protocol (VoIP) service based in the United States and paid for by a Javed Iqbal, who gave a Pakistani passport as proof of his identity. The VoIP services route phone calls over the Internet, making it difficult to trace them. For example, a person might have a New York City telephone number, but calls made to that number are routed over the Internet, allowing a client to answer from anywhere there is online access. Therefore, the chief plotter of the 26/11 attacks, Zakiur Rehman Lakhvi, spoke from two Internet phone numbers to six different Indian mobile numbers. The Internet numbers were paid by wire transfer by someone using a fake ID.

As per the Indian dossier, the last call was made at 10:26 p.m. on 27 November 2008 [between a gunman who was holding several Jews hostage inside the Nariman House] and his interlocutor. The handler is talking to his agent: "Brother you have to fight. This is a matter of the prestige of Islam. Everything is being recorded by the international media. Inflict the maximum damage. Keep fighting. Don't be taken alive", a caller has been quoted in the Indian dossier as saying to a gunman inside the Oberoi Hotel close to 4 a.m. on the first day of the three-day siege.

"Throw one or two grenades at the navy and police teams, which are outside", one of the callers reportedly instructed the gunmen inside the Taj Mahal Hotel. "Keep two magazines and three grenades aside and spend the rest of your ammunition", went another set of instructions as per the dossier to the attackers inside the Nariman House, which housed an Orthodox Jewish centre, on the second evening, with a directive to conclude the operation the next morning. "There are three ministers and one secretary of the cabinet present in your hotel. We don't know in which room," a caller tells a terrorist at the Taj at 0310 hrs on 27 November 2008, as per the dossier. "Oh! That is good news. It is the icing on the cake," he replies. "Find those 3-4 persons and then get whatever you want from India", he has instructed. "Pray that we find them," he answers.

At the Oberoi Hotel at 0353 hrs on 27 November 2008, a handler phones and says: "Brother Abdul. The media is comparing your action to 9/11. One senior police official has been killed." In another call, to the Taj Mahal Hotel this time, a handler says: "The ATS chief has been killed. Your work is very important. Allah Almighty is helping you. The Wazir (minister) should not escape. Try and set the place on fire." By the morning of 29 November 2008, the Indian security forces had killed nine of the ten Mumbai attackers besides arresting a wounded Ajmal Kasab alive.

Later, during the trial of Mohammad Ajmal Kasab in a special Mumbai court, a senior Nokia representative testified that the five mobile phones used by the LeT terrorists during the assault had been manufactured in China and shipped to Pakistan in June 2008. The enforcement manager of Nokia in the United States, whose name was withheld for security reasons, deposed in the Mumbai attacks trial through video-conferencing from the FBI office in Washington on August 14, 2009. She said the five mobile phones used by the 26/11 attackers to communicate had been ferried from China to Pakistan five months before the 2008 strikes. "I believe these phones were shipped from China to Pakistan," the witness had said on being examined by the special public prosecutor Ujjwal Nikam.

Five Nokia mobile phones were recovered by the Mumbai police from the nine slain terrorists and FBI's help was sought to ascertain from where the phones had been procured. Asked how she could identify the phones, the Nokia representative said that the international mobile equipment identification (IMEI), a unique number allotted to each mobile phone manufactured by Nokia had helped her trace the origin of the mobile sets. The Nokia representative was the third foreigner to have suggested that the terror perpetrators had Pakistani links. While an FBI forensic expert had earlier told the Mumbai court that the perpetrators used GPS to navigate from Karachi to Mumbai by sea, a Yamaha representative, during examination by special public prosecutor Ujjwal Nikam, confirmed that the *Lashkar-e-Toiba* terrorists had used an outboard engine manufactured by them and delivered in Pakistan to power the dinghy on which they landed on Mumbai coast.

Meanwhile, investigations by Indian agencies further showed that the planners of the 26/11 had used for the first time Hindi words to convey their threat message through media houses. Interestingly, the mail, sent in the name of the Deccan *Mujahideen* and claiming the attacks was generated from an email account created in Russia but was used by a computer based in Pakistan. The author of the mail had used voice recognition software to dictate the mail which would in turn type it in Devnagri font. The attackers had made the mail jump from one server to another to hide the identity of the master server. Analysing the Internet protocol addresses that were used to send the said mail, the Indian experts found that the Russia-based e-mail address which was used to send the document was opened early on 26 November 2008 by a computer user in Pakistan.

In the second section of the 70-page dossier, India pointed out the contradictory nature of the Pakistani response to the Mumbai attacks, Islamabad's failure to respond appropriately to Indian requests for cooperation when evidence was provided in the past about terrorist acts, and an outline of Pakistani bilateral and international commitments and obligations to take terrorists to task. The third and last section of the Indian dossier contained an outline of what the Congress government expected Islamabad to do in the aftermath of the assault. "This was a conspiracy launched from Pakistan. Gaps in knowledge can be filled by investigation and interrogation of conspirators there," the dossier concluded.

On 12 February 2009, Pakistan finally acknowledged for the first time, almost 80 days after the Mumbai terror attacks, that they were partly planned in Pakistan and that it has arrested six suspects, including the "main operator". Pakistani Interior Minister Rehman Malik said at a press conference that criminal cases had been registered against nine suspects on charges of "abetting, conspiracy and facilitation" of a terrorist act. He told the media that FIR No: 01/009 had been lodged with the Special Investigation Group (SIG) in the Federal Investigation Agency (FIA) against nine suspects. He added that the Pakistani investigators have already identified Hammad Amin Sadiq as the mastermind of the whole conspiracy.

Rehman Malik said the cases against nine persons had been registered under the Anti-Terror Act (ATA) and the Cyber Crime Act and they would be tried under these two sets of laws. He said six of the nine accused named in the FIR have already been arrested and being interrogated, two have been identified but not arrested so far while investigations are still under way in the involvement of the ninth accused. He identified those taken into custody as Commander Zakiur Rehman Lakhvi who was arrested from Muzaffarabad, Javed Iqbal, who was arrested from Barcelona, Spain, Hammad Amin Sadiq, believed to be the main operator belonging to southern Punjab, Zarar Shah, Mohammad Ashfaq and Abu Hamza. However, the name of Ajmal Kasab was not included in the FIR.

He also conceded that 'some' of those arrested by the Pakistani security agencies for possible involvement in the Mumbai attacks belonged to the LeT. Rehman Malik said Javed Iqbal, who was based in Barcelona, Spain, was the person who paid $200 for the 'Internet Domain' that was also used for communication and planning for the Mumbai attacks. Having ascertained the involvement of Javed Iqbal, we somehow lured him into coming to Pakistan and he was arrested on his arrival," Malik said and added that the e-mail sent by 'Deccan *Mujahideen*' claiming responsibility for the Mumbai attacks was believed to be prepared and sent by Zarar Shah, who was responsible for communication links in the whole operation.

Rehman Malik said the money to fund the Mumbai attacks was transferred from Pakistan and was received in Italy. The transaction was reportedly made through a Pakistani bank. "The Pakistani agencies have concluded that the terrorists operated from two bases – one inside Karachi and the other outside but not very far away from Karachi. The people involved in Mumbai attacks used three boats for traveling to Mumbai, one named 'Al-Huseini' and the other 'Al-Ghaus'. For communication, these culprits used 'Call Phonic' system and they also bought Indian cell phone SIMs for communication from inside India". Malik ruled out the possibility of the involvement of any Pakistani state agency in the Mumbai attacks, saying that the attackers apparently wanted to sabotage the Indo-Pak peace process and both the neighbouring countries should not allow it to happen.

On 25 February 2009, the Crime Branch of the Mumbai police filed the charge sheet in the 26/11 terror strikes before a local court, naming two Pakistani army officers – Colonel (retd) Saadatullah and Khurram Shahdad – among the 35 suspects wanted in connection with the carnage. In a summary of the 11,280-page charge sheet filed at the Esplanade court, the police gave the addresses of the two Pakistan army officers and said they facilitated communications between the dead terrorists and the accused while the attack was being unleashed. "Two suspected army names cropped up during our investigations. The name of one of the army men starts with major general but it is a matter of investigation to ascertain whether they belong to the Pakistan Army or the *Lashkar-e-Toiba*", said Rakesh Maria, Joint Commissioner of Mumbai Police (crime), who headed the 26/11 investigation.

All the wanted suspects named in the charge sheet were from Pakistan, as were the 10 young men who landed in Mumbai on the evening of November 26 to let loose a reign of terror that lasted 60 hours. Among them were the LeT founder Hafiz Mohammad Saeed, the LeT chief operational commander, Zakiur Rehman Lakhvi, Zarar Shah, Abu Sanas, Abu Hafiz, and Abu Hamza. The charge sheet categorically denied that the attackers had any local help aside from two men – Fahim Ansari and Sabauddin – who had carried out the recee for the attacks in 2007 and are already in police custody. Rakesh Maria said that the charge sheet was clear that the planning, training, and logistics for the attacks were provided by entities in Pakistan. These entities extended local support to the Mumbai attackers by providing maps of important locations, including targets in Mumbai.

The Mumbai attacks charge-sheet gave in detail the sequence of events from the moment the *Lashkar-e-Toiba* terrorists set sail from Karachi in a fishing trawler. The evidence contained in the charge sheet included satellite phone intercepts and GPS data, excerpts of telephonic conversations, statements of more than 2,200 witnesses, the SIM cards from mobile phones and a Thuraya satellite phone. The evidence also included photographs of guns and grenades that were used by the Mumbai attackers which bore markings linked to the Pakistan Ordnance Factory in Wah Cantt near the garrison town of Rawalpindi.

The Mumbai attackers and the planners were charged under Indian Penal Code (IPC) sections 121A (conspiracy to wage war, abet, or attempt to wage war against the government of India) and 122 (collecting arms with the intention of waging war). The evidence submitted to the Mumbai court also included Kasab's confessional statement (which he had retracted later), stating that the *mujahideen* were told to fight to liberate Jammu & Kashmir. In the statement, *Lashkar* leader Zakiur Rahman Lakhvi is reported to have said: "Now we have to wage a war with India and conquer Jammu & Kashmir."

On 11 July, 2009, Pakistan handed over a fresh dossier on its probe into the Mumbai attacks to New Delhi ahead of a meeting between Prime Minister Yousuf Raza Gilani and Prime Minister Manmohan Singh in Egypt. The dossier, handed over to the Indian High Commission officials in Islamabad, gave an update on the Pakistani investigations into the November 26/11 attacks. The 36-page dossier was the first official admission from Pakistan that its citizens were involved in the terror attacks. The Pakistani dossier named Zakiur Rehman Lakhvi as the mastermind of the Mumbai attacks and four others as his accomplices.

According to the dossier, a man named Hammad Amin Sadiq facilitated funds and hideouts for 26/11, another man called Mazhar Iqbal was the handler of the LeT terrorists who had carried out the operation, a man named Abdul Wajid was facilitator as well as computer network expert, Shahid Jamil was a crew member on board Al Huseini and Al Fouz, the boats that brought the Mumbai attackers up to the INS Kuber. The document listed Mohammad Amjad Khan, Ifthikar Ali, Shahid Ghafoor, Abdul Rehman, Mohammad Usman and Ateequr Rahman as proclaimed offenders in the case. The dossier said that the action taken against the accused includes the arrest of the five men, including Zakiur Rehman Lakhvi, while a hunt was on for 13 other accused involved in the Mumbai mayhem.

The Pakistani dossier was followed by a book titled "Investigating the Mumbai Conspiracy", claiming that the Mumbai terrorist attacks were first conceived on the third floor of the Inter Services Intelligence (ISI) headquarters at the Zero Point in the garrison town of Rawalpindi. Published by the Delhi-based Pentagon Press, the book made sensational claims – that the Mumbai terror attack was planned and executed by the Pakistan Army and its different agencies including the Inter Services Intelligence and the Special Services

Group (SSG) and that the Pakistani Army Chief General Ashfaq Pervez Kayani was not only in the know of the attack but had planned every detail of the assault with his close confidants in the Pakistan Army's top leadership. The book claims that the Pakistan army top brass including former President General (retd) Pervez Musharraf had been playing one of the deadliest games in recent history to provoke a disastrous war among the two nuclear armed nations.

The book then claimed: "From the evidence gathered by the various intelligence and security agencies, it is quite clear that *Lashkar-e-Toiba*, an *Al-Qaeda* affiliated Lahore based terrorist group which trained and dispatched the attackers, do not have the ability to plan and execute such a major armed assault across the seas. Operations like the Mumbai terrorist attack are never discussed in official meetings [of the ISI]. Such meetings remain unlisted and no minutes are kept. Nor are they planned in a day. Only a handful of the senior officers decide the details, over a period of time, going back and forth over details and more details".

Co-authored by Wilson John, a senior fellow with *Observer Research Foundation* and Vishwas Kumar, a senior Indian journalist with special interest in crime and terrorism, the book stated that a highly classified operation like 26/11 could not have been shared among more than four people would have known about the plan besides the Chief of Army Staff, who at the time of the planning was President General Pervez Musharraf. "The DG ISI was Lt General Ashfaq Pervez Kayani. Among General Kayani's close confidants were four Major Generals – Sikander Afzal, Asif Akhtar, Muhammad Mustafa and Tahir Mahmood – all of whom played major roles behind 26/11. Akhtar headed ISI's Operations Wing which handled terrorist groups operating in Jammu & Kashmir and other parts of India. Afzal was the Deputy Director General External and headed all sections which dealt with terrorist groups and India. One of his close confidants was Brigadier Riazullah Khan Chibb, one of the key masterminds of the Mumbai attack. Mustafa was in charge of the Evaluation wing and Tahir Mahmood was General Officer Commanding. Special Services Group (SSG), which sometimes acted as the armed wing of the intelligence agency. Tahir Mahmood, as the Brigade commander of Brigade 62 at Skardu, had launched terrorists from LeT and other Army supported groups across Indian territory to camouflage the movement of regular troops".

The book claimed that a whole lot of homework had gone into before the Pakistani jehadi Generals laid out the plan for the Mumbai attacks. "They knew which terrorist group they could rely on to carry out the task. They had notes on previous attacks, the modus operandi used, the local support network and they knew the names of Brigadiers who could control the operation through satellite phones. Three retired Pakistan Army Brigadiers who had played a key role in the Mumbai terror attacks are Riazullah Khan Chibb, Ijaz Shah and Haji. Though names of other Brigadiers and other retired officers have time and again emerged during various investigations – Major Wajahatullah and Colonel Kayani – there are fewer details in open source about their past and present activities. There are, however, some details about Shah and Chibb, largely thanks to the emails which former Prime Minister Benazir Bhutto wrote before her assassination in 2007. Both Shah and Chibb had retired from ISI a few years ago and have vast experience in running and handling terrorist groups targeting India. They are also confidants of Musharraf".

The book added: "Generally, no serving officer is given control of terrorist operations as the discovery of such links, run the risk of attracting sanctions from international donors. Terrorist operations are always left to the 'irregulars'. These are retired officers who are reemployed on contracts for specific missions for the Army which can be easily denied. They operate out of private offices in different locations in Pakistan, have access to weapons and equipment and are paid through slush funds maintained by the Inter Services Intelligence".

Going by the book contents, it was a motley crowd of committed trainers, cartographers, communications experts and ideologues who worked on the front end of the deadly mission. "The principal trainers were Zakiur Rehman Lakhvi (alias Abu Wahid Irshad Ahmad); Muzammil (aka Yousuf aka Abu Gurera aka Abu Mohammad); Faheem Ahmad Ansari (alias Abu Jarar). Apart from them, Azam Cheema, better known as 'Babaji', taught recruits how to spot vital installations on the map and uses satellite phones to keep in touch. Another Abu Qahafa, an expert commando trainer who joined the group in 2006, was the chief instructor for the Mumbai attackers. A confidante of Muzammil, he is an expert commando trainer and led the select recruits through the toughest training schedule at LeT's Maskar Aksa camp. Abu al Qama, an old hand at training new recruits, and was in charge of LeT's training camp, Ibn-e-Tamia, PoK, which received the Indian recruits across the Kashmir border".

The book further claimed that the ideologue behind the 26/11 operation was Abdur Rahman Makki, who is actually the LeT's supremo Hafiz Saeed's cousin and brother-in-law. "He is second only to Saeed in the hierarchy and is known as a firebrand proponent of suicide missions, having penned a popular book called *Tehrik-e-Islam ke fidayeen dastay* (The suicide squads of the Islamic movement). Another relative of Saeed, Ibrahim (aka Ali), a computer expert and fund distributor, put together the assault team. He recruited Faheem Ahmed Ansari (aka Abu Jarar), who trained under Muzammil, and was briefed extensively about the targets subsequently and selected for the attack in November 2008. Ansari was made to go through Google Map and other maps to pinpoint targets like the Chhatrapati Shivaji Terminus and the Taj Hotel. Ansari drew maps for Muzammil and was later tasked to extensively videotape and photograph the locations after he returned to India. Abu Hamza (aka Ramzan aka Aamir) was a trainer at Baitul *Mujahideen*. Hamza and had a role in previous terror strikes in India like the ISI (Bangalore) attack of 2004. His inputs about making entry, traveling and then exiting the target areas were critical to the success of the Mumbai attack".

The book claimed that while Lakhvi and Abu Qahaf remained in touch with the terrorists from Karachi, it was Muzammil who was coordinating the attack pattern from Lahore, most probably from an ISI Forward Detachment at 7 Lawrence Road, Lahore. "Muzammil's satellite phone conversations with the Mumbai attackers after they had set sail from Karachi was intercepted by the US electronic and communication intelligence service, NSA (National Security Agency) and passed on to the Indian intelligence agencies on 18 November 2008, six days before the attack took place. Zarar Shah (aka Abdul Wajid), LeT's communications expert and urban combat trainer, confessed later of his involvement and said he had stayed with the attackers in Karachi for a few weeks to train them in urban combat skills. US agencies had intercepted his telephone calls to the attackers at the Taj Mahal Palace and tower. Shah, the intercepts showed, was directing the attackers almost minute-to-minute".

The authors of the book claimed that once the plan was finalized by the ISI, the LeT supreme Hafiz Saeed was contacted and his two key operational commanders Zaki Lakhvi and Abdur Rehman Makki were briefed about the requirements of the Mumbai operation. "They wanted two dozen men all fresh recruits, to be trained intensively in commando operations hostage taking and mass killing. These men had to be new; the handlers did not want to risk renegades or freelancers among the attackers. They wanted men who would obey them to the tee. They wanted martyrs. They knew none of them would come back alive. The LeT heads were told they had a year to train these recruits. During the training, the Mumbai attack team was briefed extensively about the movement of ships in the sea. They were told to use boats similar to Indian fishing boats to avoid suspicion and detection. They knew that fishing boats traveled in groups of 50 to 100 and it would be easy to dodge the India Coast Guard and the Indian Navy if enough precautions were taken during the journey. More than 10000 fishing boats travel across the Arabian Sea in a day", the book further claimed.

On 29 July, 2009, an exclusive news report published by *Los Angeles Times* and filed by a Pakistani journalist Zahid Hussain, claimed that Pakistani investigators have found substantial evidence directly connecting *Lashkar-e-Toiba* to the Mumbai terrorist attacks. While citing an updated report on Pakistani investigation handed over to India on 11 July, 2009, the *LA Times* report said the material recovered from LeT camps in Karachi and the coastal town of Thatta indicated that the terrorists were provided training and weapons by the militant outfit.

"The investigation conducted by the FIA gives some new and startling details about people involved in training and providing finances for the worst terrorist attack in India which heightened tensions between the two South Asian nations. The investigation has established beyond any iota of doubt that the defunct LeT activists conspired, abetted, planned, financed and established communication network to carry out terror attacks in Mumbai", said the report. According to the new details, the report said, training sessions, codenamed 'Azizabad', were held in an LeT camp in Karachi from where the investigators seized jehadi literature, inflatable lifeboats, detailed maps of the Indian coastline, handwritten literature on navigational training and manual of an intelligence course. Another training camp in Thatta was housed about two kilometers from a creek from where small boats sail to the sea.

On 27 August 2009, the Indian media reported that an investigation into the geographical locations of Internet Protocol (IP) addresses used for the Mumbai terror attacks led the police to places in Pakistan, Russia, Kuwait and the United States. Mumbai Crime Branch Cyber Cell inspector Mukund Pawar said in his testimony before the 26/11 trial court that five of the 10 locations traced were in Pakistan. The US Federal Bureau of Investigation actually gave the Indian police a list of 10 IP addresses and it was from these addresses that the email id kharak_telco@yahoo.com was accessed to make payments to CallPhonex, a US-based Internet communication service provider. Mukund Pawar said he was tasked with finding the actual locations from where the IPs were accessed. He said the Cyber Cell officials used the services of the website www.all-nettools.com to trace the physical addresses.

"I downloaded the information available on the website in respect of the 10 addresses. Five of the IPs – 58.27.167.153, 118.107.140.138, 203.81.224.201, 203.81.224.202, and 203.81.224.203 were traced to Pakistan. The IP 118.107.140.138 threw up the names Col. (retd) Saadat Ullah and Khurram Shahzad from SCO Qasim Road, Rawalpindi. Another IP led to Sajid Iftikhar, seventh floor, EFU House, Jail Road, Lahore. The rest of the three IPs were traced to the World Call Network Operations, 16-S, Gulberg, Pakistan. The remaining five addresses were proxies, traced to Chicago, Moscow and Safat in Kuwait", Mukund Pawar said in his testimony.

On 21 August 2009, India handed over a fresh dossier to Islamabad with specific information Hafiz Mohammad Saeed's alleged role in the Mumbai terror attacks. Having provided the fresh dossier, Indian External Affairs Minister S.M. Krishna said in a television interview: "Whatever evidence that we have gathered in our opinion and subsequently provided to Pakistan, is enough to get a person convicted if it is presented through proper advocacy before a court of law". But the Pakistani Interior Minister Rehman Malik responded by saying that India's only evidence against Hafiz Saeed is based on statements given by three accused detained in the 26/11 Mumbai attack case, and claiming that the banned outfit's leader had overseen their training and urged them in his sermons to carry out attacks. He said although Hafiz Saeed had been included in the Mumbai investigation, he would only be arrested after availability of solid evidence against him. "I assure my Indian counterpart, if there is evidence found against (him) during our investigation, he will not escape from the clutches of the law. We will take action," he added.

On the heels of the first anniversary of the 26/11 terror episode, a picture began to emerge of the planning that was behind the attacks and of a projected attack on the offices of the Danish newspaper Jyllands Posten, infamous for the publication of blasphemy against the Holy Prophet (PBUH). On 20 November 2009, the US media reported that two former students of the Hasan Abdal Cadet College in Pakistan, who are currently living in Chicago, have been arrested and are being interrogated by the FBI for their possible involvement in Mumbai attacks. David Coleman Headley and Tahawwur Hussain Rana were actually arrested for allegedly planning an attack on a Danish newspaper, which published cartoons of the Prophet Mohammad (PBUH) in 2005. But the investigations were widened into a global terrorism inquiry that led to arrests and implication of Abdur Rehman Hashim Syed, alias Pasha, a retired major of the Pakistan Army.

David Headley, who had changed his name from Daood Gilani in 2006, was identified as a US citizen who lived in Pakistan but was mainly a resident of Chicago. Tahawwur Hussain Rana was identified as a Canadian citizen living legally in Chicago, where he operated a travel agency. After subsequent investigations by the FBI, it transpired that Headley and Rana are graduates of a military academy in the town of Hasan Abdal in Pakistan, and they maintained e-mail contact with other former students, including officers in Pakistan's military. They belonged to a group of the school's graduates who referred to themselves as the "*abdalians*" in Internet postings. Both of the detainees were accused of reporting to Ilyas Kashmiri, the *ameer* of the Pakistan-based pro-Kashmir jehadi group – *Harkatul Jehadul Islami* (HUJI). Indian officials in Mumbai subsequently claimed that Headley and Rana had visited the Indian port city of Mumbai in the months before the 26/11 assault, and may have visited some of the sites that were attacked.

REFERENCES

1. *Asia Times Online* (AToL), Syed Saleem Shehzad, 4 December 2008.
2. *New York Times*, 5 December 2008.
3. *Dawn*, 12 December 2008.
4. Confessional Statement : Ajmal Amir Kasab, 23 December 2008.
5. *Mumbai Terrorist Attacks* (Nov. 26-29, 2008), Indian dossier sent to Pakistan as evidence of the *Lashkar-e-Toiba*'s role in the Mumbai terror attacks, 5 January 2009.
6. Investigating the Mumbai Conspiracy, Pentagon Press, New Delhi.
7. *Los Angeles Times*, Zahid Hussain, Report, 29 July 2009.
8. Rahman Malik, Press Conference, 12 January 2009.
9. Mumbai Terrorist Attacks (Dossier handed over by Pakistan to India in reply to the information gained by the Indian Dossier), 5 July 2009.
10. Indian Media Reports, 27 August 2009.
11. American Media Reports, 20 November 2009.

CHAPTER 3

The Rise and Fall of Commander Zakiur Rehman Lakhvi

Passion for jehad against India has been the defining feature of the life of Zakiur Rehman Lakhvi alias Chacha Jee, the chief operational commander of *Lashkar-e-Toiba* (LeT), already named by the Indian authorities as the mastermind of the 26/11 Mumbai terrorist attacks and now being tried by a Pakistani anti-terrorism court in the garrison town of Rawalpindi.

In the aftermath of the Mumbai attacks, it was Ajmal Kasab, the lone surviving 26/11 attacker, who had first named Zakiur Rehman Lakhvi as his trainer as well as the chief plotter of the attacks. The next development was that the US Federal Bureau of Investigation (FBI) provided Pakistan with a taped conversation between Lakhvi and the Mumbai attackers when the 26/11 operation was still on. The American investigators had already analysed the tape and concluded that Lakhvi was one of the speakers and that he was the handler of the LeT terrorists who carried out the Mumbai carnage. It was on 3 December 2008 that the Indian government officially named him as one of the four possible major planners behind the 26 November 2008 attacks. He reportedly offered to pay the family of Ajmal Kasab the sum of Rs. 150,000 for his participation in the deadly attacks.

On 7 December 2008, the Pakistani armed forces arrested Zakiur Rehman Lakhvi along with 12 other LeT operatives from the

Muzaffarabad headquarters of the organisation, situated in the Shawai Nullah area. Yet, despite an Indian demand for his immediate extradition, the Pakistan government refused to hand over any of them to India, saying it would hold the trial of the alleged 26/11 planners on its own, as per the law of the land since all those arrested were Pakistani citizens. As things stand, Zaki Lakhvi and four other *Lashkar-e-Toiba* operatives – Zarar Shah, Hammad Amin Sadiq, Abu Qama and Shahid Jameel Riaz – are being tried by an anti-terror court in Rawalpindi, inside the premises of the high-security Adiala Jail.

The importance of Zaki Lakhvi to the LeT's jehadi network comes from the awe he inspires among the *Lashkar* cadres who describe him as 'imam' of the jehadis due to his family's personal contribution to the 'cause'. As a matter of fact, two of his sons had lost their lives in the Indian-administered *Jammu & Kashmir* while waging jehad against the Indian security forces. Lakhvi's two sons – Abu Qatal and Abu Qasim – were gunned down in the Bandipora area of *Jammu & Kashmir* by Indian security forces in 2003 and 2005 respectively. His wife reportedly looks after widows and orphans of *Lashkar* men gunned down by security forces, in addition to other charity work due to which the LeT has succeeded in building a loyal cadre by caring for the families of dead militants.

Considered to be a close associate of the *Jamaatul Daawa* (JuD) Chief Prof Hafiz Mohammad Saeed, Zaki Lakhvi was born on 30 December 1960 to Hafiz Azizur Rahman, a cleric linked to the neoconservative *Jamiat Ahl-e-Hadith* (*Wahabi*). His family used to live in Chak 18L of Rinala Khurd area in the Okara district of Punjab – the same district where Ajmal Kasab grew up. Lakhvi's stock in the shadowy world of jehad zoomed through a marriage between his sister and Abu Abdur Rahman Sareehi, a well-off Saudi who was considered to be a trusted lieutenant of Osama bin Laden. Sareehi is believed to have contributed a hefty amount of Rs. 10 million for the construction of the Muridke headquarters of the *Lashkar-e-Toiba* in the Punjab province called the *Markaz Daawa Wal Irshad*, way back in 1988.

The same year (1988), Abu Sareehi founded an organisation in the Afghan Kunar Valley which recruited Afghan and Pakistani youths in the Bajaur Agency on the Pak-Afghan border, to fight the Russian occupation forces in Afghanistan.

The organisation flourished in the Kunar Valley and in the Bajaur tribal agency as hundreds of youths from Pakistan belonging to the *Salafi* school of thought instantly joined the organisation, besides hundreds of Afghans. Lakhvi was one of the main trainers at the Kunar camp of the anti-Soviet militants who became the chief operational commander of the *Lashkar-e-Toiba* upon its formal launching by the Pakistani military establishment in 1991. It was essentially the outbreak of insurgency in Jammu & Kashmir that indeed prompted the Pakistani establishment to bring the huge Sareehi network of Wahabi militants under its patronage and make Kashmir their new battleground.

Being the supreme commander of the military operations in Jammu & Kashmir, Zaki Lakhvi's prime responsibility was to identify young men, indoctrinate them in jehad and train them for specific missions across the border. On 7 April 1999, almost four weeks before the first shots of the Kargil conflict rang out, Lakhvi told the Pakistani English daily *The Nation* in an interview that another Indo-Pak war was already imminent: "We are extending our *mujahideen* networks across India and carried out attacks on Indian installations successfully in Himachal Pradesh last year. To set-up *mujahideen* networks across India is our one target. We are preparing the Muslims of India and when they are ready, it will be the start of the disintegration of India".

A few months later, at the three-day annual congregation of the LeT held at its Muridke headquarters, 30 kilometers from Lahore, Lakhvi justified the launching of the *fidayeen* missions in Jammu & Kashmir in these words: "Following the Pakistani withdrawal from the Kargil heights and the Nawaz-Clinton statement in Washington, it was important to boost the morale of the Kashmiri people as well as the freedom fighters. These *Fidayeen* missions have been initiated to teach India a lesson as they were celebrating the Pakistani withdrawal from the Kargil heights. And let me tell you very clearly that our next target would be none other than New Delhi".

On 13 December 2001, Zaki Lakhvi's dire threats, willy-nilly, were implemented through a brazen attack on the Indian Parliament, raising the grim spectre of war in the subcontinent. However, the

Parliament attack and mounting international pressure prompted then President Pervez Musharraf to ban the *Lashkar-e-Toiba*. On 24 December 2001, hardly ten days after the Parliament attack, Hafiz Saeed addressed a press conference in Lahore, resigned as the LeT chief and announced the launching of an Islamic charity organisation with the name of *Jamaatul Daawa*. He also announced the appointment of Maulana Abdul Wahid Kashmiri as his successor, but retained Commander Zakiur Rehman Lakhvi as *Lashkar's* supreme operational commander.

Nevertheless the separation between the *Jamaatul Daawa* and the *Lashkar-e-Toiba* engendered animosity between Lakhvi and Saeed. Lakhvi believed Saeed had floated the JuD to corner the massive funds that had been collected to wage jehad in Kashmir. He claimed that the JuD had no right to the jehadi funds as its charter was to preach and propagate Islam. Those close to Lakhvi, however, say he fell out with Saeed because of his decision to marry at the age of 58 a 28-year-old widow of a jehadi commander whose husband had died fighting in Kashmir. Saeed justified the betrothal saying he was providing shelter to the widow and her two kids.

The discord provoked Zaki Lakhvi to rebel against Hafiz Saeed and float his own group, *Khairun Naas* (KuN) and shift to Muzaffarabad, the capital of Pakistan-administered Azad Kashmir. Their animosity grew to such an extent that some of the Lakhvi-led rebel group members largely consisting of LeT fighters reportedly took an oath to assassinate Hafiz Mohammad Saeed. However, almost a year later, Hafiz Saeed and Zaki Lakhvi finally mended fences on the intervention of their handlers in the Pakistani intelligence establishment. Zakiur Lakhvi continued to reside in Muzaffarabad, where he kept training militants to wage jehad in Jammu & Kashmir.

In July 2006, India alleged that Azam Cheema, a *Lashkar-e-Toiba* operative who was accused of being the ring leader in the 2006 serial bombing of the Mumbai rail network [that killed over 200 people] was trained and sent to the Indian port city by Lakhvi. The Mumbai Police Commissioner A.N. Roy was reported as saying at a news conference that Lakhvi's subordinates planned the 11 July 2006 serial bombings, financed their architects, and trained the perpetrators. The men who carried out the serial attacks were allegedly trained at a five-room building located on Multan Road in Bahawalpur. The Mumbai Police Commissioner also claimed that an arrested militant, Abu Anas, had confessed to be the body guard of Lakhvi.

On 27 May 2008, the US Treasury Department under the Bush administration moved to impose financial sanctions against four people (including Zaki Lakhvi) who were accused of being leaders in a Pakistan-based jehadi group allegedly linked to Osama bin Laden and *Al-Qaeda*. The Treasury Department notification said that all the four held leadership positions in *Lashkar-e-Toiba*. The four included Hafiz Muoammad Saeed, the LeT's overall leader who plays a key role in the operational and fundraising activities of the group worldwide; Zakiur Rehman Lakhvi, the LeT's chief of operations; Haji Mohammad Ashraf, the Chief of the LeT's finances and Mahmoud Mohammad Ahmed Bahaziq, a main financier of the *Lashkar-e-Toiba*.

Stuart Levey, US Treasury Department's Under Secretary for Terrorism and Financial Intelligence, claimed while imposing financial restriction against the four LeT leaders that the LeT is a dangerous *Al-Qaeda* affiliate that has demonstrated its willingness to murder innocent civilians. "The LeT's transnational nature makes it crucial for governments worldwide to do all they can to stifle its fundraising operations", he added. Following the 26/11 Mumbai terrorist attacks, India once again alleged that Zaki Lakhvi, usually based in Muzaffarabad, had moved to the port city of Karachi in August 2008, from where the LeT militants set-off, so that he could direct operations.

As things stand, Zaki Lakhvi is reportedly extremely furious over the *Jamaatul Daawa* (JuD) leadership's decision to publicly disown him in his hour of trial instead of trying to bail him out. According to circles close to Lakhvi's interrogators, he is much hurt over the JuD spokesman's statement that neither Zakiur Rehman nor Zarar Shah had any link with either Hafiz Mohammad Saeed or the JuD. In a bid to shield Saeed, the JuD spokesman Abdullah Muntazir told the *Times of India* on 9 January 2008: "In any case, Lakhvi and Zarar, the two men India is talking about, were never associated with the JuD which has always been into charity work only".

This had been conveyed by Hafiz Saeed himself after the Mumbai attacks, the spokesman said, adding that there are "elements in the Pakistan government that wanted to target religious organisations". Circles close to Hafiz Saeed say there was nothing new in the JuD spokesman's stance as its leadership has repeatedly denied any link with them. However, a former LeT officer bearer who is now a part of the JuD confirmed that Lakhvi is extremely upset over the U-turn taken by his former JuD associates and complains that they have abandoned him at a time when he desperately needed their support.

However, one year after the 26/11 Mumbai terrorist attacks, the court trial of Zakiur Rehman Lakhvi alias Chacha Jee is progressing at snail's pace at the Adiala Jail in the garrison town of Rawalpindi. The sluggish pace at which the trial is progressing can be gauged from the fact that the Anti-Terrorism Court (ATC) of Rawalpindi consumed one full year to frame charges against Lakhvi and six others for their alleged role in 26/11 attacks. It was on 25 November 2009 that Justice Malik Akram Awan of the Special Anti-Terrorism Court, Rawalpindi Division formally indicted the seven LeT suspects. The accused – Zakiur Rehman Lakhvi, Hammad Amen Sadiq, Shahid Jamil Riaz, Abdul Wajid alias Zarar Shah, Mazhar Iqbal, Yousuf Anjum and Muhammad Jamil subsequently challenged their indictment in the Lahore High Court, saying the prosecution did not have enough evidence against them. But they failed to get any reprieve as the court disposed-off their petitions after directing the Rawalpindi's anti-terrorism court to consider their objections against indictment under provisions of the Criminal Procedure Code.

But as things stand, it appears that the ongoing trial of Zaki Lakhvi and his associates is not expected to conclude in the near future in view of the extremely sluggish pace at which the case proceedings are moving. Confusion had first surrounded the status of the trial on 23 May 2009 when the contract of the judge hearing the case expired the day the seven accused were likely to be indicted by the anti-terror court judge Sakhi Mohammad Kahut. Almost five months later, on 21 October 2009, in yet another setback to the ongoing trial, Judge Baqir Ali Rana of the anti-terrorism court No. 2, who was hearing the case, simply expressed his inability to continue with the proceedings, citing unavoidable reasons. His close circles were of the view that the judge was left with no other option but to quit after the lawyers of the LeT accused had expressed their no-confidence in the judge on 10 October 2009 and boycotted the case proceedings to protest his decision to formally charge all the seven suspects in their absence.

But there are those who believe that Justice Rana took the extreme step as he felt he was under pressure from "both the sides" with regard to the trial of the LeT suspects. There are also reports that the judge had received threats of dire consequences from some close associates of the under trial LeT leaders after he had indicted the seven suspects in the absence of their lawyers during a hearing on 10 October 2009. On 24 October 2009, Malik Akram Awan replaced Baqir Ali Rana as the trial court judge on the orders of chief justice Lahore High Court Khwaja Mohammad Sharif. On 25 November 2009, on the heels of the first anniversary of the 26/11 terror attacks, the defence lawyers of the accused sought the extradition of Ajmal Kasab, the lone surviving terrorist being tried in India, in an apparent bid to further prolong the already prolonged court trial. They were of the view that since Kasab was the lone surviving attacker, and his confession to Indian authorities formed a crucial part of the case built up by Pakistani authorities against their clients, he should be brought to Pakistan to face trial.

On 6 January 2010, the Rawalpindi trial court rejected the acquittal plea of the seven LeT accused. On 13 January, Zakiur Rehman Lakhvi approached the Lahore High Court, seeking his shifting from Rawalpindi to Lahore, saying he fears for his life by the Indian agencies. On 22 January, the Lahore High Court dismissed Lakhvi's petition, seeking transfer of the case from Anti-Terrorism Court of Rawalpindi to Lahore. On 27 January 2010, a Pakistani Federal Investigation Agency (FIA) report presented to the Rawalpindi trial court stated that there was sufficient incriminating evidence against the seven accused arrested for their involvement in the November 26, 2008 Mumbai attacks.

All the seven 26/11 accused, except Jamil and Yunas, have already been charged with setting up training camps at Yousaf Goth in Karachi and Mirpur Sakro in Thatta and training Ajmal Kasab and his nine accomplices. Jamil, Yunas and five absconders – Usman Zia, Mukhtar Ahmed, Javaid Iqbal, Ghufran Zaffar and Abbas Nasir –

have been accused of providing Rs. 398,722 to Shahid Jamil Riaz through cheque No. 2338-2 of MCB Bank, Drig Road branch, Karachi, in the account No 2464-0 of Hammad Amen Sadiq at ABL, Drig Road, Karachi. Jamil is also accused of obtaining a SIM card from Thuraya satellite phone in Jeddah and giving it to the attackers. Yunas is accused of being chief of the *Jamaatul Daawa*'s Multan chapter. All the seven arrested LeT men and 20 others are accused of planning, designing, instigating and providing all the required aid and abetment through common intention. The accused allegedly provided funds, arms, bombs, grenades and other items such as life jackets, inflatable boats, Yamaha motor boat engine, cell phones, GPS, and pumps for reaching India. Mazhar Iqbal and Abdul Majid are accused of remaining in touch with the accused killed in India and giving them instructions for carrying out the attack.

Ajmal Kasab – from a Street Criminal to a LeT Fighter

In his very first confessional statement given to the Crime Branch of the Mumbai Police, the 21-year-old 26/11 Mumbai attacker Mohammad Ajmal Amir Kasab had described his conversion from an aspiring street criminal to a loyal soldier for *Lashkar-e-Toiba*. He came to the LeT while looking around to buy guns to commit robberies after quitting a low-paying job at a catering business. The search led him to several *Lashkar-e-Toiba* stalls at a bazaar in the Pakistani city of Rawalpindi.

In his confessional statement, Ajmal Kasab gave a detailed account of his family background, his terrorist training and trainers, his role in the terror strike as well as the role of the nine other LeT militants in the Mumbai attacks. Born on 13 July 1987, the 21-year-old resident of Pakistani Punjab's Faridkot village is the third of five siblings. His family is from the underprivileged Kasai/Kasab (butcher) caste. Ajmal's father, Mohammad Amir Kasab, runs a *pakora* cart while his mother Noori Tai is a homemaker. Kasab's 25-year-old brother Afzal Kasab lives near *Minar-e-Pakistan* (Lahore Minaret) in Lahore. His sister, 22-year-old Rukaiyya Husain is married in her home town while his younger siblings, 14-year-old Suraiyya and 11-year-old Munir, live at home.

Kasab said in his confessional statement: "I had been residing in

Faridkot village of the Okara district of the Pakistani Punjab since my birth and I studied up to class IV in a government school there. In year 2000, however, I left the school and went to stay with my brother in Tohid Abad Mohalla, near *Minar-e-Pakistan* in Lahore. I worked as a labourer at various places till 2005, visiting my native place once in a while. In 2005, I had a quarrel with my father. I left home and went to the shrine of *Data Darbar* in Lahore, where boys who run away from home are given shelter. The boys are sent to different places for employment".

"One day, a person named Shafiq came there and took me with him. He was from Jehlum and had a catering business. I started working for him for Rs. 120 per day. Later, my salary was increased to Rs. 200 a day. I worked with him till 2007. While working with Shafiq, I came in contact with Muzaffar Lal Khan, 22... Since we were not getting enough money, we decided to carry out robbery to make big money. So we quit the job and went to Rawalpindi, where we rented a flat. Afzal had located a house for us to loot... We required some firearms for our mission... While we were in search of firearms, we saw some LeT stalls at Raja Bazaar in Rawalpindi on the day of *Eidul Azha*. We then realised that even if we procured firearms, we would not be able to operate them. Therefore, we decided to join LeT for weapons training".

"We reached the LeT office and told a person there we wanted to join the LeT. He noted down our names and addresses and directed us come the next day. The next day, there was another person with him. He gave us Rs. 200 and some receipts. Then he gave us the address of a place called Markaz-e-Toiba, Muridke, and told us to go to there. It was a LeT training camp. We went to the place by bus and showed the receipts at the gate of the camp. We were allowed inside... Then we were taken to the actual camp area. Initially, we were selected for a 21-day training course called *Daura Aam*. From the next day, our training started... After *Daura Aam*, we were selected for another training program which was also for 21 days. We were taken to Mansehra in Buttal village, where we were trained in handling weapons...."

"After that, we were told that we will begin the next stage involving advanced training. We were taken to a LeT camp in Shawai

Nullah near Muzaffarabad for advanced training... We were then taken to Chela Bandi Pahari area for a training program, called *Daura Khaas*, of three months. It involved handling weapons, using hand grenades, rocket launchers and mortars... There were 32 trainees in the camp, of which 16 were selected for a confidential operation by one Zakiur Rehman Lakhvi alias Chacha. But three of them ran away from the camp. Chacha sent the remaining 13 with a person called Kafa to the Muridke camp again. At the Muridke camp, we were taught swimming and made familiar with the life of fishermen at sea. We were given lectures on the working of Indian security agencies. We were shown clippings highlighting atrocities on Muslims in India. After the training, we were allowed to go to our native places. I stayed with my family for seven days. I then went to the LeT camp at Muzaffarabad..."

"After the training Chacha selected 10 of us and formed five teams of two people each on September 15.... The date fixed for the operation was 27 September [2008]. But the operation was cancelled for some reason. We stayed in Karachi till 23 November and then left from Azizabad in Karachi, along with Zaki and Kafa. We were taken to the nearby seashore.... We boarded a launch. After traveling for 22 to 25 nautical miles we boarded a bigger launch. Again, after a journey of an hour, we boarded a ship, Al-Huseini, on the high seas. While boarding the ship, each of us was given a sack containing eight grenades, an AK-47 rifle, 200 cartridges, two magazines and a cell phone".

"Then we started towards the Indian coast. When we reached Indian waters, the crew members of Al-Huseini hijacked an Indian launch. The crew of the launch was shifted to Al-Huseini. We then boarded the launch. An Indian seaman was made to accompany us at gunpoint; he was made to bring us to the Indian coast. After a journey of three days, we reached near Mumbai's shore. While we were still some distance away from the shore, Ismail and Asadullah killed the Indian seaman in the basement of the launch. Then we boarded an inflatable dinghy and reached Badhwar Park jetty".

"I then went along with Ismail to VT station [in Mumbai] by taxi. After reaching the hall of the station, we went to the toilet, took out the weapons from our sacks, loaded them, came out of the toilet and started firing indiscriminately at passengers. Suddenly, a police officer opened fire at us. We threw hand grenades towards him and opened fire at him. Then we went inside the station threatening the commuters and randomly firing at them. We then came out of the railway station searching for a building with a roof. But we did not find one. Therefore, we entered a lane. We entered a building and went upstairs. On the third and fourth floors we searched for hostages but we found that the building was a hospital and not a residential building. We started to come down. That is when policemen started firing at us. We threw grenades at them…"

"A bullet hit my hand and my AK-47 fell out of my hand. When I bent to pick it up another bullet hit me on the same hand… Ismail was injured in the firing too. The police removed us from the vehicle and took us to a hospital where I came to know that Ismail had succumbed to injuries. My statement has been read to me and explained and it has been correctly recorded", Ajmal Kasab's confessional account concluded.

While quoting Kasab, the Indian authorities also claimed that four days prior to the Mumbai attack, Lakhvi gave a final pep talk to the group of 10 terrorists in Karachi, before bidding them adieu on their deadly mission. "My brave soldiers, with sanity in conscience and enlightened souls, you have endured enough penance for the ultimate goal. The time has come. From now on, you all are *fidayeen* for the greater cause." These were the last few words Lakhvi reportedly uttered to the group of 10 LeT militants. Kasab told his interrogators that Lakhvi gave them the final lesson on '*Shahdat*' (martyrdom) in Karachi on 22 November 2008. "We had been taken to a small house in the Azizabad area where the sermon was delivered. Lakhvi then embraced each one of us and repeatedly asked us to be prepared for the *fidayeen* mission", Ajmal Kasab purportedly told his interrogators.

Nevertheless, when the trial of the 26/11 accused was formally initiated on 17 April 2009, Kasab pleaded not guilty and sought retraction of his confessional statement. Defence lawyer Abbas Kazmi told Justice ML Tahiliyani that his client was retracting his confession as it was obtained under duress. After the charges were read out to him by Justice Tahiliyani, the court officials recorded Kasab as saying: "I do not plead guilty". His lawyer subsequently told the court that the confession, made to a local magistrate by Kasab while he was in police custody were indeed extracted out of coercion and that it was not a voluntary confession.

However, almost three months later, on 20 July 2009, Ajmal Kasab stunned everybody in the Mumbai courtroom by making a surprise guilty plea, admitting his role in the three-day Mumbai rampage. "I plead guilty", Kasab told the Special Court in the Arthur Road Jail of Mumbai which was trying him for various charges including the shooting in the Chhatrapati Shivaji Terminus railway station that killed over 50 people and injured 90. He recorded a three-hour confession by recounting his actions and narrating to the court the entire plot behind the Mumbai terror attacks, confessing that he and his nine other accomplices had traveled to the Indian commercial capital Mumbai in a boat all the way from the port city of Karachi.

Among his new statements was that an Indian he identified as Abu Jundal had taught him and his accomplices Hindi before the attack. Kasab told the court: "I was firing and Abu was hurling hand grenades. I was in front of Abu who had taken such a position that no one could see him. I fired at a policeman after which there was no firing from the police side." Talking to newsmen outside the court room after Kasab's dramatic confession, prosecutor Ujjwal Nikam said: "Ajmal Kasab had realised that the cat was out of the bag after 134 witnesses gave evidence against him since the trial began in April. The DNA, fingerprint and closed-circuit television evidence had already been produced before the court, being some irrefutable evidence".

The sudden confession of Kasab, who had earlier pleaded not guilty and claimed he was a minor, came after a brief consultation with his lawyer Abbas Kazmi as the prosecution's 135th witness stepped into the box for giving evidence on the 65th day of the trial. As the judge asked him why he was confessing now after having retracted his earlier confessional statement given to the Mumbai police, Kasab reportedly said: "*Ab ye saabit ho chukaa hai, aur mai chahtaa hun ki mujhe mere gunaah ki saza di jaaye* (Now it has been proven that I am guilty and I should be given punishment for my crime)".

Significantly, his confession came a few days after Pakistan had acknowledged that besides Ajmal Kasab, two more of the ten LeT terrorists who attacked Mumbai on 26 November 2008 – Imran Babar and Abdur Rehman – were Pakistani nationals. The acknowledgment was part of the 26/11 dossier Pakistan handed over to India on 11 July 2009, which said that determination about the nationality of Imran Babar and Abdur Rehman had been made on the basis of their DNA samples.

During subsequent court proceedings on 22 July 2009, Ajmal Kasab told the judge that he was prepared to be put to death. "Please go ahead and hang me," Kasab told Judge M.L. Tahaliyani in the court. The judge was considering how to proceed after Kasab's sudden decision to confess, in lengthy detail, to being one of the 10 gunmen in the November attacks. "Whatever I have done, I have done in this world. It would be better that I be punished in this world. It would be better than God's punishment," Kasab said.

"If anyone is worried that I am trying to escape death by hanging, I am not. If that is the punishment, so be it." In his admission, Kasab told the court he had orders to take hostages at the city's main railway station, where he and an accomplice, Abu Ismail, opened fire and threw grenades. Prosecutor Ujjwal Nikam offered a skeptical take on Kasab's confession, arguing that the 21-year-old had made only a partial and 'half-hearted' admission, which did not cover all the charges.

Nikam also suggested that his apparent bravado over the death penalty was part of a strategy to save him from the hangman. "Very shrewdly and cleverly, Kasab has tried to save his own skin by showing he was acting as a subordinate to Abu Ismail," the lawyer said. "He knows that by denying a major role, no Indian court is going to award the death penalty," he added. Nikam claimed that Kasab, who said he was trained by the *Lashkar-e-Toiba*, could be trying to help his paymasters. "This is a very clever move made by accused Kasab just to save his bosses," Nikam added.

But Ajmal Kasab's defence lawyer Abbas Kazmi rejected the prosecution's concept of a partial admission and argued that his client's confession should either be accepted or completely rejected. Judge Tahaliyani earlier said he was 'absolutely satisfied' that Ajmal Kasab's statement had been made voluntarily and that he was aware of the consequences. "He did not give a statement with a view to getting a lesser sentence," he told the Mumbai court.

A subsequent editorial on 23 July 2009 by English daily *The News*, titled 'Destiny's child' stated: Although we do not know what Ajmal Kasab had to say regarding his indoctrination, the fact that he used the word indicates that he is very much a child of his time. Ours is a society riddled with indoctrination of one form or another from top to bottom and side to side, in every segment of society. It can be found in school textbooks in every province, and the foundations of our animosity towards India are laid in early life…We know that Kasab came from humble beginnings, his family are poor and when his trainers caught him in their web he was looking to pursue a life of crime – to hone his criminal skills the better to 'earn' his living. He would have been easy prey for them".

Like many other rootless or criminally minded young men, the editorial added, Kasab had little education and is open to every kind of half-baked conspiracy theory; open to being convinced that it is somehow worthy to enter a railway station and open indiscriminate fire on unarmed civilians, to kill and maim and terrorise in the name of whatever morally squalid doctrine had been planted between his ears. "He now has his metaphorical 'fifteen minutes of fame' before the court and the cameras of the international media. A finding of guilt seems inevitable and another young life will have been wasted, sacrificed on the altar of extremism and the product of a process of indoctrination that is pervasive and insidious. Whether we like it or not – and many find it difficult to come to terms with – Ajmal Kasab is one of our own. We made him. He was born and raised here by simple ordinary parents and went astray as many do in a country where opportunity is determined by what strings you can pull and how rich you or your family are. There are millions of potential Kasabs out there, and those who seek to turn their minds to the dark paths will have no difficulty finding a replacement for him", the editorial concluded.

On 12 October 2009, Ajmal Kasab told the Mumbai trial court that he had no faith in the Indian judiciary and that his case should be transferred to an international court. He had moved the application written in his own hand in Urdu language. The application was filed through jail authorities who translated it into Marathi and produced before the court. But Judge M.L. Tahaliyani rejected Kasab's plea saying "it is misconceived". On 31 October 2009, a Pakistani anti-terrorism court conducting the trial of seven *Lashkar-e-Toiba* suspects in connection with the Mumbai attacks declared 14 other accused, including Ajmal Kasab, absconders.

On 31 November 2009, the Mumbai trial court judge removed Abbas Kazmi, the lawyer of Ajmal Kasab, after he indicated that he was likely to cross-examine all 340 formal witnesses in the 26/11 case. Kazmi is determined to consume time of the court unnecessarily and the issues are being raised only with a view to drag the trial, Judge M.L. Tahaliyani observed.

In a dramatic turn around on 18 December 2009, a year after the 26/11 terror attacks Ajmal Kasab retracted his earlier confession saying that he had come to Mumbai to work in Bollywood films and had never seen an AK-47 rifle in his life. Retracting the confession made before a magistrate on 20 February 2009, Ajmal Kasab told the court that he had come to Mumbai almost 20 days before the 26/11 attacks. Kasab told the trial court judge that he had confessed before the magistrate but it had been recorded wrongly. He rejected the evidence of a witness, Bharat Tamore, that he was seen with 10 LeT terrorists at Badhwar Park when they got down from a dinghy there.

Kasab said that "*do baatein bolkar katham karna chaahtha hoon, aaj bhi mujhe bolne ka mauka nahin mila tho...*" (I want to finish by saying two lines, if I don't get a chance to speak then...) The judge cut him short and told him he had to answer questions the court put to him. Kasab disagreed with Tamore's version that he had seen the 10 terrorists at Badhwar Park wearing saffron jackets and carrying bags on their back and also a handbag. Tamore had told the judge in his evidence he saw two of the 10 terrorists closely and that Kasab was one of them. Several questions were put to Kasab based on the evidences given by witnesses. Asked about the dinghy, Kasab said he did not know anything about the dinghy. "I saw the dinghy for the first time in the court", he said.

The case of the prosecution is that the terrorists had reached Mumbai while using the dinghy. Ajmal Kasab denied having told the magistrate that he and Abu Ismail had hired a taxi. He also denied having told the magistrate that Abu Ismail was in the driver's seat and he himself was sitting behind and that he planted a bomb underneath the driver' seat while Abu Ismail was talking to the driver. To a question that witness Natwarlal, father of an 11-year-old girl, who was injured in the 26/11 attack, had seen him and another terrorist at CST, Kasab replied that he was not present there. "Maybe Natwarlal had said that there was firing on people but I was not there – I dont' know", Kasab said. To another question that Natwarlal had recognised him in court, he said anybody could recognise him by having seen my pictures in newspapers. About Abu Ismail, Kasab said that "I don't know who he is. Ismail may have been involved in the attack but I don't know him".

Kasab further claimed that he was arrested on the night of 25 November 2008 and that he was falsely implicated in the 26/11 case. "I was roaming in Juhu on the night of November 25, 2008. I had gone to see a movie when the local police arrested me. I had a passport and I'm not the first one to come from Pakistan to Juhu area. I was arranging for a house here. The local police first arrested me and then handed me over to the Mumbai Crime Branch. On 27 November 2008, I was produced before a magistrate. But I did not make any confessional statement before the magistrate and the one submitted with the trial court has been simply fabricated. The police have actually killed the main accused who resembled me and told me that his name was Abu Ali. I am his look-alike. His height and face resembles mine. I totally deny the confession made before the magistrate – I was beaten up by the police and was interrogated by foreigners and one of them was David Headley". Headley, a suspected LeT operative, was arrested by the FBI in October 2009 for plotting terrorist attacks in India and Denmark.

On 22 December 2009, Ajmal Kasab further claimed before the trial court that he was never given training in Pakistan. He told the court, which was recording his final statement on the prosecution evidence, that he was not a jehadi and had not undergone any training at any of the LeT camps. "I was actually a cook with a catering company in Jehlum and had never met Hafiz Mohammad Saeed, Zakiur Rehman Lakhvi, Abu Kahfa or Abu Hamza. I heard these names from the police after my arrest". When the trial judge asked Kasab if he was introduced to any Major General at the training camp, Kasab said, "This is absolutely wrong." When the special judge referred to his confessional statement that Hafiz Saeed had told 30 boys at the LeT training camp that they would have to lay down their lives for liberating *Jammu & Kashmir*, Kasab said: "This is absolutely wrong. As a matter of fact, the Mumbai police had threatened to administer electric shocks to me if I did not give a confessional statement to the magistrate. The statement you are referring to had actually been prepared by the Mumbai police and I was forced to recite it."

REFERENCES

1. *Times of India*, 9 January 2008.
2. Destiny's Child, Editorial *The News*, 23 July 2009.
3. Warning letter by the Crime Investigation Department (CID) of Punjab, Secret Communiqué, 22 January 2009.
4. Ahmed Rashid, *Daily Telegraph*, 4 March 2009.
5. News Report, *The News*, 15 July 2009.
6. News Report, *Dawn*, 22 July 2009.
7. Editorial, Destiny's Child, *Daily News*, 23 July 2009.
8. Court Statement, Ajmal Kasab, 18 December 2009.

CHAPTER 4

A Journey in Terror: From *Lashkar-e-Toiba* to *Jamaatul Daawa*

Dreaded for its guerrilla operations in the Indian-administered Jammu & Kashmir and known for the infamous suicide attack on the Red Fort in New Delhi, the *Lashkar-e-Toiba* (LeT) or the Army of the Pure once again hit international media headlines in the wake of the 26 November 2008 terrorist attacks in Mumbai and the subsequent allegations of its involvement.

Founded by Prof Hafiz Mohammad Saeed in 1991 in the Kunar province of Afghanistan, the LeT has proved to be one of the most dangerous jehadi organisations operating out of Pakistan and fighting the Indian security forces in Jammu & Kashmir. The lethal *Lashkar* happens to be an *Ah-le-Hadith* (*Wahabi*) jehadi group which was born as an armed wing of *Markaz Daawatul Irshad* (MDI) or Centre for Proselytisation and Preaching. The MDI was set-up in 1988 by three Islamic scholars – Hafiz Mohammad Saeed and Zafar Iqbal, who were professors of Islamic Studies at the University of Engineering & Technology, Lahore, and Dr Abdullah Azzam, a professor of the International Islamic University, Islamabad. Azzam was also the ideologue for the Palestinian militant group, Hamas, besides being the political mentor of *Al-Qaeda* chief Osama bin Laden. But the moving spirit behind the military might of the *Lashkar-e-Toiba* had always been Commander Zakiur Rehman Lakhvi, the prime accused in the 26/11 Mumbai terror attacks.

The main purpose of the MDI was to promote the purification

of society in accordance with the teachings of the holy Koran and *Shariah*. However, towards the end of the Soviet war in Afghanistan, the MDI set-up an armed wing called the *Lashkar-e-Toiba*. The militant group's objectives included establishing an Islamic state in South Asia and uniting all Muslim majority regions in countries that surround Pakistan. With the launching of the *Lashkar*, several military training camps were set-up in the eastern Afghanistan provinces of Kantar and Paktia, both of which had a substantial number of *Ahl-e-Hadith (Wahabi)* followers of Islam, with the aim of participating in the US-sponsored jehad against the Soviet occupation of Afghanistan. Since the LeT had joined the Afghan jehad at a time when it was winding down, the group did not play a major part in the fight against the Soviet forces, which had pulled out in 1989. But the participation of the *Lashkar* cadres in the Afghan jehad helped its leadership gain the trust of the Pakistani establishment.

Insurgency in Jammu & Kashmir beginning in 1989 came at an appropriate time to provide an active battleground for the LeT militants when its top brass was made to turn its attention from Afghanistan and devote itself to waging jehad in Jammu & Kashmir. The LeT almost immediately shot into prominence by launching several deadly guerilla attacks against the Indian security forces in Jammu & Kashmir, thereby establishing itself as an effective jehadi organisation operating in the troubled valley. Twenty years later, the *Lashkar* today is undoubtedly considered to be one of the most effective jehadi organisations operating in Jammu & Kashmir and involved in guerilla activities, largely due to its extraordinary growth in size, vast resources as well as fame.

The outfit has more than 3,000 offices across Pakistan and over two dozen launching camps for the militants along the Line of Control (LoC). Its jehadi network also has greater independence than other militant groups since the *Markaz Daawatul Irshad's Wahabi* orientation does not have to follow any of the four Muslim religious leaders or imams, unlike three other important Pakistan-based jehadi organisations – the *Harkatul Mujahideen* led by Maulana Fazlur Rehman Khalil, the *Hizbul Mujahideen* led by Pir Syed Salahuddin, and the *Jaish-e-Mohammad* led by Maulana Masood Azhar.

The *Lashkar-e-Toiba* operations in Jammu & Kashmir were given form at the annual convention of the *Markaz Daawatul Irshad* in November 1993, when Hafiz Saeed announced that Kashmir was the gateway to the liberation of Indian Muslims. On 5 February 1993, an armed group of 12 LeT insurgents attacked the headquarters of the 11 Jammu & Kashmir Light Infantry at Balnoi in Poonch district. Two soldiers and three *Lashkar* insurgents were killed in the attack. Since then, the LeT has been held responsible for hundreds of deaths and a large number of communal massacres in Jammu & Kashmir. In 1997, the LeT shifted its militant operations from the Kashmir Valley to the Jammu region. Consequently, there was a rise in militant activities all along the border districts of the Kashmir, particularly in the districts of Poonch and Doda.

While the primary area of operations of the *Lashkar-e-Toiba* is Jammu & Kashmir, it has been accused of carrying out terror attacks in other parts of India too, including New Delhi, Mumbai, Bangalore, Hyderabad, Varanasi, Kolkata and Gujarat. The *Lashkar* has been able to network with several Islamic extremist organisations across India, especially in *Jammu & Kashmir*, Andhra Pradesh, Tamil Nadu, Maharashtra, Karnataka, and Gujarat. The Indian authorities allege the LeT is actively engaged in subversive activities in the States of Maharashtra, West Bengal, Bihar, Hyderabad, New Delhi, Haryana and Uttar Pradesh at the instance of the Pakistani intelligence establishment to expand the frontier of violence outside J&K by subverting fringe elements.

Apart from waging battle, the *Lashkar* also focuses on conducting a war of nerves. This, according to Hafiz Saeed, has demoralised the Indian army so much that it has ended up using heavy fire, destroying its own buildings and causing the deaths of its own men in misguided attacks. Also, the *Lashkar* militants, unlike others, prefer to die in an encounter with the Indian security forces rather than get caught. For instance, in 1997, the largest group of militants killed in clashes with the Indian security forces belonged to the *Lashkar*. However, the LeT claims that it can sustain such losses as around hundred militants join the corps every month and a fresh batch of 'freedom fighters' queues up. The *Lashkar* prefers not to reveal the exact number of militants it has currently deployed in Jammu & Kashmir. What is known, however, is that the *Lashkar* recruits and trains many more men that it actually requires for fighting in Kashmir at any given time.

Compared to other Pakistani jehadi organisations, the *Lashkar* has proven to be a great success. Since its inception, it has managed to attract thousands of committed young men to its fold. And the driving force behind its success in recruitment is deceptively single. It uses its impressive organisational network which includes schools, social service groups and religious publications, to create a passion for jehad. But its militants are not sent to war just to die as martyrs; they are trained to kill: taught the use of infantry tactics and small arms – from handguns to assault rifles and rocket-propelled grenade launchers. They are also trained in shoulder-fired Surface to Air Missiles (SAMs) like the Stingers, taught through a 21-day basic course called *Daura Aam* and a three-month advanced course called *Daura Khas* that are geared towards guerrilla warfare and equip students to use arms and ammunition besides providing ambush and survival techniques.

A 2005 issue of the international edition of the *Lashkar-e-Toiba*'s mouth piece Voice of Islam even taught readers how to use swords, spears and daggers; how to set up an ambush and lay siege to camps and cantonments; and the rudiments of attacking the forces of 'disbelievers'. 'Learn all these things through Holy Koran,' said the Voice of Islam in its recruitment pitch for jehad. The *Lashkar* is never short of manpower or resources because of its affluent patrons, both internal and external, despite a so-called ban imposed on the group as well as its activities in 2002 by the Musharraf regime, in the aftermath of the 9/11 attacks. That is because the *Lashkar-e-Toiba* has innovative ways to raise funds.

One is by advertisement: "It costs millions to make a tank but only a few rupees to defend against it," says a *Lashkar* advertisement asking Muslims to pay for the *mujahideen* fighting in 'Held Kashmir'. The *Lashkar* advertisement concludes with a borrowed reminder: "If you are not part of the solution," it says, "you are part of the problem." Even by Pakistani standards, the advertisement is direct. And successful. Funding to the *Lashkar* has increased, coming mostly from Pakistani businessmen and those settled abroad.

Interestingly, the *Lashkar* is an extremely secretive organisation and takes great care to conceal the identities of its members. For this purpose, the LeT follows Palestinian organisations in the use of '*Kuniat*', which are Arabic pseudonyms adopted from the '*Kuniat*' of the Companions of the Prophet and later Islamic heroes. There are some distinguishing characteristics of the hardcore LeT militants. They neither shave, nor have a haircut, allowing their beards and hair to grow long. Like fighters of many other jehadi groups operating in Jammu & Kashmir, they generally wear *shalwars* that do not cover the ankles.

The *Lashkar* is believed to be the only jehadi group operating out of the Pakistan-administered Azad Kashmir that still keeps a comparatively large group of activists at its Khairati Bagh camp in the Lipa Valley. Another camp is said to be functional at Nala Shui in Muzaffarabad from where young militants are launched after being indoctrinated and given initial training at the Muridke headquarters near Lahore in the Punjab province. Unlike the past strategy of launching large groups comprising 25 to 50 militants on a regular basis from the camps located on the LoC, the *Lashkar* launches smaller groups of not more than five to ten people into the Indian-administered Kashmir, especially after the Mumbai terror attacks, and that too, at intervals.

Compared to other militant groups active in Jammu & Kashmir, the *Lashkar* has commanded significant attention because of two reasons. Firstly, for its well planned and well executed *fidayeen* attacks on Indian security forces in J&K and secondly, for the dramatic massacres of non-Muslim civilians. These two strategies had been designed not only to achieve maximum publicity but also to extract public allegiance, albeit out of fear. *Fidayeen* or life daring attacks are the *Lashkar*'s hallmark. The LeT prefers the term *fidayeen* to the more common 'suicide attack' because the ultra-orthodox Islam favored by its *Wahabi* leadership strictly prohibits suicide. The *fidayeen* attackers seldom return from these penetrate-and-kill missions as their aim is not to save their own lives but to maximize the frightening psychological impact on the enemy by inflicting death and destruction on their targets.

After the Kargil episode of 1999, when the Pakistani troops and militants, including those of the *Lashkar*, were forced to withdraw from peaks on the Indian side of the LoC, the LeT launched its suicide attacks strategy whereby small groups of *fidayeen* would storm a security force camp or base. The first *fidayeen* attack in Jammu & Kashmir was carried out in July 1999, shortly after the end of the Kargil war, when two guerrillas simply barged into a Border Security Force camp in Bandipore, a northern Valley town, firing indiscriminately from automatic rifles and lobbing grenades. Between mid-1999 and the end of 2002, at least 55 *fidayeen* attacks, usually executed by two-man teams, were carried out against police, paramilitary and army camps as well as government installations in Kashmir. Of these, 30 took place in 2001, making that year the high point of the *fidayeen* campaign. A total of 161 military, paramilitary, and police personnel died in these attacks (the Indian army alone lost 82 men), and 90 militants perished while executing them.

On 13 December 2001, a heavily armed five-man *Lashkar* squad managed to enter the compound of the Indian Parliament building in Delhi, where hundreds of elected members and government ministers were present at the time. Yet all the attackers were killed by Indian security officers after a forty-five-minute battle with guns and grenades. Nine others, including security staff, parliament stewards, had also died. The Indian government subsequently began a massive military buildup on Pakistani borders. As international pressure mounted on the Musharraf regime, especially from the US to act against the LeT, General Pervez Musharraf announced on 13 January 2002 launching a crackdown on jehadi organisation operating across the LOC from the Pakistani territory, besides banning the *Lashkar-e-Toiba* and several other militant and sectarian organisations.

The Pakistani action actually came a few weeks after the US State Department's December 2001 decision to designate the *Lashkar* a foreign terrorist organisation and freeze its assets. The LeT subsequently renamed itself *Jamaatul Daawa* (JuD) in a bid to separate its military actions in Jammu & Kashmir from its religious undertakings in Pakistan. While addressing a press conference in Lahore on 24 December 2001, a few months after the 9/11 attacks in the US, Hafiz Saeed announced his resignation as the LeT *ameer* and appointed a comparatively unknown Maulana Abdul Wahid

Kashmiri, as the new *ameer* of the *Lashkar*. The new LeT Central Executive Council comprised Maulana Abdul Wahid Kashmiri (the Supreme leader) with Zakiur Rehman Lakhvi as the Supreme Commander of the military operations in Jammu & Kashmir.

Hafiz Mohammad Saeed had stated at that time that his stepping down was aimed at countering strong Indian propaganda that the Pakistani government had been sponsoring the jehad in Jammu & Kashmir, though he added, in the same breath, that his departure from the high office of the LeT *ameer* was not due to any internal or external pressures, be it Islamabad or Washington. He further announced he would now lead an Islamic charity organisation, *Jamaatul Daawa* (or Party of the Calling), which was thought to be a front for the proscribed *Lashkar-e-Toiba*. Having stepped down as the LeT chief, Hafiz Saeed had to look for such a role for the newly-launched JuD that could be more acceptable to the world.

A week later, however, [on 31 December 2001], Hafiz Saeed was detained, on flimsy charges of making inflammatory speeches and inciting people to violate law and order. But according to the *Jehad Times*, one of the LeT mouth pieces, "Hafiz Sahib knew he was to be arrested and had reorganized the organisation in anticipation". Subsequent news reports in the American media alleged that Saeed was closely associated with Osama bin Laden's "International Islamic Front for Jehad against United States and Israel". However, on 19 November 2002, almost a year later, the Lahore High Court finally let off Hafiz Saeed, who had been put under house arrest at his Johar Town residence in Lahore. Soon after being freed, Hafiz Saeed launched the *Tulaba Jamaatul Daawa* (TJD), the student wing of the JuD, currently working aggressively across Pakistan to take its mission to youngsters.

The JuD survived a number of restrictions and threats from the Pakistani authorities in the next couple of years mainly because of the fact that it had already dissociated itself from the *Lashkar-e-Toiba*. In a bid to prove that the Kashmir insurgency was an indigenous freedom struggle – the *Lashkar* hierarchy had to announce in 2002 that it was formally shifting its base from Pakistan to Indian Administered Kashmir. The JuD further chose to camouflage its jehadi agenda by giving an impression that it was concentrating more on extending the invitation of Islam. According to Saeed's close associates, the cautions exercised by him helped their group survive a fresh ban imposed by the Musharraf regime on several other extremist organisations in November 2003.

Elaborating on the establishment's uninterrupted love for Saeed, Pakistani intelligence circles say the JuD *ameer* is more amenable to ISI control compared with the leader of any other jehadi outfit as Hafiz Sahib could readily agree to wage a 'controlled jehad' in the Kashmir Valley whenever asked to do so. Similarly, they say, the JuD's militant wing – the *Lashkar-e-Toiba* – is perceived to be more dedicated to the cause of Kashmir liberation and hence more useful, given the fact that it had the largest Pakistani component when compared to many other jehadi cadres. The rise of the *Lashkar* in the establishment's priorities is also attributed to its Punjabi base which helps easy mixing of its militants with the local population of Jammu & Kashmir, linguistically allied to Punjab.

Interestingly, despite being declared a terrorist outfit by the US State Department and placed on the terror watch list of the Pakistani government, the *Jamaatul Daawa* has been enjoying considerable freedom to raise funds and recruit cadres. Despite a government interdiction, banners can easily be seen in the urban and rural areas of Punjab province, urging young boys to enroll themselves with *Jamaatul Daawa* and *Lashkar-e-Toiba* for waging jehad against infidels. The banners usually carry the telephone numbers of the area offices so that the young men interested in military training can contact local agents of the jehadi group. The prospects of free education, free food and free lodging are very attractive in rural Pakistani society where people live under extreme poverty. And the JuD leadership knows how to exploit the situation.

Similarly, the LeT and the JuD activists can usually be seen outside mosques in the rural areas of Punjab, distributing pamphlets and periodicals preaching the virtues of jehad in Kashmir, Palestine, Chechnya, Kosovo and Eritrea besides vowing that it would plant the flag of Islam in Washington, Tel Aviv and New Delhi. The *Lashkar* leadership describes India and Israel as well as Hindus and Jews to be the enemies of Islam. The donation boxes of the *Lashkar* and the *Jamaat* that had disappeared soon after the Mumbai terror attacks and a subsequent government swoop against the LeT have already reappeared on public places as well as mosques across Pakistan. However, most of the funds still come in the form of anonymous donations being sent directly to the JuD accounts from various parts of the world.

Western media reports say the *Jamaatul Daawa* uses all these funds to run dozens of training camps for the LeT militants along the LoC, being the front organisation of the LeT. In its 2008 annual report on global terrorism, the US State Department said that after being outlawed, the LeT and Hafiz Saeed continue to spread ideology advocating terrorism, as well as virulent rhetoric condemning the United States, India, Israel, and other perceived enemies. The report noted, when a senior *Al-Qaeda* commander Abu Zubayda was captured from Rawalpindi in March 2002, he was located at a *Lashkar* safe house in Faisalabad. "This suggested that some LeT members were facilitating the movement of *Al-Qaeda* members in Pakistan", the US State Department report added.

However, Yahya Mujahid, a close associate of Hafiz Saeed and the central secretary, information, of the JuD, simply laughs off the State Department findings, saying the Americans are obsessed with *Al-Qaeda* and Osama bin Laden. In the aftermath of the 26/11 Mumbai terror attacks, the western media reports described the *Markaz-e-Toiba* (Holy Centre) compound of *Markaz Daawatul Irshad* at Muridke, 35-kilometres north of Lahore, as a symbol of General Pervez Musharraf's unfinished business where the LeT recruits undergo initial indoctrination before being dispatched for military training to its camps spread across Pakistan, especially in Muzaffarabad, the capital of the Pakistan-administered Jammu & Kashmir.

Spread over 200 acres of land, the *Markaz-e-Toiba* complex at Muridke houses both teaching as well as residential facilities, complete with its own farms, mosques, fish-breeding ponds and stables. Bearded men with Kalashnikovs and camouflage jackets guard the entrance to the *Markaz-e-Toiba*, which is surrounded by barbed wire and protected from view by tall trees. The education being imparted there – Islamic and Western – is from the primary to the university level for both men and women. Students are indoctrinated towards propagating Islam.

The *Markaz* also has a modern-looking, computerised religious university, which has five related institutions. At least two dozen thoroughbred horses are being used for training the MDI students between the ages of eight to twenty. Literally dressed in military uniforms, these students are imparted compulsory training in shooting and swimming. In fact, they are not allowed to cross the barbed periphery wire on the Line of Control until they are 'mature'. Photography of all living things which is anathema to Hafiz Mohammad Saeed is strictly prohibited. The *Markaz Daawatul Irshad* describes photo cameras, television sets and films as un-Islamic and its students carry out periodic campaigns for the public destruction of cameras and televisions.

Visitors are frisked for cigarettes and any other addictive substances, which are banned in the complex. The Muridke complex is also not just restricted to the *Markaz Daawatul Irshad*. The organisation has bought land around the *Markaz* for supporters, who have built houses, shops, more mosques and centres of Islamic learning. "We want like-minded people to get together", says a Muridke resident. Evidently that is happening. The JuD has transformed the land between Lahore and Gujranwala cities [at Muridke] into an Islamic state that has literally banned music, television and smoking on its heavily guarded premises. Not even passing vehicles are allowed to play music which, Hafiz Mohammad Saeed believes, is strictly forbidden in Islam.

Markaz Daawatul Irshad runs a huge network of social services, including 20 Islamic institutions, 140 secondary schools, eight *madrassas* or religious seminaries and a $300,000-plus *Daawa* medical mission that includes mobile clinics, ambulance service and blood banks. The *Markaz* complex also has a garment factory, an iron foundry, a wood-works factory, a swimming pool and three residential colonies. So far, Rs. 50 million had been spent on the *Markaz* projects. Where has the money come from? *Al-Qaeda* chief Osama bin Laden, whisper rumours. It is alleged that the Most Wanted FBI Saudi billionaire, a figure who has grown from being demonised by the West to being mythologised, rolled out (through his close associate Abu Abdur Rahman Sareehi), a thick wad – Rs. 10 million – for the construction of the *Markaz* complex. Bin Laden is even said to have financed Hafiz Saeed, his low-key, comrade-in-arms Prof Zafar Iqbal, and a short-lived founder, Abdullah Azam, to launch the *Markaz Daawatul Irshad.*

Abdullah Azam was a killed in a powerful car explosion in Peshawar a year after the MDI was launched. Prof. Zafar Iqbal, who used to head the Islamic Studies Centre at the government-run University of Engineering and Technology, Lahore, the same one where Hafiz Saeed served for 22 years as a teacher, now looks after the *Markaz* affairs, being its vice-chancellor. Saeed, however, will not speak of Osama, even though he is an ardent supporter of his anti-west jehadi agenda. He denies that *Markaz Daawatul Irshad* is a foreign-funded project and says the funds came from a group of affluent traders who had offered money to buy cheap farm land near a Muridke village – Nangal Saada, about one kilometer from the main Grand Trunk (GT) Raod. As per his claim, a Saudi trader, Ahmed, contributed Rs. 10 million (the same figure as Osama's) while another, Saudi Sheikh, donated more millions for the construction of *Daawa* Model School inside the *Markaz.*

The Indian investigators probing the 26/11 Mumbai terror attacks have already alleged that it was at the Muridke *Markaz* that Ajmal Kasab, the lone surviving attacker captured alive, started getting influenced by films on the Indian atrocities in Kashmir and by impassioned speeches the preachers used to make, including Hafiz Saeed. But the JuD spokesman refutes that the *Markaz* complex has ever been used for any jehad-related activity. Yahya Mujahid, the JuD spokesman, who had been the LeT spokesman till 13 December 2001, insists that Kasab's confessional statement was recorded by the Mumbai police under duress, which he has already retracted before the court.

These claims apart, international media keeps saying that the students at the *Markaz* are indoctrinated towards propagating extremist and conservative Islam since the syllabus of the JuD-run schools and colleges is guided by Hafiz Mohammad Saeed's own philosophy of jehad against the infidels. His extremely conservative beliefs are propagated through scores of JuD publications, including a multi-lingual (Urdu, Persian and English) website, an Urdu monthly journal, *Al Daawa* (the call), an Urdu weekly, *Gazwa* (the battle), a children's monthly, *Nanhe Mujahid* (infant militants) and an English monthly, Voice of Islam. As a result, Hafiz Saeed, despite having stepped down as the LeT *ameer* way back in 2001, is still considered to be the *Lashkar* ideologue and hardly anyone either in India or in Pakistan knows Maulana Abdul Wahid Kashmiri – his so-called successor.

Subsequently, the Indian authorities continue to attribute most of the major terrorist strikes on their soil – from Jammu & Kashmir to New Delhi and Gujarat to Mumbai – to the *Lashkar* besides seeking the extradition of its founder – Hafiz Saeed. December 2008 was not the first time that the Indian authorities had demanded from Pakistan the extradition of Hafiz Saeed for his involvement in the 26/11 Mumbai attacks. Hardly 15 months before the 26/11 assault, both the LeT and the ISI had been accused of carrying out the 11 July 2006 serial blasts in the Indian commercial capital which killed over 200 people. The Congress government had promptly demanded the extradition of Hafiz Saeed.

The then Mumbai Police Commissioner A.N. Roy had alleged that 15 persons had been arrested in connection with the serial blasts of whom 12 were directly involved in the blasts. "A top LeT cadre, Azam Cheema, who reportedly runs a training camp at Bahawalpur in Pakistan, has been identified as the principal conspirator of the Mumbai serial blasts. Many of those arrested in connection with the Mumbai serial blasts had received training in the use of arms and explosives at Bahawalpur in Pakistan on more than one occasion", he said.

The Police Commissioner added that the interrogation of two *Lashkar* militants has brought to light direct links between the ISI and the terror outfit, which strengthens the Indian case that Islamabad was actively supporting anti-India terrorist activities. "One of the arrested militants Abu Anaz has revealed he was the body guard of the *Lashkar's* second-in-command Zakiur Rehman Lakhvi and given detailed descriptions about the functioning of the terror outfit and the monthly meetings that take place between Pakistan Army officials and LeT leaders. Zakiur Rehman and some others of LeT used to meet Pakistan Army's Major Wajahat, Brigadier Riaz and Brigadier Haji every month in Muzaffarabad, the capital of Pakistani-administered Kashmir", he had added while narrating his findings.

On 14 August 2006, almost a month after the Mumbai serial blasts, Hafiz Saeed was put under house arrest in Lahore for a period of one month and his so-called Islamic charity – *Jamaatul Daawa* – was banned from all public activities for the time being, after the unearthing of a plot to blow up US-bound trans-Atlantic airliners taking off from London. The American and British intelligence sleuths had expressed fears that the JuD, which is also active in the mosques of Britain's largest cities, might have provided the money that was to be used to buy plane tickets for Islamic militants to bomb several US-bound passenger jets from Britain.

As a matter of fact, following the October 2005 earthquake in parts of Pakistan, the JuD had raised funds in several British Pakistani areas in London, Birmingham and Manchester. The *Jamaat* had also urged British people of Pakistani origin to go to the region to help in the relief efforts and hundreds did. Therefore, the British and the American intelligence agencies had claimed that five million British pounds or $10 million was transferred to Pakistan for the earthquake victims, but that less than half was used for relief operations. They claimed that if they had failed to foil the trans-Atlantic terror plot, the world may have witnessed the worst terrorist attacks ever, causing even more carnage than 9/11 or the 7/7 events. They alleged that from the 7 July 2005 bombings in London to the Virginia Jehad Network in the United States and an Australian cell broken up by police in 2007, a common denominator has been the *Lashkar-e-Toiba*.

The US State Department subsequently added the *Jamaatul Daawa* and its subsidiary – *Idara Khidmat-e-Khalq* to the Specially Designated Global Terrorist list in a bid to checkmate the *Lashkar-e-Toiba* from operating in any part of the world under disguise. A few months later, however, addressing a huge gathering at *Jamia al Qadsia Mosque* in Lahore on 5 February 2007, Hafiz Saeed declared: "The jehad in Kashmir will end when all the Hindus will be destroyed in India. Jehad has been ordained by Allah Almighty. It is not an order of a general that can be started one day and stopped the other day", he observed.

Exactly a year later, on 5 February 2008, addressing thousands of youngsters at the 'Kashmir Solidarity Conference' in Lahore, Hafiz

Saeed said that the time was ripe to take the war onto the Indian soil for liberating Jammu & Kashmir. "Washington and New Delhi are already engaged in a proxy war against Pakistan and it is high time Islamabad declare jehad against them to protect the security and integrity of Pakistan."

Six months later, international media reported in the first week of August 2008 that the 7 July 2008 suicide bombing outside the Indian embassy in Kabul [that killed 40 people including a serving Brigadier of the Indian Army] was masterminded by the Inter Service Intelligence with the help of *Lashkar-e-Toiba*. These reports stated that the suicide bomber who carried out the car attack was 22-year-old Hamza Shakoor, a Punjabi activist of the LeT and recruited by the Gujranwala chapter of the *Jamaatul Daawa* as a jehadi operative.

Almost five months later, the *Lashkar-e-Toiba* was once again accused of carrying out the 26/11 Mumbai terrorist attacks that killed over 175 people, undoing in less than 60 hours what the Indian and Pakistani governments had been struggling for over four years to achieve – peace and stability in the troubled region. On 11 December 2008, acceding to an Indian request, the United Nations Security Council (UNSC) designated the *Jamaatul Daawa* a global terrorist organisation while describing it as the frontal organisation of *Lashkar-e-Toiba*. The UNSC's *Al-Qaeda* and Taliban Sanctions Committee also declared its leader Hafiz Mohammad Saeed a terrorist in the wake of his group's involvement in the Mumbai attacks.

The UNSC Sanctions Committee further designated two other LeT leaders – Zakiur Rehman Lakhvi, chief operational commander of the group and Haji Mohammad Ashraf, the chief of the LeT finances – as terrorists. The Sanctions Committee also designated Mahmoud Ahmed Bahaziq, an India-born Saudi national, as a terrorist. He reportedly served as *Lashkar's* leader in Saudi Arabia and raised money for the terrorist outfit. However, despite the UNSC ban on the *Jamaatul Daawa* activities, its countrywide vast educational and healthcare network continues to run without any restrictions.

It was in the second week of December 2008 that the Pakistan government was made to launch a crackdown on the JuD, detaining among others Hafiz Mohammad Saeed and Zakiur Rehman Lakhvi.

But the JuD continued to use print and electronic media for propaganda purposes, in a flagrant violation of federal government orders. The JuD spokesperson Abdullah Muntazir issued a statement on 6 January 2009 threatening the Pakistan government with dire consequences should it decide to act against the *Jamaat's* infrastructure.

Incidentally, by that time, the American FBI had already identified Muntazir as the one who had been impersonating as the Srinagar-based *Lashkar-e-Toiba* spokesman Abdullah Ghaznavi. The Pakistani intelligence officials were told by a visiting FBI team that Muntazir had adopted this ruse – ringing up journalists from masked numbers – because of the JuD's official stance that it has severed links with the LeT, once it shifted base to Srinagar. Within the next few weeks, Muntazir was stripped of his position to avoid any further complications for the JuD. The only concrete action taken by the government against the JuD was the shutting down of its Urdu and English websites by the Cyber Crime Wing of the Federal Investigation Agency (FIA).

However, the JuD's Urdu-language weekly, *Ghazva*, kept hitting the newsstands, featuring hate material. *Ghazva* treated the Mumbai attacks as its lead story in the first week of December 2008, describing the gory incident as a historic victory for Muslim warriors who had actually avenged the grave atrocities being committed by the Indian establishment against the Muslim minority in several parts of India and in Jammu & Kashmir. In the same issue, Ghazva claimed that over 4,500 Pakistani mothers donated one son each and 83 mothers two sons each to the JuD this year (2008). Their goal: promoting, preaching and defending Islam, besides waging jehad against the forces of the infidel.

International terrorism experts believe that the focus of *Lashkar-e-Toiba*, which is inspired by *Al-Qaeda* in large measure, has expanded beyond India because it sees itself as a saviour of Islam. Once focused narrowly on the conflict in Jammu & Kashmir, they say, the *Lashkar* is evolving into a global exporter of terror today as its leadership has now opened its training camps to foreigners. Terrorism experts say Afghanistan may be off-limits to Western Muslims' yearning for jehad, but the terrorist training camps still operate in Pakistan and their graduates are proving troublesome for the West.

On 3 February 2009, the outgoing director of the Central Intelligence Agency (CIA) Michael Hayden declared that the Pakistan-based *Lashkar-e-Toiba* will be among the top ten security challenges for the agency in 2009. "Iran, North Korea and *Al-Qaeda* are the others that he and his successor Leon Panetta will have to deal with. This is an informal list that I kind of jotted down, what are the things I would fret about over the next 12 months", Hayden told FOX News in an interview about the nation's greatest security challenges. He said top of the list is still *Al-Qaeda*, which has been working on expanding its associations with other terrorists groups around the world.

"This development is particularly troubling because groups like *Lashkar-e-Toiba*, which was responsible for the attacks in Mumbai, start to think outside their region and focus on the United States and elsewhere. There was a migration in *Lashkar-e-Toiba* thinking over the past six, 12, 18 months, in which they began to identify the United States and Israel as much as being the main enemy as they have historically identified India. That is a troubling development and suggests that the migration of *Lashkar-e-Toiba* to a merge point with *Al-Qaeda* is probably taking place", Hayden added.

On 10 February 2009, a detailed study report into the Mumbai attacks, prepared by the RAND Corporation, a US public policy research organisation, said those behind the Mumbai attacks demonstrated a significant level of strategic thought that makes their group particularly dangerous. The study titled 'The Lessons of Mumbai' and conducted by 10 RAND researchers and terrorism experts argued that safe havens continue to be key enablers for terrorist groups. "Safe havens allow terrorist leaders to recruit, select, and train their operators and make it easier for terrorists to plan and execute complex operations."

"The defining characteristic of the Mumbai attack and what makes it so alarming, is not just the ruthless killing, but the meticulous planning and preparation that went into the operation," said Brian Michael Jenkins, a leading terrorism expert and senior adviser at RAND who worked on the study. "The goal was not only to slaughter as many people as possible, but to target specific groups of people and facilities with political, cultural and emotional value. This indicates a level of strategic thought – a strategic culture – that poses a difficult challenge: not whether we can outgun the terrorists, but can we outthink them?"

The researchers of the RAND study argued that the level of thought devoted to the Mumbai attacks demonstrated a strategic approach present in the planning, and the implementation of the attack that has not been seen before the attack by this group, and may indicate the development of an escalating terrorist campaign in South Asia. The study said given the terrorists' effort to maximize the psychological impact of the attacks, future attacks from this group of terrorists would aim for large-scale casualties and greater symbolic targets.

"At the strategic level, the Mumbai terror attacks show the urgent need for addressing the transnational sources of regional terrorism. And there is a danger in this type of terrorist attack that the attackers had local assistance from segments of the population that have become radicalized, which remains a significant political and social challenge", said the study. It went on to state: "The attackers designed the assault to do what the authorities were not expecting: seek a high casualty count, go after significant local targets and cause economic damage", the RAND study report concluded.

In a related development, the Obama administration has already charged the Inter Services Intelligence of "continuously maintaining links with terror outfits like the *Lashkar-e-Toiba* and *Jamaatul Daawa*". Bruce Reidel, a former top official of the American Central Intelligence Agency (CIA), said on 6 June 2009 in Washington that the US needs to be tough with the Pakistani establishment by sending a clear message to it that it cannot pursue a policy of selective counter-terrorism.

Pointing out that the ISI today is in a mortal battle with the Pakistani Taliban in the restive Swat valley, Bruce Riedel, who co-chaired the inter-agency committee of Obama administration which formulated the Af-Pak policy, said Islamabad has been pursuing selective counter-terrorism measures. "The problem is that ISI continues to have relations with groups like *Lashkar-e-Toiba*, with whatever its new name is and with the Afghan Taliban. It is selective counter-terrorism because the Saeed-led terrorist organisation continues to enjoy cosy relations with the ISI. What we need is uniform counter-terrorism", Bruce Riedel added.

On 1 July 2009, the US Treasury Department imposed sanctions on four leaders of the proscribed *Lashkar-e-Toiba* for their alleged *Al-Qaeda* links. The US Treasury Department said it was imposing an assets freeze on Fazeel-a-Tul Shaykh Abu Mohammed Ameen al-Peshawari, Arif Qasmani, Yahya Mujahid and Nasir Javaid. "Peshawari allegedly provided assistance, including funding and recruits, to *Al-Qaeda* and the Taliban militia fighting to regain control of Afghanistan and battling government forces in Pakistan. Qasmani is believed to be the chief coordinator for the *Lashkar-e-Toiba,* Mujahid the head of the group's media department while Javaid had served as a LeT commander in Pakistan", the US Treasury Department's announcement said.

Despite all these accusations and reservations being expressed by the international community, the *Jamaatul Daawa* once again sprung back as a charity organisation in mid-2009, providing food and shelter to the millions of people fleeing the fighting between the military and the militants in Swat and some other parts of the NWFP (following a military operation there), and moving out to safer places. The people of Pakistan had witnessed the same phenomenon in the aftermath of the October 2005 earthquake in Azad Kashmir when many proscribed jehadi groups had re-emerged under new names, especially the JuD. By actively taking part in the post earthquake relief activities, the JuD was able to paint itself in the minds of people as a charity group engaged in good work.

However, more than one year after the 26/11 terrorists attacks in Mumbai that literally shook the Indian commercial capital, the *Lashkar-e-Toiba* (LeT), which is the prime accused of carrying out the gory episode, largely remains unbroken and is determined to pursue its jehadi agenda under the guise of *Jamaatul Daawa* (JuD). Reeling under intense international pressure in the wake of the Mumbai attacks, the Pakistan government did incarcerate a clutch of the LeT/JuD leaders, detained Hafiz Saeed and Zaki Lakhvi, besides raiding militant camps countrywide. These actions fanned hopes that the *Lashkar-e-Toiba* and its parent body, the *Jamaatul Daawa* – would now be dismantled and defanged. However, no concrete action seems to have been taken at the official level to contain the JuD activities – amidst frequent international media reports that they continue to raise funds and recruit fresh cadres to wage jehad in Jammu & Kashmir.

That the LeT is still functional and carrying out its activities freely in Pakistan has already been confirmed by Abdullah Muntazir, the former JuD spokesman who was sacked by Hafiz Saeed following international media reports that he was also impersonating as the LeT spokesman with the name of Abdullah Ghaznavi. In a 24 November 2009 news report run by the Reuters and carried by the Pakistani print media, Abdullah Muntazir was quoted as saying that the *Lashkar-e-Toiba* has opened several new training camps in Azad Kashmir.

"The Pakistan authorities had closed many LeT training camps in Azad Kashmir after the Mumbai terrorist attacks but that had had a limited impact", the report stated, adding that though the LeT is officially banned in Pakistan, the group is unofficially tolerated as the only militant group not believed to have been involved in attacks inside the country. "The LeT cadres are seen as a kind of civil defence force in the event of war with India and going after the group now would create a new enemy when Pakistan is concentrating on defeating the evil of Taliban in northwestern regions".

On the first anniversary of the Mumbai terrorist attacks, Pakistan's renowned English Monthly magazine *Herald* reported in the title story of its December 2009 issue that the *Jamaatul Daawa* is still not an outlawed organisation in Pakistan even after a year of official rhetoric. "The report titled "Sleight of Ban" stated: "The *Herald* has not been able to identify any official notification that states that the JuD has been banned since none exists. The only notification pertaining to it is the one issued by the foreign ministry, which neither calls it a terrorist organisation nor bans it. Some legal experts, including international law expert Ahmer Bilal Soofi, insist that the UN resolution does not demand the Pakistan government to declare JuD a terrorist organisation. In Soofi's opinion, "Resolution 1267 only says that there is a list being maintained of associates of *Al-Qaeda* and Taliban ... this is not a list of international terrorists ... the idea is to put pressure on them so that they can dissociate from *Al-Qaeda.*" He even goes so far as to add: "Pakistan doesn't have a corresponding obligation to prosecute the organisation the moment its name appears on the list."

The *Herald* report further stated: "The Pakistan government of course seems to have a slightly different viewpoint which could be seen as unclear and contradictory. Federal Information Minister Qamar Zaman Kaira claims that the organisation is banned though he says the interior ministry would have the details about the legality of the ban and the notifications issued. (The interior ministry did not respond to the *Herald's* written request for an interview on the issue.) For the cynical, this could simply be evidence of deliberate obfuscation. And the most compelling circumstantial evidence of this is the fact that when asked by the Lahore High Court to provide a notification on the ban of JuD (in the Hafiz Saeed detention case) the government failed to submit any document – not even the Foreign Office notification. This then gives rise to the following question: what is the legal basis of putting the *ameer* of the JuD in detention and for closing and shutting down the organisation's offices and schools? That Saeed's detention has put the government in a fix is evident and it seems as if the judiciary is not satisfied with legalities of the issue. The status of the organisation's installations and immovable infrastructure is even less clear. A.K. Dogar, a Lahore-based senior lawyer who represents Saeed in the court, tells the *Herald*: "The action against the organisation is an administrative embargo but it has dubious legal status because the government has so far failed to notify under which law it has taken such a step."

The report added: "It could be argued that schools, offices and such infrastructure could come under "groups, undertakings and entities associated with" that the Foreign Office notification said would be 'frozen'. However, this cannot be assumed. Soofi, who specialises in international law and has followed the JuD case since it began, argues that this is a point of fact and not law and would have to be decided by the courts. However, this would require either the JuD or the government to bring the issue to the courts. This is why many feel that if the state was serious about the crackdown it carried out in December 2008, it could have avoided all these legal pitfalls by taking the steps needed and issuing a notification banning the organisation. This could be done under the Anti-Terrorism Act, 1997. This is exactly what the Foreign Office notification implies as well. The document states that "bank accounts, funds and financial resources ... of groups, undertakings and entities ... shall stand frozen with effect from the date of implementation of instructions issued by the State Bank of Pakistan or any other federal or provincial authority duly authorised in this regard under the law..."

"This makes it quite clear that if financial assets are to be frozen then the State Bank of Pakistan needs to issue a notification once the Foreign Office one was provided to it. In the same vein, if the state was serious about shutting down the offices and other entities run by the JD, either the federal government or the provincial ones could have issued a notification under the existing laws of the country. Soofi claims that this lack of real action is because the Pakistan government has been somewhat confused. There was tremendous Indian pressure which possibly unnerved the government."

But Haider Rasool Mirza, a Lahore-based lawyer representing JuD and Hafiz Saeed, has a more controversial explanation. "The government didn't issue a notification because it didn't believe JuD to be a terrorist organisation." Even senior government officials testify to this. "They are not clear on what to do," says a senior official of the foreign ministry. Others claim that the state is hampered by domestic opinion. A senior ministry official says that the state has no option but to act when the UNSC passes a resolution, "but at the same time we do not want to do things that don't sit well with domestic public opinion." The *Herald* report, therefore, concluded that the government crackdown was a knee-jerk reaction under international pressure and the state never thought through its actions.

To tell the truth, what position the government takes on this issue is directly related to what is happening in Indo-Pak relations. As long as the Pakistan government was eager to bring India to the negotiating table, its law officers were instructed to take the case very seriously. Indeed, the state's inconsistent stance towards JuD and its leaders since December 2008 has done nothing to restore international faith in the willingness of the Pakistan government to be transparent in the fight against militancy.

As the sprawling Muridke headquarters of the JuD came under intense media scrutiny after the Mumbai attacks, the federal government directed the provincial government of Punjab to bring under its administrative control the educational institutions functioning there and to ensure that they are not used by the JuD to advance its jehadi agenda in future. However, going by another *Herald* report published in its December 2009 issue and titled "Business as Usual", it is evident that the Muridke headquarters of the JuD are functioning normally. "Nothing has changed for those living, working, studying and getting medical treatment at the sprawling headquarters of the JuD outside Muridke town, about 20 kilometers north of Lahore. No one has been forced out of their houses inside the massive compound that also contains two schools, a hospital, a *madrassa* and administrative offices; nor has anyone working there as a teacher, doctor, clerk or accountant been told to quit. Children attend school regularly and patients get their check-ups and medicines without a hitch", the report stated.

But there is one difference, said the *Herald* story: the headquarters is, on the surface, no longer run by JuD itself. Since January 2009, it has been under the supervision and administrative control of the Punjab government, a change resulting from last year's United Nations Security Council Resolution 1267 against JuD. But a debate on the validity and the legal implications of the resolution aside, the administrative change has simply shifted the work – that JuD chief Hafiz Saeed and his close aides were doing – to Khaqan Babar, a civil servant, whom the government appointed as administrator. Even Saeed continues to visit the place regularly because "one part of his family lives inside the headquarters."

According to Khaqan Babar, the government hasn't changed a lot as far as running the headquarters is concerned. "We couldn't have fired all the staff working here before I took charge; there are hundreds of people. The government does not have the resources to replace them all," he told the *Herald*. "The government staff working under him consists of less than half a dozen individuals. And although Babar says that all the government departments including the police are at his beck and call, if and when he needs them, the fact remains that he does not have a permanent police presence at the otherwise heavily barricaded entrance. During a visit to the place in the middle of November 2009, the *Herald* found two stern-looking activists of JuD manning the entrance. They categorically stated that no outsiders could get in unless they had permission from top government functionaries or were accompanied by senior JuD leaders. Putting them on the phone with a prominent member of the organisation did not work either".

Inside the headquarters, as far as the *Herald* correspondent could see while roaming around the compound outside it, life appeared to be functioning as usual. "Small children in school uniforms were running into classrooms and a handful of bearded youngsters were standing in front of a half-built office block engrossed in some serious discussion." Curious clerks cast furtive glances at a frustrated reporter from behind their desks in reception rooms next to the blocked entrance, and a couple of dozen *madrassa* students were completing a late afternoon running drill in the large playground. Except for strangers and outsiders, people moved freely in and out of the headquarters. "The Punjab government has only taken over the administration there; they have not occupied the place. How can they put a ban on people's movement?" a JuD source asked.

The report added: "This is as far as the government's administrative control can go here. More surprisingly, government authority does not hold at all at the organisation's premises in Lahore near Chowburji crossing – where Hafiz Saeed regularly meets people and delivers Friday sermons when he is not under house arrest. The main gate is closed with a heavy steel barrier and rights of admission are as strictly reserved as at the Muridke complex. To get in, one has to prove that one has serious business inside the building; be accompanied by some responsible member of the organisation; be a regular member of the congregations that attend daily and Friday prayers there; or be a *madrassa* student. Otherwise one can try to plead with the men inside the small reception room next to the barrier for hours without success. The official JuD line, however, claims that the organisation is being treated unfairly and that the group will launch a legal challenge to the appointment of the administrator at the Muridke headquarters".

"The government has frozen all the bank accounts of the JuD

and its senior members. All six of our periodicals and newspapers have been stopped from being published and all our offices in towns and cities across Punjab have been shut down," said a JuD insider. "We have the right to move the court and ask if all these actions are legal and under what laws have they been taken." He also claimed that the government action is creating a lot of hurdles in the way of our work, although he insisted that the spirit among his colleagues remains high. "Although our offices are closed, our members are still active in their respective areas in raising money, running social welfare projects and spreading the JuD's mission. This is something no administrative action and curbs can stop us from doing."

Hardly a few days after the *Herald* story was published, US Defence Secretary Robert Gates said that *Al-Qaeda* was providing operational support to militant groups seeking to destabilise Pakistan, including the *Tehrik-e-Taliban Pakistan* and the *Lashkar-e-Toiba*. He singled out the grave threat posed to stability in South Asia by *Al-Qaeda* leaders having a free run in Pakistan, while opening a second day of contentious hearings on President Obama's new Afghan strategy aimed at tackling the Taliban. "Apart from the Taliban, we know that *Al-Qaeda* is helping the LeT, the terrorist group that carried out the 26/11 bombings in Mumbai," Robert Gates told the House Armed Services Committee on 5 December 2009. "*Al-Qaeda* is supportive of the *Lashkar-e-Toiba* and providing them with targeting information and helping them in their plotting in India, clearly with the idea of provoking a conflict between India and Pakistan that would destabilise Pakistan."

As India and Pakistan decided in February 2010 to restart the stalled peace talks, Hafiz Saeed suddenly resumed his activities by taking to the streets, holding a chain of public meetings, mouthing venomous anti-India slogans, promising to liberate *Jammu & Kashmir*, and stoking jehadi passions with impunity. And he was allowed to do all this from the platform of *Jamaatul Daawa*, already banned by the United Nations Security Council. For the first time after being banned by the UNSC in the aftermath of 26/11, the JuD was allowed [on 5 February 2010] to hold a protest rally on The Mall in Lahore under its original name. It is true such rallies are quite common on the Kashmir Solidarity Day, observed officially on

February 5 every year. But ever since the UN Security Council sanctioned the JuD, this was the first time the Pakistani authorities had allowed it to hold a rally under its own name. Although the JuD had restricted its public activities after the UNSC ban, it kept appearing on important occasions, but using dummy names - a common tactic used by the banned jehadi groups to keep them operational.

For instance, the JuD had observed the Kashmir Solidarity Day last year (2009) under the banner of the *Tehreek-e-Azadi-e-Kashmir* or Kashmir Freedom Movement. The Saeed-led so-called welfare group held yet another protest rally on 6 February 2009 under the forged name of the *Tehreek-e-Qibla-e-Awwal* (Movement to Safeguard the First Center of Prayer) to condemn the Israeli attacks on Gaza. Almost a year later, on 5 February 2010, hundreds of JuD supporters who came from various districts of Punjab province, took out "*Yakjehti Kashmir Karwan*" (Kashmir solidarity rally) from the *Markazul Qudsia* to Faisal Chowk in Lahore, walking or driving in vehicles and lustily shouting slogans against India and the United States - and in praise of the LeT. At the Mall could also be seen banners extolling Hafiz Mohammad Saeed, and makeshift stalls hawking literature on the ongoing jehad in Jammu & Kashmir.

Waving the black and white flag of the group and dummy Kalashnikovs and raising anti-India slogans, the JuD activists first gathered at *Markazul Qudsia*, the new headquarters of Hafiz Saeed, and began the rally after the Friday prayers. February 5 was also the first occasion Saeed had made a public appearance since his release from house arrest in October 2009. To the throng, the JuD *ameer* disclosed in his address to the rally that militant groups waging jehad in Kashmir were considering of renewing their armed struggle there. He then demanded, "Therefore, no talks with India should be held unless it pulls out its occupation forces from Kashmir and releases the water of Pakistani rivers... Any future Indo-Pak dialogue should include all contentious issues including unjust division of Punjab at the time of Partition, the Indian army's terrorism in East Pakistan, the demolition of *Babri Masjid* and Indian occupation of Hyderabad Deccan and Junagadh. As the Americans plan their exit strategy for

Afghanistan, the Indian security forces will have to retreat from *Jammu & Kashmir* in the same fashion..."

On 4 February 2010, a day before the JuD rally in Lahore, the *Jamaatul Daawa* had organised a Kashmir conference in Muzaffarabad, the capital of Azad Kashmir, which was attended by several key leaders of the pro-Kashmir jehadi groups, including the former ISI chief Lt Gen (retd) Hameed Gul, the *Hizbul Mujahideen* chief Commander Pir Syed Salahuddin and the *Al-Badr* chief Bakht Zamin. In his address, Salahuddin said the Kashmiri *Mujahideen* should flex their muscles to wage a renewed jehad if they want to get the Kashmir issue settled as per their aspirations. Rejecting Indian allegations about involvement of the LeT and the JuD in the Mumbai attacks, he urged the Pakistan government to lift the ban on the JuD and release LeT's Commander Zakiur Rehman Lakhvi. "He (Lakhvi) is our aide and an active member of the United Jehad Council who is behind bars for quite long, though no charges have been established against him so far," he said.

The Kashmir solidarity conference further adopted a declaration asking Pakistan to revoke the ban on Kashmiri militant groups so that Azad Kashmir could once again become the base for waging the freedom struggle in *Jammu & Kashmir*. The declaration also warned Islamabad that friendship with India won't be tolerated, and that the Indian army should be taken to the international court of justice for committing war crimes in Kashmir. "If the Pakistan government can't extend any political, diplomatic and moral support to the people of Kashmir, it should at least give a free hand to *mujahideen* to tackle India on their own", the jehadi declaration concluded.

Indeed, Hafiz Mohammad Saeed was just about everywhere in the first week of February. On 2 February 2010, he attended a seminar organised by a fanatic Urdu newspaper (*Nawa-e-Waqat*) and warned India that it would be held accountable for every single Muslim martyred in Jammu & Kashmir. He accused India of illegally constructing 62 dams on the rivers flowing into Pakistan, with the sinister aim of turning the country barren. But Indian design would fail because these dams are bound to become Pakistan's once *Jammu & Kashmir* is liberated - which, he said, has to happen one day. On 5 February, the same Urdu daily published an article by the JuD *ameer*, stating: "India has been trying to malign the freedom struggle in *Jammu & Kashmir* by falsely implicating Pakistani jehadi groups in the 26/11 attacks despite the fact that it has miserably failed to prove any Pakistani involvement in these attacks so far. Under the present circumstances, the Pakistan government should adopt an aggressive stance and expose all Indian conspiracies besides internationalizing the Kashmir issue", Saeed concluded.

The subliminal message from the Pakistani establishment, therefore, seems: anti-India jehadi groups like the *Lashkar-e-Toiba/Jamaatul Daawa* can't be hounded as the *Tehrik-e-Taliban Pakistan*. Hence, the Pakistani establishment is in no mood to act against the vast jehadi infrastructure of the JuD as well as its leadership which is actually the moving spirit behind the military muscle of the LeT. As a result, the LeT continues to survive and morph into something that threatens both India and Pakistan, amidst fears that as long as the JuD leadership is allowed to move freely and the jehadi infrastructure of the group is there to exist, somebody is going to do something sooner or later.

REFERENCES

1. *Voice of Islam*, 2005.
2. *Ghazva*, December 2008.
3. Interview, *FOX News*, 3 February 2009.
4. The Lessons of Mumbai, *RAND Corporation*, 10 February 2009.
5. Bruce Reidel, Central Intelligence Agency (CIA), Statement, 6 June 2009.
6. *Reuters*, 24 November 2009.
7. *Herald*, Report, December 2009.
8. Robert Gates, Statement, 5 December 2009.
9. Public Speech, Hafiz Saeed, 5 February 2010.
10. Seminar Speech, Hafiz Saeed, 2 February 2010.

CHAPTER 5

Hafiz Mohammad Saeed: A Professor who Turned Aggressor

"Jehad is not about Jammu & Kashmir only. About 15 years ago, people might have found it ridiculous if someone told them about the disintegration of the USSR. Today, I announce the break-up of India, Insha-Allah. We will not rest until the whole of India is dissolved into Pakistan". – Hafiz Mohammad Saeed, the founder of Lashkar-e-Toiba (LeT) on 3 November 1999, in Lahore.

Some people don't evolve. They only ride the crest of passion hoping to realise their dreams of destruction. Nine years after the above-quoted rabble-rousing in Lahore, the former professor of Islamic Studies at the government-run University of Engineering and Technology, Lahore, was back to spewing vitriol against India. In his Friday sermon on 17 October 2008, again in Lahore, at *Jamia al Qudsia Mosque*, which is touted as the second JuD headquarters, a visibly charged JuD *ameer* ranted: "India has blocked the Chenab waters and constructed the Baglihar Dam. The only reason all this has happened is because jehad-e-Kashmir has been abandoned by the rulers. India understands only the language of jehad, which cannot be suppressed. In fact, with some support, jehad can break up India like the former USSR".

Hardly 40 days later, on 26 November 2008, the *Lashkar-e-Toiba* – founded by Hafiz Saeed almost two decades ago – carried out the lethal 26/11 Mumbai terrorist attacks. A cursory glance at Saeed's public speeches of the last ten years indicate that India, Israel and the United States – Hindus, Jews and Americans, in that order, have been his three main targets as he believes they are the main enemies of Islam and Pakistan. A *Lashkar-e-Toiba* pamphlet titled 'Why Are We Waging Jehad?' clarifies matters further and establishes the Muslim right to revenge in history. "Jehad is obligatory, it pronounces, for taking back Spain where Muslims ruled for 800 years. The same goes for Nepal and Myanmar. Of course, the whole of India, including Jammu & Kashmir, Hyderabad, Bihar, Junagarh and Assam, also has to be retaken".

To most of us, Prof Hafiz Mohammad Saeed's jehadi zeal may seem appalling. But there are hundreds of young men who find that kind of rhetoric inspiring and are willing to sacrifice their lives to rain destruction on India. Perhaps it was his fiery speeches that persuaded Hamza Shakoor, a suspected *Lashkar-e-Toiba* militant from Gujranwala district, to ram an explosives-laden vehicle into the Indian embassy in Kabul in July 2008. And the lone surviving Mumbai attacker Ajmal Kasab has already confessed having been indoctrinated at the Muridke headquarters of the *Jamaatul Daawa* where Hafiz Saeed and his jehadi associates used to deliver lectures on the attributes of jehad. But legally speaking, Saeed can't be blamed for the violence the LeT perpetrates since he now heads the JuD which he claims has nothing to do with the *Lashkar*.

At first sight, Hafiz Saeed is an academician, jovial man who wears an easy smile on his face and, invariably, a Turkish cap on his head ... a *shalwar kameez*-clad man, thoroughly Eastern in dress and habit, who is friendly and humble towards those who listen carefully to him ... probably a person whose only introduction to cosmetics has been the *henna* that is regularly applied to his long beard – a regular feature on a regular face in this part of the world. At first sight – it is a face that hardly begs for the camera. Look closer – it is a face that shies away from cameras as a rule. It has good reason to: Islam, the much un-photographed man says, forbids the capture of human images. Human lives, however, are another matter. The *Lashkar-e-Toiba* is the Professor's brainchild, crafted through an interpretation of militant Islam. For him, killing infidels is a pious man's obligation: it is his duty "to destroy the forces of evil and disbelief." And the

Professor is a very pious man. His kind of piety has also given him dubious distinctions.

Hafiz Saeed, who likes to give the impression of a scholarly man, is much more than that. Outwardly a simple Punjabi, who speaks the tongue of the region, has broken a fifty-five-year-old tradition: before him, the Pushtuns always led the jehad against India. Now, the LeT ranks have just a few Pushtuns and even fewer Kashmiris. Though he cultivates simplicity, Saeed always moves under tight security due to safety concerns. His preferred vehicle is the hardy Land Cruiser.

The Professor is generally surrounded by young followers with whom he is quite frank. The leader and his keen young group talk freely. Most of the youngsters are from big families that count close to ten members. The Professor favours the big-family norm, reasoning that greater Muslim numbers translate into many more fighters of jehad against the infidels. Once in the *Lashkar*, the youngsters are drawn into a pattern of community life, epitomised by the shared, common meal. All young men eat together using their fingers to pick food from a big, shared bowl. This simple occasion is like a rite, symbolising and encouraging fraternity among the comrades-in-arms.

The Professor himself comes from a close-knit family. He is married to the daughter of his maternal uncle, Hafiz Mohammad Abdullah Bahawalpuri, a well known religious leader and renowned *Ahl-e-Hadith* scholar. But, interestingly, he heads a very small family unit: one son and one daughter. Three members from among his widely dispersed family have been drawn into the organisation's ranks. Before the 26/11 Mumbai terror attacks, his only son, 35 year-old Talha Saeed, used to look after the JuD affairs at its base camp in Muzaffarabad, the capital of Pakistan administered Kashmir. His brother-in-law, Abdul Rehman Makki, is his close partner and holds an important position in the *Markaz-e-Toiba* at Muridke. Makki spent many years in Saudi Arabia before settling down in Pakistan. Saeed's son-in-law Khalid Waleed is also associated with the *Lashkar's* organisational set-up in Lahore.

Three of Hafiz Saeed's real brothers – Hafiz Mohammad Hamid, Hafiz Mohammad Masood and Hafiz Mohammad Hannan – used to live in the United States till June 2007, running three separate

Islamic centers in Massachusetts as prayer leaders. However, on 4 June 2007, Hafiz Mohammad Hamid, who was being tried by a US federal immigration court on charges of committing immigration irregularities, finally lost his case and was ordered to leave the US along with his family. The US immigration authorities had arrested on 15 November 2006 all the three Boston-based prayer leaders – Hafiz Hamid, Hafiz Masood and Hafiz Hannan as part of a wide swoop carried out by the US Immigration and Customs Enforcement agents in connection with an investigation into a specific visa fraud scheme that was designed to help large numbers of illegal aliens, primarily from Pakistan, fraudulently obtain religious worker visas to enter or remain in the United States.

Hafiz Mohammad Masood was a prayer leader at the Islamic Centre of New England, Sharon, Massachusetts, Hafiz Mohammad Hannan was an Imam at the Islamic Society of Greater Lowell, Massachusetts, while Hafiz Mohammad Hamid was a prayer leader at the Islamic Society of Greater Worcester, Massachusetts. According to the US Immigration and Customs Enforcement findings, the three came to the United States in 1988 on student exchange visas to Boston University and studied there till 1990, but stayed on, violating their visa status. Although the three were released on bail, they were facing legal proceedings especially after their family relations with the *Lashkar* chief Hafiz Saeed had been confirmed. Interestingly, Hamid lost his case despite the fact that he had disowned his real brother Hafiz Saeed before the court and sought asylum in the United States.

His other brothers, Hafiz Masood and Hafiz Hannan, are also facing deportation proceedings. But as far as Hafiz Saeed is concerned he has never traveled to the US or set foot anywhere in the West. And unlike most fundamentalists, he does not express deep hatred for it. But his critics say his past has been bloody, with a cause for revenge. Thirty-six members of his family were killed during the Partition of the Indo-Pak sub-continent in August 1947 when his father, Kamaluddin, an ordinary landlord, moved to Pakistan. Kamaluddin first tried to settle his family in Sargodha district of Punjab, but finally chose Village 126 Janubi, in the Mianwali district. A government land grant to the settlers and hard work soon brought prosperity to the family, an effect that Hafiz Saeed credits to Allah's bounty.

The Professor's parents were religious-minded and his mother used to teach the Holy Koran to her seven children, five of whom are still alive. Saeed was a good learner, and memorised the Koran. His favourite verse is: *Wajahidu Fee Sabilallah*: Wage a holy war in the name of Allah. In college days, he furthered his religious interests. After graduating from the Government College at Sargodha, he came to Lahore and was admitted to the Punjab University Lahore. According to writer and analyst Arif Jamal, Hafiz Saeed started his political career as a student and rose to become the *Nazim-e-Aala* (Chief Organiser) of the *Islami Jamiat Tulaba* (the student wing of the *Jamaat-e-Islami*) at the Punjab University Lahore in the early 1970s.

After completing his education at Punjab University, Saeed went to Islamabad and worked in the Islamic Ideological Council as a research officer for a couple of years after which he joined Islamic Studies Department of the University of Engineering & Technology, Lahore as a teacher of Islamic Studies. Afterwards, he went on a scholarship to study at the King Saud University, Riyadh in 1982 and came back in 1984. He frequently met religious scholars and even received special religious instruction. Indeed, his first job in Pakistan was as a research officer for the Islamic Ideological Council (ICI) and his last job was with the University of Engineering and Technology (UET), Lahore from where he took premature retirement as professor of Islamic Studies to fully devote himself to his organisation *Markaz Daawatul Irshad*, which was launched in 1988.

Before that, Saeed had been involved in *Dawat* (call to Islam) and formed a small *Ahl-e-Hadith* group in Lahore along with his University colleague Zafar Iqbal. The group used to organise small *Daroos* (lectures) gatherings. Arif Jamal writes in *The News* that Saeed had become convinced of participating in the Afghan jehad by this time, but could not decide which group to join because the Afghan jehad had not attracted any big *Ahl-e-Hadith* group from Pakistan. "His dream came true when Maulana Zakiur Rehman Lakhvi invited him to join his small group to wage jehad in Nooristan region of Afghanistan. Hafiz Saeed reinvigorated the *Ahl-e-Hadith* jehadi group in Nooristan. The group reorganised itself under the name of *Daawatul Irshad* to systematically wage jehad in Afghanistan. The group chose Hafiz Mohammad Saeed as its *ameer* because he distinguished himself among the group".

He further writes: "The existing *Ahl-e-Hadith party, Jamiat-Ahl-e-Hadith (JAH)*, opposed the formation of the *Markaz Daawatul Irshad* tooth and nail. The *Markaz Daawatul Irshad* apparently failed to win official Saudi support because of the efforts of the *Jamiat-Ahl-e-Hadith*. The *Markaz* was also barred from recruiting students from the *Ahl-e-Hadith madrassas* because a majority of them were under the control of the *Jamiat-Ahl-e-Hadith*. However, some Saudi sheikhs privately helped the *Markaz*. Under the leadership of Hafiz Saeed, the *Markaz* found alternative solutions to the emerging problems. Instead of recruiting from amongst the students of religious seminaries, as had been the traditional practice in Pakistan, the *Markaz* recruited from amongst the have-nots. Instead of looking for official financial support, *Markaz Daawatul Irshad* turned to the affluent classes both in Pakistan and the Middle East".

However, the brightest moment for Hafiz Saeed and his group came after they formed the *Lashkar-e-Toiba* to wage jehad in Jammu & Kashmir. That was also the time when it attracted the attention of the Pakistani military and intelligence establishment. The *Markaz* grew into one of the biggest militias in the Muslim world in the 1990s. As the *Lashkar-e-Toiba* grew into a formidable anti-India jehadi group, *Markaz Daawatul Irshad* also revived the old theory of jehad with all its hidden and abandoned dimensions. The *Markaz* faced the most serious crisis since its creation in the aftermath of the 9/11 terrorist attacks. However, Hafiz Saeed was asked by his spy masters in the ISI to save his party by dividing the *Markaz* into two groups – the *Jamaatul Daawa* and the *Lashkar-e-Toiba*. The JuD was to act like an Islamic charity organisation while the LeT was confined to the Jammu & Kashmir region.

However, the Professor is at pains to deny the widely held belief that he is or had ever been on the payroll of Inter Services Intelligence to wage the Kashmir jehad. "We do not get a single rupee from the Pakistan government," says Saeed. His critics, however, say neither the *Lashkar-e-Toiba* nor Hafiz Saeed would have been able to grow from strength to strength had they not been enjoying the ISI's backing. The LeT is one of the most active militant groups working inside the Jammu & Kashmir valley today, with operations based on the Pakistani side of the border. And the *Lashkar* is quite daring and vocal in claiming responsibility for its terrorist activities in Jammu & Kashmir.

"Be it the camp at Bandipura or the headquarters of 15 Corp Badamibagh, Red Fort at Delhi or the Srinagar airport," its website boasts, "the *mujahideen* have proved that no place on the Indian soil was out of their reach." Such glaring admissions, followed by the attack on Indian Parliament on 13 December 2001, provided the Indian government with an ample opportunity to pressurise the US State Department to designate the *Lashkar* a terrorist organisation. However, despite being banned, the *Lashkar* moves on and claims to have acquired Chinese anti-aircraft guns and 60 mm heavy mortars.

"Our cadres have procured the latest Chinese-made guns which can be used against fighter aircraft and to destroy bridges and buildings," trumpets the *Lashkar-e-Toiba* mouthpiece, *Jehad Times*. The *Lashkar* also has heavy mortars that are accurate up to 2.5 kilometers. These sophisticated arms have already been pushed into *Jammu & Kashmir*. The LeT does not lack communication lines either: militants use the latest technology to keep in touch with their commanders across the border. The group reached this level of sophistication after receiving significant covert aid from the US Central Intelligence Agency (CIA) during the early 90s to fight the Soviet invaders inside Afghanistan.

Hafiz Saeed has no qualms in admitting that he participated in the US-sponsored jehad against the Russians in Afghanistan. "The US supported us with guns during the Afghan jehad. If we were not terrorists at that time, then why are we terrorists now? Maybe because of Kashmir", he had stated in a 2002 interview. The Professor likens the Indian occupation of the disputed territory to the Soviet occupation of Afghanistan. For him Kashmir is a battlefield for jehad, a fifty-three-year-old 'custody battle', an open-and-shut case with Pakistan in the right. Not only does he want Jammu & Kashmir to become a part of Pakistan, he also wants Pakistan to become a part of a global Islamic state – in the true sense. Because the Professor, an avid student of religion in college, believes that there is no Islamic government in the world. His worldview, knocked down into two basic sentences, is straight and simple: "God has ordained every Muslim to fight until His rule is established. We have no option but to follow God's order", he pleads.

Therefore, the Professor is following God's order and the instrument of God's order is jehad. The *Markaz Daawatul Irshad* website [which was shut down by the Pakistan government in the aftermath of the 26/11 Mumbai attacks] used to quote a saying of Prophet Mohammad (*Peace Be Upon Him*) that elaborates its interpretation of jehad. "Islam will live forever and for the sake of it", quotes the website, "a class of Muslims will continue jehad until the dawn of Doomsday. By means of jehad", the site said, "Prophet Mohammad spread light in the Arabian Peninsula". By dint of this factor of jehad, he captured even *Qaisar* and *Kisraa*. Keeping themselves on the same path, the followers of the Holy Prophet (*Peace Be Upon Him*) trampled under their feet the two superpowers of their time – Iranian fire-worshippers and Roman Christians. Hence, they raised the flag of the Koran and *Shariah* so high.

And Hafiz Saeed undoubtedly, wants to do the same. The *LeT*'s 2001 *fidayeen* attack on the Red Fort in New Delhi is seen as a significant step in this direction. The *Markaz* website used to point out that the Fort was the symbol of Muslim power in the subcontinent and later the main target of the East India Company's machinations. The Red Fort is also the site from where India's Independence day speeches are made on 15 August every year. Saeed confirms this: "The *fidayeen* attack at the Red Fort was a symbolic activity intended to warn India that it should withdraw its forces from Jammu and Kashmir and stop the farcical show of talks", he had stated in a speech soon after the attack.

Ideologically, it helps that God's orders as believed by Saeed do not countenance democracy. "I reject democracy. The notion of the sovereignty of the people is anti-Islamic. 'Only Allah is sovereign,' says the Professor. Democracy is a menace we inherited from an alien government. It is part of the system we are fighting against. Many of our brothers feel that they can establish an Islamic society by working within the system. They are mistaken. It is not possible to work within a democracy and establish an Islamic system. You just dirty your hands by dealing with it. If God gives us a chance, we will try to bring in the pure concept of an Islamic Caliphate".

So, when it comes to the affairs of his organisation, it is the Professor, the faceless man of horror, who allegedly decides how many militants have to be sent to the Valley. But the Professor has only a little know-how of ordinary weapons and has, so far, kept his distance from combat training. Surprisingly, he has never been found involved in any act of violence or terrorism in Pakistan. However, a decision to send in fighters is calculated on the number of deaths that have taken place and the requirement and capacity of the *Lashkar* to absorb new fighters. The LeT and the JuD have been calling for many years for the expansion of jehad to the rest of India to create two independent homelands for the Muslims of South and North India.

The jehadi strategy of the *Lashkar* has repeatedly been articulated by its leaders in public speeches. Thus, Nasar Javed, a trainer of the LeT suicide attackers, delivering a speech after the evening prayer at the *Quba* Mosque in Islamabad on 5 February 2008, stated: "India is also afraid of jehad. India fears that if the *Mujahideen* liberated Kashmir through jehad, then, it will be very difficult to keep the rest of India under control. Jehad will spread from Kashmir to other parts of India. The Muslims will be ruling India again." He added, further, "We want to tell the Kashmiri brothers that the government of Pakistan might have abandoned jehad but we have not. Our agenda is clear. We will continue to wage jehad and propagate it till eternity. No government can intimidate us. Nobody can stop it – be it Bush or Musharraf."

Post 26/11: Hafiz Saeed in the Dock

However, the Professor's over-ambitious and equally unbridled jehadi agenda finally landed Pakistan in serious trouble in the aftermath of the 26/11 Mumbai terrorist attacks, placing massive international pressure on Islamabad to proceed against the *Lashkar-e-Toiba* and the *Jamaatul Daawa* as well as their leadership. The Mumbai attacks also prompted the United Nations Security Council to ban on 10 December 2008 the *Jamaatul Daawa* as a terrorist organisation and tag its *ameer* a terrorist. He was subsequently named by the Mumbai police in a charge sheet for his suspected role in hatching the criminal conspiracy to execute the 26/11 terror strikes on the Indian financial hub. On 11 December 2008, a day after the UNSC action, Hafiz Saeed addressed a hard hitting press conference at *Jamia al Qadsia Mosque*, declaring that he would approach the International Court of Justice (ICJ) against the UN decision.

The Professor's harsh criticism of the UN Security Council and India could not have been possible without the consent of the government which had apparently decided to ease curbs on him in a bid to counter the flood of Indian allegations against Islamabad in the wake of the Mumbai attacks. Saying that the UNSC was playing into the hands of India, a furious Saeed said he has decided to write to the global body to clarify that the *Jamaatul Daawa* has no links with terrorism and the UNSC action is actually motivated by false Indian propaganda despite the fact that New Delhi has failed to provide any evidence of the JuD's involvement in the Mumbai attacks.

He said in an aggressive tone that the UNSC decision was in fact a blatant attack on Islam and Pakistan since the only mission of his organisation was to spread the message of Allah Almighty. To a question, the JuD *ameer* went to the extent of disowning the *Lashkar-e-Toiba*, saying that he had never been its *ameer* as being reported now. The wily Professor regretted that India had been accusing the *Lashkar-e-Toiba* of the Mumbai terror attacks, which is a Srinagar-based Kashmiri militant outfit, but, the UNSC has proceeded against the *Jamaatul Daawa* which is a Pakistan-based Islamic charity organisation which has nothing to do with the LeT.

"It is a pity that regardless of the tremendous trust shown in the JuD by leading international humanitarian organisations including the United Nations [in the aftermath of the October 2005 quake in the northern areas of Pakistan], the UNSC has chosen to portray it negatively at the behest of India", he said. Asked about reports saying Ajmal Kasab, the lone surviving Mumbai attacker, had been to the Muridke headquarters like ten other members of the terror squad as a part of their training, Saeed said he had never met anyone with the name of Kasab. To another query, he simply disowned his closest confidant, the chief operational commander of the LeT, Zakiur Rehman Lakhvi, the alleged mastermind of the Mumbai attacks, saying Lakhvi was a Kashmiri militant while he was a Pakistani national.

His hostile utterances immediately invited the wrath of the international community, making the Pakistan government to place him under house arrest at his Johar Town residence in Lahore the same evening – 11 December 2008. Almost six months later, however, while deciding a habeas corpus petition, a three-member full bench of the Lahore High Court (LHC) ordered the government on 3 June 2009 to release Saeed, saying the authorities did not have proof to detain the petitioner for preventive measures. Rejecting the government's contention that Hafiz Saeed had been put under house arrest due to his alleged *Al-Qaeda* and Taliban links and that he should remain behind bars in the larger interest of Pakistan, the court declared his detention illegal and unconstitutional, adding that the government has no evidence of the JuD leaders' links with *Al-Qaeda* or their involvement in any anti-state activity except allegations leveled by India that they were involved in the Mumbai attacks.

The three member LHC bench, comprising Justice Ijaz Ahmad Chaudhry, Justice Hasnat Ahmad Khan and Justice Zubdatul Hussain, heard arguments of A. K. Dogar, the counsel for petitioner after those of the then Attorney General of Pakistan Latif Khosa and decided the habeas corpus petition in Saeed's favour, saying it had not been provided with substantial evidence to continue the detention of the banned JuD *ameer.* A few days earlier, on 30 May 2009, while pleading that Hafiz Saeed should remain under house arrest the Attorney General of Pakistan had presented documentary evidence to the Lahore High Court, linking his JuD to *Al-Qaeda* and Taliban. The court was told that the JuD leader was detained after the United Nations declared his group a terrorist outfit in the wake of the Mumbai attacks.

The Attorney General pleaded that the action of the UNSC Sanctions Committee obliged the Pakistan government to act against the JUD leadership. When the court did not agree with his contention and asked him whether the government had any independent evidence of its own, Latif Khosa met the three LHC judges privately and told them that one of the culprits involved in the Mumbai attack has known links with Saeed. He further said

Ajmal Kasab has already admitted to being a Pakistani national and to being trained for the 26/11 attacks by Zakiur Rehman Lakhvi, the LeT's chief operational commander and a close associate of Saeed. Latif Khosa then showed the judges what he claimed was independent evidence of the JuD's links with *Al-Qaeda*.

Interestingly, however, the LHC judges wanted to see a copy of the government notification under which *Al-Qaeda* had been declared a terrorist organisation. Two days later, the Attorney General reportedly went back to the court and told the judges that the Pakistan government had not yet declared *Al-Qaeda* a terrorist organisation. The court subsequently told him if that was the case, Hafiz Saeed's having links with *Al-Qaeda* was no offence under the law of the land. The LHC released its detailed verdict on 6 June 2009, making public the grounds on which it had ordered the release of Saeed. One of the grounds says: "The security laws and anti-terrorism laws of Pakistan are so far silent on *Al-Qaeda* being a terrorist organisation".

The Lahore High Court judgment further added: "Even after the perusal of the documents presented by the government, we do not find any material declaring that Hafiz Saeed's detention was necessary for the security of the petitioners and there was no evidence that the petitioners had any links with either *Al-Qaeda* or any other terrorist movement. The material provided by the government to the court in chamber against petitioners was mostly based on reports of intelligence agencies which had been obtained after their detention, but even then, there was no solid evidence or source to supplement the reports".

"As regard the contention of the Attorney General of Pakistan that the petitioners are being blamed to be involved in Mumbai attacks, not a single document was brought on the record showing that the JuD or the petitioners were ever involved in the incident. About the legality of the detention orders, the bench observed that as per Article 10(5) of the Constitution, it was mandatory on the detaining authority to provide grounds for detention on which the order had been made within 15 days, but the authority made clear violation of express provisions of the Pakistani Constitution, which deprived the petitioners from assailing their detention before the competent forum and also to know the allegations against them".

Concluding the verdict, all three judges on the bench observed with a unanimous view that the writ petition in form of habeas corpus was maintainable as prima facie the Pakistan government had no sufficient grounds to detain the petitioners for preventive measures. "So far as resolution of the UN is concerned, there was no matter before this court about its vires and the federal government can act upon the same in letter in spirit, if so advised, but relying upon the same their detention cannot be maintained as it was even not desired thereby. Hence the writ petition is allowed and the impugned detention orders are quashed", the bench concluded its verdict.

Soon after his release, the freed JuD *ameer* said that his freedom became possible due to an independent judiciary, adding that due to the grace of Allah Almighty, all the Indian allegations leveled against him and the JuD have been set aside by the Lahore High Court. Saeed declared that the moment would come soon when India would be forced to put an end to its occupation of Jammu & Kashmir. Talking to a private television channel, Saeed said US President Barack Obama was not serious in reshaping America's relations with Muslims. "If the US President wants to prove that he is serious, he should pull out his forces from Afghanistan and Iraq and pressurize Israel to liberate the Palestinian territory.

"Let me remind the world powers, the Kashmiri Muslims had to take up arms after the failure of the international community to help them liberate *Jammu & Kashmir* from the illegal occupation of the Indian security forces through negotiations. Even the Pakistani authorities are not fulfilling their responsibilities to make the ongoing freedom movement in Jammu & Kashmir a success. I believe that Azad Kashmir should be used by Pakistan as the base camp for intensifying the freedom movement in *Jammu & Kashmir*", said the JuD chief.

The court orders and the subsequent release of Hafiz Saeed raised serious doubts in India about the Pakistani establishment's sincerity in bringing the Mumbai terror suspects to book. The newly-elected Congress-led government in India handed over to the Pakistani high commissioner in New Delhi a protest letter, saying it was disturbed by the release of Hafiz Saeed and wanted Pakistan to act against those responsible for the 26 November 2008 Mumbai terror attacks. However, Islamabad blamed India for failing to pin Hafiz Saeed down, saying the Pakistan government could not provide evidence in the Lahore High Court owing to the non-cooperative attitude of New Delhi.

However, such excuses appear feeble considering the fact that Pakistan has failed several times in the past to keep Hafiz Saeed in custody for any length of time. For instance, Musharraf had detained him in January 2002 in the wake of the Indian accusations of his involvement in the December 2001 *fidayeen* attack on the Indian Parliament, but he was quickly released within a few weeks on flimsy grounds. At India's insistence, he was arrested again on 15 May 2002, and placed under house arrest, but had to release him five months later on a court order in October 2002. In the aftermath of the July 2006 serial train bombings in Mumbai, Saeed was again detained, but released hardly a few days later on the orders of the Lahore High Court like in the previous instances.

On 24 June 2009, an Indian court issued arrest warrants for 22 Pakistani nationals accused of masterminding the Mumbai terrorist attacks, including Hafiz Saeed. The arrest warrants were issued in response to an Indian prosecutors' motion in the trial of the under detention LeT terrorist Ajmal Kasab, followed by an Indian demand that Islamabad extradite all the 26/11 suspects to New Delhi. However, Pakistan ruled out the possibility of handing over to India any of its nationals linked to the Mumbai attacks and made it clear that such persons would be brought to justice within Pakistan.

Hafiz Saeed's release and Pakistan's refusal to extradite him to India again came as a serious blow to the international community's renewed efforts to help resume the stalled peace talks between the two nuclear armed South Asian neighbours. To tell the truth, when the state wants to detain an individual in countries like Pakistan, no matter how influential he or she is, nobody is beyond its reach. Therefore, when people like Hafiz Saeed are released by the superior courts on grounds of insufficient evidence, the affected parties have the right to ask what is going on. The Congress government in India subsequently told Pakistan that the peace process would resume only after the Pakistan government acts on its two key demands: dismantling the infrastructure of terrorism from its soil; and the speedy prosecution and punishment of all the Pakistani suspects involved in the Mumbai terror attacks.

Therefore, almost three weeks after the release of Hafiz Saeed on the orders of Lahore High Court, the federal and Punjab governments jointly challenged the LHC decision in the Supreme Court, saying the JuD chief needed to be detained in his own interest as well as in the interest of Pakistan. The two petitions maintained that by seeking his house arrest, the Pakistan government was only trying to ensure the implementation of the restrictions that had been imposed on the *Jamaatul Daawa* by the United Nations Security Council.

However, in a surprised move on 15 July 2009, the Punjab government decided to dissociate itself from Hafiz Saeed detention case in the Supreme Court, saying that the federal government lacks considerable evidence against the JuD *ameer* to convince the apex court to allow his continued preventive detention. As a three-member Supreme Court bench, comprising of Chief Justice Iftikhar Chaudhry, Justice Sair Ali and Justice Jawad Khawaja, was hearing two identical petitions filed by the federal and Punjab governments against the June 3 release of Hafiz Saeed, the Advocate General Punjab Raza Farooq surprised almost everyone in the court room by seeking withdrawal of the Punjab government's appeal. Stating that it was not possible to pursue the petition on the basis of the evidence that the provincial government had against Saeed, the Advocate General said he had instructions from the provincial government of Punjab to withdraw the petition. However, the court proceedings continued.

On 28 July 2009, Pakistan said it cannot arrest Hafiz Saeed since there was no proof of his involvement in the 26/11 assault. Interior Minister Rehman Malik told Geo News that Hafiz Saeed would not be arrested merely on the basis of statements linking him to the attacks and the Indian government has been asked to provide solid proof of his involvement. "We have demanded from India that if you have proof, give (it to) us, but do not do propaganda. I assure we will take action. If Delhi wants some credible action from Pakistan, it needs to provide us substantiated evidence", he added.

On 2 August 2009, Indian officials said they had given Pakistan more details from their investigation of the Mumbai terrorist attacks, in the hope that this will prompt Pakistan to prosecute a suspected mastermind of the plot. Indian Home Minister Palaniappan Chidambaram, told reporters in New Delhi that Pakistan has been provided four sets of information and evidence about the 26/11 attacks. "All of Pakistan's previous questions about the case investigation now have been answered and there is enough evidence for Pakistan to prosecute Hafiz Saeed", he added.

However, on 6 August 2009, Pakistan said that evidence given by India failed to build a case for the arrest of Hafiz Saeed. Pakistani Foreign Office spokesman Abdul Basit said at a media briefing that the information provided by India had not helped although Islamabad was still proceeding with the 26/11 attacks case. "The material contained in that dossier apropos Hafiz Saeed is not really enough and doesn't really strengthen our hands to proceed against him legally, as has been expected," he added.

On 17 August 2009, Indian Prime Minister Manmohan Singh said that militants in Pakistan were plotting new attacks on India and the security forces should stay on high alert. "There is credible information of ongoing plans of terrorist groups in Pakistan to carry out fresh attacks", Dr. Singh told a summit on internal security. However, the Pakistan government rejected the statement, saying the Indian Prime Minister was actually playing to the gallery under domestic pressure from the BJP-led opposition parties in the parliament.

On 21 August 2009, India handed over yet another dossier to Pakistan with new information on Hafiz Saeed's alleged role in the 26/11 terrorist attacks, after Islamabad had stated that it has insufficient evidence to prosecute the JuD chief. The information contained in the fifth dossier that India had provided to Pakistan since the terror attacks, included transcripts of conversations between the attackers and their handlers in Pakistan. Islamabad confirmed having received the fresh dossier, saying: "Our legal experts would examine it to see whether it was legally tenable".

Meanwhile, the *Press Trust of India* (PTI) reported that Hafiz Saeed was not only present at an *iftar dinner* gathering hosted by the 10 Corps of the Pakistan Army on 12 September 2009, but he was allowed to freely mingle with the guests, which included the pro-Taliban, anti-US *ameer* of the *Jamiat Ulema-e-Islam* (JUI) Maulana Fazlur Rehman as well as with the Corps Commander Rawalpindi Lt Gen Tahir Mehmood.

The PTI report stated: "At no point during the iftar, held at the 10th Corps headquarters in Rawalpindi, was there even the slightest hint of pressure, either on Saeed or the Corps leadership playing hosts. When asked about the pressure from India for his arrest and the red corner notice against him issued by the Interpol, a senior officer present at the *iftar dinner* commented that the Pakistan army owes a lot to Hafiz Saeed. The 10th Corps has especially close ties with Saeed and closely interacts with him in Kashmir operations. The JuD chief is seen to be virtually a part of the military-ISI set-up and his views can even count in army postings in the sectors that face J&K. Pakistan Army's hobnobbing with the JuD chief is only one indication of Islamabad's unwillingness to bring Saeed to book".

On 20 September 2009, ahead of the scheduled meetings of the foreign secretaries and the foreign ministers of India and Pakistan in New York on the sidelines of the United Nations General Assembly session, the Pakistani police registered cases against Hafiz Mohammad Saeed and his close aide Abu Jandal under the Anti Terrorism Act of 1997 for making inflammatory speeches and placed curbs on their movements. Three First Information Reports (FIRs) – two against Saeed and one against Abu Jandal – were registered at police stations in the Faisalabad district of Punjab for allegedly inciting people to wage jehad against infidels. The cases were filed in connection with Hafiz Saeed's visit to Faisalabad on 27 and 28 August 2009. According to the contents of the FIRs, Saeed had attended *iftar dinners* and held a meeting with activists of his banned organisation during which he had asked the people to wage a jehad against India, besides seeking donations from the gatherings for jehad. The FIRs were registered in the police stations at People's Colony, Madina Town and Sadar in Faisalabad.

On 23 September 2009, Hafiz Saeed filed a constitutional petition in the Lahore High Court, seeking quashment of two FIRs registered against him on charges of instigating people to launch a jehad against the US, India and Israel. His counsel advocate A.K Dogar said in the petition that the release of Saeed by the LHC had caused uproar in India which had been pressing Pakistan to take action against him. He added that the cases registered against Saeed were actually meant to appease India and these should be quashed immediately. On 12 October 2009, the Lahore High Court quashed all cases against Hafiz Saeed and set him free. The court further notified that the JuD was not a banned organisation and can work freely in Pakistan to collect funds, carry on membership and hold congregations.

On 26 November 2009, on the first anniversary of the 26 Mumbai terrorist attacks, Hafiz Saeed condemned armed activities and suicide attacks in Pakistan, saying they were damaging the image of Islam and Pakistan. In a letter written to a select group of Pakistani journalists having soft corner for the LeT/JuD combine, the alleged mastermind of the Mumbai attacks sympathised with the families of all those who had lost their lives in the Mumbai attacks and said Islam does not condone random blasts at public places, nor does it endorses the killing of innocent people.

Expressing disappointment with some Pakistani journalists who are "propagating" against him, the JuD *ameer* stated: "I am indeed extremely saddened at the loss of innocent lives in the Mumbai attacks, and I fully sympathise with the families of those who lost their lives, but it remains a fact that India has deceitfully associated me with these attacks. Although India succeeded in associating the JuD and me with these attacks in the media, yet it has been unable to prove these allegations in any free and independent court of the world…. The fact is that India desires to suppress the Kashmir issue, which is the real dynamic behind all this Indian propaganda. My real crime is that I have vociferously and comprehensively highlight the Kashmir issue. Kashmir is Pakistan's jugular vein and we can never close our eyes to it. India is extremely averse to our stance regarding Kashmir and instead of resolving the issue; it resorts to unleashing propaganda in order to cover up the matter".

Hafiz Saeed further stated in his letter: "Another reason for India's personal vendetta against myself, accompanied with all the usual racket, is evident in what every Pakistani man, woman, and child is saying these days, and which I have claimed for several years now;

that India is the real sponsor of all the acts of terror and carnage in Pakistan. My crime is that I reveal India's real face to the people of Pakistan and I expose its two-faced policy of overtly appearing all smiles and geniality, while it conceals a dagger in its sleeve, waiting to stab one in the back at the first opportunity. India cannot stand my existence for another reason too, and that is that I speak about the rights of Muslims of the whole subcontinent. Moreover, I do not stay silent when Muslims are slaughtered in Gujarat and Maharashtra".

He went on to state: "Not only my religion, but, in fact, no law in the entire world forbids me from raising my voice at the massacre of innocent Muslims in India, or anywhere else in the world for that matter. It is also noteworthy that my parents had migrated from India when Pakistan gained independence and, hence, apart from the ties of Islamic brotherhood, I also have a geographical association with the Muslims of India. We lost many of our loved ones during the migration to Pakistan and, therefore, have a much clearer and comprehensive understanding of the difficulties and problems faced by Muslims in India. India's double-faced policy is also evident from the fact that it had been constructing dams on rivers flowing into Pakistan while it overtly negotiated confidence-building measures. My organisation exposed this Indian conspiracy in every corner of Pakistan. India, therefore, considers my group and me the biggest obstacles in its path of nefarious designs against Pakistan and that is why it incessantly points the finger at me without providing any tangible evidence. Alas! It is unfortunate that our government continues to pursue a meek and self-protective foreign policy *vis-a-vis* India instead of defending the JuD and me. The Pakistan government dreams of friendship with an enemy, though its dream will never be realized".

Hafiz Saeed concluded his letter by stating: "The object of writing these lines is to call for an end to negative propaganda against the *Jamaatul Daawa* and to allow it to fully resume its humanitarian and public welfare projects. Perpetual negative propaganda against us, despite our evident past and our open present is beyond our comprehension. We obviously do not expect anything from others, but we do believe we have a right to expect that the Pakistani media will support us against the innumerable injustices being committed against Pakistan's major humanitarian relief organisation and will cooperate with us in presenting the truth to the international community".

On 1 December 2009, Wilson John of the *Observer Research Foundation* raised a pertinent question in his article titled 'General Hafiz Saeed' – "Why is Pakistan Army so much interested in protecting him despite global pressure after 26/11". He then addressed his question himself in the same article: "The answer is not difficult to find. There is enough evidence to show that the Pakistan Army today protects Hafiz Saeed and his empire with such diligence that *Lashkar-e-Toiba* has transformed into a major international terrorist training centre since the Mumbai terror attack. Saeed has been so useful to the Army in the past that he enjoys the privilege equivalent to a retired General with the Army ensuring that he is provided with a fully armoured Land Cruiser imported from Dubai. It was therefore not surprising that he was among the special guests at a recent *iftar dinner* hosted by the Rawalpindi Corps Commander Lt. General Tahir Mehmood...It is quite clear that the Pakistan Army has gone to extraordinary lengths to protect LeT? The *Lashkar-e-Toiba*, with its vast network of trained jehadis, commanders and training infrastructure, is the Pakistan Army's key strategic instrument in keeping terrorism active in Jammu & Kashmir and other parts of India. Since the Army cannot justify its stranglehold over Pakistan without projecting India as the arch enemy, the LeT and its affiliates will remain long-term investments in keeping the proxy war alive".

Following the holding of an unsuccessful meeting between the foreign secretaries of India and Pakistan [in February 2010] – the first ever since the 26/11 attacks – Hafiz Saeed said on 27 February in an interview to Pakistani news channel: "Pakistan will have to fight a war at all costs if New Delhi is not prepared to hold talks. The JuD chief's face was not shown during the interview and he was filmed over his shoulder from the back. Asked about the Indian accusations about his involvement in planning the Mumbai attacks, Saeed replied: "Let India prove these allegations in any court, I will be ready to accept whatever punishment is given to me".

On 3 March 2010, the *Press Trust of India* (PTI) reported that the renewed bid to bridge the trust deficit between India and Pakistan has taken a serious knocking with Pakistan deciding not to arrest Hafiz Saeed. Pakistani English daily *The News* reported on 4 March 2010 that during the 25 February Indo-Pak foreign secretary level talks, the Indian foreign secretary Nirupama Rao had handed over three dossiers to her Pakistani counterpart Salman Bashir which contained the names of 34 terrorists wanted by India, including Hafiz Saeed. "However, after a careful study of the dossiers, the Pakistani authorities maintained that the JuD chief could not be arrested on the basis of new dossiers from India as they do not contain actionable intelligence", the news report added.

REFERENCES

1. Arif Jamal, Fighters among warriors, *The News on Sunday,* 2003.
2. Interview, Hafiz Saeed, *Weekly Outlook*, 2002.
3. Letter, Hafiz Saeed, 26 November 2009.
4. General Hafiz Saeed, Observer Research Foundation, I December 2009
5. Abdul Basit, Media Briefing, 6 August 2009
6. *Press Trust of India* (PTI), 12 September 2009.
7. Hafiz Saeed, Open Letter to the Press, 26 November 2009
8. Wilson John, General Hafiz Saeed, 1 December 2009.
9. *Press Trust of India*, Report, 3 March 2010.
10. *The News,* Report, 4 February 2010.
11. TV Interview, Hafiz Saeed, 27 February 2010.

CHAPTER 6

The Glory and Doom of the Jaish-e-Mohammad

The *Jaish-e-Mohammad* (JeM) or "the Army of the Prophet Mohammad," is one of the deadliest militant groups operating from Pakistan and waging 'jehad' against the Indian security forces in Jammu & Kashmir. It was launched by Maulana Masood Azhar at the behest of the ISI in February 2000, shortly after he was released from an Indian jail, in exchange for hostages on board an Indian Airlines plane which was hijacked by five armed Kashmiri militants and taken to Kandahar in December 1999.

While resuming his activities in Pakistan almost immediately after his release, Maulana Masood Azhar announced the formation of his own militant group, *Jaish-e-Mohammad,* with the prime objective of fighting the Indian security forces in Kashmir. Masood Azhar was the ideologue of another militant group, the *Harkatul Ansar,* which was banned in 1997 by the US State Department, due to its alleged link with Osama bin Laden. Therefore, the *Jaish* is ideologically an extension of *Harkatul Ansar* which rechristened itself as *Harkatul Mujahideen* in 1998, a year after being banned.

While the *Harkatul Mujahideen* was never the same after the split, the *Jaish-e-Mohammad* grew rapidly as the more radical militant group because of its links with two major *Sunni* sectarian groups – the *Sipah-e-Sahaba Pakistan* and the *Lashkar-e-Jhangvi.* The formation of the *Jaish-e-Mohammad* was widely supported by the country's top

Islamic *Deobandi* scholars, especially Mufti Nizamuddin Shamzai of the *Jamia Binoria* in Karachi, who was known for his pro-Taliban leanings, and Maulana Yusuf Ludhianvi, chief commander of the *Sipah-e-Sahaba* at that time. Some other religious scholars who had supported the *Jaish* formation included Maulana Mufti Rashid Ahmed of the *Darul Ifta wal Irshad*, and Maulana Sher Ali of the *Sheikhul Hadith Darul Haqqania.*

While Nizamuddin Shamzai became the chief ideologue of the *Jaish-e-Mohammad*, Maulana Ludhianvi was made its supreme leader and Masood Azhar himself became chief commander. The dramatic emergence of the new jehadi group was seen by many in Pakistan as an ISI ploy to keep the network of jehadi groups divided so that they could be managed easily for waging a controlled jehad in Jammu & Kashmir. The creation of the *Jaish* soon caused the first serious split within the *Harkatul Mujahideen.* Unable to comprehend Masood's decision to launch his own group, the leadership of the *Harkat* (with which Masood Azhar had been affiliated as the secretary general till his arrest in India) unanimously decided to distance itself from their ex-secretary general.

However, hostility developed between the two groups when a large number of the former *Harkat* activists managed to wrest control of over a dozen *Harkat* offices in Punjab. The *Harkat* leadership reacted sharply and accused Masood of being "a greedy Indian agent who was out to damage the Kashmiri jehad". On the other hand, the Maulana got an unprecedented response from the former *Harkat* cadres, primarily because of his oratorical skills, his recognition as a scholar and the four-year jail term in India. Masood's image was greatly enhanced by his spymasters in Punjab when he was allowed to travel to Lahore with scores of Kalashnikov-bearing guards. He was restrained only when his anti-Musharraf statements became too aggressive.

Strong *Deobandi* creed forms the primary religious and ideological base for the *Jaish-e-Mohammad* as well as the Taliban. In fact, the Taliban movement was launched by the students of the very network of 9,000 *madrassas* which the *Jaish's* parent organisation – *Jamiat Ulema-e-Islam* led by Maulana Fazlur Rehman (whose name resembles with Maulana Fazlur Rehman Khalil) – runs across

Pakistan. Masood knit the ties stronger when he toured Kandahar after his release to secure the blessings of the Taliban leadership for launching the *Jaish*. His former associates in *Harkat* say by launching the *Jaish*, Masood actually wanted to become the ultimate leader of the *Deobandi* pan-Islamist militants in Jammu & Kashmir. Delivering speeches at various cities and towns in Pakistan after the launch of the group, Masood Azhar said his group would eliminate Indian Prime Minister Vajpayee who he termed as '*Abu Jahal*' (One of the key enemies of Prophet Mohammad). In its fight against India, he said, the outfit would not only liberate Kashmir, but also take control of the *Babri Masjid*, a mosque in the state of Uttar Pradesh in the Indian heartland.

The *Jaish* carried out its first terrorist activity in Jammu & Kashmir on 19 April 2000, hardly two months after its formation, when one of its members drove a hijacked car loaded with explosives into the main gate of the Badami Bagh Cantonment. The deadly strike marked the first suicide bomb attack in the 13-year-old history of Kashmir militancy. Since then, the *Jaish* has largely confined its operations within Kashmir and the only recorded instance of its operations outside J&K had been the 13 December 2001 attack on the Parliament building in New Delhi. Earlier, on 10 October 2001, a month after the 9/11 terror attacks, Masood Azhar renamed the *Jaish* as *Tehrik-ul-Furqa*. The move was motivated by reports that the United States was contemplating to declare it a foreign terrorist outfit because of its involvement in the 1 October 2001 explosion outside the Jammu & Kashmir Legislative Assembly.

Despite being renamed, the US State Department designated the *Tehrik-ul-Furqa* as a foreign terrorist organisation in December 2001. However, within no time, Masood Azhar got his outfit registered under the new name of *Khudam-ul-Islam*, (Servants of Islam) although it is still operationally known as the *Jaish-e-Mohammad*. Masood was arrested by the Pakistani authorities on 29 December 2001, after pressure from India and other foreign countries following the attack on the Indian parliament building. His outfit was also banned by the Musharraf regime in January 2002. However, a three-member Review Board of the Lahore High Court ordered his release on 14 December 2002.

Pertinent to mention here is a significant statement by a close aide of Musharraf and a former Director General of the ISI, Lt. Gen. (retd) Javed Ashraf Qazi. He was quoted as saying by the Lahore-based *Daily Times* on 7 March 2004: "We must not be afraid of admitting that the *Jaish-e-Mohammad* was involved in the deaths of thousands of innocent Kashmiri Muslims, in the bombing of the Indian Parliament, in Daniel Pearl's murder and in attempts on Musharraf's life." Javed Qazi further said that both the *Jaish-e-Mohammad* and *Lashkar-e-Toiba* had harmed the Kashmir cause the most.

The startling statement came three months after the December 2003 twin suicide attacks on General Musharraf in Rawalpindi, in which one of the bombers was later identified as Mohammad Jameel, an activist of the *Jaish*. Afterwards, there were many in the intelligence circles who started giving statements that Masood Azhar was actually a turncoat, who after spending time in the Indian jails, was turned by the Indian intelligence and whose sole purpose upon his return to Pakistan was to defame the 'indigenous freedom movement' in the Occupied Jammu & Kashmir.

In the aftermath of the twin suicide bombings, Maulana Masood Azhar had to face the wrath of his spy masters because of suicide bomber Mohammad Jameel's connection to *Jaish*. He tried to clear his position by maintaining that the bomber had already defected to *Jaish's* dissident group – *Jamaatul Furqaan*, led by Maulana Abdul Jabbar alias Maulana Umer Farooq. However, the Maulana from Bahawalpur soon fell out of favour with the establishment and was made to go underground in the wake of Washington's allegations about his *Al-Qaeda* links and because of the American belief that he, along with some other jehadi leaders, had been providing logistical support to fugitive *Al-Qaeda* and Taliban leaders.

Prior to that, Masood Azhar had been among the establishment's most trusted jehadi leaders, one of those who walked the credibility tightrope gingerly. One season he would be mouthing impassioned anti-India rhetoric, sending his militants across the Line of Control (LoC) to wage jehad in Jammu & Kashmir; the next would see him lying low and smouldering. In return, the *Jaish* chief used to receive the patronage of the Pakistani intelligence apparatus, both financially and morally. But all this seemed to be changing towards the end of 2003 – and not entirely because of the diplomatic pressure Delhi and Washington have mounted over the years.

To begin with, a glimpse of the clout Maulana Masood Azhar used to enjoy: Nothing illustrates this more vividly than the Pakistani government's decision to decline a request by the Interpol for taking Masood Azhar into custody. Interpol had been prompted to act at the behest of the US department of justice which wanted charges filed against the Maulana from Bahawalpur and Sheikh Ahmed Omar Saeed for their involvement in at least two crimes committed against American citizens – the 2002 murder of journalist Daniel Pearl and the 1999 hijacking of Indian Airlines flight IC-814 (one of the passengers was an American citizen, Jeanne Moore). The US authorities claim that under the American law, they have the right to investigate crimes committed against their citizens anywhere in the world.

However, the Pakistani authorities turned down the requests of both Interpol and the Americans to interrogate Masood Azhar. The Musharraf regime argued that Masood Azhar did not have a role in the murder and the principal culprit, Sheikh Ahmed Omar Saeed and three accomplices had already been tried and sentenced to life imprisonment by a Pakistani court. The government of Pakistan rejected the Interpol request saying Masood Azhar was not a hijacker and his incarceration in India had been illegal. "Otherwise, he would have been tried and convicted by the Indian courts while he was behind the bars in India". In other words, Masood Azhar could not be accused of any crime.

Ordinarily, the reprieve should have emboldened Maulana Masood Azhar to brazenly espouse the jehadi cause. However, he had to suffer a major setback on 15 November 2003 when his *Jaish* was banned by the Musharraf regime for the second time in nearly as many years. While the government outlawed *Khudam-ul-Islam* (earlier called *Jaish-e-Mohammad*), *Jamaatul Daawa*, the political offshoot of the already banned militant outfit namely the *Lashkar-e-Toiba*, was only placed on the interior ministry's watch-list. Five days later, the government banned three more jehadi organisations – *Jamiatul Ansar* (formerly known as *Harkatul Mujahideen*), the *Jamaatul Furqa* (a sister organisation of *Jaish-e-Mohammad*) and *Hizbul Tehrir*.

Significantly, the move to ban these outfits came a day after the US ambassador to Pakistan Nancy Powell said during a visit to Karachi that Washington was concerned about the re-emergence of several banned militant organisations in Pakistan. "These groups pose a serious threat to Pakistan, to the United States and to the region. We are particularly concerned that these groups are re-establishing themselves with new names," said Nancy Powell. She noted that Hafiz Mohammad Saeed, founder of the outlawed *Lashkar-e-Toiba*, was also addressing rallies across the country as the leader of a new group, *Jamaatul Daawa*. "He is up to his old habit of urging holy war against Indian forces in the disputed Kashmir region," she said. *Jaish-e-Mohammad* renamed as *Jamaatul Furqaan*, Nancy Powell added, was one of the groups blamed for the December 2001 attack on the Indian Parliament building. The ambassador then urged Pakistan to enhance its efforts to stop these jehadi groups from infiltrating into the Indian-controlled part of Kashmir.

However, intelligence circles maintained the banning of the *Jaish* twice had more to do with the December 2003 suicide attacks on Musharraf rather than American pressure. Those attacks were followed by a major swoop in which hundreds of Masood Azhar's followers were arrested and *Jaish* offices sealed across Pakistan. Many other *Jaish* activists had been arrested earlier for carrying out suicide attacks on churches and missionary institutes in Islamabad, Murree and Taxila in the aftermath of the 9/11 terror attacks and the subsequent invasion of Afghanistan by the US-led Allied Forces. However, Masood Azhar's close circles insist that those involved in these attacks were in fact dissidents headed by Maulana Abdul Jabbar who had already been expelled from their outfit for violating party discipline.

When Maulana Masood Azhar expelled Maulana Abdul Jabbar alias Maulana Umer Farooq and 12 commanders, they launched their own faction, *Jamaatul Furqan*, and started confronting their parent group. Abdul Jabbar became the chief of the *Furqan* while Abdullah Shah Mazhar was nominated as the *nazim-e-aala* (chief organiser) and secretary general. The dissidents were adamant to carry out suicide missions against the US interests in Pakistan to avenge the fall of the Taliban regime in Afghanistan. However, some militants say Maulana Abdullah Shah Mazhar was the first one to leave Masood Azhar in October 2001 to launch his own faction, *Tehrikul Furqaan* and was later joined by Maulana Abdul Jabbar and the 12 expelled commanders.

Unnerved by this development, Masood Azhar informed his handlers in the ISI that the new group had nothing to do with his outfit and he was not to be held responsible for their future actions, adding that most of the expelled members were sectarian terrorists who should be arrested instead of being allowed to regroup. But according to Abdullah Shah Mazhar, Masood Azhar was himself ousted from his position by the very people who made him the *Jaish* chief – Mufti Nizamuddin Shamzai, Maulana Shabbir Ali Shah and Maulana Wali Ullah, the moving spirits behind the creation of *Jaish.*

These scholars have already deprived Masood Azhar of that position. Seven out of ten members of the *Jaish* Supreme Council, which Maulana Azhar claimed to have favoured him, had dissociated from him. "I am one of them. ... We are all united and running the party for the very cause for which it was actually launched. Masood Azhar has nothing to do with the cause of jehad now. Our main difference with Masood Azhar was that he deviated from the cause of jehad while the organisation was ostensibly created for waging jehad to liberate Occupied Kashmir. Unlike Masood Azhar and his masters in the Pakistani intelligence agencies, we are not ready to compromise jehad for the sake of funds."

On the other hand, Masood Azhar's younger brother and the *naib ameer (assistant chief)* of *Khudam-ul-Islam,* Maulana Abdul Rauf, were of the view that Jabbar and Mazhar had no concern for jehad and just wanted to grab the organisation's assets. "We have taken up the grabbing of several mosques owned by the *Jaish* at the higher level and will get their possession sooner or later," Rauf was quoted as saying after being questioned in connection with the 2003 Rawalpindi suicide bombings against Musharraf.

Insiders tell a long story about the division of the *Jaish* and the vested interests, corruption, greed and deep conflict that eventually led to the group's split. *Jaish-e-Mohammad* and Al-Rasheed Trust, both blacklisted by the US State Department are considered quite close. When the *Jaish* was founded, the Karachi-based Al-Rasheed Trust donated Rs. 20 million ($360,000) as seed money. Later, thousands of people joined the *Jaish* and helped to raise funds, to the estimated tune of Rs. 1 million a day. A substantial amount of this money was spent on establishing training camps and paying to the families whose sons had been killed in J&K. Simultaneously, the lifestyle of many of the *Jaish* leaders had become incredibly lavish.

For instance, Masood, who hails from a lower-class family that resided in a slum area of Bahawalpur, moved to the city's posh Model Town area. He and his cohorts began driving around in Land Cruisers and Land Rovers along with their retinues of gunmen. The Jabbar faction alleged that Masood appointed his relatives and friends to supervise the *Jaish's* mushrooming assets – seminaries, publications, offices and bungalows. His blatant favouritism and lavish lifestyle irked those who had spent grim years in Afghanistan and Kashmir, eventually making them part ways.

In 2007, the slowing down of the Indo-Pak peace process by the decision makers in New Delhi made the Musharraf regime reactivate the *Jaish-e-Mohammad* – apparently to re-launch cross-border offensives in Jammu & Kashmir. According to Pakistani intelligence circles, the *Jaish* was reorganised under the command of Mufti Abdul Rauf, the younger brother of Masood Azhar who had proved his mettle by carrying out successful militant operations inside Jammu & Kashmir. Mufti Rauf was allowed to establish a transit camp in Rawalpindi for recruits traveling from southern Punjab to the training camp at Kohat, a medium-sized town in central NWFP. It was decided that the Mufti would supervise the *Jaish* training camps as the acting *ameer* of the group while his elder brother – Masood Azhar – would continue to manage the organisational affairs while remaining underground.

Links to Maulana Masood Azhar and his *Jaish* continued. In July 2005, the British intelligence agencies investigating the 7/7 suicide bombings in London informed their Pakistan counterparts that two of the four bombers Shehzad Tanweer and Siddique Khan, had met Osama Nazir, a *Jaish-e-Mohammad* suicide trainer, in Faisalabad, Pakistan a few months before the 7/7 attacks. Information provided by Osama Nazir after his arrest revealed that Shehzad Tanweer had stayed at another extremist *Sunni* religious school, *Jamia Manzurul Islami* situated in the Cantonment area of Lahore, and being run by its principal, Pir Saifullah Khalid, who is considered close to Masood Azhar.

The *Jaish* once again became the focus of world attention in August 2006 after it transpired that Rashid Rauf, a brother-in-law of one of Masood Azhar's younger brothers and an alleged *Al-Qaeda* member, was the main plotter of a terrorist plan to blow up US-bound British airliners with liquid explosives. He was accused of helping to train terrorists in the use of the liquid explosives. Rashid Rauf was arrested on 9 August 2007 from a *Jaish*-run religious seminary – *Madrassa Madina* – situated in the Model Town area of Bahawalpur, a couple of days before the British crackdown and arrests of the main plotters in London. On 17 August 2007, a senior Pakistani official conceded that the British airport terror plot was sanctioned by *Al-Qaeda*'s No. 2, Dr Ayman al Zawahri and that Rashid Rauf was the plotter of the attacks.

Information provided by British intelligence to their Pakistani counterparts showed that Rauf was born in Mirpur and went to England in 1981 when he was hardly one year old. He fled to Pakistan in 2002 to escape questioning in the murder of his uncle Mohammad Saeed. The frequent use of text messages to Britain by Rashid Rauf actually led to his arrest. On 12 August, the British authorities said Rashid Rauf had a key operational role in the attacks and should be extradited to Britain.

Despite his closeness to the *Jaish-e-Mohammad* leaders, they disowned him in public. In the aftermath of Rashid Rauf's arrest, the father of Masood Azhar and Abdul Rauf, told media people in Bahawalpur that Rashid Rauf was indeed a member of the *Jaish-e-Mohammad* but had left the group. "He was a member of our group but later he deserted us and joined the *Jamaatul Furqan*, led by a *Jaish* dissident, Maulana Abdul Jabbar," Hafiz Allah Bukhsh was quoted by *Dawn*. "Our cause is liberation of the Occupied *Jammu & Kashmir*, while their main cause is Afghanistan. They are anti-America but we are not," he said. However, on 13 December 2006, the terrorism charges on Rashid Rauf were dropped as the court ruled that there was no evidence that he was involved in planning any terrorist activity.

Two days later, as pressure mounted from British authorities for his extradition, Rashid Rauf escaped from police custody in Rawalpindi under mysterious circumstances. An inquiry report disputed the claims of Islamabad police that Rashid Rauf had escaped while he was being taken to the Adiala jail Rawalpindi and termed his mysterious disappearance story totally fictional and baseless. Subsequent reports said the escape pointed to a deal between the authorities in Islamabad and the *Jaish* leadership. Mufti Abdul Rauf, the younger brother of Masood Azhar was named as one of those who might have masterminded and facilitated Rashid Rauf's escape.

On 22 November 2008, Rashid Rauf was reportedly killed in a US predator strike in the North Waziristan area of Pakistan. However, almost four months later, in April 2009, the British authorities sought intelligence cooperation from Pakistan for the arrest and extradition of Rashid Rauf. The British request said that the previous assessment that Rashid had been killed has now been revised keeping in view credible intelligence information which has surfaced recently. The British authorities said a key *Al-Qaeda* operative detained in Belgium has confessed that besides plotting terrorist attacks in Belgium, France, England and Holland, Rashid Rauf had trained him and dispatched him to Brussels to conduct a suicide attack during a meeting of the European leaders.

The *Jaish* connection emerged once again during the July 2007 *Lal Masjid* crisis when Masood Azhar's younger brother Abdul Rauf disowned *Jaish* militants present inside the *Lal Masjid* and *Jamia Hafsa* as disgruntled elements of *Jaish*. He also distanced his outfit from the fanatic Ghazi brothers of *Lal Masjid*, saying they had only brought huge embarrassment to Islamists. On 5 July 2007 – the second day of the *Lal Masjid* operation, Abdul Rauf described the *Lal Masjid* clerics as 'lackeys' of the government, adding they had accumulated heavy weapons with the connivance of the authorities.

The fact, however, remains that the *Jaish* decided to withdraw its support to the *Lal Masjid* clerics only after the Musharraf regime turned its guns towards the Ghazi brothers. Hardly a week before the operation was launched the *Jaish* had been reiterating its support to the Ghazi brothers' demand for the enforcement of *Shariah*. In an article published a few days before the *Lal Masjid* operation, Maulana Masood Azhar wrote in the *Jaish* publication *Al Qalam:* "Now, there are hundreds of jehadi organisations and hundreds of *ameers*, most of whom are computer operators, who have become jehadis by watching CDs of jehad. They have received jehadi training through websites. They think that via the internet, they have become *ameers*. If they come across a gullible youth, they tie a bomb around his body and send him to jehadi battlefields. Some of the jehadis are in the business of drugs, human smuggling and kidnapping for ransom. Therefore, jehad has become everybody's business. It is, therefore, difficult to control these jehadis."

Before the 26/11 Mumbai terror attacks, the two brothers had distributed their duties equally. Mufti Abdul Rauf was stationed in the twin cities of Rawalpindi and Islamabad as in charge of the *Jaish* training camps, Maulana Masood Azhar used to oversee the group affairs of the organisation from his headquarters in Bahawalpur. A 23 June 2008 article in *The News* titled 'Another *Lal Masjid'*, gave a clear idea of Maulana Masood Azhar's activities at that time. The writer had returned to Bahawalpur after spending many years abroad and narrates the state of the present state of *Jaish* affairs there:

"Bahawalpur was always a laidback small town where everyone knew everyone else. Maulana Masood Azhar was a neighbour of my cousins and used to have a small house which wasn't even visible from the road. I remember when he was released. The *BBC* wanted to film his return, from the terrace of my cousins' house, but they refused due to privacy concerns. Since then we heard little about him, in the news or in local gossip. In general, people didn't give him much credibility.... The walls were filled with anti-West hate slogans, with '*Al-Jehad al-Qital*' (holy war, bloody battle) written everywhere around the central mosque in the city. This was not the Bahawalpur I knew. As we got closer to the mosque, I saw the adjacent ground filled with bearded men in white robes, with more of them reaching there in buses, chanting the slogans written all over the city. A number of men were uniformed, and they had closed the road to facilitate the movement of the buses into the place.

"The purpose of the conference was to distribute a new book of

Masood Azhar, which had supposedly substantiated that the jehad these men thought they were preparing for was actually sanctioned by the verses of the Holy Koran, based on their strict politically-motivated interpretation. We reached the house of our family friends with mixed thoughts. Disturbed by these developments, I asked them what was going on in the city. They said it had been silently going on for a long time. Over the years, Masood Azhar had converted his small house into a multi-storied concrete compound housing 700 armed men, who freely did target practice there. All this was located in a central part of the city, ironically called Model Town. The local police dared not touch these men, and instead of putting pressure on them to stop their militant activities, local politicians actually hired these men as bodyguards during the general elections.

"After leaving their house, as we got closer to my cousins' house, a strange tall building with the same white flags on top was visible from a distance. This was Masood Azhar's compound. A few blocks away from my cousins' house our car got stuck in a crowd of the same bearded men in white robes who flocked outside the compound and watched us suspiciously as we drove through them. For a moment, I felt like a stranger in my own hometown. Everyone at my cousins' house thought of all this as something normal and didn't seem to be bothered. Talking to people about this, I had some interesting conversations with some of the people who were involved in local politics and the internal politics of Islamabad. Their understanding was that Maulana Masood Azhar was like Maulana Abdur Rashid Ghazi of the *Lal Masjid.*"

In December 2008, almost a week after the 26/11 Mumbai terror attacks, the Pakistani authorities placed restrictions on the movement of Masood Azhar by confining him to his multi-storeyed concrete compound in the Model Town area of Bahawalpur. The action was taken in the wake of the Indian government's demand to hand over three persons to Delhi – Masood Azhar, Dawood Ibrahim and Tiger Memon. India had sought their extradition by citing a 1989 agreement signed by the Director General of the Central Bureau of Investigation and the Director General of the Federal Investigation Agency which binds both the agencies to collaborate with each other to trace out the most wanted terrorists and criminals and hand them over to their respective counterparts. The Indian demand said that Masood Azhar was wanted for his alleged involvement in the 2001 attacks on the Indian parliament.

An 18 January 2009 report in the English daily *The News* said Masood Azhar has abandoned his *Jaish* headquarters in the Model Town area of Bahawalpur and temporarily shifted his base to the trouble-stricken South Waziristan region in the wake of the mounting Indian pressure for his extradition. However, in the second week of April 2009, Masood Azhar was declared 'officially' missing from Pakistan. A 13 January 2009 new report in *Daily Times* quoted official sources in Islamabad as having said that the *Jaish* chief has abandoned his headquarters in Bahawalpur and was missing now. Pakistani Interior Minister Rehman Malik officially declared that Masood Azhar and Dawood Ibrahim were not in Pakistan adding that Islamabad would not provide protection and refuge to any criminal. However, Indian External Affairs Minister Pranab Mukherjee ridiculed Pakistan for denying the 'obvious presence' of the *Jaish* chief, saying: "India had several times got different information from Pakistan on Masood Azhar and it was not unusual to hear such denials from Pakistani officials".

On 7 May 2009, a day after Prime Minister Yousaf Raza Gilani asked the armed forces to eliminate terrorists and extremists, Pakistani military spokesman Major General Athar Abbas told *Dawn News channel* in an interview that the members of the *Jaish-e-Mohammad* and militants from the South Waziristan tribal region are fighting alongside some 5,000 Taliban fighters in the restive Swat valley. On 5 June 2009, barely seven months after the 26/11 Mumbai terrorist attacks, the Indian efforts to place UN sanctions on Maulana Masood Azhar and his several associates in the JeM received a major setback, after Britain surprisingly joined hands with China, blocking New Delhi's move to proscribe them under the United Nations' *Al-Qaeda* and Taliban Sanctions resolution (1267).

The Indian government actually wanted Massod Azhar, Azam Cheema and Abdul Rehman Makki, to be included in the list just like the *Jamaatul Daawa* and its head Hafiz Saeed were added along with other LeT operatives after the Mumbai attacks. The banning under UN resolution 1267 meant freezing of assets, travel restrictions and embargo on arms. However, what stunned India was the UK's position because the *Jaish* as an outfit is already banned by the UN and, therefore, it was only logical for Masood Azhar to be placed on that list also. Britain, while placing the Indian request on a procedural hold, had sought fresh evidence and more details from New Delhi while China had taken a similar position. In the third week of June, however, Britain withdrew its hold on the Indian resolution to place sanctions on Masood Azhar, leaving China the only country standing in the way of the ban. India had strongly taken up the matter with the UK, providing additional information on the reasons for seeking the ban on the *Jaish* leaders. New Delhi argued that Masood Azhar benefited from a terror act – the hijacking of an Indian airliner in December 1999 – and, therefore, there can be no objections on the grounds of evidence.

On 17 June 2009, following the arrest of five JeM activists from the Sialkot district of Punjab, some Pakistani newspapers reported that Masood Azhar is also among those detained by the police. However, the Pakistani authorities were quick to deny the news of his arrest, saying the whereabouts of the *Jaish* chief are still unknown and the official stance of the government remains that he is missing after abandoning his Bahawalpur headquarters.

On 12 September 2009, the Britain-based *Sunday Telegraph* reported that the *Jaish-e-Mohammad* has revived its jehadi activities in Bahawalpur by establishing a sprawling new base outside the city, spanning over 4.5 acres, possibly to serve as a training camp for its jehadi activists. "The Pakistani authorities have turned a blind eye to the new base, in the far south of Punjab province, even though it is believed to have been built to serve as a radical *madrassa* or some kind of training camp...While world attention has been focused on the menace of the Taliban in the north west of Pakistan, the bases of *Jaish* and a string of other similar jehadi groups in southern Punjab have gone largely unnoticed", the *Sunday Telegraph* report stated.

It further added: "Bahawalpur is a backwater, a dusty, dirt-poor town which is swelteringly hot in summer. Its isolation allows it to function quietly as a centre for ideological indoctrination and terrorist planning, a jehadi oasis which is surrounded by parched fields. Once mentally prepared, promising students are dispatched to camps for training jehadis in warfare, in the north west of the country. The *Jaish* has its central headquarters in Bahawalpur and it openly runs an imposing *madrassa* in the centre of town, called *Usman-o-Ali*, where it teaches its extremist interpretation of Islam to hundreds of children every year... However, *The Sunday Telegraph* was prevented from entering the *madrassa*, which also has a mosque that should be open to everyone. *Jaish's* new site, about 5km out of Bahawalpur at Chowk Azam, is much larger, with evidence that it could contain underground bunkers or tunnels. Surrounded by a high brick and mud wall, little can be seen from the road. But *The Sunday Telegraph* discovered that it has a fully-tiled swimming pool, stabling for over a dozen horses, an ornamental fountain and even swings and a slide for children – all belying claims by the group and Pakistani officials that the facility is simply a small farm to keep cattle. There were signs of construction activity. A man at the site, who gave his name as Abdul Jabbar, who wore a visible ammunition vest under his shirt, would not allow *The Sunday Telegraph* to enter, and suggested it was time for the newspaper to leave", the report stated.

It added: "We are not hiding anything. Nothing happens here. We have just kept some cattle for our milk" said Mr Jabbar, who sported the long hair that is typical for Pakistani and Afghan Taliban. A man on a motorbike followed as *The Sunday Telegraph* drove away. The new facility is known to the administration and, with a hefty army cantonment in Bahawalpur, the military would also be aware. It has deeply worried some Pakistani security personnel. One described it as a "second centre of terrorism", to complement the existing *Jaish madrassa* in the middle of town. The officer, who requested anonymity because of the sensitivity of the issue, said that the *Jaish* should never have been allowed to buy the land. He said they initially acquired 4.5 acres, and then they forced the adjacent landowner to sell them another two acres. He said it was big enough for training purposes. On the inside walls, there are painted jehadi inscriptions, including a warning to Hindus and Jews, with a picture of Delhi's historic Red Fort, suggesting they will conquer the city.

The report then quoted Mushtaq Sukhera, the Regional Police Officer (RPO) for Bahawalpur, and the most senior police officer of the district, as having admitted that the *Usman-o-Ali madrassa* in the middle of Bahawalpur belongs to the *Jaish*. He said the *Jaish* also owned the facility out of town. Yet he added that there is nothing over there except a few cows and horses. "No militancy, no military training is being imparted to students at *Usman-o-Ali*", said Sukhera, adding that: "There is no problem with militancy in south Punjab, and there no problem with *Talibanisation*. It's just media hype".

A well known Pakistani defence analyst Dr. Ayesha Siddiqa maintained in the September 2009 issue of Monthly *Newsline* that while official sources continue to claim that the *Jaish-e-Mohammad* was banned and does not exist, or that Maulana Masood Azhar is on the run from his hometown of Bahawalpur, the facts prove otherwise. She wrote in her cover story titled 'Terror's Training Ground': "The outfit continues to acquire real estate in the area, such as a new site near Chowk Azam in Bahawalpur, which many believe is being used as a jehadi training site. Junior police officials even claim seeing tunnels being dug inside the premises. The new facility is on the bank of the Lahore-Karachi national highway, which means that in the event of a crisis, the JeM could block the road as has happened in Kohat and elsewhere. Furthermore, the outfit's main headquarters is guarded by AK-47-armed men who harass any journalist trying to take a photograph of the building. In one instance, even a police official was shooed away and later intimidated by spooks of an intelligence agency for spying on the outfit".

Ayesha Siddiqa then added: "Is it naivety and inefficiency on the part of officialdom or a deliberate effort to withhold information? The government claims that Masood Azhar has not visited his hometown in the last three years. But the fact remains that he held a massive book launch of his new book *Fatah-ul-Jawad*: Quranic Verses on Jehad, on 28 April 2008, in Bahawalpur. Moreover, *Jaish's* armed men manned all entrances and exits to the city that day – and there was no police force in sight. The ISI is said to have severed its links with the JeM for assisting the Pushtun Taliban in inciting violence in the country. But sources from FATA claim that the *Jaish-e-Mohammad*, *Harkat-ul-Mujahideen* and *Lashkar-e-Toiba* are suspected by the Taliban for their links with state agencies. In addition, intelligence agencies reportedly ward-off anyone attempting to probe into the affairs of these outfits. In one case, a local in

Bahawalpur City invoked daily visits from a certain agency after he assisted a foreign journalist. Similarly, only six months back, a *BBC* team was chased out of the area by agency officials".

On 15 September 2009, *Daily Times* wrote in its editorial note titled 'Non-state actors in South Punjab' that although the government of Pakistan claims they do not know the whereabouts of Masood Azhar, it is rumored that he is with the new *ameer* of the *Tehrik-e-Taliban Pakistan* Commander Hakeemullah Mehsud in South Waziristan. "A majority of the non-state actors now operating in the region and also targeting the state of Pakistan have come from South Punjab, with Bahawalpur as epicenter, because first *Sipah-e-Sahaba* and then *Jaish-e-Mohammad* have found the backwardness of the region suitable for recruiting terrorists. In 1998, the SSP boys were part of the Taliban force that took Mazar-e-Sharif and killed Iranian Revolutionary Guards personnel stationed in the city under diplomatic cover and assisting the Northern Alliance which the Taliban were fighting. Later, the JeM emerged as the outfit that fought Indian occupation forces in Jammu & Kashmir but also feasted itself bloodily by attacking *Shias* inside Pakistan".

The editorial added: "Pakistan has reason to be worried about *Jaish* and South Punjab because there are 3,000 to 8,000 youths from this region fighting on the side of the Taliban and *Al-Qaeda* in Afghanistan. Masood Azhar was once very close to Osama bin Laden and went with him to Sudan when *Al-Qaeda* relocated there after the jehad against the Soviet Union....What is most worrisome about the dominance of *Jaish* and other terrorist groups in South Punjab is the fact that the local centres of power in the region are likely to succumb to it in the same way that the people did in Swat after warlord Fazlullah was allowed by the NWFP government to establish his satrapy there. Therefore, effective measures should be taken to check the increasing activities of the non-state actors in South Punjab. This is not a good trend. Pakistan must re-evaluate its options in regard to regional security and review the policy which gave rise to the phenomenon of non-state actors. Our internal security demands that".

However, informed sources in the Pakistani establishment say the Pakistani intelligence establishment is still not in a mood to discard

Masood Azhar and there is a strong possibility that he would be allowed to stage a come back when the Indian pressure for his extradition is eased out.

REFERENCES

1. Javed Ashraf Qazi, *Daily Times,* 7 March 2004.
2. Another Lal *Masjid, The News,* 23 June 2008.
3. News Report, *The News,* 18 January 2009.
4. News Report, *Daily Times,* 13 January 2009.
5. Interview, Athar Abbas, *Dawn News Channel,* 7 May 2009.

CHAPTER 7

Maulana Masood Azhar: The Slayer from Binori Mosque

The Most Wanted, not only for the weapon he wields, but also for his mind, the *Jaish-e-Mohammad* chief, Maulana Masood Azhar, received his Islamic education at the *Jamia Islamia*, considered to be one of the largest and the most influential centre of *Deobandi* Islam in the Indo-Pak subcontinent. *Jamia Islamia*, which is also called the *Binori Mosque* and *Darul Uloom Islamia*, has long been the nerve centre of the infamous Mullah-Military enterprise in Pakistan. And Maulana Masood Azhar's jehadi mentor had been none other than Mufti Nizamuddin Shamzai, the chief of the religious seminary and a co-founder of the *Jaish-e-Mohammad*.

Like many other religious seminaries, *Jamia Islamia*, located in Karachi's Binori Town area, too has been a key component in the Pakistani jehadi infrastructure which has been churning out extremist jehadis since 1951. The *Jamia* has the distinction of having produced a number of leading jehadi leaders including the chief of the *Harkatul Mujahideen*, Maulana Fazlur Rehman Khalil, the chief of the *Harkatul Jehadul Islami*, Qari Saifullah Akhtar and the late chief of the *Sipah-e-Sahaba* Pakistan, Maulana Azam Tariq. The *Jamia Islamia* was promoted during the dictatorial rule of General Zia-ul Haq, who deemed it fit to make Maulana Yusuf Binori, the founder of the *Jamia Islamia* in Karachi, the chairman of the Council of Islamic Ideology (IIC) in 1979, when the so-called Afghan jehad was about to be launched.

The *Jamia Islamia* or *Binori Mosque,* which imparts religious education to more than 5000 students at a time, has led the anti-*Ahmadiya* or anti-*Qadiani* and anti-*Shia* movements in Pakistan for the last 50 years. Curiously, a bulk of the *Jamia* students is not drawn from the Sindh province, where it is located, or even Punjab, which provides the ballast to Pakistan. A majority of the Binori Mosque students are Afghans and Pushto-speaking Pushtuns from the North West Frontier Province (NWFP) and the Federally Administered Tribal Areas (FATA) of Pakistan. Smaller numbers come from Bangladesh, Africa, Philippines and Malaysia.

The *Jamia* has a large number of smaller affiliated *madrassas* in the port city of Karachi and outside and is largely funded by *Deobandis* in Saudi Arabia, the United States, Britain, France, Germany and Switzerland. *Jamia Islamia,* which is also referred to as *Jamia Binoria,* has also been accused of advancing the political-Islamic and geo-strategic agenda of the Pakistani military and intelligence establishment. The *Jamia's* aim in *Jammu & Kashmir* is also linked to the greater Kashmir idea which rode on extremist militant organisations like the *Harkatul Ansar* and its two reincarnations, the *Harkatul Mujahideen* and the *Harkatul Jehadul Islami,* and finally, the *Jaish-e-Mohammad.*

As far as Maulana Masood Azhar is concerned, he became a teacher at the *Jamia* after completing his education from the same institution. At the age of 20, when most youth were plotting their professional future, Masood Azhar, deeply influenced by his teachers at the *Jamia,* went to Afghanistan to take part in a military training course, after which he participated in the last stage of the Afghan jehad against the Russian forces in Afghanistan. Masood Azhar returned to Pakistan in mid-1989 and started writing Islamic books, the most known of which is "The Virtues of Jehad". Religious indoctrination from a young age and the fact that Maulana Fazlur Rehman Khalil, the chief of the HuM, spotted him at the *Jamia Islamia* – from where the organisation was recruiting cadres for Pakistan – ensured Azhar's entry into the battlefield of jehad.

A few years later, Maulana Masood Azhar was elevated as the secretary general of the *Harkat,* and was dispatched to India for an important mission – to ensure that the *Mujahideen* belonging to the two separate groups of the *Harkatul Jehadul Islami* and the *Harkatul Mujahideen* merge under the new name of *Harkatul Ansar* and work under one umbrella. But the mission failed as the Maulana was arrested from Srinagar on 1 February 1994 along with his right hand man Sajjad Afghani after their car broke down and they were trying to hail an auto rickshaw to reach a nearby mosque to deliver a Friday sermon.

Their arrest came as a big blow to the Pakistani intelligence establishment that had embarked on the new strategy of pushing foreign mercenaries into Jammu & Kashmir to give the militants a cutting edge. By that time, Masood Azhar was a recognised leader of the *Harkatul Mujahideen* and was regarded in the *Deobandi* militant circles as one of the most promising jehadi commander ever produced by the *Jamia Binoria*. It was at the *Jamia* that Masood Azhar had later announced the formation of the *Jaish-e-Mohammad* to fight out the Indian forces from J&K. And remember, jehad against India, Israel and the United States has also been a guiding principle of the *Jamia Islamia* ideology.

One of the two men who announced the establishment of the *Jaish-e-Mohammad* [after Masood Azhar's release from Indian captivity] in a congregation at *Jamia Islami* in Binori Town, Karachi on 4 February 2000, Mufti Nizamuddin Shamzai had previously denounced the United States. *Jasrat*, the Urdu-language Pakistani daily being run by *Jamaat-e-Islami*, quoted Mufti Shamzai as having declared that the Americans were warring infidels and it was, therefore, permissible to kill them, loot their wealth and enslave their women. On 30 May 2004, the *Deobandi* cleric was shot dead when armed assailants ambushed his vehicle in front of the *Jamia Islamia*. Shamzai was the third head of the *Jamia* to have been assassinated in succession. Before him, Mufti Habibullah was shot dead in 1998 and Maulana Yusuf Ludhianvi in year 2000.

Mufti Shamzai was considered to be one of the most powerful men in Pakistan during the rule of the Taliban under Mullah Mohammad Omar in Afghanistan. Mullah Omar and Osama bin Laden are alleged to have met for the first time in at *Jamia Islamia* under the auspices of Shamzai. Along with the Akora Khattak seminary near Peshawar, being run by Maulana Samiul Haq, the

Binori Town seminary in Karachi had imparted doctrinal training to many leading Taliban commanders. That Shamzai wielded immense influence over the Taliban came to the fore when the Musharraf regime had sent a delegation of Pakistan religious scholars, including Mufti Shamzai, to Kandahar in October 2001 to prevail upon Mullah Omar to hand over Osama bin Laden to the US.

The American intelligence agencies had later reported to the Bush administration that the delegation, which also included the then director general of the ISI, Lt. Gen. Mahmood Ahmed, instead of pressurizing the Taliban *ameer* to hand over the *Al-Qaeda* chief, congratulated Mullah Omar for resisting the US pressure and encouraged him to keep up his defiant posture. Among the 2,000 odd *fatwas* issued by Shamzai, the most infamous was the one he gave against the United States in October 2001 to wage jehad against 'the force of infidel', after the fall of the Taliban regime.

The slayer in his own words

Khudamul Islam chief and *Jaish-e-Mohammad* founder Maulana Masood Azhar was arrested by the Indian authorities in February 1994 after traveling to Srinagar from New Delhi. But his name first hit the headlines after the December 1999 hijacking of Indian Airlines Flight IC 814, when he had to be released from an Indian jail in return for the lives of people who were held hostage on the plane.

During lengthy interrogations by the Indian Central Bureau of Investigations (CBI), Masood Azhar had provided fascinating insights into the world of Pakistani religious right. He provided a graphic account of the use of seminaries as factories that produce cadre for the wars in Afghanistan, Jammu & Kashmir, and several other regions. Reproduced below is one of Masood Azhar's interrogation reports, which reveals the story of the making of the man heading one of the most-feared militant organisations in the Jammu & Kashmir.

"I was born in Bahawalpur, Pakistan on 10 July 1968. My father worked as the headmaster of the government school in Bahawalpur. I have five brothers and six sisters. My father had *Deobandi* leanings, and was extremely religious. One of my father's friends, Mufti Sayeed, was working as a teacher at the *Jamia Islamia* at the Binori Mosque in Karachi. He prevailed upon my father to admit me to the *Jamia*. Accordingly, after Class VIII, I studied at the *Jamia Islamia* and passed the *almia* (Islamic) examination in 1989.

A number of the *Jamia* students were under the influence of *Harkatul Mujahideen* (HuM) leaders who had been students there. I was also influenced by the work of the *Harkat* in the Afghanistan jehad. The *Jamia* had on its rolls Arab nationals, Sudanese and Bangladeshis apart from Pakistanis. All of them believed in the *Deobandi* ideology, and many were recruited for the Afghan jehad. I was also sympathetic to the cause. When I met Maulana Fazlur Rehman Khalil, the *ameer* of the HuM, he invited me to participate in training at Yavar, in Afghanistan. Partly because of my poor physique, and also because of my literary skills, I did not complete the mandatory 40 days of training. I was instead asked to bring out a monthly magazine for the HuM.

From around August 1989, I started bringing out *Sada-e-Mujahid* (the voice of the militant). I used to bring out about 2,000 copies, most of which were distributed free at public meetings, Friday prayers and so on. We used to carry news of our activities in Afghanistan, our functions and the opening of new offices. By 1990, the HuM had offices in almost all important cities of Pakistan, including Karachi, Hyderabad, Lahore, Gujranwala, Islamabad and Lahore. .

In 1993, 400 United Arab Emirates' nationals and other militants were arrested by the Pakistani government at Peshawar. Because of international pressure, they were expelled from Pakistan. Some of the Arab governments, expecting trouble, did not want them back in their own countries. As such, a majority of them went to Sudan and Somalia, where they joined the ranks of the *Ittehad-e-Islami*. These people continued to correspond with us, describing the plight of the Muslims in Somalia. They told us that Pakistani troops under the United Nations forces had been placed at the central positions of trouble, guarding the life and property of Americans. If one American vehicle moved, its armed guards were Pakistanis.

As such, the *Ittehad-e-Islami* was in a dilemma about when they should engage the Americans, who are the biggest enemies of Islam, because they also faced their brothers. In the attack on the Adib Radio Station in Somalia by the Pakistani troops, many persons of *Ittehad-*

e-Islami lost their lives. As such, the Pakistanis, who until now were champions of Islam, found themselves unwelcome. I used to publish these letters and also organised for a team of journalists to meet these militants in Nairobi. After our return from Somalia, a number of news stories appeared, condemning the role of Pakistani troops in Somalia. I also brought out a booklet on the issue, and distributed 5,000 copies.

In January 1993, I, along with Maulana Rahman-ul-Rahman and Maulana Farooq Kashmiri, was asked to visit Bagh, Abbaspora and Rahim Yar Khan to meet the families of our militants who had laid down their lives in Jammu & Kashmir. Sajjad Afghani also accompanied us on this trip. It was then he was told to take up command of the organisation in Jammu & Kashmir. He was told to go there via Bangladesh, since there was heavy snow on the Indo-Pak border. I traveled along with Sajjad Afghani by an Emirates flight to Dhaka. While Sajjad Afghani was handed over to some people for his crossing into India, I simply returned to Karachi.

After the formation of the *Harkatul Ansar* by merging the *Harkatul Jehadul Islami* (HUJI) and *Harkatul Mujahideen* (HuM), a number of messages were sent to the chief commanders of both outfits in Kashmir to join hands. We did not, however, receive any compliance to these orders. In January 1994, I decided to visit the Kashmir valley. Meanwhile, we learnt that our orders had been implemented. However, I still decided to proceed to Kashmir to ascertain the ground position, besides boosting the morale of our cadre and resolving any differences between HUJI and HuM. I landed in Delhi by a Bangladesh Biman flight that arrived from Dhaka early on the morning of 29 January 1994. I used a Portuguese passport, and the duty officer at the Indira Gandhi Airport commented that I did not look Portuguese. But when I told him I was Gujarati by birth, he did not hesitate to stamp my passport."

The story of my arrest in Jammu

Maulana Masood Azhar narrates the story of his 1994 arrest from Jammu & Kashmir.

On the eve of Friday, our old friend Abu Ghazi Shaheed, along with 15 armed *mujahideen* had come to call upon us (i.e. Sajjad

Afghani Shaheed and myself) at a small house in a remote village of Islamabad (Anant Nag, Occupied Kashmir). We greeted them warm-heartedly and soon a *majlis-e-jehad* (meeting of jehadis) was in full swing. What an exhilarating scene it was! In front of me and around, were faces shining with the spirit of jehad. In their hearts was a deep yearning for martyrdom and in their eyes dreams of the glory and revival of Islam. Decorating the chests of these young men were magazines and grenades and within them burned the flame of courage and bravery. All of them were listening intently to what I was saying. Their Kalashnikovs lay in their laps as children in their mothers' laps. Some of them had rocket launchers as well as carbines which they had seized from the Indian army. Two or three of the *mujahideen* were guarding the door downstairs.

For an hour I spoke and then asked them if they had any questions to ask. The *majlis* ended at about two. Some stretched out on the floor while others dozed-off with their backs against walls. I quietly took up one of the Kalashnikovs and went downstairs to join the *mujahideen* on guard. Half way down, in the darkness, I felt the weapon in my hands and found that it was ready and willing to talk to the infidels. It was cocked, and the bullet was in the chamber. A feeling of ecstasy descended upon me. My joy knew no bounds as I held the loaded gun in my hands. It was the wee hours of the night and a cool refreshing breeze was blowing. It was the time when Allah's besieges descends upon the earth. All praise to Allah who granted me an opportunity to perform guard-duty on the front of Kashmir. For this greatest of blessings He cannot be thanked enough. The memorable night came to an end. According to the English calendar the year was 1994.

The day, i.e. Friday was bringing a message for me of which I was completely unaware. Brother Sajjad Afghani wanted me to deliver the Friday sermon in the city's *Jamia Masjid*. Therefore, at nine in the morning, we left the house. As luck would have it, our car broke down in the way. We hired an auto rickshaw. It was nearly 12 o' clock; we were not very far from the mosque when we were suddenly arrested! The Indian soldiers literally danced with joy and shouted with glee at the prize they had caught. We were blind-folded and our hands were tied behind our backs and we were driven to an army camp. A crowd very soon gathered there and we could hear them cheering, "*Jai Hind! Bharat mata ki jai!*" (long live India), at the top of their voices. An exercising pain ripped through my heart. What an agonizing moment it was! The enemies of Allah, the enemies of Islam, the murderers of Muslims were rejoicing and we were helplessly waiting for the coming hours when the torture would begin.

Come; now let us raise the curtain upon another scene. This is the eve of Friday. Situated on the outskirts of Jammu and Kashmir, in Kot Bhalwal jail, ward No. 9, seventeen of us are offering our prayers. Maulana Abu Jandal leads the prayers. Afterwards, I come back to my cell with Abu Jandal. At 8:30 the prison guards arrive, count us and lock our barrack. Most of our companions come into my cell where I have turned on my radio. We listen to the news. Later we comment upon the hijacking of the Indian plane. The incident has given rise to a new fragile hope. Our conversation is strange indeed. The ray of hope seems to be tangible, seems to disperse the gloom in the cell. Till nearly 10 o' clock the *majlis* in my cell continues. Then I am all alone. I don't know why sleep evades me. May be the events of the coming day are casting a shadow over me.

The long night somehow passes. At dawn I meet my companions again. The sun of Friday rises. Tired, I now fall asleep. As I wake up at ten, prison officials swarm into my cell. They tell me they have come to take me away and I should take my belongings. I ask them where we are going. I get a confused reply. Someone says, "Kandahar". My companions tie my few belongings together and then start saying farewell. Tears of love fell from their eyes. Some are crying as if their hearts will break. I try to say something but tears overwhelm me. At that moment it is borne upon me with intensity how deep is the love, how strong is the bond which binds us together. We have been a need, a comfort for each other. Together we have suffered tortures at the hands of the infidels, heard each others shrieks and cries of pain, bandaged each others wounds, and together confronted the enemy. So close have we become that we have become each other's identity. All these young men have been my students too. The love and respect they have showered upon me will be impossible to forget. As Allah is my witness, till all of them are free and with me I cannot consider my freedom to be complete.

At 11:30, leaving my companions crying, I come out of the ward. At the threshold I am blind-folded and handcuffed. I am pushed into a jeep. We travel for a long time and then I am put on a plane which lands in Delhi. We come off the plane and then, in what seems to be a convoy of cars I am taken somewhere. On our arrival I ask them to remove my blindfold and give me my Koran so that I can recite it. Their refusal fires my temper and I tell them a thing or two. My outburst seems to have an effect and my blindfold is removed. As I open my eyes I see an Airbus of Air India in front of me with strange people running here and there. Later I learn that they are officers of secret agencies. We board the plane. I sit surrounded by armed and alert commandos. I tell them to give me my Koran from my bag and started reciting it. The plane taxis and within minutes takes-off, leaving the land of the cruel oppressors far behind. Anxious, I listen to the announcement, "Ladies and gentlemen, we welcome you on board the flight to Kandahar".

"Allahu Akbar" (God is great), I shout with joy and tears of sheer joy come to my eyes. But I hold them back lest seeing me cry might give the enemy some relief. The plane is on its journey – from *darul Kufr* (the land of infidels) to *darul Islam* (the land of Islam). The believers are getting ready to celebrate. The Islamic world is rejoicing with a sense of victory, a sense of pride. The world of infidel is in despair. The preface to a new chapter of history is being written.

My journey to freedom

Maulana Masood Azhar narrates the story of his 2000 release from the Indian custody.

The plane was now flying high and heading for Pakistan, where crossing over *Baluchistan* it would enter Afghanistan. I turned to look back and caught the curiosity-filled glance of Kashmir's notable commander Mushtaq Ahmad Zargar who was seated a few feet away. He raised a questioning eyebrow asking me our destination. Perhaps because of the blind-fold which had covered his ears too he had not heard the announcement over the passenger address system. The joy in my eyes was enough to make him realize that we were free at last. Immediately a sense of deep contentment spread over his face too. I turned back and saw another of our militant companion, Sheikh Ahmed Omar Saeed, who was sitting a few rows in front of me. Each of us was surrounded by three guards. I counted the others and there were about ninety guards in the plane with us. In the very first row sat Jaswant Singh, the foreign minister of India. I saw him getting up three or four times and go into the cockpit. He had a personal physician with him too who was making him take some tablets. The cabin crew politely asked us for refreshments but we declined saying we were fasting. Had we not been fasting we would still have refused for with freedom only a few hours away, we felt neither hungry nor thirsty. Moreover, we found it unacceptable to eat anything of theirs.

After an hour and forty five minutes, the plane changed direction and started descending. Then the historic moment arrived when the Indian plane with the stigma of defeat and humiliation, with head bowed down landed at Kandahar airport, in Islamic Republic of Afghanistan. The runway flashed by and I was a mixture of emotions. The land where the plane had landed, everything belonging to it was intensely dear to me. The blood of the martyrs was running in the veins of this city. The person whose deep love filled my heart, on whose unseen hand I had taken oath in jail, he lived here. Kandahar, the city of *Ameerul Mumineen* (the Taliban *ameer* Mullah Mohammad Omar), who in these times has made Islam proud; whose presence is a true blessing for the Muslims. When I was in prison, I desperately yearned to behold this city, to kiss the hand of *Ameerul Mumineen*. It was the greatest wish of my life, a wish I had often expressed in my writings.

O Allah, praise be to you indeed! You chose a city from where the rays of Islam were emanating and spreading all over the world. This is the place where your words rein supreme, where Islam and the Muslims are free where the leaders are your beloved ones. The plane was racing towards the airport building and the sight of the beautiful faces of the thousands of Taliban armed guards was adding joy to my heart. I was surprised to see such a vast number of guards lining the runway. I later learnt that on that day it was the earnest wish of every citizen of Kandahar too to be present at the airport. The Taliban had banned entrance into the airport premises and so only a few thousand people had managed to gain entry.

Though the Taliban had no connection with the plane hijacking, yet the people of Kandahar were jubilant that Allah Almighty had granted their three Muslim brothers release and that the crises had been solved so peacefully. Upon them had been revealed the sanctity of Islamic brotherhood and so their faces shone with welcoming joy. The hundreds of armed Taliban guards at the airport, their discipline, their shining cars, tanks and weapons were inviting Indian officials to thought, and the thought could be seen on the face of every infidel sitting in India.

For many years now India has given refuge to the robbers and thieves of the anti-Taliban Northern Alliance. It is providing full material and financial support to this gang of murderers based in New Delhi. The leaders of the opposition have impressed upon India that the Taliban are just a disorganised band whose power is only temporary. But today, the Indian foreign minister had landed at the Kandahar airport to acknowledge and pay tribute to the superiority and political acumen of the Taliban. He must have been witnessing the organised, controlled power, the quiet efficiency and dignity of the Taliban ranks.

When the plane came to a stop we thought that it would necessarily take a few hours for our exchange and subsequent release to take place. Unknown fears clutched at our hearts too. The delay of next few hours weighed like a mountain upon. I felt like getting up, breaking the door of the plane and run like a mad man down the Tarmac. The smell of the martyrs' blood was irresistibly calling me, tugging at my heart strings. The stairs were brought and as soon as the door of the plane was opened a man came running in. I later came to know that he was the head of the Indian negotiation team. He quickly came up to me and said: "Maulana Sahib, come with me quickly". I told him to wait so that I could tie my turban on my lead, for this was the land of the Taliban. Having calmly completed my task, I took Mushtaq Ahmad Zargar and Ahmad Omar Sheikh with me and we all made our way down the steps. As soon as my feet touched the ground my heart was transformed!

The Taliban high ups greeted us at the foot of the stairs. The Corps Commander of Kandahar, Maulvi Muhammad Akhtar Usmani was among them, as I found out later. With a cordial handshake and a warm embrace he took me to a car and bade me get inside. I saw that to my right, a few feet away stood the Indian plane which had been hijacked a week ago. I could not turn my gaze away. Our car came to a stop. The Taliban Corps Commander got down, walked under the plane and said something to the hijackers above. As I watched mesmerised, two masked men came down from the plane by a rope ladder. One of them was wearing a beautiful suit while the other was in a safari dress. Both of them were armed with revolvers and grenades. They came running towards our car and inside hugged me in a warm embrace.

A storm of emotions washed over us. Those hijackers who were being called extremists and terrorists were overcome with emotion. Tears welled from their eyes. Had the world seen those tears, it would have been forced to think what was it that had driven these soft-hearted young men into taking that extreme step? A step which was condemned by the whole world? Certainly it was the atrocities committed by India, its barbaric, inhuman treatment which had driven these young men. Oblivious of their surroundings they clung to me, pressing themselves into my chest.

Suddenly the Taliban Corps Commander intervened from the front seat and quietly asked, "Are both of you satisfied"? His voice broke the spell and startled the hijackers. They quickly asked my a few questions and said 'yes'. Then the well-dressed one who seemed to be their leader beckoned from the car window, and the others who were still in the plane came running down and got into the car. In spite of the fact that they had been overcome by their emotions, I noted that the hijackers had not for a single moment let go of their weapons. In an astonishing manner all of them carried out to the letter the short orders fired at them by their leader. As a security measure they made a Taliban official get in and the car raced out of the airport building.

I realized how tense I had been until now; fearful of the last-minute hitches that might take place; of the hours it would take before we would at last be free. Nothing had happened. Everything had gone-off amazingly smoothly due to the Taliban's excellent, political acumen and their superb handling of the situation. What would necessarily have taken a few hours; was accomplished within a few minutes. The Taliban had thus proved to the world they had a keen perception of international matters and had the ability to solve crises of every kind. That day had been a Friday too. When, with both my hands tied behind my back I had been pushed into a truck. The truck had headed for the prison where my long life of captivity had started and to-day was a Friday too! Both of my hands were free and I was sitting in a Taliban car heading towards freedom – a freedom about which my prayer is: "O Allah make it a precursor of the liberation of Kashmir, *Babri Masjid* and *Masjid-e-Aqsa!*"

Advani! I am back!

On gaining his freedom in February 1994, Masood Azhar visited Karachi to meet his teachers and associates. On his arrival at Darul Ifta wal Irshad, giving in to the demands of the thousands of his admirers gathered there, he delivered a short speech, a summary of which is being reproduced below:

"My proud Muslim elders, brothers and friends! It was the year 1992, the cold month of December and the sixth day of the month the infidels put us to the test. Thousands of them, chanting the names of their idols, raising slogans against Islam, challenging the honour of the Muslims advanced upon the *Babri Masjid* in Ayodhiya to demolish it. The entire Muslim world stood transfixed, as many of them were crying with anguish and pain. Finally, the heavens witnessed the scene, the earth watched too as defying the one billion and two hundred twenty million Muslims, the Hindus attacked and martyred the 550 year old *Babri Masjid.*

By demolishing the *Masjid*, the Hindus were testing the Muslims, watching what they would do; what the Muslim governments would do, the Muslim citizens would do. India, which was already shedding the blood of the Muslims in Kashmir, India which had tried with all its might to break Pakistan into two, had launched a fatal attack that was to be the forerunner of many other similar attacks.

Having demolished the *Babri Masjid*, the Hindus saw that no army advanced upon them, they saw that no one fell upon them. They saw that the Muslims did shed tears but took no action and so the very next day, Lal Krishan Advani announced that he would demolish 3000 more mosques and then 3000 more. The Hindus planned to first demolish all the mosques in India and then advance upon the sacred land which Allah has given us – Pakistan. My dear friends! In those painful days, in those distressing times a weak person, a lone man used to shout, some times form a mosque in Karachi, sometimes from the rural areas of Sindh.

He went to the religious scholars and begged them with outstretched hands and to the Afghan *mujahideen* too he pleaded in the name of Islam. Then this weak person, with complete faith in his Allah, here in this very city of Karachi, issued a challenge to the seemingly much more powerful Lal Krishan Advani. Advani, he said, you shall not be able to desecrate our mosque any more. Advani! you will not be able to demolish even three mosques now. Advani, you talk of three thousand mosques, we shall take away *Babri Masjid* from you, we shall wrest away Jammu & Kashmir from you too. This weak person, this unarmed man went from door to door, begging each and everyone to do something.

This defenceless young man went to Kashmir. Lal Krishan Advani ordered his forces to arrest him. But after six years and twenty-four days, the Indian foreign minister had to hand over the defenceless young man to the Islamic Emirate of the Taliban, saying, "Take him back. We are unable to keep him any longer in our jails". India's Jaswant Singh and Lal Krishan Advani later had alleged that the plane was hijacked by Pakistan. Listen! I tell you the truth. No one in Pakistan had even an inkling of the hijacking. Your death warrant was issued somewhere else!

You now demand of Pakistan to hand over the hijackers to you. But where has your army of 30,00,000 gone? Where have all your agencies vanished? O drinkers of the urine of cows, in front of idols! O agents of RAW! You failed to catch the five people only and you shall never catch them. You shall not be able to catch them for possibly they are sitting upon your own chest waiting to slit your throats with their knives again. It is possible that they are people of your own country, whom we have never seen or known. You had conquered and subjugated the Muslims of India and you had thought that you had suppressed them completely. But there are embers in that dying fire. When they shall blaze again they shall teach you a lesson you shall never forget!

My dear friends! Today, I am back with you again. Holding you as my witness I am telling Advani again, Advani, I have come back. And today, an Islamic Emirate had been established in the world. What you wanted to destroy has reached glorious heights to-day. You wanted to destroy Islam, but Islam has reached indestructible heights. I am just an insignificant servant of Islam. You have not seen our real people. Advani! My young men, my dear young men, my *mujahid* companions, my respected elders have snatched me away from you, in the same way I shall wrest away the *Babri Masjid*, and Kashmir from you, *Insha Allah* and I shall not rest till then".

CHAPTER 8

The ISI, Taliban and the 1999 Air India Hijacking

In the post-Taliban era, the war-torn, impoverished landscape of Afghanistan has become the new arena for India and Pakistan to score strategic points over each other. Having expanded its presence and influence in post-Taliban Kabul, New Delhi has made substantial progress in its efforts to make the international community believe that Islamabad is using terrorism as an instrument of foreign policy to pressurise its neighbour for initiating talks on the lingering dispute of Jammu & Kashmir.

Having established its consulates in the Afghan cities of Herat in the West, Kandahar in the South and Jalalabad in the East, the Indian government is still making renewed attempts to get hold of any evidence that could prove the involvement of Pakistani intelligence agencies in the hijacking of Indian Airlines flight IC-814. On 24 December 1999, the Indian plane was on its way to Delhi from Kathmandu when five armed men hijacked it over Varanasi. They first took it to Amritsar and from there to Lahore. After refueling in Lahore, the plane took off for Dubai where the hijackers allowed 21 passengers to disembark before they took it to Kandahar in Afghanistan.

Although an Indian national, Rupin Katyal was murdered by the hijackers, the rest of the passengers returned home safely after spending a week [from 24th to 31st December] in captivity before they were set free in exchange for the release of three key Pakistani militants detained in Indian jails on terrorism charges – Maulana Masood Azhar, Sheikh Ahmed Omar Saeed and Mushtaq Ahmed Zargar.

The authorities in both India and the United States had registered criminal cases against the hijackers. It was in October 2003, almost three years after the hijacking episode, that the FBI and CBI investigative agencies reached the epicenter – Kandahar. Two Deputy Inspectors General of the Indian Central Bureau of Investigation and a couple of the US Federal Bureau of Investigations officials had actually reached Kandahar to interrogate those Taliban masterminds of the operation that saw the Indian plane seized by hijackers immediately after it took-off from the Katmandu airport. Before proceeding to Kandahar, the Indian officials got prior permission from the Northern Alliance government to question several captured Taliban leaders, especially Mullah Wakil Ahmad Muttawakil, Afghanistan's last foreign minister in the Taliban government.

Muttawakil had served as spokesman and secretary to the Taliban *ameer* Mullah Mohammad Omar. Being a key witness in the hijacking case, he was interrogated by the FBI and the CBI officials and it is largely believed that he had furnished some vital information to his interrogators pertaining to the role of the Pakistani intelligence establishment in the hijacking incident. Muttawakil was finally set free on 8 October 2003 after eighteen months of detention in Bagram and allowed to return to his family home in Kandahar. On 21 October 2003, hardly two weeks later, a Taliban spokesman disowned him, saying he had lost the confidence of his seniors.

It later transpired that after the invasion of Afghanistan by the US-led Allied Forces in October 2001, the FBI sleuths had seized exceptionally revealing tape-recorded conversations between the hijackers of IC-814 plane and the Air Traffic Control in Kandahar. Some of the information contained in those tapes was then shared with the CBI, pursuing which a joint FBI and CBI team visited Kandahar to follow up on those leads. The FBI had extended full cooperation to the CBI because a US national, Ms. Jeanne Moore, a psychotherapist from Bakersfield, California was also amongst the passengers of the ill-fated flight.

Subsequently, a criminal case was registered in the US against the hijackers. Having recorded Moore's testimony, the FBI teams had visited New Delhi thrice to discuss her abduction and progress in the hijacking case. Determined to get to the bottom of the hijack in order to unmask the masterminds, the FBI then shared with the CBI the record of the incoming calls at the Air Traffic Control of the Kandahar airport.

French writer Bernard Henri-Levy writes in his famous book "Qui a tué Daniel Pearl?" (*Who Killed Daniel Pearl*), *published 2002.* "Two high-ranking officers of the ISI were present on the tarmac in Kandahar when the Indian negotiating team landed there. They were later joined by colleagues, from the special operations wing of the ISI's Quetta station. Negotiations were being conducted over wireless sets. The five hijackers got careless and inadvertently allowed Indian negotiators to overhear them, taking instructions from Urdu-speaking men. Eventually, the episode had ended with the release of Maulana Masood Azhar, Mushtaq Ahmed Zargar and Sheikh Ahmed Omar Saeed, the man who was later convicted for the brutal murder of American journalist Daniel Pearl. The Indian aircraft and its passengers were released in exchange".

During and after the hijack drama, Islamabad strongly denied having any role in it and went to the extent of offering to negotiate on New Delhi's behalf. The fact, however, remains that Mufti Abdul Rauf, the younger brother of Masood Azhar and his brother-in-law, Yusuf Azhar were among the hijackers.

The Indian CBI believes that Mullah Wakil Ahmed Muttawakil had played an adverse role during the plane hijack leaving the then Foreign Minister Jaswant Singh red-faced by going back on many commitments he had made during the negotiations with the hijackers. Going by several Indian media reports, Wakil, who acted as an interlocutor at Kandahar after the IC-814 plane landed there, was hostile during the negotiations. When Jaswant Singh landed in Kandahar with the three terrorists (Maulana Masood Azhar, Omar Sheikh and Mushtaq Zargar) Wakil had made it a point to assure him that the hijackers and terrorists would be held in Afghan custody until all the Indians left Kandahar. However, as soon as the three Pakistani militants were handed over to the hijackers, they were provided with a jeep in which they victoriously drove away. The CBI believed that Muttawakil would be able to divulge more details about the intricacies of the hijack such as contacts that the hijackers had with the outside world including instructions and logistical support they received from Pakistan.

Therefore, during the Indo-US Joint Working Group on Terrorism meeting held on 11 July and 12 July 2003 in Washington, India requested the Bush administration to make the FBI give permission to the CBI to grill Wakil Muttawakil. After being denied access for almost two years, Indian investigators finally succeeded in debriefing Mullah Wakil Ahmad Muttawakil and a few other Taliban leaders as well. What is not known to the Pakistani intelligence establishment is whether Muttawakil was questioned for reconstructing the hijack drama or he had agreed for a statement to be recorded as a witness in the ongoing trial in a Patiala court in India.

The FBI investigators are convinced that on several occasions, Wakil Muttawakil had used the Air Traffic Control (ATC) channel to speak to the hijackers and to some Pakistani officials. Therefore, he, more than any other Taliban official, had a holistic picture of how the hijack was facilitated by Pakistan and where the five hijackers were headed after the scenario came to an end. The Indian authorities insist that Pakistan's role in the hijacking should be seen within the context of the Taliban's official spokesman, Abdul Haj Mutmaen's 1 January 1999 statement that the hijackers and terrorists released from Indian jails were left on the Pak-Afghan border near Quetta, Baluchistan.

From Indian point of view, any evidence that could establish the role of Pakistani intelligence in the hijack could put enormous pressure on Islamabad for the custody of the IC-814 hijackers. Under the South Asian Association for Regional Cooperation convention on extradition and mutual assistance in tackling criminal activities, the Indian government had made two formal requests for the extradition of the five hijackers. But Pakistan refused to oblige, maintaining if any person suspected of being involved in the Air India hijacking was to be found on its territory or in Pakistan-administered-Kashmir, Islamabad would undertake to apprehend and prosecute the suspect.

The CBI subsequently raised the issue with Interpol, prompting the latter to issue a red corner alert (look-out notice) to Pakistan, Britain, the United Arab Emirates, Nepal and Bangladesh against the five hijackers and two accomplices who are believed to be the key conspirators in the hijacking. However, the Indian side is not very hopeful about getting their custody even after issuance of a red corner notice given the fact that several countries did not comply with the warrant from the international organisation. The CBI has already filed a charge sheet against ten people in the hijacking case, including three Indians – Abdul Latif alias Patel, Bhupalmar Damai alias Yusuf Nepali and Dilip Kumar Bhujel.

The other seven accused, all Pakistani nationals, were Ibrahim Athar, Sunny Ahmed Qazi, Zahoor Ibrahim, Shahid Akhter Sayed and Shakir and accomplices Yusuf Azhar and Abdul Rauf. Yusuf Azhar and Abdul Rauf are believed to be the key conspirators. The CBI charge sheet alleged that the hijackers possessed a very sophisticated satellite telephone to communicate with their mastermind in the garrison town of Rawalpindi. "And when the Taliban authorities in Kabul refused to allow the hijacked aircraft to land, which was communicated by the hijackers to the authorities in Rawalpindi, they were instantly asked to proceed to Kandahar", the charge sheet said. Islamabad, however, has vehemently denied these charges time and again.

CHAPTER 9

Daniel Pearl's Murder – A Major Blow to Jehadis

No other single factor has forced the powerful Pakistani military and intelligence establishment to undo its decades-old pro-jehad policy in Jammu & Kashmir and Afghanistan than the gruesome murder of the American journalist Daniel Pearl, who was beheaded in Karachi in January 2002 after being abducted by a group of Islamic fanatics, led by Sheikh Ahmed Omar Saeed.

At the time of his kidnapping, Pearl was serving as the South Asia Bureau Chief of the *Wall Street Journal*, stationed in Mumbai, and had been investigating the case of Richard Reid, the shoe bomber and alleged links between *Al-Qaeda* and the Inter Services Intelligence (ISI). Investigations into the Pearl murder unraveled for the first time the deadly cocktail of radical Islamic groups and intelligence operatives in Pakistan, something that had been hinted at for years by international media. The involvement of an ISI agent in the murder generated enormous US pressure, forcing Musharraf – their most trusted ally at that time – to ban several jehadi groups in Pakistan besides disbanding (for the time being) the Afghanistan and Kashmir desks of the ISI, considered to be the invisible government of Pakistan which had known links with Islamic militant groups.

American intelligence sleuths involved in the Pearl murder investigations along with their Pakistani counterparts believe the journalist was kidnapped and killed because he had uncovered some vital links between the Pakistani intelligence establishment and *Al-Qaeda*. At the same time, they are convinced that Sheikh Ahmed Omar Saeed, convicted for Pearl's murder, was actually a double agent of the Pakistan intelligence establishment as well as *Al-Qaeda*. The Pearl killer was a key operative of the *Jaish-e-Mohammad* (JeM) and a close confidant of its chief, Maulana Masood Azhar, who was released by the Indian government in 1999 following the hijacking of an Indian passenger plane.

The *Wall Street Journal* reporter came to Pakistan in the aftermath of the 9/11 attacks to cover the US-led war on terror. But unlike most Western journalists who after coming to Pakistan seek official contacts and get hooked up with local journalists, Pearl decided to remain independent of any official patronage in uncovering the 'whole truth'. Besides visiting Islamabad and Karachi, he was spotted in many other cities – Bahawalpur, Peshawar and Quetta where no ordinary foreign journalist dared to tread, in view of the violent anti-American sentiments there. With this background in mind, the somewhat overexcited movements of a hyper Pearl made the Pakistani intelligence agencies suspicious of him and his agenda, making them to follow and keep him under close surveillance.

While Pearl had in general told people who came into contact with him in the days prior to his abduction and murder that he was completing a story on shoe-bomb terrorist Richard Reid, there is now increased evidence that he was also looking at far more sensitive matters. Some of those who had spoken to Pearl during his stay in Karachi believe that his main interest was to look into the links between intelligence agencies in Pakistan with religious militancy. The ISI, the most powerful intelligence agency in the country, had also received Daniel Pearl's attention during this investigation.

For instance, on 24 December 2001, Pearl had filed a story about ties between the ISI and *Ummah Tameer-e-Nau*, a Pakistani NGO that was allegedly working on giving bin Laden nuclear secrets before the 9/11 terror attacks. The introduction of the story entitled '*Military elite is linked to activities of nuclear scientist*', stated: "Pakistan has pledged to clamp down on a humanitarian organisation headed by a nuclear scientist, but the nation's military government also has ties to the organisation which is accused of sharing nuclear information with terrorists. The organisation, *Ummah Tameer-e-Nau*, used an ex-military officer to pursue a large agricultural project near Kandahar, according to three people involved in the venture".

Moreover, Pearl's story stated, a former head of the ISI, Lt Gen (retd) *Hameed Gul*, admitted that he was *Ummah Tameer-e-Nau's* honorary patron and encouraged Pakistani businessmen to invest in the group. "Gen Gul saw Pakistani nuclear scientist, Dr. Bashiruddin Mahmoud, in Kabul, the Afghan capital, in August 2001 – the same month Dr. Mahmoud is alleged to have traveled to Afghanistan and discussed nuclear weapons with Osama bin Laden, whom the US blames for the 9/11 terror attacks".

A few days later, Pearl reported in the *Wall Street Journal* that the ISI-backed militant organisation *Jaish-e-Mohammad* still has its office running and bank accounts working, even though President Musharraf claims to have banned the group. This may have brought him on the ISI radarscope. He was doing another story on the whereabouts of India's Most Wanted fugitive terrorist Dawood Ibrahim, who is considered to be a well-connected jehadi gangster allegedly hiding in Pakistan and enjoying the protection of the Pakistani intelligence establishment.

On 22 March 2002, General Musharraf said in Islamabad that Daniel Pearl had been over intrusive. Unfortunately, Musharraf said, "Daniel Pearl had come from Mumbai and made intrusion into the areas which are dangerous and he should have avoided it. Perhaps he was over-intrusive. A foreign journalist should be aware of the dangers of getting into dangerous areas. Unfortunately, however, he got over-involved". Yet the million dollar question remains: what exactly had Pearl got himself 'over-involved' in?

Noted French writer Bernard-Henri Levy writes in his best seller book 'Qui a tué Daniel Pearl?' (Who killed Daniel Pearl?): "US journalist Daniel Pearl was kidnapped and then murdered by Islamist groups manipulated by a faction of the (Pakistani) intelligence services – the most radical, the most violent, the most anti-American.... This faction, from the beginning to the end of the affair, behaved itself as if it was very much at home in (General) Musharraf's Pakistan". Bernard started his book on 31 January 2002, when Daniel Pearl was tortured and decapitated in Karachi, after being kidnapped by a bunch of jehadis. On 15 July 2002, a special anti-terrorism court of Hyderabad, Sindh, found Ahmed Omar Sheikh, Syed Salman Saquib, Sheikh Muhammad Adil and Fahad Naseem guilty of the kidnapping and murder of Pearl.

Bernard Levy, who describes his book as a romanquete – an investigative novel – was fascinated by two main themes: the flower of evil (personified by Sheikh Ahmed Omar, the mastermind of Pearl's ordeal) and the double (Omar the killer as the double of the sacrificial lamb Daniel Pearl). Most of all, Bernard was fascinated by Pearl as his own double. Pearl was an American Jewish journalist trying to come to grips with radical Islam. Bernard had one year, plenty of time and resources and at least four trips to Pakistan to weave his plot. Bernard reconstitutes the last days and minutes of Pearl before being beheaded. Omar Sheikh was to arrange the interview Daniel Pearl was so obsessed with. The interviewee would be Sheikh Mubarak Gilani, head of a small extremist political faction named *Tanzeem-ul-Furqa*.

On 23 January 2002, Pearl left his Karachi home to meet British-born Islamic militant Ahmed Omar Saeed Sheikh at a local restaurant. Pearl hoped that Omar Sheikh would arrange a subsequent meeting with Sheikh Mubarak Shah Gilani. Having initially met Omar Sheikh along with his colleague and local journalist Asif Farooqui, Pearl chose to venture out alone. According to a taxi driver who drove Pearl to the restaurant, the US journalist met his man and stepped into a white car along with Omar Sheikh and three others, and he was not seen since then. In an e-mail to the US authorities four days later, an unknown group The National Movement for the Restoration of Pakistani Sovereignty sent ransom demands along with pictures of the 38-year old reporter in shackles.

On 20 February 2002, three men approached a Karachi-based journalist working for the Pakistani media group Online International News Network, offering to sell a compact disk depicting Pearl's death for US$ 200,000 as well as a promise of global coverage. Lacking the equipment needed to play the CD-ROM as proof, the three men returned the next day with the footage converted to videotape. With a camera purchased from a local video store, the journalist was able to view and confirm the tape's gruesome images.

In the video, Pearl's body is shown naked from the waist up with his throat slit at about 1 minute and 55 seconds into the video, by which time he would have bled to death. A man then cuts his head off. A few more images, such as captives held at Guantánamo Bay detention camp, are shown near the image of Pearl's head. The last 90 seconds of the videotape shows the list of demands scrolling, super imposed on an image of Daniel Pearl's severed head being held by the hair. The videotape entitled "The Slaughter of the Spy-Journalist, the Jew Daniel Pearl" also showed the US journalist stating his identity: "My name is Daniel Pearl; I am a Jewish-American".

The English transcript of the text reads:

> *"My name is Daniel Pearl. I am a Jewish American from Encino, California US."*
> *"I come from, uh, on my father's side the family is Zionist."*
> *"My father's Jewish, my mother's Jewish, and I am a Jewish."*
> *"My family follows Judaism. We've made numerous family visits to Israel."*
> *"Back in the town of Bnei Brak there is a street named after my great grandfather Chayim Pearl who is one of the founders of the town."*

The second part of the video shows Daniel Pearl stating his captors' demands. A caption in Urdu is shown along the way. Pictures of dead Pakistanis and similar scenes are superimposed around the image of Pearl. Other images shown are those of George Bush shaking hands with then Israeli Prime Minister Ariel Sharon and those of the Palestinian boy Muhammad al-Dura, of whose death the Sharon regime had been accused.

The message reads: "We give you one more day if America will not meet our demands we will kill Daniel. Then this cycle will continue and no American journalist could enter Pakistan". Photos of Pearl handcuffed with a gun at his head and holding up a newspaper were attached. There was no response to pleas from Pearl's editor, nor from his wife Mariane.

On 17 May 2002, three activists of the *Lashkar-e-Jhangvi* (LeJ), a banned militant group, were arrested. The three were among the six alleged associates of Omar Sheikh and had revealed during interrogation that the US journalist had been kept in a house in

Orangi Town, Karachi when he was alive. Their information finally led to the recovery of Pearl's body, which had been cut into ten pieces, and buried in a vacant plot in Gadap Town off Super Highway. Incidentally, the plot belonged to *Al-Rasheed* Trust, founded in the 1980s by Mufti Ahmed as one of several ostensibly humanitarian relief organisations, but known to finance leading jehadi outfits like *Jaish-e-Mohammad* as well as the Taliban rulers in Afghanistan.

In October 2003, fifteen months after Sheikh Ahmed Omar Saeed was convicted for Pearl's murder by a special anti-terrorism court of Hyderabad, the case took a new turn. A senior White House official called Mariane Pearl and Paul Steiger, the managing editor of the *Wall Street Journal*, to report a new, key development in the investigation into Pearl's death. "We have now established enough links and credible evidence to think that Khalid Sheikh Mohammad – the mastermind behind the 9/11 attacks – was involved in your husband's murder", the official reportedly told Marianne. "What do you mean 'involved'?" Mariane asked. "We think he committed the actual murder", they said. They told her that Khalid Sheikh Mohammad was one of three Arab men known to have arrived with video equipment and knives at the location where Pearl was held after his abduction in Karachi that day.

On 15 March 2007, the American media reported that according to a Pentagon transcript, Khalid Sheikh Mohammad, who has already claimed responsibility for the 9/11 attacks, has further confessed to having slaughtered Daniel Pearl. "I decapitated with my blessed right hand the head of the American Jew Daniel Pearl," Mohammad said in a statement, according to the Pentagon transcript. "For those who would like to confirm, there are pictures of me on the Internet holding his head," said the statement read by a US military staffer assigned to assist the 9/11 mastermind.

REFERENCE

1. Daniel Pearl's New Report, "Military elite is linked to activities of nuclear scientist", *Wall Street Journal*, 24 December 2001.

CHAPTER 10

Sheikh Ahmed Omar: No ordinary terrorist

Convicted in American journalist Daniel Pearl's murder, Sheikh Ahmed Omar Saeed is a British citizen of Pakistani descent. He served five years in prison in New Delhi in the 1990s in connection with the 1994 abduction of three British travellers. However, he was released from captivity in 1999 along with Maulana Masood Azhar, the chief of the defunct Islami militant group *Jaish-e-Mohammad* and provided safe passage to Pakistan, with the alleged support of the Pakistani intelligence establishment and the then Taliban regime in Afghanistan, after the BJP government in New Delhi acceded to the demands of the hijackers of Indian Airliner IC-814.

Omar was put on trial on 22 April 2002 for the kidnapping and murder of Daniel Pearl, the 38-year-old reporter who was abducted from Karachi on 23 January 2002. Presently languishing in a Pakistan jail after being awarded the death sentence, Omar awaits the outcome of his appeal against the sentence. This was the second time the British-born Omar had been charged with kidnapping of a US citizen. In November 2002, Omar was secretly indicted in the United States for the 1994 kidnapping of four Westerners in India, including Bela Nuss, a school teacher of California. Omar has been described by the Western media as "no ordinary terrorist" but a man who has connections that reach high into Pakistan's military and intelligence elite and into the innermost circles of Osama bin Laden and the *Al-*

Qaeda. An in-depth investigative report carried by *The Sunday Times* on 21 April 2002 revealed links between the ISI and Omar.

The report said the Britain-born Omar knows too much about this connection to ever be allowed to leave Pakistan alive. One "bizarre clue" the report mentioned is the demand by Pearl's kidnappers to honour an agreement to sell F-16 fighter aircraft to Pakistan. 'This hardly squared with the outlook of a militant Muslim organisation fighting a jehad in Afghanistan and Kashmir,' the report said. The next clue came with the revelation that Omar was in custody. On a visit to the US, Musharraf announced on 12 February 2002 that Omar had been captured by the police authorities in Lahore. However, Omar reportedly shouted out in court that he had turned himself over to the then Home Secretary Punjab Brig. (retd) Ejaz Hussain Shah (who had earlier served the Musharraf regime as the director general of the ISI Punjab and eventually retired as the director general of the Intelligence Bureau (IB) in March 2008).

'It would appear that the ISI had its own reasons for holding Sheikh for a week before announcing to the world that he was in custody,' the *Sunday Times* report said. 'One thing it would have wanted to do was to make sure its protégé did not give more away than absolutely necessary about his relationship with Pakistani intelligence services.... Omar Sheikh was their (the ISI's) man and he was brought in to deal with Pearl; the ISI knew everything.' *The Sunday Times* added that the Karachi police, who deeply distrust the ISI, leaked details of their interrogation of Omar Sheikh in which he talked about his ISI links.

The Sunday Times report quoted MJ Gohel of the Asia-Pacific Foundation, a security and terrorism policy assessment group that has been researching Pearl's murder, as saying: 'Omar Sheikh is a vital key that can open all the doors to the *Al-Qaeda* network, to the links between the Pakistani military and intelligence establishment and the terror groups, and can destroy Musharraf's credibility with Washington.' The report said the full story of the kidnapping of Daniel Pearl would probably never come to light.

Yet another report appearing in the *Newsweek* in the first week of April 2000 said: 'The ISI has been so powerful for so long that it seems to play by its own rules. In the Pearl case, the ISI may have had mixed motives. According to well-informed sources, ISI agents were confident that they could cut a deal for Pearl's release by offering to let Omar Sheikh go in return. The American authorities believe Omar himself was an ISI asset at one point, most likely an operative in Kashmir. The ISI would have had good reason not to burn one of its former contacts. That could send a message to other present and future intelligence assets that the ISI doesn't protect its agents. The ISI always wants to keep its options open.'

Interestingly, journalist Daniel Pearl and jehadi Omar Sheikh were both highly educated individuals from privileged backgrounds, but who saw the world very differently. While Daniel Pearl was a humanist who became an accomplished journalist and spent most of his career reporting from the Muslim world as part of a quest to promote cross-cultural understanding, Omar Sheikh was radicalized by events that he regarded as the global persecution of Muslims, and became an Islamic militant who chose a deeply violent method to achieve what he believed in. After the 9/11 terror attacks in the US, their paths crossed in Pakistan, with tragic consequences.

Omar Sheikh was born on 23 December 1973, six years after his father, Saeed Sheikh, a cloth merchant, moved to London from Lahore, the provincial capital of Pakistani Punjab, to pursue a Chartered Accountancy course. Having worked as an accountant with a record company for a short while, Saeed Sheikh started his own wholesale garment business under the name 'Perfect Fashions'. His family owns a house (bought in 1977) in London, some shops and land. Omar Sheikh is the eldest of three children. His younger sister, Hajira Sheikh, was a medical student at Oxford, while his younger brother, Awais Sheikh, was a student of 'A' levels. All the three children are known to be brilliant and are recipients of scholarships.

Omar Sheikh did his schooling at Nightingale Primary School and later at Forest School at Snaresbrook. Former English cricket team captain Nasser Hussain was his classmate at school. In 1987, Omar's father wound up his business and moved back to Lahore because of his son's interest in older girls and his drinking and smoking habits. Once in Pakistan, Omar attended the prestigious Aitchison College in Lahore for three years between the age of 14 and 16. While his contemporaries concentrated on achieving careers in the Pakistani civil service, Sheikh began to develop an unhealthy interest in the idea of a jehad, a holy war in defence of Islam. Alarmed, his father again wound up his business and moved back to London in 1990. Omar went back to the Forest School and finished his Senior Cambridge in 1992.

By the time he returned to England to complete his sixth-year at Forest, his twin obsessions were Islam and body-building. During his Forest School days, Omar had a short-lived romance with an English girl. He then became a chess champion and a keen arm wrestler who took part in the 1992 World Arm Wrestling Championships in Geneva. Omar then moved to the London School of Economics, yet the lure of the classroom was not as strong as his burgeoning interest in the fundamentalist Islamic groups dotted around London. He would regularly skip lectures to attend a variety of mosques and it was there that he was invited to join a Muslim charity, the Convoy of Mercy, which was working in Bosnia at the height of the conflict. Moved by a documentary on Bosnia in 1992, Omar took to jehad and went to Bosnia with the Convoy of Mercy.

Interestingly, former President Pervez Musharraf, in his book "*In the Line of Fire*" states that Omar Sheikh was originally recruited by British intelligence agency, MI6, while studying at the London School of Economics. He alleges Omar Sheikh was sent to the Balkans by the MI6 to engage in jehadi operations. According to Musharraf: 'At some point, he probably became a rogue or double agent.'

Whatever the fact of the matter, what is known is that Omar suddenly dropped out of the Bosnia adventure in 1993, only to travel to Pakistan where he joined the *Harkatul Mujahideen*, a militant organisation fighting in Jammu & Kashmir. After being trained by the HUM in Afghanistan, Omar reportedly flew to India on his first mission. In October 1994, he kidnapped six Western tourists from a low-budget hotel in New Delhi. Posing as Rohit Sharma, a British student of the London School of Economics who had inherited a village in his father's will, he invited the three Britons, Myles Croston, Paul Rideout and Rhys Partridge, to accompany him to the village.

When the party arrived, they were greeted by armed terrorists. They spent the next few weeks chained to a stake and tortured by Sheikh Omar. Using the name Al-Faran, another militant group linked to HUM, Omar Sheikh had demanded the release of 22

Islamic terrorists jailed in India, many of whom were the most wanted and dangerous, including *Jaish-e-Mohammad* chief, Maulana Masood Azhar. This was the second kidnapping episode to secure the release of Masood Azhar. The Indian government refused despite Omar threatening to behead them. The breakthrough came on 30 October 1994 when Omar Sheikh and his accomplice, Pakistani national Abdul Rahim, were arrested after a brief shootout, in which an Uttar Pradesh Police commando was killed. The four hostages were brought out unharmed.

According to Western media reports, Omar Sheikh is also known as Mustafa Mohammad Ahmad aka Mustapha Ahmad Al-Hawsawi and was mentioned in a public transcript of the trial on the Kenya Embassy bombings of August 1998. Under his alias Al-Hawsawi, as mentioned in the indictment of Habib Zacarias Moussaoui, the so-called "20th hijacker" in the 9/11 attack, he wired $100,000 to the official ringleader of the 11 September attack, Mohammad Atta from a Saudi Arabian account of the Standard Chartered Bank. On 6 October 2001, a senior-level American government official told *CNN* that American investigators had discovered that Omar Sheikh, while using the alias "Mustafa Muhammad Ahmad" had sent about $100,000 from United Arab Emirates to Mohammed Atta.

Investigators said Mohammad Atta then distributed the funds to conspirators in Florida in the weeks before the deadliest 9/11 acts of terrorism on US soil that destroyed the World Trade Center, heavily damaged the Pentagon and left thousands dead. In addition, the finding showed that Atta had sent thousands of dollars – believed to be excess funds from the operation – back to Omar Sheikh in United Arab Emirates in the days before the September 11 attacks. The 9/11 Commission's Final Report states that the source of the funds "remains unknown."

More than a month after the said money transfer was discovered, the ISI director general, Lt Gen Mahmood Ahmad was made to resign from his position. It was later reported by the US media that the FBI was investigating the possibility that Lt Gen Ahmed Mahmood ordered Omar Sheikh to send the $100,000 to Atta; there were also claims that Indian intelligence had already produced proof to Pakistan that this was so. The *Wall Street Journal* was the only

Western paper to follow up on the story with these words: 'The FBI's examination of the hard disk of the cell phone company Omar Sheikh had subscribed to led to the discovery of the link between him and the deposed chief of the ISI, Lt Gen Mahmood Ahmed. US authorities sought Lt Gen Mahmood Ahmad's removal after confirming the fact that $100,000 was wired to WTC hijacker Mohammed Atta from Pakistan by Omar Sheikh at the instance of none other than Mahmood.'

A July 2002 *Washington Post* report quoted a senior US law-enforcement official as having said that Omar Saeed bragged to FBI agents during investigations that he would never be extradited to the United States, and in fact would serve only three or four years if convicted of Pearl's murder in Pakistan. The only remorse he expressed was over Daniel Pearl's unborn child: "He said he felt bad because he realised Pearl was going to be a father soon, and he had a 2-month-old son," the American official quoted the convicted militant as having said.

Yet his complicity in the execution of Daniel Pearl and the reasons behind it are still disputed, despite the fact that he has been convicted in that case. At his initial court appearance, Sheikh Omar stated, 'I don't want to defend this case. I did this ... Right or wrong, I had my reasons. I think that our country shouldn't be catering to American needs.'

Interestingly, despite being sentenced to death almost seven years ago by an Anti-Terrorism Court in Karachi for the gruesome murder of Daniel Pearl, Sheikh Ahmed Omar Saeed is lucky enough to have dodged the gallows during all those years, mainly because the Sindh High Court has yet to decide his appeal against the sentence, even though the case hearing has been adjourned for over 100 times since 2002. However, Omar's defence lawyer Rai Bashir sees nothing unusual despite all these adjournments, saying that appeals in murder cases usually last for years and years.

Rai Bashir, the defence lawyer, further maintains that the Pearl case has already taken a new twist, proving his contention that his client was innocent. He intends to use the confessional statement of Khaled Sheikh Mohammad he had made in the FBI custody that he was the one who had beheaded Pearl. "What we were saying for so many years in the appeal is that Omar was innocent and he has not committed that murder. We are happy that this version has been verified by none other than the Americans after the arrest of Khaled Sheikh Mohammad", maintains Rai. But contrary to his lawyer's contention, the hard fact remains that at his initial court appearance in April 2002, Sheikh Omar had almost confessed to his crime by stating before the court: "I don't want to defend myself. I did this".

In a sensational development in November 2008, the Pakistani authorities foiled a clandestine assassination plot being hatched by Sheikh Ahmed Omar Saeed from his Hyderabad death cell, against the former Pakistani dictator Musharraf. The plot was unearthed after Musharraf received a threatening phone call from none other than Sheikh Omar on his personal cellular phone in the first week of November, saying, 'I am after you, get ready to die'. Subsequent investigations revealed that the threatening phone call was made by someone from the Central Jail, Hyderabad. Being an obvious suspect, Omar was placed under observation before it transpired that he was the one to have hatched a plot to physically eliminate the General with the help of his jehadi associates with whom he had been in touch on phone since long. As Omar's cell was thoroughly searched, three mobile phones and 18 SIMS of almost every mobile phone company were recovered from his possession. Further scanning of his phone records revealed that he had been making calls all over Pakistan to his former jehadi associates as well as his relatives in Lahore, Karachi, Rawalpindi and Peshawar. Interestingly, however, his mobile phone records revealed that besides having revived his contacts to the outer world, Sheikh Omar had also been in touch with Attaur Rehman alias Naeem Bokhari, a key *Lashkar-e-Jhangvi* operative who had been arrested by the Karachi police in June 2007 for his alleged involvement in the murder of Daniel Pearl.

In yet another breathtaking development, daily *Dawn* reported on 26 November 2009 that it was Omar Sheikh who had made hoax calls to President Asif Zardari and Chief of Army Staff General Ashfaq Kayani almost a year ago, in a bid to heighten Pakistan-India tensions after the 26/11 terrorist attacks on Mumbai. The report said that Sheikh Omar was the hoax caller who had threatened the civilian and military leaderships of Pakistan over phone, and that too from inside his death cell in Hyderabad jail. The Pakistani media had reported on 27 November 2009 that a hoax caller claiming to be then Indian foreign minister Mr. Pranab Mukherjee was making threatening calls to President Zardari. It was on the night of 26 November 2008 that Saadia Omar, the wife of Omar Sheikh, informed him about the 26/11 carnage in Mumbai. The information was reportedly passed on to Omar in Hyderabad jail through his mobile phone, which he was secretly using without the knowledge of the administration.

Saadia kept updating Omar about the massacre through the night and small hours of the morning. On the night of 28 November 2008, when the authorities had regained control over the better part of Mumbai, Sheikh Omar, using a UK-registered mobile SIM, had made a phone call to Indian External Affairs Minister Pranab Mukherjee. He told an operator handling Mukherjee's calls that he was the President of Pakistan. Indian officials started verification as part of security precautions and, after some time, the operator informed Omar Saeed (who was posing to be Pakistan's president) that the foreign minister would get in touch with him soon. Omar now made a call to President Asif Zardari and then the Chief of Army Staff. He also made an attempt to talk to the US secretary of state, but security checks barred his way.

The presidency swung into action soon after President Zardari's conversation with the adventurous militant. President Zardari first spoke to Prime Minister Yousaf Raza Gilani and informed him about the episode. He also took Interior Minister Rehman Malik into the loop. In Rawalpindi, General Ashfaq Kayani immediately spoke to the chief of the Inter Services Intelligence, Lt Gen Ahmed Shuja Pasha. According to the news report, not only President Asif Zardari was taken in by Omar Sheikh's audacity but the Army Chief was also baffled by his cheekiness. General Ashfaq Kayani, sharing his thoughts with close associates, reportedly said he had been bewildered by the caller's threatening tone.

Sheikh Omar was subsequently shifted from the Hyderabad Jail to the Karachi Central Jail. Reports emanating from the Karachi Jail say the guards stationed outside Omar's death cell are rotated almost daily because he has the ability to influence anyone he meets. Omar had actually managed to convert the first four police constables deployed outside his cell, with all of them growing beards within days after they were assigned to guard his ward. The jail authorities say if the guards outside his cell are not rotated every day, Omar is fully capable of converting the entire jail staff. He is currently reading books on history, particularly on World War-I and II, the Cold War and the Afghanistan and Iraq wars.

Face to face with Sheikh Omar

Sheikh Ahmed Omar Saeed had several brushes with the Indian news media in 1994. On one occasion he walked into the *BBC* offices in New Delhi to deliver a note about the kidnapping of four foreigners. Later that year (1994) – after being wounded in a gun battle with Indian police – he was visited by Zubair Ahmed, now of *BBC* World, who recounts the experience:

"We stumbled upon Sheikh Omar Saeed by chance. I was leading a three-man television crew from a private Indian news channel. He appeared repentant, but clearly not enough. While on the trail of a crime and kidnapping story in Ghaziabad, just outside the Indian capital, Delhi, we found Sheikh Omar. He had been involved in a fierce gunfight with Indian police in the northern Indian town of Saharanpur. Police said he was part of a group of Kashmiri militants who had kidnapped some Western tourists. A senior police officer died in the gunfight and some of the militants, including Sheikh Omar, were wounded. So that is where I found him, with a bad shoulder wound in a room in a swanky private hospital under heavily-armed guard.

I thought he had not even been interrogated. The authorities clearly had no idea who he was, as he was not on the list of wanted men. Though at first reluctant, the police finally allowed us in to speak to him, but he was not keen to play along. The camera was rolling anyway as we came face to face with the tall, bearded young man, propped up against hospital pillows but still belligerent. "Do you have the doctor's permission to speak to me", he snapped. I confessed I did not, but I showed him my identity card. That seemed to do the trick and he started to talk".

Sheikh Omar looked extremely worried and he told me he would give anything to return to life in Britain. He was strikingly young and his accent was distinctly British. He said he was 20 years old and had spent two years taking part in jehad in Bosnia. But over an over, he repeated, he had made a mistake. "Please get me out of here", he pleaded. He said he had been fooled by the hard-luck stories he had heard about the plight of Muslims and Kashmiris in India. He said he had been part of a group charged with kidnapping some foreign tourists to barter for militants held in prison in India. He said he had been in Delhi for more than a month before the kidnapping and was struck by the religious freedom he saw. "I had been told that Muslims in India had no religious rights and Kashmiri Muslims were being subjected to torture and rape by the Hindu army", he said. I asked him, if he was released, would he go back and tell people in Britain that we Indian Muslims were free to build mosques, say our prayers and work in government offices. He said he would. He appeared repentant, but clearly not enough.

REFERENCES

1. Report, *The Sunday Times*, 21 April 2002.
2. Report, *Newsweek*, April 2000.
3. Report, *Washington Post*, July 2002.
4. Zubair Ahmed, *BBC World.*
5. *Daily Dawn*, 26 November 2009.

CHAPTER 11

The Terror Trail of a Londoner Turned Holy Warrior

In October 1994, Sheikh Ahmed Omar Saeed organised the abduction of one American and three British tourists from a low-budget hotel in New Delhi to press for Maulana Masood Azhar's release. The hostages were driven to a safe house near Saharanpur in Uttar Pradesh, where police officers located them on October 31 that year. Sheikh and his accomplice, Pakistani national Abdul Rahim, were arrested after a brief shootout, in which an Uttar Pradesh Police commando was killed. The four hostages were brought out unharmed. The kidnapping was the second in a series of three kidnappings of foreign tourists to secure Azhar's release. How the prime suspect in Daniel Pearl's murder case, Sheikh Ahmed Omar Saeed, entered New Delhi to free the now detained *Jaish-e-Mohammad* chief Maulana Masood Azhar – below are the details, in his own words

It's a 35-page note handwritten in English, gathering dust for over five years in New Delhi's Patiala House courts. For, the author of this note is Omar Sheikh, a British national who studied at the London School of Economics and was one of the three militants released by New Delhi in the Kandahar hijack drama in December 1999. Now languishing in a Pakistani Hyderabad jail in connection with Daniel Pearl's murder trial, the FBI is exploring leads that Sheikh could have been involved in the transfer of $100,000 to Mohammad

Atta, one of the hijackers in the September 11 attacks in the US.

Omar Sheikh's note, written in Tihar Jail and part of the records in his TADA case, describes, in almost diary-like detail, how he went about his "kidnapping mission" in India at the behest of his superiors in Pakistan. His mission: to kidnap a group of foreigners in India and then demand, as ransom, the release of several Kashmiri militants, the most high-profile being Maulana Masood Azhar. The mission failed, Omar Sheikh was arrested, only to be released by the Indian authorities five years later when he was delivered to the Taliban rulers of Afghanistan along with Maulana Masood Azhar.

Following are excerpts from Sheikh Ahmed Omar Saeed's note.

"On July 26, 1994, I arrived at Indira Gandhi International Airport. I went by auto rickshaw to Connaught Palace. My instructions had been to spend the first night in some good hotel and then contact the two phone numbers I had been given the next day. I was to ask for a "Farooq." Maulana Abdullah (a *Harkat* operative) had given me these instructions over the phone. When I got to Connaught Palace, I stopped a passer-by and asked which was a "good hotel" to stay in. He mentioned a few names – one of which was Holiday Inn. I chose to go to this because the name was familiar.

I registered under my own name and gave my passport number. The bill was an astounding $ 210/night. I did not know I had picked the most expensive hotel in town – I thought all Delhi hotels were this expensive and that my money would soon run out! Therefore, I decided I had better contact Farooq straightaway. I phoned both numbers from the hotel. Both answered there was no Farooq there. This worried me even more and I debated whether to contact Maulana Abdullah but decided against it since it would have been grossly against principles to phone head-office from a hotel...

Sultan (an accomplice) took me to a guesthouse in the *Jamia Masjid* bazaar area. After we checked in, Sultan became much friendlier. I asked him if Mr Zubair Shah (the chief of my mission) had arrived and he said not yet but he would soon. He said he had been very pleased to hear of him coming since they had fought many battles together in Afghanistan. Back in the guesthouse, we chatted for a while. Sultan had instructed several of the lads I had been a co-instructor with. I asked him about conditions here and he said they were not going well mainly because Farooq and he were not getting on – they didn't know who was in charge between them and they didn't have clear directions. I asked them what they had in terms of weapons and he said that he had an AK-47 and a couple of pistols. He said that Farooq had a couple of pistols and some grenades also. I asked him where the stuff had come from but he was evasive. Later on I learnt that they had come from Kashmir – but by which route or other details I do not know.

I managed to persuade Sultan to take me to where he lived – the Ganda Nala house in Nizamuddin. At that time Sultan, Farooq and Nasir were staying there. We sat down and discussed what our steps should be. Sultan and Farooq wanted to wait until Shah Saab arrived before starting anything. I said we should seriously consider buying a house in Delhi. They said that some Aswat Darr – who had betrayed after the arrest of Maulana Masood, had taken the money that had been sent to them. I said I wanted to see him. They reminded me that I was supposed to do the job I was sent for, namely kidnapping, and not interfere in what they were doing.

(Over the next one month) every place I visited, I analysed from various points of view – a "future conqueror" I fondly imagined myself to be, a social scientist, a traveller, noting down the intricacies of a new country and as an introspector. I went to mosques and *madrassas* and talked about ideas pertaining to jehad. Among the *madrassa* students, I felt there was great potential for an Islamic movement to emerge but the great obstacle was that the students were generally not capable of independent conclusions – they concluded what their teachers told them to.

In September-October 1994, Sheikh combs Delhi to kidnap foreigners as part of the conspiracy to force the release of *Jaish* chief Masood Azhar. He catches a Briton but loses an American.

I was at ISBT when I saw a foreign chap wandering about. I asked him where he was going. He said Dehra Dun. I quickly made up my mind. My experience with Akhmir had shown that journeys together gave an excellent opportunity to initiate friendships. So I said, "What a surprise – I'm going there too!" and got with him on the bus. His name was Richard and he was a British student who had arranged to have teaching experience at Doon School, Dehra Dun. He will be a teacher there now. By the time we got to Doon School, I had not only initiated a friendship – I had put forward the idea of spending time together touring India. I spent the night at Hotel Relax at Dehra Dun but failed to start up a conversation with the foreign couple staying there.

Back to New Delhi, Shah Saab told me to leave the tourists aside and look for foreigners under the protection of the Indian government as he called them, i.e. diplomats and engineers based here. One night Nasir said he was moving out. He left. I had the room to myself. Now, since I had been in India, the sight of emaciated beggars everywhere particularly round the (Nizamuddin) *Markaz* had posed a serious dilemma for me. I had never seen so much poverty first hand in my life before. But I had soon realised that superficial help was only perpetuating the problem – most of the money they received was spent on cigarettes or charas. But they were genuinely needy people.

Anyway, that night I decided that since I had the room to myself, I offered to share it with an old one-legged man who sat outside the *Markaz*. I went and brought the old man to the room. We had dinner and I was enjoying one of his stories when Farooq arrived. He declared that the old man had to leave the house. I tried to reason with him but he said that my "antics" were putting everyone in risk. I lost my temper, packed up my stuff and left – taking the old man with me – and telling Farooq I was sorry I had such a cowardly set of companions.

I had taken Salahuddin and Siddique to meet Shah Saab at *Jamia* mosque. Shah Saab talked to them in turns. He had told me that they were suitable for sentry duty over whoever was kidnapped. My search for foreign employees based in India took me to the Chanakyapuri side. But I didn't see much scope since security was tight – even to my optimistic eyes.

It was about the third week of September when Shah Saab told me in a *Jamia Masjid* meeting to bring Salahuddin and Siddique early the next day. He said that he had finally managed to arrange a house in a remote area in Saharanpur where the neighbourhood was Muslim and undeveloped to the extent that it was unlikely to have an effective system of informers. Siddique and Salahuddin were to be left in the house and be on the ready. I was to go and see the house and cook up a story accordingly to entice people there the same way as I had bought the Israeli. Sultan would be taking us there and would have two pistols with him – so we have to be alert on the way.

We got to Saharanpur, the four of us, and from the bus stand we went by cycle rickshaw to a place called Katha Keri. From there it was a short walk to the house. When I saw the house, my heart sank. How the hell was I supposed to bring a foreigner all the way here? And that too unnoticed by the local people? Salahuddin was aggrieved at the prospect of himself having to stay virtually prisoner there for may be weeks to come. Siddique was jumping up and down in joy and making little gestures with the pistols. Sultan beamed at me and said, "Like it?" "No," I said sharply. He was surprised. I didn't bother to start to explain. I'd explain to Big Man himself. But then I cheered up. This wasn't far from Dehra Dun and I'd give ole Richard a shot any day. So I told Sultan I wouldn't go back with him to Delhi and would go out "on the hunt" straightaway.

I stayed the night with Sid (Siddique) and Sal (Salahuddin) – and set off for Dehra Dun the next day. I met Richard at the school and he had got over his cultural shock and was involved with school activities such that he couldn't take time off to visit my "relatives". After Richard refused, I went onto Mussoorie, the hill-station and checked most of the hotels there but due to the agitation at that time; there were no foreigners there at all. I stayed at a hotel in front of the mosque there. Next morning, I went to Woodstock School – an American school situated even higher up – and applied for a job as a teacher. I did this partly because if I got it, I could easily bring one of my co-teachers down to visit my "relatives" and partly because I wanted to see whether cutting short my academic career had greatly affected my competitiveness on the job-market. I had an interview with the vice-principal and I didn't get offered the job!

So I returned to Saharanpur, spent another night there and then returned the next day to Delhi. I went to Kale Khan as instructed where Farooq met the next morning and took me for the first time to Shah Saab's hideout. It was between *Jamia Masjid* and Turkman Gate. I told him that I had had no success with Richard and that I was fed up this friendship business – especially with a house in the middle of nowhere like that and that we stop wasting time and grab whoever we needed. He told me to be patient – he was just in the process of purchasing a van (I mentioned that we could have borrowed one a long time ago) and in any case, he was waiting for the reports of the other channels before he made a final decision.

We finally came to a conclusion. I was to have one final thrust at befriending foreigners and if there was no result by the end of four days, we would carry out the snatch option. So, next morning I left. I went by cycle rickshaw to Turkman Gate and took an auto rickshaw to Paharganj. There I checked in at Ankur Guest House (I can't remember by what name but I said I was from Bombay). I sat around at the four or five cafes in that stretch, slowly sipping or eating something and gradually developed a knack for opening up conversations. I would introduce myself as an Indian-blooded British national who was thrilled to come to India for the first time since he had left as a child. Then I would go on to tell them that my uncle had died and because of some grievance against his son, he had left his village on my name. Given that the feudal system had died out in India for a long time – it seems amazing that the story was greeted with such credible enthusiasm but the newly arrived traveller to India yearns to hear extraordinary stories, which will increase his insight into this strange and colourful culture.

That night we arranged to meet the next evening at Hare Krishna. Next morning I told Shah Saab at the *Markaz* that I had two Britishers on the pipeline, did he want them? He answered affirmatively and we arranged to meet next morning when I would hopefully have made the arrangements.

That evening I went to Hare Krishna restaurant, met the two guys and casually mentioned I was going down to my village the next day, would they be interested in accompanying me? They agreed and I arranged to meet them the next morning in the hotel they were staying at (the name of which I can't remember). So next morning, at the *Markaz* I told Shah Saab and he had the van arranged in a couple of hours.

We met at the petrol pump behind the *Markaz* and set off. The van parked outside Delhi Railway Station and I went inside to fetch the two guys, guitars and all. So we set off to Saharanpur, the two, the driver and myself and it was almost exactly like the first time (with Rhys) except that I didn't talk about revolutions on the way – we discussed more complicated issues like women.

At Saharanpur, Siddique opened the door. He saw that two guests accompanied me and so he immediately called the others to attention telling them the Maharaja was here. There was Sultan, Salahuddin and Maulana Saab. The same drama as before happened except that this time there was an AK-47 in the picture – brandished by Sultan. I don't know how it got there. The two were shocked to see Rhys, who we'd talked about on the way. Rhys was rather pleased that he was no longer alone.

Next day, after taking their passport details and reassuring them as best as I could, I returned to Delhi. I met Shah Saab that evening at the *Markaz* and informed him of what had happened. He said that I should make one last thrust for an American. He told me that he'd arranged a house in Ghaziabad (near Delhi) and so it should be easier for me. I told him I'd go the next morning to Vasant Kunj and check out Michael. Our meeting was fixed for the following afternoon.

Next morning, 18th October, I popped down to Vasant Kunj and this time managed to go inside the apartment and meet Michael. He was a mousish sort of chap and I perceived that it would be virtually impossible to convince him to go anywhere.

So, when I met Shah Saab I requested him that we could only do a grab-job on Michael. He said that I would first have to do a complete reconnaissance, which included observing the Vasant Kunj area at different times. We decided Amin would meet me that evening and take me to the Vasant Kunj area on the motorbike.

After the meeting, I went down to the Paharganj area. My mind was fixed on the Michael-task so I didn't try terribly hard to browse round the foreigners there. I just sat at a cafe opposite the Ankur Guest House and ordered a drink. The person in front of me started talking to me and with a shock I realised he was American.

This was Bela Nuss. He was staying at Ajay Guest House and was about to leave India. He was a lonely sort of fellow who found in me someone he could talk to. I told him I was staying at Galaxy

Guest House and after the conversation in which we agreed to meet later, I went and booked a room at Galaxy under the name of Rohit Sharma from Bombay.

In the evening, I met Amin at the *Markaz* and he had with him the motorbike. We went to Vasant Kunj and I noted down what was going on and also the nearest police station. I decided that morning was a better time for the job. I returned to Paharganj to find that Bela had left a message for me saying that we should meet the next day in the afternoon.

Next morning, I made my way to the *Markaz* and told Shah Saab that we could postpone the Michael programme since I had another in prospect. In the afternoon, I met Bela and we went and had dinner at some pizza place in Connaught Place. I told him I was having dinner at an Indian family's house the next day and asked him whether he'd like to come along. He was delighted.

Next day I met Shah Saab at the *Markaz*. He took me for the first time to the room in Nizamuddin behind the tomb. Farooq and Amin were present. Amin was sent to get dinner. I let Shah Saab know that the chap was set up for that evening. Shah Saab then sent Farooz to buy a burqa. He told me that I had to put it on the American since there would be a check post on the way to the house in Ghaziabad.

I slept for a few hours while Shah Saab and Farooq went and made arrangements. They were going to lock me inside but I promised I wouldn't leave the house. When Shah Saab returned, he said the driver would be there in a couple of hours. He had decided that he and Siddique would be involved as well – they would thumb a lift on the way.

I went to the house and told the guys there that I had come to take photographs. Some hours later, after sunrise, Maulana Saab went and bought a newspaper. He and Khan Saab stood in the background, veiled, with the newspaper and AK-47. Sultan took the photos – six of them. I went back by train and arrived at Shah Saab's house absolutely exhausted. Farooq was there with him. He told Farooq to take the camera to Ghaziabad and get the same of the American. I had slept a few hours when Farooq returned with the photos. Shah Saab and I then sat down to make adjustments to the letters for the photos. Our deadline was 72 hours, starting from midnight (26th October).

I went off to Kashmiri Gate and speed-posted one letter. Then I went to Daryaganj and faxed another, asking the owner of the shop to turn his back since the contents were confidential. Next day, I went with Farooq and posted the remaining letters from Connaught Place. Then I returned to Shah Saab's. It was going to be a waiting game, said the Big Man. I was forbidden from leaving the house so I settled myself down to catch up with my Arabic.

For the next couple of days, I stayed with Shah Saab. Farooq had gone off somewhere. Amin was with us and would do errands like fetch dinner, etc. Each morning Shah Saab went off and came back saying that he had phoned Pakistan and the comrades were still not freed. On the 29th he said that the threat would have to be carried out, so I wrote out the letter to the *BBC*, VOA, Hindustan Times and British and American embassies.

Shah Saab added some more names to confuse the authorities even more. Next day, which was a Sunday, Shah Saab instructed me to go to Meerut and post them (in case the authorities put watchers at Kashmere Gate and Connaught Place). I was on the way to ISBT when I decided it wasn't worth wasting all that time so I got off at Kashmere Gate, took a quick look around to see if any security zones were there, went in and hurriedly got the letters posted all except the ones to the *BBC* and the *HT* – since Shah Saab and I had agreed they should be hand posted in case the authorities are watching the post at the press organisations.

Next morning, I set off with the last two letters. At Shah Saab's instruction, Amin was behind me watching to see if everything went OK. I went to Nizamuddin East but found that the *BBC* office had moved. A chap there gave me the new address: Rafique Marg. So off I went, Amin behind me, and gave the letter to the rather nice girl at the reception. 'Tell the Editor I want an answer by 3 p.m." I said thinking tonight she'll be telling the whole world that this big, monstrous, terrorist-looking sort of chap came to me in person and tomorrow I'll ring her up and say 'Actually, my dear, I'm not like that at all...

I left the building speedily and went to *HT* in K G Marg. I found my way to the Chief Editor's office – he wasn't there himself so I gave the letter to his public affairs manager and asked him to give it to him. To my consternation, he started opening it. I speedily withdrew from the room and ran down the stairs (I only just refrained myself from sliding down the banister!) and out of the entrance and across the traffic-jammed road where Amin was. We got into a rickshaw and I told him to go to Okhla since Shah Saab had instructed me to go to my Okhla hideout and show it to Amin also. On the way, when we got to Nizamuddin, I spied Siddique. So we got off, greeted Siddique and the three of us got on a bus for Okhla. I went to that place in Haji colony, which I'd had for over a month but had hardly used. Amin left, Siddique stayed.

For my part, I thought, it was finally over, success or failure lay with Him above. Siddique and I wandered about the nearby roads and talked philosophically and not so philosophically. We talked about Afghanistan, Kashmir, Bosnia, and England. We talked about Shah Saab and the other comrades and the great days we had had in India, the jokes that would be remembered for years to come. He told me about the girl back home he was engaged to, I told him about the one I wasn't engaged to. We talked about the comrades who'd be getting free any day now... now their families would meet and what they'd be likely to do next. So evening came.

It was just after sunset that Shah Saab and Amin arrived. Shah Saab told us to get ready. Amin left, Shah Saab then said that the American had stopped eating and that we were to go and convince him that it was a matter of a few days only. We left the boarding house and went towards *Jamia Millia*. Shah Saab asked me as we walked whether it had gone all right and I replied in the affirmative. He cautioned me not to talk about pertinent matters in front of the driver.

The driver and the van were waiting near Okhla. We got in and sped off towards Ghaziabad. We got down there and instructed the driver to return at 9 o'clock. We got off on the main road and had turned into the lane that took us to the house when two armed policemen came towards me and asked gruffly who we were and where we were going. I thought it was a routine patrol and asked what the matter was. The policeman swore at me and tried to drag me to one side by the collar – at which I (got) furious and started hitting him. The next thing I remember, I felt a stinging blow on my back and I looked around to see the other swinging his rifle at me – my comrades had disappeared. I turned towards him and Bang! I felt the anger drain out with the blood. I thought it was the end. It was the end ... of one era and the beginning of another".

CHAPTER 12

Dawood Ibrahim: The Militant Don from Mumbai

Dawood Ibrahim Kaskar is one of the most fascinating figures in the world of international terrorism, a criminal mastermind linked to everyone from *Al-Qaeda* to Bollywood starlets to East African drug cartels. Few have heard of him despite his status as a billionaire gangster, an alleged global terrorist and an Islamic extremist who is currently on the 'most wanted' list of Interpol for organised crime and counterfeiting and ranks No. 4 on the Forbes' World's Top 10 most dreaded criminals' list for 2008.

Largely believed to be living in Pakistan and accused of heading a vast and sprawling empire, Dawood's name has become a byword in political, business and law enforcement circles. An impoverished street toughie from Indian commercial capital Mumbai, who grew up to possess international influence, Dawood formed the infamous 'D-Company', probably one of the most feared international crime organisations in the world. Accused of heading a vast and sprawling illegal empire, his name has become a byword in political, business and law enforcement circles.

A colourful mobster with powerful friends ranging from Bollywood movie stars to members of Pakistan's intelligence establishment, his alleged crimes include murder, kidnapping, drug-smuggling as well as trafficking in nuclear secrets. The underworld don is also accused of having masterminded the 12 March 1993

Mumbai serial blasts, at the behest of the Pakistani Inter Services Intelligence, when twelve car-bombs killed almost 300 innocent people and injured over a thousand more. Until the 9/11 terror attacks, the Mumbai serial bombing was the single most destructive terrorist act committed in modern history.

Dawood Ibrahim later absconded from India and now, according to the Indian government, is hiding in Pakistan, which Islamabad denies. The bombings were believed to be carried out in revenge for the deaths of hundreds of Muslims in riots in 1992 blamed on the right-wing Hindu Shiv Sena party. He is also suspected to have connections with jehadi groups like the *Lashkar-e-Toiba* (LeT), and was linked to the financing of terrorist attacks in Gujarat (India) in 2002. As the global consensus against terrorism grew post-9/11, in October 2003, the US State Department declared Dawood a specially designated global terrorist with *Al-Qaeda* links. The US decision created ripples in Pakistani intelligence circles which had cared little about the security implications of harbouring a mafia don wanted by an ever-hostile neighbour. Not only did the US action change the complexion of its relationship with India, but it also brought Washington into conflict with Islamabad, its ally in the war against terror, for the latter's alleged covert support to terrorists.

Much to Islamabad's embarrassment, the Treasury Department amongst its reasons for naming Dawood in the list of the world's worst terrorists, cited intelligence reports of his connection with *Al-Qaeda* and *Lashkar-e-Toiba*. The fact sheet on Dawood placed on the Treasury Department's website states: "Dawood Ibrahim, son of a police constable, has financially supported Islamic militant groups working against India such as *Lashkar-e-Toiba*. Information as recent as Fall 2002 indicates that Ibrahim had been helping finance terrorist attacks in the Indian state of Gujarat by *Lashkar-e-Toiba*, the armed wing of *Markaz Dawatul Irshad* – an anti-US *Sunni* missionary organisation, formed in 1989".

According to media reports, soon after India's then deputy Prime Minister L.K. Advani returned from his American visit in June 2003, New Delhi received information about Dawood Ibrahim's alleged links with LeT and the Taliban, and through the latter, to *Al-Qaeda*. During his June 2003 trip to Washington, Advani had told US leaders that India needed a visible, non-reversible action from Pakistan to demonstrate its sincerity in curbing terrorism, and what could be a more visible action than handing over Dawood Ibrahim and others from the list of twenty most wanted terrorists who according to India, are based in Pakistan. This list was handed over to Pakistan after the December 2002 attack on the Indian parliament.

Advani told the American leaders, "The name Dawood Ibrahim had the same kind of resonance in India as the name Osama bin Laden had in America." The US leaders were also told that any movement on the 'most wanted' list could completely change the dynamics in the region. In early 2002, Islamabad was repeatedly asked to hand over those named in the list, but it stonewalled, predictably rubbishing media and intelligence claims of Dawood residing in Pakistan. Among other things, India provided details of the 1993 Interpol red corner notice (A 135/4-1993) on Dawood and of the Pakistani passport issued to him on 12 August 1991.

However, in Advani's own words, the US showed lack of enthusiasm in getting Dawood Ibrahim deported to India from Pakistan despite making some initial efforts. Advani had claimed while talking to Indian newsmen after his US visit that he was assured by Colin Powell that Pakistan would hand over Dawood Ibrahim to India with some strings attached and also that Musharraf needed 15 to 20 days more for doing so. But Advani regretted that no Pakistani action was made the following months. "There was only fibbing and foot-dragging. In my interactions with visiting Americans, I began to see, strangely, a certain lack of enthusiasm. They started saying we do not have the clout to compel Pakistan to act. I suspected, not without basis, that somebody in the bureaucratic system was trying, in India's dialogue with Americans, to de-emphasise or derail the issue of getting Ibrahim and other Indian terrorists back from Pakistan. India was denied a major success in its war against Pakistan-supported terrorism by way of bureaucratic non-cooperation that I have not been able to fully fathom", Advani had stated.

Curiously, when the US Treasury Department terrorist listing was made public in 2003, it mentioned Dawood's passport number as G 869537; the number New Delhi had provided was G 866537. There was also a discrepancy in Dawood's telephone numbers: the

American list said the number was 021-5892038; the numbers provided by India were 021-7278866 and 7272887. Though the US treasury did not list Dawood's address, his passport mentions his permanent residence as: 6/A *Khayaban Tanzeem*, Phase 5, Defence Housing Area, Karachi. It is a posh Karachi address where retired army officials live and it underscores the intimate links between Dawood Ibrahim and the establishment there. These discrepancies in US Treasury Department listing perhaps enabled Islamabad to claim that it had checked out the details but that they did not tally with their records. Indian officials, however, say the discrepancies were an error and would presumably be rectified by the US.

Obviously, it was not just Advani's prodding that pushed the US into moving against Dawood Ibrahim. The latter had already crossed Washington's path during the investigations into the massive bomb blasts in Riyadh on the eve of the then Secretary of State Colin Powell's visit there in May 2004. American sleuths were tracking *hawala* or money laundering operations, so it is not surprising that Dawood's name cropped up, considering the control he exercises in the region. American investigations in Riyadh, to begin with, focused the spotlight on one of Dawood's shadowy henchmen, Saud Memon. Otherwise known as a wealthy Karachi garment exporter, it was Memon who, in January 2002, drove Daniel Pearl into a compound that he owned. It was here that Pearl was murdered. Memon subsequently disappeared from Karachi. Meanwhile, in June 2003, when Musharraf was in the US, the FBI nabbed eight suspected LeT operatives in the US. Charged with stockpiling weapons and waging war against India, these eight activists had apparently received arms training in Pakistan and some of them had even seen action in Kashmir.

A set of official documents released by the FBI in June 2003 in Washington stated that some of those arrested had even fought against Indian troops in Kashmir and were being funded by the Dawood syndicate to conduct terrorist activity in the Indian state of Gujarat. The documents disclosed that one of the arrested men was a Pakistani citizen working as an electrical engineer in the US. FBI action subsequently led to more arrests in several other American states.

Several Pakistani and Western writers, including the slain

American journalist Daniel Pearl, attempted to write about Dawood Ibrahim, but they were made to repent their decision. Author Gilbert King has attempted to reveal the secrets of Dawood's life in his book entitled '*The Most Dangerous Man In The World.*' After his expulsion from the UAE, says the book, no country other than Pakistan was willing to accord him asylum. "But his power and capability in the underworld remain undiminished; he can still do what he wants," the author claims.

The book also paints a disturbing picture of Pakistan's ISI and its involvement with Dawood Ibrahim. The author believes that Dawood is as dangerous as Osama bin Laden, though few in the West know of him. The book tries to connect the Karachi killing of US journalist Daniel Pearl to Dawood. According to King, the journalist was trying to ferret out information about Dawood and "Mr Ibrahim was alarmed and had Mr Pearl kidnapped and killed." However, no one had so far linked the Pearl murder to Dawood. As for the Mumbai don's future, the author says that for now he is safe in Pakistan but he could be affected on account of the close cooperation between the US and Pakistan in the war against terrorism.

According to the US Treasury Department's fact sheet: "Ibrahim's syndicate is involved in large-scale shipment of narcotics in the United Kingdom and Western Europe. Its smuggling routes from South Asia, the Middle East and Africa are shared with Osama bin Laden and his terror network. A financial arrangement was also brokered to facilitate bin Laden's use of these routes. In the 1990s, Ibrahim traveled to Afghanistan under the protection of the Taliban." During his much trumpeted 2001 Agra visit, Musharraf had vehemently denied that Dawood had taken refuge in Pakistan, though the Vajpayee administration believed otherwise.

The truth is Pervez Musharraf was right in his claim because Dawood had left Pakistan in early July 2001, before Musharraf's trip to India. According to the FBI's investigations, the mafia don had left with a fake Pakistani passport for Singapore and then gone on to Hong Kong. He returned to Karachi from Dubai later in July, but only after getting clearance from Islamabad. Taking strong exception to the US observations that Dawood, holding a Pakistani passport, was hiding in Pakistan, the foreign office spokesman in

Islamabad said the US had been asked to rectify its mistake. "Dawood Ibrahim is not in Pakistan. I would like to point out here that we do not have any Indian suspects on our soil. Second, India has not provided any evidence or proof of their presence on Pakistani soil", the spokesman added.

The Don in the Dock

From Mumbai to Dubai to Kuala Lumpur to Karachi, the stories associated with Dawood Ibrahim and his war with his underworld rivals can beat the best Bollywood thrillers. It is the nature of the crimes attributed to Dawood that place him at the top of India's most wanted wish list. Dawood figures in a list of twenty fugitives that India wants Pakistan to hand over and is suspected to be the prime player used by Pakistani intelligence to foment cross-border terrorism in India.

Since Dawood Ibrahim's branding as a global terrorist by the United Nations, the Pakistani intelligence establishment has been under intense pressure and feels extremely uneasy at persistent media reports about his presence in Pakistan. It was in September 2000, that monthly *Newsline* ran for the first time a detailed story claiming that Dawood was, indeed in Karachi and under the protection of the ISI. The cover story drew an extremely harsh reaction from the Pakistani authorities. During a meeting with the editors of several Pakistani newspapers after the story was published, Musharraf himself described it as an "indiscretion that had seriously hurt Pakistan's national interest".

The *Newsline* report was followed by yet another cover story a few months later carried by the Indian weekly *Outlook* in its 20 November 2002 issue and titled 'Donning a Monarchy'. The report stated: "Dawood Ibrahim has a passion for beautiful girls, designer clothes, expensive watches, *nehari* (trotters soup), *biryani* (fried rice with meat) and spicy food like *aaloo chana* (chickpea and potato salad) and *pani puri* (crackers with tamarind syrup). Dawood is said to be a moderate drinker. Favourite poison – Johnny Walker Black Label. Though said to keep his cool, his colleagues (who always address him as *Bhai* and *Jee Bhai*) never question his decisions. But they avoid him when he is in a bad mood. In such a mood, he can simply ask to kill some person or the other. It is after his evening round of meetings which end at 8 pm that Dawood and associates, under heavy armed escort, head for his old house in the Defence Officers Housing Authority in Karachi. Dawood's vehicle, often a Mercedes, is usually in the middle of the cavalcade and is escorted by at least 15 armed guards in two four-wheel-drive vehicles".

According to one story doing the rounds in Pakistani intelligence circles, Dawood was drawn into the communal infighting that swept India after Hindu zealots pulled down the *Babri* Mosque in Ayodhya in 1992. Mumbai was badly hit by communal rioting and hundreds of Muslims were butchered in the city. It is not clear why Dawood chose to retaliate on behalf of the Mumbai Muslims (the Indians allege he followed instructions from the ISI while the Pakistanis feel his motivation was primarily religious) but the CBI regards him as the mastermind behind the subsequent Mumbai bombings.

The story the Indian intelligence circles has spun regarding Dawood's alleged connections with the Pakistani intelligence has all the elements of a thriller. The CBI claims it learnt of Dawood's alleged involvement in anti-India espionage while investigating the Mumbai blasts. According to the CBI, the perpetrators went to Dubai using their Indian passports where Dawood allegedly provided them with Pakistani visas on plain pieces of paper so that their passports would not carry any records of their entry into Pakistan. They landed in Karachi and were taken to a training camp in the NWFP. The CBI concludes that they were sent back to Mumbai after being trained in the use of explosives by the now defunct *Harkatul Ansar.*

According to the Indian government's claim, shortly after Dawood left Dubai for Karachi in the wake of the 1993 Mumbai bombings, he was issued a Pakistani passport backdated to 12 August 1991. Soon afterwards, he moved into a 6,000 square yard house in Karachi. He later smuggled his family, comprising his wife, four daughters and a son, certain close associates, and their family members out of Mumbai. While in Karachi, Dawood, then known as David or Bhai (brother), came in contact with members of the former Mumbai community (Memons, Kathiawaris, Gujaratis and Konkanis) who had settled in the port city before and after the partition of India in 1947. They introduced him to some business-*cum*-religious-*cum-*

political figures, such as Haji Hanif Tayyab, a religious leader of the *Sunni* sect, known for his *Barelvi* leanings.

The Barelvi sect is diametrically different from the *Wahabi* (*Salafi*) and *Deobandi* schools of thought that characterize religious militancy. The *Barelvi* school places emphasis on paying respect to tombs and shrines, and it believes that the bodies in shrines can bestow blessings on those who visit them. The *Barelvi* school does not deal much with the issues of vice and virtue, and jehad has never been a part of this sect. Conversely, the *Wahabi* and *Deobandi* schools do not believe in shrines, indeed, they would like to see them all demolished, and they preach that only Allah can bestow blessings if one prays to him. They are also very strict on matters of vice and virtue, and jehad is one of the most emphasized chapters of their teachings.

Interestingly, it is said that when Maulana Masood Azhar, the founder *ameer* of the banned pro-Taliban militant *Sunni Deobandi* jehadi group *Jaish-e-Mohammad* was detained in India, the ISI people asked Dawood Ibrahim to use his contacts to have him released. However, his straight response had been: 'Impossible, he is a *Deobandi*'. Being a *Barelvi*, Dawood buried one of his daughters [who had died of malaria while in Karachi] in the premises of the Abdullah Shah Ghazi's shrine in the port city, which is situated close to the Moin Palace, where Dawood used to live before 9/11.

However, the strange thing is that he, the D-Company boss, is considered close to the *Lashkar-e-Toiba* leadership, which is even more extremist compared to the *Deobandis*. It does not even accept clean-shaven people into its organisation. However, as a matter of fact, the *Lashkar*-Dawood nexus is purely a tactical thing, orchestrated by the intelligence agencies, which has nothing to do with the sectarian leanings.

Born on 31 December 1955, Dawood Ibrahim is the son of a former criminal investigation department *havaldar*, Ibrahim Kaskar. The collapse of the Mumbai textile industry in the 1980s and the urban despair that it caused provided the backdrop for Dawood Ibrahim's spectacular rise to riches. After falling out with Amirzada Pathan and his brother Alamzeb Pathan, two major figures in Mumbai's underworld associated with the Karim Lala gang, Dawood set out on his own. In 1981, his elder brother Sabir was shot dead by the Pathan brothers. Dawood Ibrahim promptly had Amirzada assassinated to avenge the murder of his brother. In 1984, under pressure from both the police and Karim Lala's gang, Dawood moved to Dubai. However, his right hand man Chhota Shakeel stayed on in India to manage Dawood's interests, which had already become substantial by the late 1980s.

By 1987, however, Mumbai had become too hot for Chhota Shakeel as well. First arrested in 1983 on charges of kidnapping and illegal possession of weapons, Shakeel was arrested again on 1 December 1988, at Dongri in Mumbai under the Indian national security laws. He was awarded bail by the Mumbai High Court on 28 March 1989 and immediately moved to Dubai. Dawood's enterprises in Mumbai continued to flourish meanwhile with the help of other key figures in his gang including Chhota Rajan. However, soon after the 1993 Mumbai serial blasts, Rajan broke away from Dawood and moved to Dubai, from where he was forced to flee to Kuala Lumpur by 1994.

Chhota Rajan's departure from Mumbai triggered one of the bloodiest gang wars in Mumbai's history. Significantly, the war that began with the serial blasts seems to have led to a transformation of the Mumbai-centred underworld alliances. Rajan's efforts to project himself as an enemy of the ISI, determined to avenge terrorism in India, are clearly aimed at winning support of both the Indian state and the politicians who believe that a 'Hindu' underworld is somehow better than a 'Muslim' underworld. While the stories connected to Dawood Ibrahim and his likes may read like Bollywood fiction, their impact is far from imaginary.

Dawood further strengthened his Pakistani connection in August 2005 when he got his eldest daughter Mahrukh Ibrahim married to Junaid Miandad, the eldest son of former Pakistani cricket captain Javed Miandad, who still holds an important administrative slot in the Pakistan Cricket Board (PCB). Dawood and Miandad's becoming in-laws gave credence to the Indian government's allegations that the most wanted CBI fugitive hides in Pakistan despite claims to the contrary by the Pakistani authorities. The engagement ceremony in Karachi in January 2005 was a hush-hush affair as the 'globally designated terrorist' is not supposed to be residing in Pakistan.

In the first week of August 2007, the Indian print and electronic media reported that Dawood has escaped an assassination attempt in the vicinity of his Kawish Crown Plaza Hotel in the port city of Karachi where he had gone on a secret visit. The story went that Dawood had moved to Karachi from Islamabad following the June 2007 release of his younger brother Iqbal Kaskar in India, with a view to inject fresh blood into the dwindling network of his D-Company and get it through to Iqbal Kaskar so that he could re-establish the D-Company's lost control over real estate business in the commercial capital of Pakistan.

On 7 August 2007, following media reports of Dawood's arrest in Pakistan, the interior ministry spokesman Brig (retd) Javed Iqbal Cheema stated: "Nobody with that name has been arrested in Pakistan. We have reason to believe he is not in Pakistan," he said, adding that Indian authorities were advised to scour their own territory for the wanted men. He said Dawood's arrest on Pakistani soil was out of the question and such reports are meant to create problems for Pakistan. "On the one hand, the Indian establishment continues to claim Dawood Ibrahim was hiding in Pakistan with the blessings of the ISI while on the other, the Indian media has come up with an astonishing claim that the Most Wanted CBI fugitive has been arrested by the ISI. Does that make sense?" asked the Pakistani interior ministry spokesman.

A few weeks later, on 18 October 2007, the Pakistan government was once again compelled to deny media reports about the presence of Dawood on its soil and his detention by the ISI. "Apprehension of Dawood Ibrahim (subject of Interpol Red Corner Notice A-135/4/93) and his presence in Pakistan has not been substantiated", a Pakistan Interpol communication to the Central Bureau of Investigations said. Extensive reports were carried in the media about Ibrahim being detained in Pakistan, following which, the CBI, which represents Interpol in India, sent a request to its Pakistani counterpart to verify them. The Interpol-Pakistan responded to CBI's request, denying reports that Dawood along with his aides Chhota Shakeel and Tiger Memon were arrested by the ISI from their hideout near the Pak-Afghan border.

On 31 March 2008, the Indian print media was splashed with

news reports that the *Lashkar-e-Toiba* has taken over D-Company. One such report carried by the *Times of India* stated: "D-Company is now officially part of the *Lashkar-e-Toiba's* network, with the Inter Services Intelligence getting Dawood to merge his gang with the fundamentalist terror group as part of a game plan to crank up its anti-India campaign. The underworld gang and the LeT jehadis have been knocked into a single entity, posing serious challenges to the Indian internal security. ISI's links with D-Company are old, going back to 1993 when the Pakistani external intelligence agency used Dawood and his henchmen to execute the 12 March 1993 terror attack on Mumbai in what marked the first instance anywhere of serial bombings".

The news report added: "There has been a shift in the dynamics of ISI-Dawood equations, reducing D-Company from a useful ally to a group of individuals dependent on ISI to escape international law agencies, especially after Dawood's having been branded a global terrorist by the US. But the hospitality has a tag attached to it: complete dependence for survival on the ISI, which does not mind displaying its leverage *vis-à-vis* the once ruthless gang... The joining of ranks with *Lashkar*, one of the most dangerous terrorist outfits which treat liberation of large tracts of India from Hindu domination as its religious obligation, can help the ISI to further its subversive agenda. Stints with *Lashkar* camps can morph Dawood's band of urban gangsters into well-armed and jehad-driven terrorists. On the other hand, the *Lashkar* benefits immensely from collaboration with D-Company which continues to attract recruits and has acquired financial muscle by venturing into mainstream business enterprises without letting go of its original money spinner, smuggling."

The return of democracy in Pakistan in the wake of the 2008 general elections seems to have made little difference to the fortunes of the underworld don. It was in the wake of the 26/11 Mumbai terror attacks, allegedly carried out by the *Lashkar-e-Toiba*, that Dawood Ibrahim was initially characterised by the Indian press as being the mastermind behind the attacks. In the second week of December 2008, India officially demanded Dawood's arrest and extradition from Pakistan.

On 5 December 2008, Interior Minister Rehman Malik conceded

that India has given a list of three persons – Dawood Ibrahim, Tiger Memon, and Masood Azhar – for extradition. But he strongly rejected the presence of the three in Pakistan, adding that Tiger Memon and Dawood Ibrahim were Indian nationals and their presence in Pakistan was out of the question. The Indian government had reacted sharply over the Pakistani denial, saying Pakistan was prepared to make all the right sounds that are designer-suggested to suit terrorists and criminals back home.

On 22 December 2008, Jeremy Hammond, the editor of the well-known American *Foreign Policy Journal,* wrote in his article titled 'Why the CIA does not want Dawood in Indian hands' that his arrest and handover to India might prove inconvenient for either the ISI or the CIA, or both. He wrote: "The planning and execution of the 26/11 terror attacks in Mumbai are indicative of the mastermind role not of either Zakiur Rehman Lakhvi or Hafiz Saeed, but of Dawood Ibrahim, an Indian who is intimately familiar with the city. It was in Mumbai that Ibrahim rose through the ranks of the underworld to become a major organised crime boss. But while Lakhvi and Saeed have continued to be named in connection with the Mumbai terror attacks, the name of Dawood Ibrahim seems to be either disappearing altogether or his originally designated role as the mastermind of the attacks being credited now instead to Lakhvi in media accounts. Whether this is a deliberate effort to downplay Ibrahim's role in the attacks so as not to have to force Pakistan to turn him over because of embarrassing revelations pertaining to the American CIA's involvement with known terrorists and drug traffickers that development could possibly produce isn't certain".

Jeremy added: "Yoichi Shimatsu, former editor of the *Japan Times,* wrote last month after the Mumbai terror attacks that Ibrahim had worked with the US to help finance the mujahedeen during the 1980s and that because he knows too much about the US darker secrets in the region, he could never be allowed to be turned over to India. The promotion of Zakiur Rehman Lakhvi to mastermind of the attacks while Ibrahim's name disappears from media reports would seem to lend credence to Shimatsu's assertion. Investigative journalist Wayne Madsen similarly reported that according to intelligence sources, Ibrahim is a CIA asset, both as a veteran of the mujahedeen war and in a continuing connection with his casino and drug trade operations in Kathmandu, Nepal. A deal had been made recently to have Pakistan hand Ibrahim over to India, but the CIA was fearful that this would lead to too many of its dirty secrets coming to light, including the criminal activities of high level personnel within the agency".

While New Delhi still hopes that the end could be in sight for Dawood Ibrahim, there are indications that the going may not be so tough for the man who still has friends in high places. But the million-dollar question remains: How long can the Pakistani establishment afford harbouring the Most Wanted jehadi don.

REFERENCES

1.   Gilbert King, *The Most Dangerous Man in the World*, 2004.
2.   Ibrahim's syndicate is involved in large-scale shipment of narcotics
3.   *Fact Sheet*, US Treasury Department, September 2000.
4.   Report, *Newsline.*
5.   Donning a Monarchy, Weekly *Outlook*, 20 November 2002.
6.   News Reports, *Times of India*, 31 March 2008.

CHAPTER 13

The *Hizbul Mujahideen* – Losing its Bite

The *Hizbul Mujahideen* (HM) or the Party of Freedom Fighters is considered to be the mother of on-going militancy in the Indian-administered Jammu & Kashmir. Led by a militant *Sunni* Kashmiri Muslim, Mohammad Yusuf Shah alias Pir Syed Salahuddin, the *Hizb* is politically mentored by the *Jamaat-e-Islami Pakistan* (JI), which considers Jammu & Kashmir an integral part of Pakistan.

The HM cadre is drawn mainly from indigenous sources, but its leaders' contacts with many Afghan *mujahideen* groups such as the *Hizb-e-Islami* of Commander Gulbaddin Hekmatyar enabled some of its cadres to receive arms training at camps in Afghanistan. However, the *Hizb* leadership has never identified itself with either *Al-Qaeda* or the Taliban. Unlike the other Kashmiri militant groups fighting in the Indian controlled state, the HM operates exclusively in Jammu & Kashmir and has been held responsible for regular attacks against the Indian security forces since its inception in 1989. Many say the *Hizb* was actually formed to keep a check on the growing influence of the pro-Independence Jammu & Kashmir Liberation Front (JKLF) and its birth marked the first ideological division of militancy in Jammu & Kashmir – total independence versus merger with Pakistan.

Well-built with long hair, Syed Salahuddin is the supreme commander of the *Hizbul Mujahideen* who keeps shuttling between

Muzaffarabad, the capital of Pakistan-administered Kashmir and the garrison town of Rawalpindi, which houses the General Headquarter of the Pakistan Army. Until 1987, Syed Salahuddin was a little known pro-Pakistan political activist who swore by the Indian Constitution, not once but thrice. He unsuccessfully contested the Jammu & Kashmir Assembly elections as a *Jamaat-e-Islami* candidate. Then he was known as Yousaf Shah. Mysterious but outspoken, Salahuddin is now a father figure, reverentially called Pir Sahib (a religious title), among the militants fighting a decade-long tenacious and bloody secessionist insurgency in the Kashmir Valley.

Born as the last and seventh child of his parents at Soibugh, Budgam, a village in the Kashmir Valley, Mohammad Yusaf Shah initially became interested in studying medicine, but later on decided to become a civil servant. While studying Political Science at the University of Jammu & Kashmir, he was influenced by the *Jamaat-e-Islami*, and become a member of its branch in the Kashmir Valley. At University, he got involved in persuading Muslim women to veil themselves and also took part in processions in support of Pakistan. After University, he decided not to join the civil service, but instead he became an Islamic preacher at a *deeni madrassa* or religious seminary.

In 1987, Yusuf Shah, a well-known Islamic preacher with three Masters Degrees, contested the J&K Assembly polls from Amira Kadal constituency of Srinagar. He was among the candidates of the Muslim United Front who had been tipped as 'sure winners' but were declared defeated in the largely rigged elections and sent to jail. Soon after his release in 1989, he picked up the gun to fight Indian rule and adopted the nom de guerre of Salahuddin, after the famous 12th century warrior who fought the Crusaders. He crossed the Line of Control into Pakistan-administered Kashmir immediately after taking over from Master Ahsan Dar as the supreme commander of *Hizbul Mujahideen* in 1991.

Salahuddin's strength lies in the fact that he heads a militant group that is largely indigenous and not one dominated by foreign mercenaries, as had been the case with many other militant groups active in Kashmir. As the supreme commander, the *Hizb* chief, who ranks No. 8 on India's 'Most Wanted' list, controls a 20,000-strong jehadi cadre from Muzaffarabad, the capital of Pakistan-administered Kashmir. The Indian government has frequently demanded his extradition from Islamabad. But a confident *Hizb* chief has publicly stated time and again that the Pakistani government would never hand him over to India because it considers him a freedom fighter and not a terrorist.

However, the US State Department added the *Hizbul Mujahideen* to its Foreign Terrorist Organisations list on 1 May 2003, after its leadership admitted having acquired shoulder-firing Estrela surface-to-air missiles being used against the Indian security forces in Jammu & Kashmir. This forced the Musharraf regime to follow suit.

Four other militant groups active in J&K and banned by the US authorities are *Al-Badr Mujahideen*, the *Harkatul Jehadul Islami* and the *Jamiatul Mujahideen*. Interestingly, the State Department's annual 2003 report highlighted the visible splits between Pakistan-based commanders and several other commanders in the Kashmir valley. The report said that *Al-Badr* was a splinter group of the *Hizbul Mujahideen*. The *Harkatul Jehadul Islami* mainly consisted of Pakistanis and foreign Islamists, who were fighting in Kashmir and the group had been linked to the mysterious disappearance of five foreigners kidnapped by *Al-Faran* from Srinagar in 1995. The *Jamiatul Mujahideen*, it said, comprised mainly Kashmiris and Pakistanis.

Currently, the *Hizb* is divided into five divisions: central division for Srinagar, northern division for Kupwara, Bandipora and Baramulla, southern division for Anantnag and Pulwama districts, Chenab division for Doda district, Gool in Udhampur district, and Pir Panjal Division for the Rajouri and Poonch districts. The group has a substantial support base in the Kashmir Valley and in the Doda, Rajouri, Poonch districts and parts of Udhampur district in the Jammu region. A 20-member council and a 5-member *Shura* run the *Hizb* which has its own news agency, Kashmir Press International and a women's wing: *Banat-ul-Islam*. Overseas, Ghulam Nabi Fai's Kashmir American Council and Ayub Thakur's World Kashmir Freedom Movement back it.

The *Hizb* has essentially three factions: The first of these was set up in Jammu & Kashmir in 1990 with the blessings of the *Jamaat-*

e-Islami (JI) and is commanded by Syed Salahuddin. The Pakistani faction of the HM was founded by the Pakistan chapter of the *Jamaat* with Usman Bhai as commander. The *ameer* of the Azad Kashmir chapter of the *Jamaat-e-Islami* Allama Rashid Turrabi launched the third *Hizb* faction under the command of Masood Sarfraz. This faction later came to be called the Pir Panjal Regiment.

The *Hizbul* story begins in 1983 when the *ameer* of J&K chapter of the *Jamaat-e-Islami*, Maulana Saad-ud-Din, came to Pakistan from Saudi Arabia. In Pakistan, he met the then military ruler General Zia-ul Haq and leaders of *Jamaat-e-Islami* Pakistan, including the then JI *ameer* Mian Tufail Mohammad, to work out a detailed strategy for armed resistance in Jammu & Kashmir. On the basis of this strategy, in 1984, the *Jamaat-e-Islami* Occupied Kashmir (JIOK), led by Syed Ali Geelani began preparing for militancy. The JI cadres were asked to migrate to the Pakistan-administered Kashmir and other areas, including Afghanistan, for military training.

This process continued until 1987 and saw the rise of many organisations such as Zia Tigers, *Al-Hamza* and *Al-Badr*, which were invariably *Jamaat-e-Islami* affiliates, guided by the ISI with branches in Azad Kashmir and Jammu & Kashmir. These organisations began operating against the Indian forces in Jammu & Kashmir from August 1988 onwards. In a September 1989 session, JI leaders formed the *Hizbul Mujahideen* by merging two groups, *Tehrikul Mujahideen* and *Hizb-e-Islami*.

The organisational structure of the *Hizbul Mujahideen* was finally put in place in October 1989. In November 1989, its formation was formally announced in the press and its constitution was promulgated in June 1990. Master Ahsan Dar, a former teacher in a *Jamaat*-run school and a militant leader from Pattan, North Kashmir, became its first commander-in-chief. The Indian authorities allege the Pakistani ISI was actively involved in coordinating all these efforts to launch the organisation. By 1991, major groups such as *Tehreek-e-Jehad-e-Islami* led by Abdul Majid Dar had merged with the new outfit.

Soon, the *Hizb* initiated a massive recruitment drive across the Kashmir Valley. For this, it first established a network of trained guides, generally residents of border villages who were engaged in cross-border smuggling before the emergence of militancy. Unlike the *Jammu & Kashmir* Liberation Front, the *Hizbul Mujahideen* leadership conducted unchecked mass recruitment drives to send Kashmiri youths across the border to Azad Kashmir for arms training. The youths were ferried in passenger buses from Srinagar to Kupwara, from where they crossed the border. Militancy, which till then was a covert hush-hush affair, came above ground.

Within a year, the *Hizb* had over 10,000 armed cadres, mostly trained in Pakistan or Pakistan-occupied Kashmir, thus becoming the largest militant group in the Valley. By now, the JKLF had been completely marginalized since the Pakistani intelligence establishment had embargoed all supply of arms and money to it. Two military training camps were established in Jhal and Dhani, in Pakistan-administered Azad Kashmir. Over the militancy-hit years, although over 100 pro-Pakistan jehadi groups mushroomed in the Valley, the *Hizb* was perhaps the only group with a large network. In fact, many of the groups existed only on paper and did little else than issue press releases.

In the meantime, the supreme advisory council of the *Hizb* met for two days in November 1991 and asked its chief commander Master Ahsan Dar to step down and make way for Syed Salahuddin. In early 1992, the HM became a member of the Popular International Organisation (PIO) under the leadership of Sudan's Dr Hassan-al-Turabi, which made it eligible for guidance, training, funds and arms from abroad and also bringing it under the scrutiny of the Indian security and intelligence agencies. The Indian government banned it under the J&K Criminal Law Amendment Act, 1983.

By that time, the hardliners in the JI and *Hizb* leadership had developed serious differences on policy, but mainly the question of independence of the State as a third option. And in November 1997, Salahuddin announced the disassociation of his group from the *Jamaat-e-Islami* Pakistan. "Our outfit is not affiliated with any particular group. Ours is an armed resistance movement of all the people of Jammu & Kashmir. We have a network from Srinagar to every important capital of the world and our supporters are all Kashmiris and expatriate Kashmiris," he declared.

Salahuddin's move infuriated the Pakistani intelligence

establishment, leading to an intense rivalry between two HM groups, one loyal to Salahuddin, a Kashmiri, and the other headed by a Pakistani, Masood Sarfraz, who was being favoured by the ISI to replace Salahuddin. However, complaints against Masood Sarfaraz, ranging from arbitrary use of the funds to mismanagement in the training camps to a high-handed attitude towards the party leadership worked against him. Next choice was *Jamaat-e-Islami* chief, Allama Rashid Turrabi, who proved no better. He refused to accept orders from Pakistan and started accusing the *Jamaat* leadership of compromising the Kashmir cause under US pressure.

Following Sarfaraz's refusal to step down, Turrabi himself took control of the *Hizbul* headquarters in Kotli district of Azad Kashmir, leading to a fierce battle between the two groups. This exposed a disturbing trend. The two armed groups fighting in Azad Kashmir were increasingly showing signs of indiscipline, a phenomenon that had already been witnessed in Afghanistan at one stage of its resistance movement against the Soviets.

The next split in the *Hizb* came in July 2000 when Abdul Majid Dar, the chief operational commander of the HM made a conditional ceasefire offer to the Indian government at a press conference in Srinagar. Interestingly, the offer was endorsed by Syed Salahuddin at a press conference in Islamabad. But it created a divide among the component parties of the United Jehad Council (UJC), the collective body of leading militant groups fighting in Jammu & Kashmir, finally leading to the removal of Syed Salahuddin from the chairmanship of the UJC.

Salahuddin saved his position by hastily dissociating himself from the ceasefire offer, although some in the jehadi circles say Dar had made the offer at the behest of his leader Salahuddin. This about-turn on the part of Salahuddin infuriated Dar but the point of no return came when Salahuddin, alarmed by Dar's efforts to initiate a dialogue with the Indian government, bypassing Pakistan, decided to replace many of his field commanders besides ordering Dar and his associates to return to Pakistan. However, matters spiraled out of hand when Dar's associates refused to comply. Eventually, at the May 2002 supreme council meeting, Majid Dar was removed as the chief operational commander with a majority vote.

Immediately after his expulsion, fissures showed up in the *Hizbul Mujahideen* field commands. By early 2003, Dar and many of his supporters within HM decided to launch their own group to take part in the upcoming Jammu & Kashmir state assembly elections. As he was preparing to come to Pakistan to announce the formation of his political group, the *Jammu & Kashmir* Salvation Movement, he was shot dead in the Noor Bagh area of Sopore Township in north Kashmir on 23 March 2003 by two unidentified gun-wielding youth.

Two organisations claimed responsibility for the Dar murder: the previously little-known, 'Save Kashmir Movement', believed to be a front of the *Al Umar Mujahideen*, and *Al Nasireen*, while describing him as "an informant of Indian agencies" and "an enemy of the Kashmiri people". However, there are those in the jehadi circles who believe that Dar's killing was the culmination of an almost three-year old battle for supremacy being waged by his followers against the *Hizb* faction led by Salahuddin and that the hit-squad that killed Dar was sent by none other than the HM chief.

Dar's assassination provoked a serious split within the *Hizb* cadre in Pakistan, though Salahuddin survived and remained firmly in control of the organisation, primarily because of ISI's support. While all the top commanders of the Dar group and a majority of its *mujahideen* decided to join the *Hizb*-e-Islami, some of them, refusing to work under the new flag and leadership, reluctantly returned to the HM led by Salahuddin. Dar's followers maintain that Salahuddin himself had betrayed the cause of jehad in J&K. Even today, they say, he is open to criticism for having made deals of his own with the Indian authorities to protect his personal interests.

For instance, they point out, not one of his five sons had joined the ranks of the hundreds of young cadres that the *Hizb* leadership trains to fight the Indian forces in Kashmir. His five sons and two daughters live with their mother in their ancestral house in Soibugh, Badgam. His oldest son, Shahid Yusuf, 35, works as a teacher, while Javed Yusuf, 31, is an agricultural technologist, who was trained at the prestigious *Sher-e-Kashmir* University of Agricultural Science and Technology. Shah's third son Shakeel Yusuf, 27, works as a medical assistant at Srinagar's *Sher-e-Kashmir* Institute of Medical Sciences. Wahid Yusuf, 24, studies in Sri Maharaja Hari Singh Government

Medical College, after the family's affluent contacts helped him obtain a seat through a quota controlled by the Jammu & Kashmir Governor. Momin Yusuf, 20, the youngest of Shah's sons, studies Engineering in Pattan town.

But far from his present base in the garrison town of Rawalpindi, Salahuddin continues to command the *Hizbul Mujahideen,* the most powerful group despite having split four times since its inception. In the words of an ex-intelligence official: "One of the oldest tricks in the book is not to allow any individual jehadi group to become too strong. This is a tried and tested mode of keeping overall control on such groups. Whenever one group is seen as getting too strong or influential, the agencies try to split it and sometimes pit one against the other. And the *Hizbul Mujahideen* is no exception."

With militancy going out of fashion and the Pakistani establishment apparently withdrawing its support to the Kashmiri militants in the aftermath of the 9/11 attacks and the subsequent U-turn on *Jehad-e-Kashmir,* Syed Salahuddin plans to assume a new role by converting the *Hizb* into a political party. Having already gotten clearance from the leadership of the *Jamaat-e-Islami,* many say Salahuddin has started groundwork to take over the mantle of Syed Ali Shah Geelani, the ailing chief of *Jamaat-e-Islami* Jammu & Kashmir chapter. The central leadership of the two *Jamaats* believes that the octogenarian Syed Ali Shah Geelani will leave a big vacuum when he passes away.

It was against this backdrop that Syed Salahuddin turned diplomatic and announced his support for the Srinagar-Muzaffarabad bus service in March 2005. On 17 August 2006, Salahuddin told the Srinagar-based *Kashmir News Service* that his group was willing to initiate a dialogue with India even as the conflict continued, mirroring experiments in Afghanistan and Vietnam. A ceasefire, he added, could come about if India brought troop levels in Jammu & Kashmir to the 1989 position, adding that it should release detainees, it should stop all military operations, and it should acknowledge before the world community that there are three parties to the dispute.

Two years later, with the installation of an elected government in Pakistan in 2008, Salahuddin once again hinted at reviewing the group's armed struggle on the condition that India changes its stance and agrees to meaningful tripartite talks for the solution of the Kashmir issue. "The armed struggle, which the people of Jammu & Kashmir initiated in 1989, is not a terrorist movement. Instead, it is a recognised movement for freedom and for the right to self-determination for the Kashmiri people. We are peaceful people and want a political solution to the problem," he told a news conference in Karachi on 1 April 2008.

A year later, however, Salahuddin gave a fervent call for boycotting the J&K state assembly elections, saying only traitors would vote in the polls. "Those voting in the national ballot will be considered traitors who are selling out the blood of martyrs. People should not participate or they would let the sacrifices of the martyrs go waste," said Salahuddin in a statement on 14 April 2009. His stern warning came two days after a surprise announcement by Kashmiri separatist Sajid Lone that he would contest the elections. "Fighting elections is a change of strategy, not ideology," said Lone, a vocal opponent of Indian rule whose father was assassinated in 2002. "My aim is to enter parliament and represent Kashmir in India," Lone said.

Three weeks later, on 7 May 2009, the very village from where Salahuddin sowed the seeds of militancy in Kashmir two decades back saw an encouraging turnout as its voters came out enthusiastically to defy boycott calls. In contrast to the 2004 general election when the voter turnout in this village [which remained the hot bed of militancy in Jammu & Kashmir and is home to many top commanders of the *Hizb*] remained less than one per cent, about 25 per cent voters spread across eight polling booths had cast their ballots. Polling booth No. 34-E adjacent to Syed Salahuddin's house saw about 156 voters out of a total 635 turn up by afternoon.

Currently marginalised to a great extent in the wake of the 26/11 Mumbai terror attacks, the Rawalpindi-based Salahuddin seems to be at the mercy of the Pakistani establishment now-a-days; for there is little that he can do as long as he is on their soil. Groaning under mounting international pressure in the aftermath of the Mumbai terror attacks, Salahuddin has already been asked by the Pakistani establishment to lie low and adopt a wait and see policy. At the same time, there are reports that in a move that signal efforts to address New Delhi's concern over cross-border terrorism, the ISI has been made to begin disarming the *Hizb* cadres at Tarbela and Haripur militant training camps in Muzaffarabad, the capital of the Pakistan-administered Kashmir.

Then there are media reports saying that the intelligence agencies of India and Pakistan have already resorted to intelligence sharing to put an end to cross border infiltration on the Line of Control (LoC) following which the *Hizbul Mujahideen* has suffered major setbacks with the killing of over 50 senior commanders and over 300 cadres in encounters with J&K security forces. Large-scale surrenders in the Kashmir Valley by *Hizb* cadres have also weakened the group. As a matter of fact, a generation of the *Hizbul Mujahideen* operatives who had founded the organisation have either died in combat or served time in prison – and those who are still at large are now in their 40s and 50s, with little inclination for active field service.

Therefore, the *Hizb* leadership's state of mind can well be gauged from a 10 June 2008 analysis by Praveen Swami, Associate Editor of an Indian daily *The Hindu*. The very first paragraph of the report quotes Salahuddin as having told a confident: "Perhaps we should start calling ourselves *Hizbul Muhajireen* (Party of Exiles or Refugees)". His playful use of words didn't conceal the bitterness behind his remark: he feared that the army of Islamist guerrillas he had once commanded has now degenerated into a 'party of exiles', who are unwanted in both India and Pakistan'.

Yet another news report, carried by *The Hindu* on 8 August 2009 claimed that disclosures made by the two suspected *Hizbul Mujahideen* militants arrested in Delhi have indicated a sharp decline in the popularity of its supreme commander Syed Salahuddin, even leading to questions over his leadership. The report said that the interrogation of the militants, Javed Ahmad Tantray and Ashiq Ali Butt, revealed that Syed Salahuddin travels in a black Land Cruiser escorted by two personal security officers armed with AK 47 series assault rifles. "While his immediate subordinate is Khalid Saifullah, Umar Javed happens to be the third and Khursheed fourth in the *Hizbul* hierarchy. A militant named Ibrahim works as secretary to Salahuddin".

But the most important revelation made by the arrested HM

militants was that Pir Syed Salahuddin is fast losing his support base as he is unable to deliver as the *Hizbul Muhjaideen* chief. Therefore, they told their interrogators that Syed Salahuddin is getting desperate to carry out attacks in India to assert himself and consolidate his position as the supreme commander. However, the task seems difficult given the fact that many of his militants have either been arrested or neutralised by the forces in Jammu & Kashmir recently.

Under these circumstances, Syed Salahuddin seems to be a virtual prisoner. Though still in communication with his jehadi cadre in Jammu & Kashmir, he is no more master of his destiny as had been the case in the past. Therefore, there are those in the jehadi cadres who now describe him as an ageing and battered beast which is rapidly losing its bite.

REFERENCES

1. News Report, *Kashmir News Service*, 17 August 2006.
2. Praveen Swami, *The Hindu*, 10 June 2008.

CHAPTER 14

Pakistani Religious Seminaries – Indoctrination to the Core

The Pakistani *madrassas,* or religious seminaries, have always been at the centre of debates on extremism and radicalisation of society. The debate intensified after the Musharraf regime had joined the US-led war on terror in the aftermath of the 9/11 terror attacks. However, it was only seven years later that the Operation silence carried out by the Pakistan Army in July 2007 against the fanatic clerics of the *Lal Masjid* in the heart of Islamabad reinforced the Western notion about the Pakistani religious seminaries being used as breeding grounds for terrorists and suicide bombers.

The much trumpeted claims by the Musharraf regime of having introduced drastic *madrassa* reforms to halt the flow of recruits into militant groups and to bring the religious seminaries into the mainstream came to a standstill after the *Lal Masjid* episode. The bloodbath proved that the traditional religious school system in Pakistan is now rotten to the core and continues to operate as the breeding factory for the radical Islamist ideology as well as the recruitment centre for jehadi terrorist networks. Having cleared the *Lal Masjid* compound after the ruthless battle, the Pakistan Army reportedly recovered piles of highly sophisticated weapons, ranging from RPG-6 and phosphorous hand grenades to suicide jackets and high-tech gas masks.

As the dust settles on the July 2007 Operation Silence, the direct link between *madrassas* and militancy has already become apparent. If clerics running religious seminaries in Islamabad can stockpile weapons, turn their mosques into hideouts for hard-core militants and engage the highly trained and well equipped security forces in a fight to the finish for a full week, the activities of their counterparts in more remote areas can only be imagined. For long considered a nursery for the global jehad, the *madrassa* system in Pakistan is closely linked to the country's foreign policy objectives in Kashmir and Afghanistan, which have dominated the country's historiography since its creation.

In his address to the nation after the *Lal Masjid* operation on 11 July 2007, Pervez Musharraf declared that establishing the writ of the state had become inevitable. Critics, however, ask as to why this was not the priority of his regime from day one despite his repeated lofty claims as the most trusted US ally in the war against terror. Allowing the *Lal Masjid* clerics and the students of its affiliated religious seminaries – *Jamia Hafsa* for girls and *Jamia Fareedia* for boys – to remain untouched for years despite their extremist activities in the federal capital only emboldened the clerics and furthered the delusion that militants wrapped in the garb of religious seminaries are above the law.

When Musharraf had made public his much-touted plans to reform the religious seminaries in Pakistan on January 2002 in a televised address to the nation, he said the move was necessary because some private Islamic schools had become breeding grounds for intolerance and hatred. He had unveiled a new strategy, which would see *deeni madrassas* teach Computer Studies, Mathematics, Science, and English alongside their traditional Islamic programme.

Musharraf said: "The day of reckoning has come. Do we want Pakistan to become a theocratic state? Do we believe that religious education alone is enough for governance or do we want Pakistan to emerge as a progressive and dynamic Islamic welfare state? My only aim is to help these institutions in overcoming their weaknesses and to provide them with better facilities and more avenues to the poor students studying there. These schools are excellent welfare set-ups where the poor get free board and lodge. And let me make it clear that very few *deeni madrassas* being run by hard-line parties promote negative thinking and propagate hatred and violence instead of inculcating tolerance, patience and fraternity."

It was presumed to be a considered and well-thought-out speech signaling an end to the decades-old strategy of the Pakistani intelligence establishments to use jehad as an instrument of foreign and defence policy. The speech was supposed to be a response to the 9/11 and also the 13 December 2001 attack on Parliament building in India. It supposedly spelt out the short and long-term measures envisaged by an enlightened military ruler to tackle the menace of extremism and fundamentalism afflicting the Pakistani society. Yet, his so-called reform campaign was soon exposed due to his one-step forward two-steps backwards approach. His oratory to modernise the religious schools met with little success mainly due to a lack of political will to enforce any of the policy decisions that were supposed to reform the *madrassas* by bringing them into the educational mainstream. Subsequently, signs of *Talibanisation* are quite evident in all parts of Pakistan, including the federal capital.

The five year *madrassa* reforms programme was launched in the four provinces of Pakistan besides Azad Kashmir (AJK), Federally Administered Tribal Areas (FATA) and Federally Administered Northern Areas (FANA) under the banner of '*Madaris* Reforms Project' (MRP) in 2002-03 whose period expired on June 30, 2007. Before that, a comprehensive survey was conducted by the Musharraf regime to ascertain the exact number of the religious seminaries operating in the country. According to the survey results, there were 20,000 religious schools in Pakistan which had been teaching an approximate number of two million youth. *Deobandi* sect had the largest number of seminaries – 12,000 followed by those being run by the *Barelvis* – 3,500. The number of the *Ahl-e-Hadith*-run seminaries stood at 380; those operated by the *Jamaat-e-Islami* were 405 while the number of the *Shia*-run *deeni madrassas* was 390.

The survey results further showed that the largest province of Punjab had the biggest number of the religious seminaries (8,000) followed by Sindh (5,500), NWFP (5,000) and 1,500 in Baluchistan, FATA and Azad Jammu and Kashmir. The survey showed that there were 150 *madrassas* in the Islamabad city alone, almost 90% of which were being operated by *Deobandis*. Having completed the survey, the

Musharraf regime eventually launched the five year *madrassa* reforms programme in the four provinces, with the prime aim of teaching formal subjects at the religious seminaries like English, Mathematics, Pakistan Studies, Social Studies and General Science along with the religious education.

Five years later, however, it was obvious that the Musharraf regime's so-called reform strategy was essentially cosmetic. The reform project was subsequently wrapped by the regime after having targeted only a small fraction of some 8,000 *madrassas* in the country. And the Federal Education Ministry was forthright in admitting its failure. "In the last five years, we could reach out to only 507 religious schools," the *madrassa* reform project director, conceded Dr Mohammad Hanif in July 2008.

The reform programme was launched by both the federal and the provincial education departments and two separate Project Management Units were set-up at federal and provincial levels. The cost of the reform project for five years was estimated at Rs 5.76 billion, to be spent by the government on providing formal subjects, computer, printers, syllabi, libraries, books, sports items, and salaries of teachers of about 8,000 seminaries in the country. Out of 8,000 religious schools, 4,000 were of primary level, 3,000 of secondary level and 1,000 of higher secondary level.

When its tenure ended in 2007, the Project Management Unit blamed the lack of coordination between the federal and the provincial governments for non-implementation of the project. In its final report to the federal ministry of education, the Project Management Unit conceded that the project was a big failure because hardly Rs. 223 million out of the total Rs. 5.76 billion funds could be utilised in five years. Critics, however, say the project was doomed to failure because Musharraf went ahead with it despite repeated warnings by many including the International Crisis Group (ICG) that its success was dependent on political will.

Two years after the *madrassa* reform campaign was launched, the ICG stated in its January 2004 report entitled, *Unfulfilled Promises: Pakistan's Failure to Tackle Extremism:* "General Musharraf's promise to drive extremism away from *madrassas* remains unfulfilled. Today, two years after he had promised his sweeping reforms, the jehadi *madrassas* remain the key breeding ground for radical Islamist ideology and the recruitment centre for terrorist jehadi networks."

The report went on: "The government pledged to firstly register all *madrassas* so that they adopt a government-approved curriculum by the end of 2002 and secondly to stop their misuse for preaching political and religious intolerance. The international community welcomed Musharraf's promise to stem jehadi ideology, but two years on, the lack of results is clear. To date, no presidential ordinance to regulate the *madrassas* has been promulgated. In fact, the government openly assures the religious leaders that it will not interfere in the *madrassas* affairs. Most *madrassas* in Pakistan remain unregistered and their sources of funding remain unregulated. The pledge to have government-prescribed curricula at all *madrassas* similarly remains unfulfilled as no national curriculum has so far been developed".

The ICG report added: "The government inaction continues to pose a serious threat to domestic, regional and international security. Musharraf's priority has never been eradicating Islamic extremism but rather the legitimisation and consolidation of his dictatorial rule. And for that, he depends on the religious right. The failure to curb rising extremism in Pakistan stems directly from the military government's own unwillingness to act against its political allies among the religious groups. Having co-opted the religious parties to gain constitutional cover for his military rule, Musharraf is highly reliant on the religious right for his regime's survival. If the US and others continue to restrict their pressure on Musharraf to verbal warnings, the rise of extremism in Pakistan will continue unchecked," the ICG report concluded.

Three years later, the ICG released its annual report titled '*Religious Pakistan: Karachi's Madrassas and Violent Extremism*'. The 28 March 2007 report stated: "More than five years after General Musharraf declared his intention to crack down on violent sectarian and jehadi groups and to regulate the network of *madrassas* on which they depend, his government's reform programme seems in shambles. Banned sectarian and jehadi groups, being supported by networks of mosques and *madrassas*, continue to operate openly in Pakistan's largest city, Karachi, and elsewhere. The international community needs to press Musharraf to fulfil his commitments, in particular to enforce genuine controls on *madrassas*. It should also shift the focus of its donor aid from helping the government's ineffectual efforts to reform the religious schools to improving the very weak public school sector".

According to the ICG report, Karachi's *madrassas* have trained and dispatched jehadi fighters to Afghanistan and held Kashmir, and offer a valuable case study of the government failures and consequences for internal stability and regional and international security. "In 2006, the city was rocked by some high-profile acts of political violence. Not all *madrassas* in the city are active centers of jehadis, but even those without direct links to violence promote an ideology that provides religious justification for such barbaric attacks. Given the government's half-hearted reform efforts, these unregulated *madrassas* contribute to a climate of lawlessness in numerous ways – from land encroachment and criminality to violent clashes between rival militant groups and the use of the pulpit to spread calls for sectarian and jehadi violence. The Pakistan government has not yet taken any of the overdue steps to control religious extremism in the country. Musharraf's periodic declarations of tough action, given in response to international events and pressure, are invariably followed by retreat. Plans are announced [by the regime] with much fanfare and then abandoned", the ICG report concluded.

As far as the largest province of Punjab is concerned, it is a known fact that South Punjab is home to the most aggressive and poisoned of all *deeni madrassas*. South Punjab stretches from Jhang to Bahawalpur, dotted with *madrassas* that private citizens from Saudi Arabia, the UAE and Kuwait fund generously, thinking they are spreading the message of Islam. This is the region where the countryside is dominated by feudal lords with large landholdings and cities teeming with the poor masses controlled by jehadi groups. Only in Dera Ghazi Khan, the origin of the *Lal Masjid* clerics, there are reportedly 185 registered *madrassas*, of which 90 are *Deobandi* (with a total of 324 teachers), 84 are *Barelvi* (with 212 teachers), six are *Ahl-e-Hadith* (107 teachers) and five are *Fiqah-e-Jaafria* or *Shia* (10 teachers). Multan is the traditional base of *deeni madrassas*, while Rahimyar Khan and Bahawalpur have seen their proliferation in recent years.

The findings of the ICG established one thing – many of the

Deobandi and *Ahl-e-Hadith madrassas* in Pakistan support militancy and foster a way of thinking that leads to acts of terrorism. While on the face of it, no *madrassa* looks either jehadi or sectarian, in depth research shows that most of the religious seminarians are more narrow-minded and intolerant than the pupils of normal schools. It was also established that like his *khaki* predecessors, the priority of Pakistan's fourth military dictator too wasn't reforming the *madrassas* sector and eradicating the Islamic extremism, but the legitimisation and consolidation of his despotic rule, for which he had made himself dependent upon the extremist religious clergy.

Following the installation of a democratically-elected government in 2008 and the subsequent ouster of Pervez Musharraf, the new President Asif Ali Zardari announced in Washington on 9 April 2009 that his government would take over all *madrassas* as part of reforms to separate students from extremists and impart them modern education along with religious education. Yet, his declaration was no different than a similar announcement made by Prime Minister Syed Yousaf Raza Gilani while taking the oath of his office in March 2008. He had announced to set-up a *Madrassa* Welfare Authority – a seminary reforms project announced under his first 100 days programme. However, despite the lapse of a full year, the Authority, which was supposed to be functional by 9 July 2008, has not yet been set-up because the task is yet to be assigned between Ministries of interior, religious affairs and education.

Therefore, senior educationist Dr A.H. Nayyar, insist that any government which announces *madrassa* reform must first identify the nature of reform. "It is clear that the present claim of reforming *madrassas* emanates from an urge to eliminate sources of extremism in the society. But even if the government succeeds in eliminating teachings of extremism from *madrassas*, it would not be enough in eliminating extremism from the society", said Nayyar who works with Islamabad-based NGO Sustainable Development Policy Institute (SDPI). He was of the view that the roots of extremism lie in so many other nooks and corners. "Almost all agree that the extremism has taken roots because of the absence of governance and justice in the society. If the government doesn't have any plan to fill this vacuum, any action against *madrassas* would be meaningless and only temporary. If it does have a plan to improve its governance and the system of justice, it will have to share it with public at large, for no scheme for good governance and justice would succeed without an active participation by the general public".

A.H. Nayyar claimed that the people behind General Musharraf's efforts were those who were influenced by *Jamaat-e-Islami*. "The *Jamaat* leadership has been trying for quite some time to convince *madrassas* to include modern secular subjects in their curriculum. Various meetings were held with the leaders of the four boards of *madrassa* education which failed. Most *madrassa* leaders argued, among other things, that if a sudden and a radical change is brought into the curriculum of religious *madrassas* it will be difficult to find people who can lead prayers, recite Koran accurately, or even perform burial rites."

Therefore, fearing opposition from *madrassas*, Nayyar said, the Musharraf regime suggested a modified curriculum that retained everything existing and added a few subjects like English, Mathematics, sciences and social studies from the public school curriculum. "A state grant was also offered for those who agreed to the federal government's proposals. Despite the monetary incentive a majority of *madrassas* spurned the offer. But those who accepted knew the modification meant added burden. In any case, what escaped everyone's mind was the fact that the *madrassas* teaching methodology centered on rote system and the added subjects would be taught and learnt in the same spirit".

On 14 July 2009, a massive explosion left 12 people, including seven children, dead in a South Punjab village 129/15-L in the Mian Channu town of Punjab. The blast was actually caused by a huge quantity of ammunition stored in a seminary that blew up, spewing death and destruction. A subsequent editorial note by daily *Dawn* on 15 July 2009, titled '*Madrassas* as a cover', stated: "This is just a small indication of what some of those who run *madrassas* do behind what would appear to be an innocuous, even laudable, activity. The man who used to run the religious seminary, Riaz Kamboh, was known to have militant links, had visited Afghanistan for training and was arrested twice but then released. Seemingly, the *madrassa* he ran was teaching the Holy Koran to the village boys and girls.

However, the recovery of propaganda literature and suicide jackets from the debris makes it abundantly clear that he was using the *madrassa* as a cover for organising a terrorist cell which brainwashed and trained young people to become terrorists and suicide bombers".

What happened at the village No 129/15-L in south Punjab, said the daily *Dawn* editorial, is symptomatic of a larger phenomenon throughout the country, for many *madrassas* have links with banned militant organisations and serve as recruiting grounds and as centers of indoctrination for both boys and girls.... There are thousands of such *madrassas* and seminaries in Pakistan, and though all of them cannot be tarred with the same brush the security agencies must be able to separate the wheat from the chaff. That Riaz Kamboh's activities remained undetected constitutes a sad commentary on the efficiency of Pakistani security agencies whose performance leaves a lot to be desired. We do not know how many other Kambohs are using *madrassas* as cells for terrorist activity".

A week later, on 20 July 2009, a group of Pakistani religious scholars demanded that the government should conduct raids on all *madrassas* to make sure that they did not have a terrorist agenda. In a subsequent editorial the next day on 21 July, yet another editorial note titled 'Checks on *madrassas*', daily *Dawn* stated: "The demand by the religious clergy serves to highlight the rising awareness in the nation of the threat to Pakistan from religious extremism... While the scholars' demand for raids can be understood in view of the gravity of the situation, what is actually needed is a system of perpetual monitoring of *madrassas*. A raid that yields no information about covert activities will be counterproductive and will expose the government to the charge of harassing *madrassas* believed to be imparting normal religious instruction. Whether it is sources of funding from abroad, propaganda or hate literature, the intelligence agencies need to closely monitor the working of all *madrassas*. Action must be taken where positive proof exists of anti-state activities. That the demand for raids has come from a section of the *ulema* is indicative of the fact that the Taliban and their supporters are becoming increasingly isolated because of their barbaric ways and the threat they pose to Pakistan".

The 7/7 London Suicide Attacks and the Pakistani *madrassa* Connection

Evidence coming to light in the wake of the July 2005 London suicide attacks – that three of the four suicide bombers were British-born youth of Pakistani origin who had traveled to Pakistan in November 2004 and visited several *Deobandi* religious seminaries – established the Western notion that many of the Pakistani *madrassas* function as training centres for radical Islamists and produce suicide bombers.

The 7/7 London attacks brought Pakistan once again at crossroads between the military and the mosque. After leaving its footprints in the United States, Afghanistan and India, the Pakistani terror trail had now moved to the United Kingdom. As news of the usual Pakistan connection flooded the international media, a somewhat embarrassed and equally nervous Pakistani military ruler, General Musharraf, convened an urgent meeting of the four provincial police chiefs and ordered them to crackdown on extremist elements. Musharraf was definitely puzzled and confused: whatever was happening on the international terror front was negating his repeated claims of having taken effective measures to reform the *madrassa* system.

The General then addressed the nation on the state-run television on 21 July 2005, giving December 2005 as the deadline to all religious seminaries to get registered with the Federal *Madaris* Board. Sharing vital administrative decisions to contain extremists, Musharraf declared that banned organisations would not be allowed to re-emerge with other names, and if some try so would be dealt with an iron hand. In a subsequent crackdown, the police force arrested hundreds of third and fourth grade suspected militants from various parts of Pakistan. But the question remained – was the crackdown for real? Apparently not. A similar crackdown had been carried out by the law enforcement agencies after the 9/11 attacks and also after Musharraf's January 2002 speech in which he had announced his plans to uproot the extremist mafia and to dismantle its jehadi infrastructure from the country. Indeed, if the number of the jehadis arrested in all these crackdowns is tallied, there should be no extremist left in the country.

Investigations into the London attacks revealed that two of the suicide bombers, Shehzad Tanweer and Siddique Khan, met one Osama Nazir, a leader of the outlawed militant organisation, *Jaish-e-Mohammad,* in Faisalabad during their 2004 Pakistan visit. Osama Nazir had masterminded the March 2002 attack on a church in Islamabad's high security diplomatic enclave, killing five people, including an American diplomat's wife and step-daughter. Osama Nazir was also involved in the 5 August 2002 attack on Murree Christian School, close to Islamabad, in which six Pakistani guards were killed, and the 9 August 2002 attack on the Christian Hospital in Taxila, West of Islamabad. Four Pakistani nurses and one of the attackers were killed in the Taxila suicide attack.

Osama Nazir's meeting with Shehzad Tanweer and Siddique Khan was allegedly held at a small *madrassa* in Faisalabad – *Jamia Fathul Raheem being* run by Qari Ahlullah Raheemi, an extremist *Sunni* Muslim cleric considered close to *Jaish-e-Mohammad.* During their stay at the *Jamia,* the sources speculate, Siddique Khan and Shehzad Tanweer might have been trained in the handling of explosives by Osama Nazir, who headed a group of trained suicide bombers at that time. They added that following the arrest of Sheikh Ahmed Omar Saeed in American journalist Daniel Pearl's murder case, Osama Nazir had become the right hand man of the *Jaish-e-Mohammad* chief, Maulana Masood Azhar, and had helped Amjad Hussain Farooqi, the *Lashkar-e-Jhangvi* linked *Al-Qaeda* lynchpin in Pakistan, in masterminding two suicide attacks on Musharraf in December 2003.

According to the Pakistani intelligence findings, following the killing of Amjad Farooqi, Osama Nazir had assumed his position and was working with the Abu Faraj al-Libbi, the most-wanted chief operational commander of the *Al-Qaeda* in Pakistan. The Americans had offered five million dollars for the arrest of either man, and Islamabad also announced two million rupees reward for the arrest of Osama Nazir, who had visited Afghanistan several times during the days of the Taliban rule in Afghanistan. Osama was finally nabbed from *Jamia Fathul Raheem* in Faisalabad in November 2004. He also admitted having met Shehzad Tanweer at the *Jamia Fathul Raheem* in 2004, before finally leaving for England in February 2005.

Osama Nazir further disclosed that Shehzad Tanweer had stayed at the religious seminary for a few weeks to get religious and spiritual inspiration from Qari Ahlullah Raheemi. According to him, over 300 Muslims of Pakistani origin living in the United Kingdom had visited Pakistan since the 9/11, received training in several *Jaish-e-Mohammad* and *Harkatul Mujahideen*-run training camps, and joined the *Al-Qaeda* suicide squad. He reportedly revealed that Shehzad Tanweer had stayed at another extremist *Sunni madrassa* – *Jamia Manzurul Islami* situated in the Cantonment area of Lahore, and being run Pir Saifullah Khalid. While the Pir insisted the school was being run by *Ahl-e-Sunnah Wal Jamaat*, there were clear indications that it was being managed and financed by a violent *Sunni* sectarian outfit – *Sipah-e-Sahaba Pakistan*, considered close to *Jaish-e-Mohammad* and led by Maulana Masood Azhar.

Information passed on to Pakistani agencies by their British counterparts say after landing in Karachi in November 2004, Shehzad Tanweer first went to Faisalabad and then reached Lahore where he got himself enrolled at the *Jamia Manzurul Islamia*. Pir Saifullah Khalid denies Shehzad Tanweer had ever visited the *madrassa*, but British agencies insist on this connection. However, apparently he could not acclimatise himself with the *madrassa* atmosphere and subsequently left after a couple of weeks.

The intelligence agencies further came to know during investigations that it was Siddique Khan, the ring leader of the London suicide bombers who had actually persuaded Shehzad Tanweer to join *Jamia Manzurul Islamia*. He also took him to *Jamia Fathul Raheem* in Faisalabad where they had a meeting with Osama Nazir. Siddique, the eldest of the four London bombers, was the likely leader of the London attacks. A Briton of Pakistani descent, Siddique Khan is believed to have drawn two of the other attackers, Shehzad Tanweer, 22, and Hasib Hussain, 18, deeper into extremism – through his work as a volunteer in community centers in the Leeds area.

On 1 September 2005, almost a year after the London attacks, *al-Jazeera* television broadcast a video message of Siddique Khan through which *Al-Qaeda* claimed responsibility for the 7/7 attacks and threatened more such attacks in Europe. Investigations showed that the message had been recorded during Siddique's visit to Pakistan in November 2004. It was the first explicit claim of responsibility for the blasts by the terrorist group headed by Osama bin Laden. The broadcast showed pictures of *Al-Qaeda* leader Dr Ayman al-Zawahri as well as the bomber, Siddique Khan, speaking in English and saying that he would take part in the attacks. In what appeared to be a defence of the 7/7 London suicide attacks on civilians, he warned westerners that they would not be safe because of electing governments that commit crimes against humanity.

The Mushroom Growth of *madrassas* and Militants

Islamic rule was introduced to the Indian sub-continent in the early 8th century when Arab warrior Mohammad bin Qasim had conquered Sindh, in what is southeastern Pakistan today. But the earliest known *madrassas* in north India were not recorded until the 13th century under the Turks. By the 14th century, Delhi alone had a thousand *madrassas*. In the 18th century, a curriculum known as the *Dars-e-Nizamia*, devised by Mullah Nizamuddin, became the standard syllabus. The curriculum was based on the rote memorising of the Koran, which was considered the highest scholastic achievement. However, this curriculum did not focus on violent jehad. In fact, the whole purpose of the *Dars-e-Nizamia* was to combine Islamic teachings with rational sciences to train the *madrassa* pupils to become lawyers, judges and administrators.

After the end of British rule and the partition of India in 1947, the *madrassas* in India and the newly created Islamic Republic of Pakistan took different courses. The Indian seminaries stayed true to their original mission of preaching Islamic scholarship, while the Pakistani ones became progressively more intolerant and aggressive in the competition to exclusively define Pakistan's Islamic nature. There are currently five broad types of *madrassas* in Pakistan, with four of them belonging to the majority *Sunni* sect and one belonging to the *Shia* minority. Among the *Sunnis*, mostly there are the *Barelvis* – a moderate group who seeks to be inclusive of local rituals and customs. Then there are religious seminaries run by the *Jamaat-e-Islami* Pakistan, which is non-sectarian but tends to be politically very active.

In the context of extremism, the remaining two streams of *deeni madrassas* are considered most important. The first one is called *Deobandi* school of thought, originating in the Indian town of *Deoband*, near Delhi. The *Deobandi* movement has long sought to purify Islam by rejecting un-Islamic accretions to the faith and returning to the models established in the Koran. Then there are *Ahl-e-Hadith* (followers of the way of the Prophet Mohammad) who have a similar emphasis on purifying the faith as *Deobandis*, but follow the *Salafi* religious jurisprudence (*fiqah*) as opposed to the *Hanafi* sect used by the *Deobandis*.

Until the 1970s, Pakistani religious *madrassas* largely followed the *Dars-e-Nizamia* curriculum and its variants established in the 1700s in India. Even the *Deobandi* alteration of this curriculum focused on purification of faith for the purposes of knowledge, rather than militancy and jehad. All this changed in the late 1970s and early 1980s. Army Chief General Zia-ul Haq, who took power after a military coup against a secular and liberal Zulfiqar Ali Bhutto's government in 1977, was an ardent Islamist, with clear leanings towards *Jamaat-e-Islami*. Zia, whose father had actually been a prayer leader, started off with some ill-fated attempts at rushing through Islamic law within Pakistan. General Zia's existing plans to turn Pakistan into an Islamic state gained urgency and a fundamentalist tone after two major events – the Iranian revolution in 1979 and the Soviet invasion of Afghanistan 10 years later.

The twin shocks encouraged a new movement within the *Deobandi madrassas*, which sought to change the way Islam was taught to the students. While it is true that many *madrassas* dropped secular subjects like Mathematics and sciences in part or whole, what was more significant than the narrowing of the syllabus was the change in focus and interpretation in the teaching of the Koran and the *Hadith* (sayings of Prophet Mohammad), drawing on the incendiary combination of Muslim Brotherhood and *Salafi* thinking developed under Saudi funding from places like the Islamic University of Medina and propagated by other Saudi-controlled foundations, such as the World Muslim League.

The emphasis in *madrassa* curriculum was subsequently shifted almost entirely from the standard pillars of faith such as prayer, charity and pilgrimage to the obligation and rewards of jehad. The *madrassas* taught the young students that the world was divided into believers and unbelievers in a black and white setting. Jews, Hindus and Christians were portrayed as evil usurpers. The curriculum started emphasising the need for Islamic warriors of jehad to liberate regions dominated by unbelievers as well as purify Islamic nations in order to establish a single Islamic caliphate where pure Islam would be followed. The students were taught that the only means to achieve this Utopian state was by waging a near-perpetual war, pursued by any and all means against unbelievers as well as impure sects within Muslims.

Subsequently, the era of the jehadi *madrassas* was born which got intertwined with politics under the military regime of Zia who promoted the *madrassa* system as a way to garner the support of the religious parties for his dictatorial rule and to recruit troops for the anti-Soviet War in Afghanistan. General Zia's Islamist policies opened the floodgates for funding to come in for the *madrassas*. Saudi Arabia, which wanted to promote its brand of *Wahabi* Islam, remained the main source of funding for the *madrassas*. The Saudi funding, which earlier used to be for the *Jamaat-e-Islami* (JI) led by Mian Tufail Mohammad, shifted to *Deobandis* being represented by the *Jamiat Ulema-e-Islam* (JUI), led by Maulana Fazlur Rahman. The *Deobandis* are actually inspired by the *Ahab* version of Islam enforced in Saudi Arabia.

It may not be a coincidence that the rise of the JUI's militant outfit, the *Harkatul Mujahideen* in the Indian held Jammu & Kashmir and the Taliban in Afghanistan was around the same time. Most of the Pakistani *madrassas* where the Taliban grew up and received education are controlled and run by the JUI. Gulf petrodollars funded a sustained spurt in *Deobandi madrassas* not only in the Pushtun areas of Pakistan near the Afghan border, but also in the port city of Karachi as well as rural Punjab. Prominent *madrassas* included the *Darul Uloom Haqqania* at Akora Khattak in the Frontier Province and the *Jamia Binori madrassa* in Karachi. The Haqqania boasts almost the entire Taliban leadership among its graduates, including Mullah Omar, the leader of the Taliban, while the Binori *madrassa* was once talked about as a possible hiding place of Osama bin Laden and is also reportedly the place where bin Laden met

Mullah Omar to form the *Al-Qaeda*-Taliban partnership.

After the Soviet withdrawal from Afghanistan in 1989, the rapid spread of jehadi *madrassas* in Pakistan continued unabated, instead of a slow-down. The first and most important reason was that Saudi money continued to flow to the *madrassa* system. The prestige and influence of the big *madrassas* encouraged wealthy Pakistanis to contribute more than ever before, sometimes as an expression of conviction and sometimes as a means of ingratiating themselves with what had become major power players. The Zia regime had grown comfortable spending massive amounts of money on defence and almost nothing on education during the days of Afghan jehad when the US and Saudi aid flowed freely.

In the 1990s, after the US imposed economic and military sanctions on Islamabad due to Pakistan's nuclear program, the national economy almost collapsed and the education infrastructure deteriorated rapidly. For the poor, the *madrassas* offered a place where their children could get free boarding, food and education and it turned out to be an irresistible option when compared to crumbling or non-existent government-funded secular schools. The successive governments in Islamabad also encouraged this to avoid spending much on the education sector. The Pakistani army on its part saw the large number of *madrassa*-trained jehadis as an asset for its covert support of the Taliban in Afghanistan, as well as its proxy war with India in Kashmir.

In October 2003, a memo from the office of the US Defence Secretary Donald Rumsfeld, actually intended for his top military and civilian subordinates, was leaked, perhaps deliberately, to the US media. In the memo, Rumsfeld wondered: Is the US capturing, killing or deterring and dissuading more terrorists every day than the *deeni madrassas* and radical Muslim clerics are recruiting, training and deploying against America?

Almost six years later, nowhere is that aspect of the war against terror more crucial than in Pakistan. The Pakistani authorities' defence for slow progress is that the *madrassa* reform in a country like Pakistan is difficult and dangerous and thus it may take a while. But experts believe that a *madrassa* reform campaign by the government must be combined with an effort to provide a meaningful alternative to the religious schools by reviving state-sector schools and pursuing students to return to mainstream education by abandoning the narrow world of extremism that exists in most of the Pakistani seminaries. Analysts believe it is important to monitor the political disposition of the faculty and administration of *madrassas*, their connections with local militant groups and, through them, with the Taliban. They say a long-term solution to extremism and militancy cannot be articulated without regulating the *madrassas*, especially those that have the reputation for supporting militant groups or openly preach religious and cultural intolerance.

REFERENCES

1. *Unfulfilled Promises: Pakistan's Failure to Tackle Extremism.* 'General Musharraf's promise to drive extremism', International Crisis Group, January 2004.
2. *Religious Pakistan: Karachi's Madrassas and Violent Extremism,* International Crisis Group, 28 March 2007.
3. News Report, *Madrassas* as a cover, *Dawn,* 15 July 2009.
4. Editorial, Checks on *Madrassas, Dawn,* 21 July 2009.
5. Videotape Message, *Al-Jazeera* TV, 1 September 2005.

CHAPTER 15

The *Lal Masjid* Operation – The Monster vs. the Creator

In July 2007, hundreds of highly trained and equally equipped Special Services Group (SSG) commandos of the Pakistan Army carried out Operation Silence to eliminate what had come to be known as the *Lal Masjid* Brigade, led by Maulana Abdul Rasheed Ghazi, the pro-Taliban fanatic cleric of the Red Mosque in the heart of Islamabad. The bloody operation, which ended in the deaths of hundreds of people, including commandos, terrorists, students and civilians, also caused a serious blow to the decades-long mullah-military-militant nexus.

The *Lal Masjid* operation acted as the divisive line between two opposing schools of thought in the country, causing a bloody backlash from the radical Islamists. The ideological fault line became obviously clear in the wake of the operation and its reverberations are still being heard in the FATA and Swat regions of Pakistan. However, there are many in Pakistani establishment circles who insist that the whole episode was stage-managed to boost Musharraf's sagging global image as the most trusted US ally in its war against terror. Although Musharraf had been verbally advocating enlightened moderation since the 9/11 attacks, his critics alleged that he himself had been responsible for systematically expanding the sphere and influence of the radical Islamist elements in national politics, and that, too, at the cost of mainstream democratic political parties – be it the Bhutto-led Pakistan Peoples Party (PPP) or the Sharif-led Pakistan Muslim League (PML).

Many believe the *Lal Masjid* movement was an extension of the growing religious extremism creeping unchecked into the urban cities of Pakistan from the North West Frontier Province (NWFP). By that time, the more extreme elements within the radical Islamist fold were no longer satisfied with their status of obedient instrumentalities of the Pakistan Army as well as the Inter Services Intelligence and renegade groups started challenging the limits that the Pakistani establishment had set for them. Since January 2007, however, a more profound shift was sought to be engineered through the *Lal Masjid* standoff, as the moderate Islamist element – hitherto firmly faithful to their patrons in the establishment – made a bid to violently renegotiate their worth and influence within Pakistan's equations of power. That eventually came to a bloody denouement on 11 July 2007 as the Musharraf regime decided to launch Operation Silence.

For six long months, the people of Pakistan had watched, with enormous concern, the clerics of the *Lal Masjid* engaging with the government in a veritable war of attrition. The conflict began with the demolition of two illegally constructed mosques in Islamabad. The *Lal Masjid* cleric brothers, Maulana Abdul Rasheed Ghazi and Maulana Abdul Aziz Ghazi, demanded the reconstruction of the demolished mosques, and that was just the beginning. When the government conceded, they made new demands, such as the imposition of *Shariah* all over the country. Backed by the male and female students of the *Jamia Hafsa* and the *Jamia Fareedia*, the two clerics then indulged in acts of grave provocations: occupying a public library, abducting policemen and issuing scandalous religious decrees. Every time Maulana Aziz and Maulana Ghazi mocked at the majesty of the state or took the law into their hands, angry voices all around demanded to know why the regime wasn't taking action against them. In diplomatic circles of Islamabad at that time the question was equally bewildering: Why should an enlightened president in uniform tolerate people who are the face of militant Islam in Pakistan?

Before Operation Silence, the Mosque had earned a reputation of radicalism, attracting Islamic hardline students from North West Frontier Province (NWFP) and tribal areas where support for the

Taliban and *Al-Qaeda* is quite strong. The mosque is also located near the headquarters of the Inter Services Intelligence, which helped train and fund the holy warriors to wage jehad in Kashmir and Afghanistan. Much before the military action was launched, the *Lal Masjid* had become known to the outside world as a centre of radical Islamic learning, housing several thousand male and female students in adjacent seminaries.

Set in the leafy suburbs of Islamabad close to the diplomatic enclave housing foreign embassies, nobody knew the extent to which the mosque had become infested with hardcore militants. Built in 1965 by the government of General Ayub Khan, the mosque is named for its red walls and interiors. Throughout its existence, it used to enjoy official patronage from influential members of successive governments, army chiefs, prime ministers as well as presidents, especially Zia-ul Haq who had a very close relationship with Maulana Abdullah, the founder of the Mosque and the father of the two Maulana brothers.

During the Soviet war in Afghanistan (1979-1989), *Lal Masjid* became a key recruitment centre of the *Harkatul Mujahideen* for sending *mujahideen* to fight the occupation troops. Maulana Abdullah was an ardent supporter of the Taliban and of Osama bin Laden, with whom he had reportedly developed special ties. During a 2002 interview with *The News*, Maulana Abdul Rasheed Ghazi had confessed that his father had special ties with Osama and the two had met on several occasions. After his assassination in the late 1990s in the courtyard of *Lal Masjid* by his *Shia* rivals, the running of the complex was taken over by his sons – Maulana Abdul Aziz and Abdul Rasheed Ghazi – who literally converted it into a centre for hard-line *Sunni Deobandi* teaching.

After the 9/11 terror attacks, Maulana Aziz delivered some of the most biting sermons from the platform of *Lal Masjid* while Maulana Ghazi led many anti-government and anti-US processions in Islamabad. Rasheed Ghazi was one of the signatories to a religious decree, or *Fatwa*, issued by prominent clergymen in which the Pakistan Army soldiers dying in US-backed military operations against fellow Pakistanis and Muslims in Waziristan tribal region were omitted from the list of martyrs. The clerics were forbidden to lead funeral prayers for them. But no action was taken against the radical clerics and they were never reprimanded because of their close proximity with the establishment, especially the ISI.

At *Lal Masjid,* students were indoctrinated and recruited as foot soldiers of several militant groups that had been harnessed to push Pakistan's geo-strategic objectives in Jammu & Kashmir and Afghanistan. However, the two cleric brothers eventually lost the backing of their spy masters for having pushed the country's enlightened military ruler – General Pervez Musharraf – too far with their much-publicized bizarre drive to enforce strict Islamic laws in Islamabad and establish their own trial courts. The Musharraf regime had been exercising restraint since January 2007, but the ambitious manner in which they sought cheap publicity had already set alarm bells ringing among the general public as well as sections of the security establishment.

Things came to a head on 22 June 2007 when a group of the *Lal Masjid* militants abducted some Chinese nationals from an Islamabad acupuncture clinic cum massage parlour. The ensuing stern message from Beijing to take strict action against the kidnappers eventually pushed Musharraf and his commanders to lay a siege to the complex. However, what was expected to be a smart and quick commando action to subdue Islamic radicals holed up in the huge complex of the *Lal Masjid* and the *Jamia Hafsa* actually turned into a marathon battle, with the elite military forces sweeping through underground bunkers in over 30 hours of intense combat.

It was the first time that Islamabad had ever seen such a pitched battle being fought in the heart of the city. Heavy smoke drifted over the mosque complex, only a few miles from the presidential palace and the parliament building. Gunfire and explosions thundered across the city. The military and the militants had their first major clash on 3 July 2007, when some militants tried to occupy a nearby government building and, during the scuffle, snatched a number of assault rifles from the policemen posted there. Within no time a fierce clash broke out between the armed seminary students and the Pakistani security forces. Ten people died and more than 150 were injured. An indefinite curfew was imposed in G-6 sector where the *Lal Masjid* and the *Jamia Hafsa* are located, following which troops from the Pakistan Army's 111 Brigade and units of Special Services Group (SSG) commandos took positions to launch a major crackdown.

Sporadic clashes continued throughout the day and by the time night fell on Islamabad, a paramilitary soldier, photo journalist, four students of the *Lal Masjid*-run religious seminaries and a number of passers-by were dead, almost all of them being victim of high velocity bullets. The next day, the *Lal Masjid* prayer leader, Maulana Abdul Aziz, known for his firebrand speeches, called for jehad and open threats in Friday sermons about having a brigade of suicide bombers inside *Lal Masjid*, was arrested by the security forces while trying to escape clad in a *burqa* (veil). He tried to slip away by posing as one of the 50-plus women students who had offered to surrender.

On the operational front, meanwhile, the government continued its strategy of massive display of military might with machine-gun mounted armoured personnel trucks laying siege to the militant-infested *Lal Masjid*. The strategy worked well and over 1,100 men and women members and supporters of the radical brigade capitulated and surrendered unconditionally. The public specter of the surrender continued throughout the day, during which everyone who came out of *Lal Masjid* and the adjoining *Jamia Hafsa* was made to walk through metal detectors and was frisked by security officials and police-women.

The next move was that unmanned predators started flying over the *Lal Masjid* and *Jamia Hafsa*, capturing images of the movements of people inside. The security forces examined the pictures and relayed the information directly to the command post on the ground. The strategic planning for the *Lal Masjid* assault was formulated by the Pakistani authorities from information gathered by the drone, provided by the Americans. Operation Silence was officially launched on 5 July 2007, with commandos scaling up the offensive through selective bombardment using helicopter gunships to flush out holed-up militants. Who knew in the 60s that the Mosque which was being built in the heart of new capital Islamabad and was named Red Mosque would actually turn red in 2007?

On 6 July 2007, Pervez Musharraf left for the flood-affected areas of Baluchistan. As his plane took-off from Islamabad airport, some militants fired anti-aircraft guns at the presidential plane from the roof of a house in the Asghar Mall area of Rawalpindi city. The security forces captured two anti-aircraft guns along with a machine gun on a roof top of a Rawalpindi high-rise, just a mile (1.6 km) away from the airport. The failed attempt was described by the Pakistani authorities as an act of retaliation for the *Lal Masjid* operation. A few hours after the failed bid on 6 July, an intense gun battle erupted between the military and the militants. The next day, on 7 July, in a blunt warning to hundreds of radical students and militants still holed up in *Lal Masjid*, Musharraf said they must surrender failing which they would all be killed.

On the morning of 10 July 2007, minutes after former Prime Minister Chaudhry Shujaat Hussain and Federal Religious Affairs Minister Ejazul Haq and their delegation left the area, declaring that negotiations via loudspeaker and mobile phone intended to end the siege peacefully had failed, the Special Service Group commandos were ordered to storm the Red Mosque. According to the official version, Shujaat had declared the failure of the talks after Ghazi refused to show flexibility. Ghazi, however, gave his own version to TV channels minutes before the operation began, saying he had agreed to all the terms of the agreement, but the talks broke down when he insisted he and his associates would surrender before the media people.

As the operation finally began, the Pakistan Army spokesman Major General Waheed Arshad said the troops are trying to breach the Mosque from the south. However, the security forces immediately came under a hail of gunfire from heavily armed militants hunkered down behind sandbagged positions on the roof and from holes in the walls of the mosque. Eventually, the SSG commandos quickly cleared the ground floor of the Mosque despite heavy fire coming from atop the mosque roof where the militants had piled sandbags at the foot of the minarets. After the minarets were taken, security forces progressed deeper into the complex, with the militants throwing petrol bombs in an attempt to set fire to the mosque to stop the assault.

However, they were unsuccessful. Once the ground floor was secured, the forces attempted to enter the *Jamia Hafsa* adjoining the

Mosque. The militants had laid a large number of booby traps that again held up the forces as they had to be disabled before they could storm into *Jamia Hafsa* complex. The forces finally entered the *Jamia Hafsa* complex which also served as the living quarters of the Ghazi brothers, causing an intense firefight in the main courtyard. Militants fired on the security forces from makeshift bunkers beneath the stairwell. The Army spokesman Arshad later claimed that the militants must have been fortifying the bunkers for several months.

Once the courtyard had been cleared, the troops proceeded inside the *Jamia Hafsa* building, which was a sprawling labyrinthine religious school for girls. Militants inside the building were armed with guns and rockets. Some areas inside were also booby-trapped. Some militants had bullet and explosion-proof vests, and other highly sophisticated and modern weapons. The SSG commandos suffered most of their casualties during the battle to take over the complex. During close quarter combat, the commandos were attacked with smoke grenades, incendiary grenades, and fragmentation grenades. Many of the SSG commandos that were injured in the operation got their injuries from fragmentation grenades. As the fighting continued, the SSG came upon a room where half a dozen militants were present; one of the militants then detonated his suicide jacket killing everyone in the room. It took several hours of intense fighting before the SSG took control of the *Jamia Hafsa*, with only the basement left to be pacified.

According to Major General Arshad Waheed, the troops had secured 80 percent of the complex building and were moving slowly when the militants decided to retreat into the basement and to use women and children as human shields. As the forces tried to move forward, the militants in the basement resisted with machine guns, rocket launchers, and Molotov cocktails. That was the time when Abdul Rasheed Ghazi [who was hunkered down in the basement along with some other militants, told a private television channel on phone that his mother had been seriously wounded by gunfire.

However, the militants continued to fire at the SSG commandos from ventilation grilles of the basement. During the firefight, Abdul Rasheed Ghazi was shot in the leg and was asked to surrender. Other militants in the room fired back at the SSG commandos, subsequently killing Abdul Rasheed Ghazi in the cross fire. Yet some in the military circles privately claim that Ghazi was shot by his own militants when he was coming out of a bunker to surrender. The gun battle lasted until the last of the militants trapped in the basement were either killed or had surrendered.

A few hours before being killed, Ghazi told ARY television channel in a live telephonic conversation, "I know I am about to be martyred. But I do believe my blood will bring about an Islamic revolution. My last message to those fighting for the glory of Islam is that they should avenge my murder besides waging jehad against Musharraf to get rid of this illegitimate American stooge who has taken hostage the entire Pakistani nation on gun point. I know I am about to be martyred, but I will fight till the last drop of my blood. I have chosen to sacrifice my life for the sake of Islam and I believe my blood will bring about an Islamic revolution in the country".

On July 11, the military spokesman announced that the *Lal Masjid* complex had been cleared of militants and troops were combing the area for booby traps and explosives. The eight-day operation was the longest ever conducted by the Special Services Group of the Pakistan Army. An Inter-Services Public Relations official later claimed that a bevy of weapons were recovered from bullet-riddled *Lal Masjid* and *Jamia Hafsa* complex, which included Russian made RPG and Chinese variant RPG-7 rockets, Anti-tank and anti-personnel landmines, suicide bombing belts, three to five .22 caliber rifles, RPD, RPK and RPK-74 light machine guns, Dragunov sniper rifles, SKS rifles, AK-47s, pistols, night vision equipment, and over 50,000 rounds of various caliber ammunition.

After the operation, the Musharraf administration was accused of suppressing the total number of casualties. A military spokesperson had claimed that nearly 80 people, including 10 commandos, died in the fighting, excluding those 21 who were killed on 3 July. However, this figure appears patently false, considering that thousands of male and female students were present in the complex on 3 July and only 1250 of them had surrendered before the operation began. The death toll became a contentious issue especially after a private television channel *Aaj* reported on 11 July that a mass grave was being dug in the Sector H-11 graveyard of Islamabad at midnight and hundreds of dead bodies were being taken to the graveyard for a mass burial.

However, Musharraf claims that no child or woman was killed in the military operation: "It is time to end the lies. Those who say women and children were killed and several hundreds died in the *Lal Masjid* operation are telling white lies. Only 94 people were killed and all of them were terrorists and extremists", said Musharraf on 18 April 2009 in Islamabad while talking to newsmen almost 22 months after the operation.

A few days after the operation, the Pakistani military authorities claimed to have found letters from Osama bin Laden's deputy, Ayman al-Zawahiri after taking control of *Lal Masjid*. They were written to Abdul Rasheed Ghazi and Abdul Aziz Ghazi and secretly directed the brothers and the militants into an armed revolt. The military sources were reported by the national media as saying that up to 18 foreign fighters including Uzbeks, Egyptians, and several Afghans had arrived weeks before the final shootout in the Mosque and had set up firing ranges to teach students, including children, how to handle weapons. Officials blamed the presence of foreign fighters for the breakdown of negotiations at the *Lal Mosque* just as they seemed about to reach a deal to end the stand-off peacefully. Some government sources claimed that the *Al-Qaeda* fighters in the mosque actually sought martyrdom instead.

On 11 July 2007, Dr Ayman al-Zawahiri, issued a videotape calling for Pakistanis to join jehad in revenge for the attack by Pakistan's Army on the Red Mosque. Zawahiri's four minute address was entitled The Aggression against *Lal Masjid*, and entirely focused on the clash between the militants and the Pakistan Army. The video was released by *Al-Qaeda*'s media wing and was subtitled in English. Zawahiri said in his message: "This crime can only be washed by repentance or blood... If you do not retaliate, Musharraf will not spare any of you. Your salvation is only through jehad".

Speaking on a televised address to the nation the same day, General Musharraf said he was determined that extremism and terrorism would be eradicated in Pakistan. "Unfortunately we have been up against our own people [...] they had strayed from the right path and become susceptible to terrorism. [...] What do we as a nation want? What kind of Islam do these people represent? [...] In the garb of Islamic teaching, they have been training for terrorism [...] they prepared the *madrassa* as a fortress for war and housed other terrorists in there. [...] I will not allow any *madrassa* to be used for extremism".

Musharraf's rhetoric apart, his critics say he will have to answer some important questions pertaining to the *Lal Masjid* episode: How could such a crisis occur in the middle of the federal capital, about half a mile from the ISI headquarters? How did so many foreign and other hardened militants find sanctuary in a mosque that is situated at a stone's throw from the seat of government? How was the *Masjid* administration able to build tunnels under the complex, without being noticed by an otherwise ever-prying intelligence apparatus? Why did it take so long for the Musharraf regime to react? Why did the *Lal Masjid* problem erupt right after the judicial crisis following the sacking of the Pakistani chief justice by Musharraf? More importantly, will the Pakistani establishment now seriously re-examine and review the whole gamut of ties between its intelligence apparatus and the militant network? Or will it wait for another *Lal Masjid* and Operation Silence to happen?

Since Musharraf has often been accused of tolerating elements in the military and the intelligence services which are known to maintain ideological and strategic links with Islamic militants, his critics doubt the *Lal Masjid* operation was meant to uproot or dismantle the jehadi network from Pakistani soil, adding that it was yet another attempt to secure his rule for the time being, both internally and externally. Almost two years later, the *Lal Masjid* is today symbolic of the jehad the Pakistani security forces are combating, not just in the violence-torn North West Frontier Province and Waziristan but in Rawalpindi and Islamabad as well, which house the GHQ as well as Parliament, respectively.

Most analysts identify Operation Silence as the turning point that led to General Pervez Musharraf's isolation. Asked why Pakistan continues to be in the grip of escalating violence and they point to the *Lal Masjid* episode. The siege and subsequent storming of a holy place of worship eventually snowballed into a crisis which even saw senior army and ISI generals turn against Musharraf. The fall of *Lal*

Masjid certainly heralded a new era in Pakistan which is marked by conflict between moderate and fundamentalist forces. The bloody operation also brought the most dreaded fallout, an unprecedented increase in suicide attacks all over Pakistan, especially targeting the security forces.

The first anniversary of the *Lal Masjid* operation proved bloodier on 6 July 2008 as 20 people were killed, mostly policemen, and 50 others injured when a suicide bomber exploded himself near the Melody Market area close to the Red Mosque. The bomber exploded himself at the end of the *Lal Masjid* Martyrs Conference, being attended by thousands of *madrassa* students and guarded by hundreds of policemen who were the actual target of the bomber.

On 16 April 2009, a three-member Supreme Court bench granted bail to former *Lal Masjid* prayer leader Maulana Abdul Aziz in the last of over two dozen cases against him and he was subsequently released. The apex court had observed that Maulana Aziz deserved bail because there was insufficient material on record against him. On 17 April, a day after his release, Maulana Aziz made a defiant return to the *Lal Masjid*, delivered the Friday sermon and called on his supporters to be ready to sacrifice their lives for enforcing Islamic law across Pakistan. While refuting reports that his release was the result of a deal with the government, Maulana Abdul Aziz demanded that the *Nizam-e-Adl* Regulation (Enforcement of *Shariah* Justice Regulation) in Swat district should be extended to the whole of Pakistan.

In an interview with English daily *Dawn* on 4 May 2009, the Maulana said that whatever situation has emerged in the troubled areas of Swat, Buner and Dir was a reaction of the military operation conducted on the *Lal Masjid* in July 2007. He said most of the mosque students who suffered due to the operation belonged to those areas where they were now avenging of the blood of their relatives by carrying out suicide bombings. To a question, he claimed that he had never supported suicide bombings and had only threatened the federal government by saying: "Any further action against the *Lal Masjid* can lead to a series of suicide bombings throughout the country".

Asked whether his students were involved in suicide bombings in the country, Maulana Abdul Aziz said: "As far as my students are concerned I know that they cannot commit suicide for any reason but I cannot guarantee what they are doing in their native towns." Asked if he will ask his students to keep themselves away from violent means, Aziz said no they were not under his control and whatever they were doing in Swat and Waziristan was their own decision. Maulana Abdul Aziz Ghazi is a free man today and back in the federal capital, leading the weekly Friday prayers at the Red Mosque and spelling out his extremist version of Islam.

On October 6, 2009, *Daily Times* claimed that the *Lal Masjid* still train militants. "It seems that the *Lal Masjid* saga is not over yet as investigators probing the recent terrorist attacks in Islamabad suspect the involvement of Ghazi Force (GF), a small but lethal militant group named after Ghazi Abdul Rashid, the deputy imam of the *Lal Masjid* who was killed in the July 2007 crackdown. Niaz Raheem alias Bilal, the *ameer* of GF, is a prime suspect in terror activities in Islamabad and Rawalpindi. The name of Niaz Raheem first crept up in May 2009, when law enforcement agencies arrested Fidaullah, the founder of the Ghazi Force, after getting some leads from Khairullah and Khurram Shahzad, who were arrested in the case of Frontier Constabulary and Special Branch suicide attacks in Islamabad in early 2009. Though Fidaullah was the founder *ameer* of the GF, it is Niaz Raheem who is leading the force. The sources said that Fidaullah had established his network in Guljo area of Hangu and he had also been accused of taking youngsters from Islamabad to turn them into suicide bombers. But the arrest of Fidaullah and a successful military operation in Swat forced the group to lie low for some time. However, the group has now re-emerged under the guidance of a new *ameer*".

A subsequent editorial by daily *Dawn*, appearing on 27 October 2009 said: "The word *Lal Masjid* evoke revulsion among many in Pakistan, shocking evidence of the growth of militancy and the state's complicity in nurturing that threat in recent decades. But *Lal Masjid* also evokes a fierce anger against the state among a small group of people who believe that a 'house of God' was attacked in Operation Silence in July 2007 and that many 'innocent' people were killed by the armed forces. Born of that rage is a small but deadly militant group known as the Ghazi Force is bent on seeking vengeance against the state. Not much is known about the Ghazi Force, but at least two things are worth bearing in mind. One, as a relatively new outfit, it has an incentive to establish itself with a series of audacious and deadly attacks. Two, *Lal Masjid's* sectarian, anti-*Shia* leanings are well known, which means that the Ghazi Force could easily forge an alliance with a range of groups operating inside Pakistan which share a similar outlook, groups that include *Al-Qaeda, Jaish-e-Mohammad* and Ilyas Kashmiri-led *Harkatul Jehadul Islami* network.

Yet another editorial appearing in *Daily Times* the same day – 27 October 2009 – said: "Examining the spoor of terrorists closely, Pakistani security agencies are increasingly worried about Islamabad being the epicentre of terrorism. Acting on the basis of this pointer, there was a dragnet taken across the numerous *madrassas* in the capital city, only to find that all was fine with them. It is not known if the mosques – where sermons laced with politics are routinely given – were also under observation. But an outfit named Ghazi Force is being mentioned, named after the deceased leader of Islamabad's *Lal Masjid*. The intelligence agencies lack scientific know-how and the students in the various high-profile educational institutions are ideologically too indoctrinated to undertake a dispassionate project like that. It would be wrong to designate certain cities or regions as "homes of terrorism".

After the GHQ attack, we have discovered that the masterminds had come from Faisalabad, a city not too often mentioned in connection with terrorism. It would not be surprising if in the coming days female suicide-bombers come on the scene and are discovered to have emerged from a mushroom growth of female *madrassas* in Rawalpindi. What is needed is sound intelligence. If intelligence is not forthcoming then anti-terrorism campaigns will seem like wild goose chases, now suspecting one city now another. And Islamabad, traditionally "in focus" more than other cities, should be the most scrutinised place in Pakistan, down to secret recordings of Friday sermons in the city's myriad mosques".

In the wake of these media reports, the *Lal Masjid* administration claimed on 14 December 2009 that the notion that the people who survived the July 2007 Red Mosque operation are launching suicide attacks is incorrect. "The administration of the mosque still enjoys emotional and moral support of religious and jehadi circles in the country," said Maulana Amir Siddiq, the *Lal Masjid* prayer leader and spokesman for Maulana Abdul Aziz, former prayer leader of the mosque. "The suicide attacks have increased because of the government's wrong policies and the survivors of the operation at the worship place have nothing to do with the ongoing spate of suicide bombings."

Siddiq claimed that under a conspiracy hatched by the US and anti-Islamic powers, suicide attacks are being linked to the *Lal Masjid*. "We still want to play the role of a bridge between the Pakistan Army and the militants. But they would listen to us only when their legitimate demands are accepted. We support the recent statement of Army Chief General Ashfaq Kayani wherein he has stated that nobody could separate Islam and Pakistan. We back the stance of the Army that it wants to see Pakistan and Islam together. But we also support the stance of the *mujahideen* that no Islamic country should support the US or any other western country against a brotherly Islamic state", Maulana Amir Siddiq added.

References

1. Telephonic Conversation, Abdul Rasheed Ghazi, *ARY Television Channel,* July 2007.
2. Dr Ayman al-Zawahiri, The Aggression against Lal *Masjid, Videotape,* July 2007.
3. Maulana Abdul Aziz, Interview, *Daily Dawn,* 4 May 2009.
4. *Daily Times,* October 6, 2009
5. *Daily Times,* Editorial, 27 October 2009.
6. *Daily Dawn,* Editorial, 27 October 2009.

CHAPTER 16

Pakistani Suicide Bombers – Chickens Coming Home to Roost

In the aftermath of the bloody Operation Silence carried out against the fanatic *Lal Masjid* clerics, Pakistan seems to have been turned into the suicide bombing capital of the world, with the security forces, especially the Army and the Police, frequently being targeted by lethal human bombs since July 2007, killing 2749 people in 190 incidents. Look at the casualty figures for the Pakistani security forces since then: over 1000 members of the armed forces, Frontier Constabulary, Rangers and police had been killed by human bombs across Pakistan between 3 July 2007 [the day the Operation Silence was launched] and 31 December 2009.

Human bombs used to be mere puzzling headlines for the people of Pakistan till the 9/11 terror attacks, a part of stories of death and destruction emanating out of troubled West Asia. Then the US-led Allied Forces invaded Afghanistan, making Pakistan personally experience the devastation a person strapped with lethal explosives could unleash. With the avowed aim of eliminating all those who are siding with "the forces of the infidel", the new breed of well trained and highly motivated suicide bombers strike not only Western targets, but Pakistani security and intelligence agencies also, especially the army, the police and the ISI, which spearhead the US war against terror.

Consequently, from the rugged, lawless terrain of the tribal areas out west to the spiffy environs of Islamabad, the suicide bombers across Pakistan have made the whole swathe of the land their laboratory, devastating lives, ruining families, imparting a murderous edge to humdrum existences. And the target of the grisly human bombs is just about anyone, anywhere, particularly if he represents in some way the symbol of the state. Today, the security situation in Pakistan seems in utter turmoil with army headquarters, offices of the Inter Services Intelligence, police stations and police training centres, military training academies, army and police check posts, mosques, hospitals, government buildings, processions and market places becoming vulnerable targets of the suicide bombers.

It was in the aftermath of the *Lal Masjid* episode that a series of deadly suicide attacks and roadside bombings rocked the four provinces of Pakistan as well as the federal capital, Islamabad, claiming over 1100 lives. The dangerous trend of suicide strikes, targeting the Pakistani security forces, touched alarming heights in 2007, averaging more than one hit a week as the mighty military and intelligence establishment gradually lost control of the extremist jehadi networks and their leaders it had nurtured to advance its so-called geo-strategic agenda in the neighbouring states of Afghanistan and India.

While Pakistan's twice-elected Prime Minister Benazir Bhutto's 27 December 2007 tragic assassination in Rawalpindi was the most high-profile suicide attack of the year 2007, the people of Pakistan suffered 56 incidents of suicide bombings during that year, mostly targeting the security forces. The murder of Benazir Bhutto, possibly by a sharp shooter, followed by a suicide bombing, represented the peak of the non-stop phenomenon of suicide bombings going on in Pakistan since the beginning of 2007. The previous attempt to kill the moderate leader of the Pakistan Peoples Party on 18 October 2007 in Karachi was also carried out by a suicide bomber who had blown himself up near Bhutto's truck during her welcome procession which she was leading from the Karachi airport upon her return home after spending eight years in self-exile.

The suicide bomber failed in his primary mission of killing Bhutto but he did kill over 140 other people, mostly PPP supporters. However, it was rare for an individual suicide bomber to kill over

140 people with a single strike. Before the 18 October attack, the deadliest suicide attack carried out anywhere in the world was the one that killed 133 people in the Iraqi capital of Baghdad on 3 February 2007 when a bomber had detonated an explosive-laden truck at a busy market place. Figures compiled by the Ministry of Interior show that Pakistan witnessed almost a ten-fold increase in the suicide bombings in 2007 as compared to 2006. The year 2007 witnessed 56 suicide hits, killing 837 people and wounding 1,227 others, mostly belonging to the law enforcement agencies.

In fact, there had been only 12 such lethal attacks all over Pakistan between 1 January and 3 July 2007, killing 75 people. Yet the turning point came with the bloody Operation Silence, which killed hundreds, including dozens of male and female students of two religious seminaries – *Jamia Fareedia* for boys and *Jamia Hafsa* for girls, being run by the extremist Ghazi brothers. The rest of 44 suicide attacks took place between 4 July and 27 December 2007 in the aftermath of the military operation, spreading to Karachi, Quetta, Peshawar, Lahore, Rawalpindi, and Islamabad, killing 567 people, many of whom were members of military and para-military forces, the Inter Services Intelligence and the police.

Hardly 24 hours after the launching of the Operation Silence [on 3 July 2007], the first suicide hit came on 4 July, killing 11 people, including six security forces personnel, as a human bomb rammed his explosive-laden vehicle into a military convoy in North Waziristan. Since then, suicide hits have been taking place non-stop in almost every nook and corner of Pakistan, taking the ensuing death toll to new heights every year.

As per the interior ministry records, the number of suicide hits rose from 56 in 2007 to 66 in 2008, killing 965 people during that year compared with the 837 people killed by human bombs in 2007. The suicide bombers killed at least 80 people a month on an average in 2008, compared with the previous year's average of 70 killings a month. Of the 965 people killed by human bombs in the 12 months of 2008, the number of civilian casualties stood at 651, the number of security forces personnel killed was 159, while 155 policemen were also among those who lost their lives. The official data shows that on an average, 55 civilians, 13 policemen and 13 security forces personnel lost their lives every month in 2008.

However, the year 2009 proved to be the bloodiest one for the people of Pakistan since Islamabad had joined hands with Washington in the war on terror as the unending spate of lethal suicide bombings killed 1217 innocent people and injured 2305 others in 80 bloody attacks carried out by human bombs in 2009. On average, the human bombs killed 101 persons a month in 2009, compared with the previous year's average of 80 killings a month. Of the 1217 people who lost their lives in suicide bombings in 2009, the number of civilian casualties stood at 863 while the remaining 354 martyred belonged to the security forces.

Of them, 137 belonged to the Police, 102 were army officers and *jawans*, 51 were the Frontier Constabulary personnel, 28 were staff members of the Inter Services Intelligence, 22 belonged to the Khasadar Force, 12 belonged to the Pakistan Rangers and two others were employees of the Pakistan Navy. On average, around 72 civilians and 30 security and law enforcement agencies personnel lost their lives every month in 2009 due to suicide bombings.

According to the official record, the twin cities of Rawalpindi and Islamabad were struck by the human bombs 28 times during the 28 months [between July 2007 and December 2009] since the July 2007 Operation Silence, killing 431 innocent people and injuring 1074 others. Of the 28 bloody suicide bombings targeting the twin cities, 16 took place in Islamabad while 12 occurred in the garrison town of Rawalpindi. Eight suicide attacks took place in the twin cities in the six months of 2007, seven occurred in 2008 while 13 such bombings took place in 2008.

Of the 431 people killed in the 28 attacks carried out by the human bombs between July 2007 and December 2009, 274 were civilians, 69 were army men, 53 were policemen, 30 belonged to the Inter Services Intelligence (ISI), eight of them were the Frontier Constabulary (FC) personnel while two belonged to Pakistan Navy.

A total of 147 people were killed and 363 injured in Rawalpindi and Islamabad in the six months of 2007 in eight incidents of suicide bombings following the July 2007 *Lal Masjid* operation. Those killed included 36 army men, 13 policemen, 30 staffers of the ISI, eight members of the Frontier Constabulary and 81 civilians. In the year

2008, a total of 126 people were killed and 337 injured in seven incidents. Those killed included 29 policemen, 12 army men and 85 civilians. In the 12 months of 2009, a total of 158 people were killed and 374 injured in 13 incidents of suicide bombings that took place in the twin cities of Rawalpindi and Islamabad. Those killed included 21 officers and *jawans* of the Pakistan Army, 11 policemen, two staffers of the Pakistan Navy and 124 civilians.

During the year 2009, at least 366 innocent Pakistanis were killed and 901 injured in seven bloody incidents of terrorism across Pakistan, targeting mosques with the help of suicide bombers and explosive-laden vehicles. According to the figures compiled by the ministry of interior, 52 people were killed on average every month in these seven gory incidents, most of which were carried out by the *Tehrik-e-Taliban Pakistan*. On average, 33 people were killed every month in the mosque-related acts of terrorism which were carried out during the 12 months of 2009. The weekly and daily average for those killed during the same period came to eight and one persons respectively. The odious ploy of targeting jam-packed mosques at prayer time is now increasingly being used by the TTP as this has become a lethal way to create horror. According to officially available data, over 50 mosques have been targeted since 9/11 either by the Pakistani Taliban or their like-minded jehadi groups like the *Sipah-e-Sahaba Pakistan*, *Lashkar-e-Jhangvi*, *Harkatul Jehadul Islami*, *Jaish-e-Mohammad* and *Jamaatul Furqaan*.

The *fidayeen*-style suicide attacks targeting the security and law-enforcement agencies were the new phenomenon introduced by the Pakistani Taliban in 2009, as they first attacked a Police Training School in Manawan area near Lahore and then the Sri Lankan cricket team in Lahore. They have carried out several such missions since then in Lahore, Islamabad and Rawalpindi. The 4 December 2009 armed attack targeting the parade ground mosque in the garrison town of Rawalpindi, which killed 44 people including 17 children, was the last such assault of the year 2009. In one of the worst incidents of terrorism in recent years, a group of six *fidayeen* attackers belonging to the *Tehrik-e-Taliban Pakistan* stormed the crowded Parade Land Askari Mosque close to the GHQ during Friday prayers and sprayed gunfire at worshippers besides throwing hand grenades.

A serving major general of the Pakistan Army, a brigadier, two lieutenant colonels, a major and a number of army soldiers were among those killed in a multi-pronged attack that was carried out while violating the sanctity of a mosque by those who claim to be fighting for the glory of Islam. The blood-spattered episode finally came to an end after two suicide bombers blew themselves up. The fatal mosque attack came just a day after a futile bombing of the Naval Headquarters in Islamabad.

In an earlier *fidayeen* attack on the General Headquarters of the Pakistan Army in the garrison town of Rawalpindi [on 10 October 2009], a highly trained and equally armed group of six TTP terrorists who were dressed in army uniforms, riding a small van bearing army number plates, approached the outer check post of the GHQ. The natural reaction of the duty staff at the check post was to approach the van and ask for identification; upon which the terrorists opened fire with automatic weapons and grenades, killing all guards at the outer check post. The inner perimeter, being warned, engaged the terrorists. In the meantime, six more terrorists, also wearing army uniforms, jumped the spiked wall. Upon hearing the sound of automatic weapons and grenades, the lieutenant-colonel in charge of administering security and the brigadier incharge holding the overall responsibility of GHQ security, who sits within GHQ, rushed out to take control of the situation. Seeing terrorists in army uniforms, both took them to be their own reserves, and were shouting instructions at the terrorists when they were shot and killed on the spot.

Out of the six terrorists approaching along the road, four were killed. Those who had scaled the wall were presumed to be reserves by the actual security personnel and, in the confusion, managed to enter the building housing unarmed personnel responsible for administering security, outside GHQ premises and take forty odd people hostage, including seven officers, none above the rank of major. The GHQ premises were never penetrated. As the situation became clear, the building was surrounded and contained and all electricity connections cut for a limited duration during the night between 10 and 11 October, during which nine hostages escaped, providing invaluable information on the numbers and location of the terrorists, particularly the ones who were suicide bombers and carrying explosives.

Armed with this vital information, the Special Services Group of the Pakistan Army attacked the building at dawn on 11 October and, targeting the suicide bombers first, killed four, and captured one alive. The commandos rescued the bulk of the remaining hostages, though three hostages lost their lives during the rescue. The entire saga took 20 hours; the dawn attack, only five minutes. The only attacker captured alive was Mohammad Aqeel alias Dr Usman, a member of the Punjab chapter of the TTP, who had served the Army Medical Corps as a nurse at the Combined Military Hospital (CMH) in Rawalpindi till 2006. Aqeel had abandoned the army service in 2006 to join the *Jaish-e-Mohammad*. He remained affiliated with the *Al-Qaeda*-linked *Lashkar-e-Jhangvi* for a brief period and later joined the Azad Kashmir chapter of the *Harkatul Jehadul Islami* led by Commander Ilyas Kashmiri who had been working in tandem with the TTP chief Baitullah Mehsud in South Waziristan.

A mastermind of several past terrorist attacks, Aqeel decided to become a part of the team that was sure to die during the GHQ raid. And that's why he had left a video which was to be aired after his "*fidayeen* mission". Going by his dossier of activities, Aqeel was not an ordinary terrorist led by the nose by his handlers. He was himself the handler and probably knew well that the GHQ attack would not get very far. The daring assault was most likely a symbolic move to reassert the power of the Pakistani Taliban in the backdrop of Baitullah Mehsud's death and the subsequent media reports about its declining might. Aqeel knew it was going to be his last act and he did try to blow himself up with an anti-personnel mine at around 9 a.m. on 11 October, 2009, but survived the explosion and was captured in a seriously wounded condition. Six commandos were killed as a result of the blast in the final phase of the GHQ operation which was carried out to rescue 42 people taken hostage, most of whom were *khakis*.

Subsequent media reports disclosed that some key leaders of several jehadi and sectarian groups, including a jailed militant, were flown from Bahawalpur, Rahim Yar Khan and Lahore districts of Punjab to Rawalpindi through special chartered flights to hold talks with the GHQ attackers. According to these reports, having stormed the army headquarters and taken hostage 42 people, the terrorists had listed their demands and expressed their desire to directly hold talks with Chief of Army Staff General Ashfaq Pervez Kayani. They gave a list of the jailed militants belonging to several *Sunni Deobandi* militant and sectarian groups, seeking their release, failing which, the hostages were threatened to be killed one by one.

However, as a time buying tactic, the negotiators decided to rope in some key leaders of several jehadi and sectarian groups to hold talks with terrorists. Special planes were subsequently dispatched to Lahore, Bahawalpur and Rahim Yar Khan to bring to Rawalpindi Malik Ishaq, a jailed leader of *Lashkar-e-Jhangvi*, Mufti Abdul Rauf, the younger brother of Maulana Masood Azhar who is the acting *ameer* of *Jaish-e-Mohammad*, and Maulana Mohammad Ahmed Ludhianvi, the chief of the *Sipah-e-Sahaba*, to hold talks with the hostage takers. It may be recalled that all the four jehadi leaders who were roped in by the military authorities to hold talks with the GHQ hostage takers had earlier been engaged by the Musharraf regime way back in July 2007 with the fanatic clerics of the infamous Lal Mosque in the heart of Islamabad.

Soon after getting hold of the security personnel and the civilians, the terrorists had threatened to kill them in batches of ten every hour if their demands were not accepted by the authorities. The negotiators had asked the attackers to wait till next morning for the release of the jailed militants so that they could be brought to Rawalpindi. However, the rescue operation was launched at 6 in the morning before the expiry of the deadline. The detainees had been divided into two groups of 20 and 22 and kept in separate rooms of the building by four terrorists each. Despite the fact that the attackers guarding the hostages had don suicide jackets, the first one to go down at the very outset of the rescue operation by the SSG commandos was shot point blank in the head who collapsed without having the chance to blow himself up. Of the remaining four, three simply blew themselves by exploding their suicide jackets up when the commandos tried to enter the building.

Interestingly, Mohammad Aqeel alias Dr Osman, instead of blowing up himself with his suicidal jacket, adopted a unique tactic.

As his fellow terrorists blew up themselves, he set ablaze his explosive-laden jacket in one room and hid himself in the false ceiling of another room inside the security offices of the GHQ. As the rescue operation ended and the clearance of the building started, everybody was looking for him because only four dead bodies of other terrorists were found. And the man negotiating with the authorities, who had identified himself as Aqeel alias Dr Osman was missing. The sources say he had camouflaged himself well and kept out of sight for a couple of hours until bad luck struck him in the face. The false ceiling couldn't bear his weight any longer and simply collapsed, throwing Aqeel on the floor and hurting his head badly. But he survived the head injury.

To cut the long story short, such *fidayeen* style deadly commando operations have not only exposed the limitations of the Pakistani intelligence network in identifying and busting the group of individuals involved in recruiting and training of suicide bombers, but also of the Pakistani security establishment in its ability to protect its own assets. More than anything else, these attacks signified the revival of *Al-Qaeda* and Taliban networks which had been forced to give up their bases of power in Afghanistan and Pakistan and flee to the Pak-Afghan border area as a result of the war on terror launched by the US-led coalition of forces in October 2001.

Pakistan, which had been hired by the US Central Intelligence Agency (CIA) during the tyrannical rule of General Zia-ul Haq to spearhead the so-called Afghan jehad against the Russian occupation troops, was itself spared by any suicide hit until 2001, except for one such attack in 1995 at the Egyptian Embassy in Islamabad. Yet the human bombs started exploding themselves in Pakistan in 2002 after the US-led Allied Forces invaded Afghanistan. There were two major suicide attacks in Pakistan in 2002 – the first on 17 March when an Islamabad church was hit during a Sunday service in the diplomatic enclave, killing five people, including the wife of a US diplomat and his daughter. The 8 May car suicide bombing outside the Sheraton Hotel in Karachi, killing 14 including 11 French engineers was the second hit of the year, placing Pakistan on the world map of countries marred by suicide bombings.

This was primarily because of the fact that in the aftermath of the 9/11 attacks, Pakistan became a key American ally in the US-led war on terror, and that too, by reversing its previous decade's policy of trying to influence Afghan politics through the Taliban. The policy reversal immediately brought the state into conflict with the jehadi organisations active in Afghanistan and Jammu & Kashmir. For years, these groups had been ideologically motivated, mobilized and trained in Pakistan, mainly for export in the neighbourhood – particularly to Afghanistan and Jammu & Kashmir.

Several major suicide attacks were carried out in Pakistan in the aftermath of the 9/11 attacks and the subsequent invasion of Afghanistan by the US-led Allied Forces. Most of these strikes were aimed at high ranking government officials including former President General (retd) Musharraf and former Prime Minister Shaukat Aziz. Two suicide bombers rammed their explosive-laden cars into the presidential convoy of Musharraf on 25 December, 2003 at a petrol station two kilometers from his army residence in Rawalpindi, adjoining Islamabad, killing 16 people and injuring 54 others. The next aim of the human bombs was Shaukat Aziz who was targeted in June 2004, weeks before he took office as the prime minister, when he was getting into his car to return to Islamabad after an election campaign rally in Attock district of Punjab. Shaukat survived although his driver was among those killed.

Within 24 hours of the attack, a statement was posted on a website known for carrying propaganda material from several Islamic militant groups. "One of our blessed battalions tried to hunt the head of one of America's infidels in Pakistan, but God wanted him to survive". The hitherto unknown jehadi group claiming responsibility for the attack identified itself as "Islambouli Brigade of *Al-Qaeda*", an apparent reference to Lt. Khalid Islambouli of the Egyptian Army, who had led a group of soldiers in the 1981 assassination of the late Egyptian President Anwar Sadat.

Initial reaction from senior Pakistani security officials was one of skepticism and not without reason. Even if Osama or Zawahiri had directly issued instructions, it was highly unusual for the terror network to use the name of *Al-Qaeda*. But then, it was no ordinary incident and clearly indicated that the group involved in the attack comprised highly motivated Islamic militants. In some ways, the attack was no different from those carried out against Musharraf in December 2003. Yet the frequency of suicide bombings increased visibly in late 2006 and early 2007 as the suicide bombers, failing to hit high profile targets, decided to go for softer ones, including religious congregations of rival sects as well as security personnel, who have limitations while operating in the civilian areas of their own country.

However, in the aftermath of the bloody *Lal Masjid* operation, it appeared as if the so-called Islamic warriors groomed by the Pakistani military and intelligence establishment had literally declared war against their former *khaki* handlers. This was evident from the fact that suicide bombers twice attacked buses in the highly sensitive garrison city of Rawalpindi ferrying ISI employees, killing 20 of them in the first incident on 4 September 2007 and 15 more in the second hit on 24 November 2007. The suicide strikes targeting the elite intelligence agency – the ISI, which is often described as a state within the state, was unique as those responsible for tracking down terror networks themselves became the victims of saboteurs.

The intensity of the deadly suicide bombings in the aftermath of the *Lal Masjid* operation could be gauged from the fact that the then commander in chief of the Pakistani armed forces President General Musharraf had to publicly direct his troops on 13 July 2007 not to wear their uniforms in public, especially in NWFP for fear of a backlash from extremists. Analysts believe the *Lal Masjid* operation was exploited by pro-*Al-Qaeda* tribal leaders to provoke attacks against the army and demoralise its soldiers in the fight against terror. And the idea was to make the intensively Islamised military rank and file realize that the army was erring in following the orders of the US under the leadership of a 'faithless' Musharraf and his fellow generals.

Investigations by the Pakistani security and intelligence agencies have shown the involvement of several kinds of jehadi groups in the ongoing spate of suicide strikes including *Lal Masjid Brigade* (LMB), *Tehrik-e-Taliban Pakistan* (TTP), *Lashkar-e-Jhangvi* (LeJ), *Harkatul Jehadul Islami* (HUJI), *Tehrik-e-Nifaz-e-Shariat-e-Mohammadi* (TNSM), *Jaish-e-Mohammad* (JeM), *Jamaatul Furqaan* (JuF), *Jaishul-Islami* (JuI), *Fidayeen-e-Islam* (FeI) and *Abdullah Azzam Shaheed Brigade* (ASB).

The human bombs coming from the *Lal Masjid* Brigade are those who have either been linked with *Lal Masjid* or *Jamia Fareedia* or had sympathies with the fanatic Ghazi brothers due to their ideological affinity. While some of the human bombs had been students of the Ghazi duo, some were relatives of those killed during Operation Silence in July 2007. Authorities probing the ongoing spate of suicide bombings that took place after Operation Silence believe that most of the suicide hits were carried out by young men in their 20s coming from the Federally Administered Tribal Areas (FATA) of South Waziristan and North Waziristan agencies.

As soon as Operation Silence came to an end, the agencies had warned that the twin cities of Rawalpindi and Islamabad could suffer from suicide attacks, as over 500 potential suicide bombers who had been studying at the *Lal Masjid*-run *Jamia Hafsa* and *Jamia Fareedia* had not returned to their homes after the ending of Operation Silence. They had warned that the potential bombers were hiding in several *madrassas* and mosques in and around the twin cities, and were determined to blow themselves up any time, anywhere to avenge the killing of kin and friends. Hardly a few weeks after the operation ended, an 18 year old human bomb killed 22 highly trained commandos of the Special Services Group of the Army by targeting their Tarbela Ghazi mess, 100 km south of Islamabad on 13 September 2007. The bomber eventually turned out to be the brother of a *Jamia Hafsa* girl student killed during the operation, carried out by Karar Company of the SSG.

The second kind of extremists involved in suicide attacks are those linked to the *Al-Qaeda* and Taliban network based in the Waziristan region on the Pakistan-Afghan tribal belt. In the rocky and far-flung region of Waziristan, Islamic rebels allied to the Afghan Taliban and *Al-Qaeda* have literally taken control of almost the entire North Waziristan area on the Pak-Afghan border, thereby gaining a significant base from which to wage their resistance against the US-led forces in Afghanistan and the Pakistani troops, especially through their highly motivated and lethal suicide bombers. Intelligence sources say Pakistani security forces have mostly been targeted by bombers trained and dispatched by the *Tehrik-e-Taliban Pakistan* (TTP) led by Commander Baitullah Mehsud, the chief of the Mehsud tribe in South Waziristan.

According to a senior official of the elite Special Investigation Group (SIG), having closely examined the heads of 26 suicide bombers who had exploded themselves in 2007, it transpired that the vast majority of the human bombs came from just one tribe – the Mehsuds of central Waziristan, all boys aged 16 to 20. In fact, most of the suicide bombings carried out after the launching of Operation *Rah-e-Haq* by the Pakistan Army in Swat in 2009 had been claimed by Baitullah Mehsud – be it the March 2009 *fidayeen* assault on the Manawan police academy in Lahore, the June 2009 Peshawar Pearl Continental hotel blast, the May 2009 twin suicide attacks on the Lahore headquarters of ISI and the Rescue 15 offices or the June 2009 assassination of the anti-Taliban religious scholar Mufti Sarfraz Naeemi in Lahore.

According to Pakistani intelligence circles, the man tasked with indoctrinating youngsters and converting them into lethal suicide bombers is Qari Hussain Mehsud, also known as *Ustad-e-Fidayeen* or the teacher of suicide bombers. He had been running his suicide training camp in Spinkai Ragzai, a small town in South Waziristan. As one such training centre was discovered by the Pakistani military authorities in May 2008 at a Government-run school in the Kotkai area of South Waziristan, General Officer Commanding of 14 Division Major General Tariq Khan told reporters on 18 May 2008 that it was like a factory, recruiting nine to 12-year-old boys, and turning them into suicide bombers. Qari Hussain is known in the TTP ranks for his strong anti-*Shia* views and close ties with the *Lashkar-e-Jhangvi* (LeJ).

The Pakistani agencies are trying to hunt him down given his status as the one who may have recruited and indoctrinated the largest number of people from Waziristan to carry out suicide hits in the country. On 17 January 2009, Qari Hussain released an unusual video of statements from purported human bombs and footage of deadly attacks they claimed to have perpetrated in Pakistan. The tape, released by none other than Hussain himself, showed youth, some in their teens, addressing the camera about their intention to carry out suicide attacks to background music of Urdu militant anthems. The two major suicide hits claimed on the TTP video were the 11 March 2008 suicide attack on the FIA building in Lahore and the

24 November 2007 twin suicide attacks in Faizabad area of Rawalpindi, in front of the ISI headquarters when a bomber rammed his explosive-laden car into a bus carrying 35 ISI officers, killing 15 of them on the spot.

According to a 2 July 2009 investigative news report published by *Washington Times*, Commander Baitullah Mehsud was involved in buying children as young as seven to serve as human bombs in the growing spate of attacks against Pakistani, Afghan and American targets. While quoting US Defence Department and Pakistani officials, the report titled "Taliban buying children for suicide bombers", filed by Sara Carter stated that the going price for child bombers being produced by Baitullah was $7,000 to $14,000 – huge sums in Pakistan, where per-capita income is about $2,600 a year.

"Baitullah has turned suicide bombing into a production output, not unlike the way Toyota outputs cars. The price of the child depends on how quickly the human bomb is needed and how close the child is expected to get to the target. Mehsud produces these suicide bombers, which are sold or bartered, which can be used by Mullah Omar's Taliban or other groups. In some cases, the children are kidnapped and then sold to Mehsud. ... There had been a convergence of militants based in the tribal areas, supplemented, financed, trained, inculcated, by *Al-Qaeda* elements and also Punjab-based Pakistani terrorist groups. It is the relationship between the three jehadi elements that is producing effective suicide bombers and sustaining a suicide-bomb campaign inside Pakistan", said the *Washington Times* report.

Another important sectarian-cum-jehadi group involved in suicide attacks across Pakistan is *Lashkar-e-Jhangvi* – a *Sunni Deobandi* organisation which was launched in 1996. The *Lashkar* today is the most violent *Al-Qaeda* terrorist group operating in Pakistan with the help of its lethal suicide squad, which was being supervised by Qari Zafar, a member of *Al-Qaeda's* hardline inner circle due to his acquaintance with Baitullah Mehsud. South Waziristan-based Qari Zafar, who was finally killed in an American drone attack in North Waziristan on 24 February 2010, was not only the suspected mastermind of the 20 September 2008 Marriot Hotel suicide attack in the federal capital Islamabad, but the most sought after *Al-Qaeda* linked terrorist is reportedly trying to target key strategic installations belonging to the ISI and the Army.

Then next in line is the Swat chapter of the *Tehrik-e-Nifaz-e-Shariat-e-Mohammadi* which is accused of carrying out several suicide attacks targeting the Pakistani security forces. The first such attack was carried out on 8 November 2006 when 45 Pakistan army recruits undergoing training at the Punjab Regimental Centre in Dargai, 100 kilometers north of Peshawar. Another major suicide attack was carried out on 25 October 2007 in Mingora, as two suicide bombers rammed their explosive-laden vehicles into a truck carrying the Frontier Constabulary personnel, killing 33 of them. The attack came following a warning by Fazlullah against the deployment of security forces.

The TNSM was also found involved in the 3 February 2010 killing of three American soldiers in a suicide bombing incident in the Lower Dir district of the NWFP which shares a border with Afghanistan and with the Swat district. The three slain US soldiers were traveling in a convoy with troops, journalists and officials to the opening of the Koto Girls' High School when a roadside bomb exploded. The school was blown up in January 2009 and rebuilt with the help of the US Agency for International Development (USAID). Dozens of girls' school were set ablaze in Lower Dir area in 2008-2009 by the private army of Maulana Fazlullah, the fugitive chief of the Swat chapter of the *Tehrik-e-Nifaz-e-Shariat-e-Mohammadi.*

The killed Americans were members of the Army Special Forces, which had been training the paramilitary Frontier Corps (FC) to improve its combat tactics to effectively fight with *Al-Qaeda* and Taliban insurgents in the Pak-Afghan tribal belt. It was for the first time since the American occupation of Afghanistan in October 2001 that any US soldier had been killed in Pakistan, that too in a terrorist act. The slain soldiers were part of a 100-member strong special US military training unit which was dispatched to Pakistan in early 2008 to raise a 1000-member strong well-trained paramilitary commando unit which could conduct guerilla operations against *Al-Qaeda* and Taliban militants active in the Pak-Afghan tribal belt and involved in cross border ambushes against the US-led Allied Forces stationed in Afghanistan.

Then there are a few relatively unknown jehadi organisations like *Jaishul-Islami, Fidayeen-e-Islam* and *Abdullah Azam Shaheed Brigade* which had claimed several major suicide bombings. The *Jaishul-Islami* had claimed the 9 October 2008 car suicide attack on the Anti Terrorist Squad headquarters in Islamabad. The *Fidayeen-e-Islami* had claimed the 20 September 2008 Marriott Hotel suicide hit in Islamabad while the *Abdullah Azzam Brigade* had co-claimed along with the *Tehrik-e-Taliban* the 9 June 2009 attack on the Marriot Hotel in Peshawar. These three groups are supposed to be based in the Waziristan region. There are three other jehadi groups which have not yet claimed any suicide attack in Pakistan but have been found to be involved in several such attacks in the past.

The first one is *Jaish-e-Mohammad* led by Maulana Masood Azhar while the second is *Harkatul Jehadul Islami* led by Qari Saifullah Akhtar, already named by Benazir Bhutto as her would-be assassin in her posthumous book. To recall, the two human bombs who had tried to kill General Musharraf on 25 December 2003 by ramming their explosive-laden cars into his presidential convoy in Rawalpindi, were later identified as Qari Mohammad Jameel Sudhan, an activist of the *Jaish-e-Mohammad* and Khalique alias Hazrat Sultan, an activist of the *Harkatul Jehadul Islami.*

The third such jehadi group, *Jamaatul Furqaan*, is led by Maulana Abdul Jabbar alias Umar Farooq, once the chief operational commander of *Jaish-e-Mohammad* and a close associate of Masood Azhar. The *Jamaat* is accused of masterminding the 17 March 2002 suicide hit inside an Islamabad church during Sunday service in diplomatic enclave, killing five people, including an American diplomat's wife and his daughter.

Interestingly, a careful study of the life history of 25 human bombs who had exploded themselves in different parts of Pakistan between 2002 and 2005 showed that the US atrocities against Muslims in Afghanistan and Iraq were the foremost motivation for a majority of the bombers. The study conducted by an elite intelligence agency had shown that none of the 25 human bombs came from the elite class: 16 of them belonged to the lower middle class while the remaining nine belonged to middle class families. Apart from their jehadi mindset, their anti-US sentiments and their poor family background, another thing they had in common was illiteracy.

Unlike in the West where most of such attackers were university graduates, like the lead pilot of 9/11 attacks Mohammad Atta – a degree holder from a German University and the operational planner of the tragedy Khalid Sheikh Mohammad who had studied engineering in North Carolina, not a single Pakistani suicide bomber could go beyond matriculation. The study showed that almost every suicide bomber was poor, illiterate and unemployed. Of the 25 attackers, 15 were aged 15-25, seven 25-30, and the rest three were above 30. There were two human bombs who killed themselves in an attack on Musharraf on 25 December 2003 in Rawalpindi – Mohammad Jameel Sudhan and Khalique alias Hazir Sultan. Jameel, 26, was an active member of the defunct *Jaish-e-Mohammad* and had spent most of his lifetime in different *madrassas*. The second bomber, Khalique was an active member of the *Harkatul Jehadul Islami* and also having close links with *Al-Qaeda*. Both of them were unemployed with education not beyond 8th grade.

Pakistani investigators say all those groups which are involved in suicide attacks follow their own techniques to achieve their objectives and use different mechanisms to attack their targets. The jehadi group comprising the toughest motivation category is to hit military installations with the help of its suicide bombers. They include trained, skilful and equally motivated terrorists. The second category of human bombs attack personnel of law-enforcement agencies and government personalities while the third one is deputed to kill the enemy through a car bombing or blast through a remote-controlled device.

Pakistani authorities say the production of suicide belts in Waziristan has become a cottage industry as one household makes the detonator, another sews the belt, a third one moulds ball bearings, and so on. These are then collected and paid for by the Taliban, who claim in their propaganda that they have hundreds of willing youngsters lined up to carry out suicide bombings. Then there are some definite patterns of the suicide attacks being carried out in Pakistan. They say the suicide bomber generally never comes alone; he is charged up, carefully brainwashed to the last moment, highly indoctrinated and fanatically intoxicated till the last moment by his handler who makes sure that the tempo and temper of the suicide bomber reaches the climax and to the extreme just as he approaches his target.

For years, the country's mighty military and intelligence establishment used to indoctrinate, motivate and train jehadi cadres for export in the neighbourhood – to the Indian-administered *Jammu & Kashmir* and Afghanistan. The human bombs had, however, excluded their home ground from the scope of their so-called holy war. But there has been a sharp decline in suicide attacks being carried out in *Jammu & Kashmir* in recent years, with Pakistan emerging as a favoured target of the human bombs. As things stand, it appears that the suicide bombers who were originally designed by the Pakistani establishment to rip apart the 'enemies of Islam and Pakistan' are now exploding themselves inside their own country, even in the Pakistan-administered Azad Kashmir, killing fellow Muslims.

Despite the ongoing spate of terrorist activities by the Taliban militants across Pakistan, there was hardly any such activity in Azad Kashmir till May 2009. However, between 26 June 2009 and 6 January 2010, Azad Kashmir witnessed four suicide attacks, killing 20 people, ten of them security forces personnel and ten civilians. In the first ever incident of suicide bombing in Azad Kashmir on 26 June 2009, four soldiers were killed and three wounded as the bomber blew himself up near an army vehicle in Muzaffarabad, the capital of Azad Kashmir. While ruling out a possible Indian involvement in these suicide attacks, the investigating agencies have found the involvement of the *Lashkar-e-Zil* (LeZ) or Shadow Army, which is a loose alliance of the *Al-Qaeda-* and Taliban-linked anti-US militant groups, which are active in Pakistan and Afghanistan.

The *Lashkar-e-Zil* reportedly consists of the *Tehrik-e-Taliban Pakistan* (TTP) led by Commander Hakeemullah Mehsud, the Azad Kashmir chapter of the *Harkatul Jehadul Islami* (HUJI) led by Commander Ilyas Kashmiri, the *Lashkar-e-Jhangvi* (LeJ) led by Qari Zafar (killed in February 2010), the Afghan Taliban militia led by its *ameer* Mullah Mohammad Omar, the *Hizb-e-Islami Afghanistan* (HeI) led by Gulbaddin Hekmatyar and the Haqqani militant network led by Jalaluddin Haqqani's elder son Commander Sirajuddin Haqqani. While the LeZ seeks guidance from Osama's

No.2 Dr Ayman Zawahiri, the chief of the HUJI (Azad Kashmir chapter) Commnander Ilyas Kashmiri is believed to be its chief operational commander, who is currently operating from North Waziristan, which borders Khost.

According to the Pakistani investigations, the 26 June 2009 attack close to the 5-AK Brigade headquarters in Azad Kashmir was carried out by one Abid, who belonged to the *Tehrik-e-Taliban Pakistan*. The 5-AK Brigade of the Azad Kashmir Regiment is taking part in the military operation against the militants in the Swat district of the North West Frontier Province and its adjoining areas. In the second incident of suicide attack on 21 November 2009, three suspected militants blew themselves up after the police gave a chase and surrounded them in a mountainous area of Muzaffarabad. All the militants seemed to be Pushtuns.

In third such incident on 28 December 2009, a suicide bomber blew himself up amid a *Muharram* procession of the *Shia* mourners, killing ten people, including three policemen. The investigators concluded that the procession was targeted by the *Lashkar-e-Jhangvi* (LeJ). In the fourth such incident on 6 January 2010, a bomber blew himself up outside a military installation in the Tararkhel town of the Sudhnoti district of Azad Kashmir, killing four soldiers of the Pakistan Army. The investigators said the bomber was a member of the *Harkatul Jehadul Islami* (Azad Kashmir chapter). In short, it appears that the Pakistani chickens have finally come home to roost.

REFERENCES

1. Tariq Khan, *Press Talk*, 18 May 2008.
2. Qari Hussain, *Videotape*, 17 January 2009.
3. Investigative Report, *Washington Post*, 2 July 2009.

CHAPTER 17

The Bhutto Murder: 'You Can Name Musharraf If I am Killed'

The tragic assassination of Benazir Bhutto, Pakistan's twice elected former Prime Minister (1988–1990; 1993–1996) and the Chairperson of the Pakistan Peoples Party (PPP) in the evening of 27 December 2007 in the garrison town of Rawalpindi, hardly a few kilometers from the General Headquarters (GHQ) of the Pakistan Army and the head office of the ISI, raised two important questions – who actually orchestrated her murder and why? Having spent eight years in involuntary exile, Bhutto had returned to Pakistan on 18 October 2007 to campaign for a third term in power, only to be assassinated barely ten weeks later.

The murder of Benazir Bhutto, who struggled against the military regimes of General Zia-ul Haq and General Pervez Musharraf for the restoration of democracy in the country, marked the end of the long political legacy of the Bhutto family. She was the fourth member of the Bhutto family to have died an unnatural death. Her father, late Zulfikar Ali Bhutto, also a popular elected Prime Minister, was sent to the gallows by Pakistan's third military dictator General Zia-ul Haq. One of her two brothers, Mir Shahnawaz Bhutto, died in 1986 after being poisoned in Paris while the other one, Mir Murtaza Bhutto, was shot dead by unknown persons in 1996 in Karachi – the commercial capital of Pakistan during her second tenure as Prime Minister. Even before Benazir decided to end her self-exile, Benazir

Bhutto was talking publicly of the threat to her life. That is probably the reason she did not bring her husband Asif Zardari and their three children back to Pakistan in October 2007.

Two years after her death, the ghost of Benazir Bhutto continues to haunt distraught Pakistanis amid allegations and counter allegations about her possible assassins, prompting the growth of a web of conspiracy theories to explain the assassination of the country's first lady Prime Minister. The people of Pakistan may never know who killed her, yet there is no dearth of probable culprits to choose from: *Al-Qaeda* and Taliban-linked Islamic extremists, rogue elements within the all-powerful Pakistani military intelligence establishment, or some contract killers hired by her political rivals, including President Pervez Musharraf? Whatever the conspiracy theory is, it keeps getting denser every day.

A few moments before the assassination, Benazir, wearing a white head scarf, addressed a mammoth election rally in the Liaqat Bagh ground of Rawalpindi; she then got into her bulletproof white Toyota Land Cruiser. She was being driven to her Islamabad residence when her vehicle was stopped by a group of cheering PPP supporters, prompting her to demand that the vehicle's sunroof be opened so she could wave out to her workers. While a smiling Benazir Bhutto was waving to the crowd amidst loud slogans of "*Jiye Bhutto*" (long live Bhutto), three gunshots were heard. Bhutto sank back into her seat, just as a suicide bomber detonated explosives to the left of her vehicle.

Seconds later, those inside the vehicle with her noticed that her face and neck were badly bloodied, apparently from the bullets. As blood poured from her wounds and pooled in the back seat, she lost consciousness, and never regained it. The vehicle raced towards Rawalpindi General Hospital, but it was too badly damaged from the blast to complete the journey. Those accompanying Bhutto had to hoist their beloved leader into another vehicle as they desperately sought to get her medical care. At the hospital, a team of surgeons worked to save her, and even resorted to open heart massage. However, she was declared dead on the operating table at round 6:30 p.m.

Doctors did not say what caused the wound

Bhutto's cause of death has been much discussed and debated. According to a team of doctors that examined her, Benazir Bhutto had open wounds on her left temporal region from which brain matter was leaking. They did not say what caused the wound, because no autopsy had been performed on the body. Despite official claims by the Musharraf regime soon after the tragedy that some Islamic extremists might be involved in her murder, Bhutto's close circles were reported by the Pakistani media as having said that rogue elements in the Pakistani establishment had persuaded religious extremist groups to pool their resources and even rehearse the fatal attack on her. A January 2007 press conference by the chief of the Rawalpindi Central Investigation Department (CID), Abdul Majeed, reinforced this view when he confirmed that the assailants had visited the site of the incident a night before in a taxi to carry out a reconnaissance. He said they visited Liaqat Bagh and reviewed the location, and decided to hit her from different directions during or after the public meeting.

The PPP leadership thus demanded an inquiry by the United Nations to establish the identity and motives of the assassins, along the lines of the one into the murder of former Lebanese Prime Minister Rafique Hariri who was killed in a car bombing in Beirut on 14 February 2005. General Musharraf, however, ruled out any UN involvement in investigating what he described as a 'simple' murder and which he insisted could be handled internally with the help of Scotland Yard. A five-member Scotland Yard team was subsequently requisitioned by the Musharraf regime. On 11 January 2008, the British High Commission in Islamabad made public the terms of the reference agreed between the Scotland Yard team and the Pakistan government, as per which the Pakistani authorities were the principal investigators while the British squad was mandated only to assist the Pakistani authorities in providing clarity about the precise cause of Bhutto's death.

'She died after hitting her head against a hard object'

A subsequent murder investigation report, made public by the

Scotland Yard on 8 February 2008, concluded that Bhutto had died after hitting her head against a hard object (possibly the sunroof of her vehicle) as a result of the suicide bombing and the gunman and the suicide bomber were one and the same. The report, however, raised more questions than it attempted to answer and subsequently was rejected by the PPP leadership, which maintained that the so-called findings only corroborated the account of events provided by the Musharraf regime immediately after the Bhutto assassination.

In fact, Scotland Yard was just repeating history. This had been the case with the 1956 assassination of the first Prime Minister Liaqat Ali Khan at the same venue, Liaqat Bagh in Rawalpindi. Half a century later, the Scotland Yard investigators were allowed to examine only the evidence that had already been collected and interview police officials on duty on the day of the tragedy and doctors who attended to Benazir Bhutto at the Rawalpindi General Hospital. Most importantly, the report said nothing as to who might have sent the killers and who might be behind the murder. The PPP leadership also questioned the Scotland Yard's conclusion that only one killer was involved, particularly given that a taped conversation of militant leader Baitullah, which was released to the media by the Ministry of Interior on 28 December 2007, had spoken of the involvement of at least two killers.

'She died of a bullet wound'

The implication was now that if the Scotland Yard findings were correct, the taped conversation was inaccurate, and its authenticity suspect. Questions were also raised on the Yard's conclusions in the absence of an autopsy and the washing away of crucial forensic evidence by Pakistani authorities. According to Naheed Khan, the political secretary to the PPP chairperson who was sitting beside her leader at the time of the attack, Bhutto died of a bullet wound which made her slump into the vehicle just seconds before the suicide bomber exploded himself. She said the sharp shooter and the suicide bomber merged into the crowd surrounding Bhutto's vehicle outside Liaqat Bagh, taking advantage of the pitiable security arrangement at the venue of her public meeting.

According to eyewitnesses, when the vehicle ferrying Bhutto was about 69 feet from the VIP gate of the Liaqat Bagh, the sharp shooter opened fire. By that time, Bhutto had become an easy target after having removed the sunshade of her bulletproof vehicle. The sharp shooter fired at her thrice, as shown in several video footages, fatally injuring her on the third attempt. Her skull cracked on receiving the bullet shot, apparently from a 7.63 mm pistol which was found from the crime scene by the authorities. Benazir Bhutto instantly collapsed into the vehicle; seconds later a powerful bomb exploded.

The PPP circles say had Bhutto still been standing, the sheer intensity of the suicide blast would have blown off her head or at least inflicted severe wounds on her. Dozens of her supporters were surrounding her vehicle at the time of the blast, and most of them died on the spot. The theory effectively belies the official claim that she died because the intensity of the explosion smashed her head against the lever used to open the sunshade of the armoured vehicle. Some senior police officials involved in the Bhutto murder investigations are convinced that the suicide bomber was sent to eliminate the shooter and obliterate evidence of his crime. They believed it wasn't the suicide bomber, who triggered the explosion, but a powerful bomb was planted at the venue and a remote device was used to trigger it.

The police insist that the Rawalpindi attack on 27 December 2007 and the Karachi carnage on 18 October 2007 had one important common feature – the legs of the purported suicide bombers in both the cases remain missing – giving broad hints that neither of the two attacks against Bhutto was suicidal. "Had her vehicles not been targeted with time bomb devices on both the occasions, the legs of the suicide bombers would have been recovered from the crime scenes," they argue. In suicide attacks, they add, the bomber is either decapitated or his head is destroyed because he wraps explosive materials around the upper body.

Bhutto recalls the previous suicide attack

In her posthumous book *"Reconciliation: Islam, Democracy, and the West"*, which she had completed just two days before being killed, Bhutto recalls in these words her landing at Karachi Airport and her subsequent journey towards the mausoleum of Mohammad Ali

Jinnah where she was scheduled to address a public meeting: "As the sky darkened and my armoured campaign truck progressed almost by inches through the growing masses, I noticed that street lights began to dim and then go off as we approached. The jamming equipment that was supposed to be blocking cell phone signals (that could detonate suicide bombs, or even remote-controlled toy planes filled with explosives) for 200 meters around my truck did not seem to be working.

"Sometime after 11 p.m. I saw a man holding up a baby dressed in the colours of my party, the PPP. He gesticulated repeatedly to me to take the baby, which was about one or two years old. I gesticulated to the crowd to make way for him. But when the crowd parted, the man would not come forward. Instead he tried to hand the baby to someone in the crowd. Worried that the baby would fall and be trampled upon or be lost, I gesticulated no, you bring the baby to me. Finally he pointed to the security guard. I asked the security guard to let him up on the truck. However, by the time he reached the truck, I was going down to my compartment in the vehicle's interior because my feet hurt. We now suspect the baby's clothes were lined with plastic explosives.

"My feet had swollen up after standing in one place for 10 hours, and my sandals were hurting. Downstairs I unstrapped and loosened them. A little while later my political secretary, Naheed Khan, and I went over the speech that I would be delivering later at the tomb – one of the most important of my life. I was saying that perhaps we should mention my petitioning the Supreme Court to allow political parties in the tribal areas to organise as part of our plan to counter extremists politically. As I said the word "extremist", a terrible explosion rocked the truck. First the sound, then the light, then the glass smashing, then the deadly silence followed by horrible screams. My first thought was: "Oh, God, no."

"A piercing pain tore my ear from the force of the blast. An eerie silence descended. Then a second explosion – much louder, larger and more damaging – went off. Almost simultaneously, something hit the truck, which rolled from side to side. (Later I saw two dents clearly visible on the left side of the truck, where I had been.) I looked outside. The dark night was bathed in an orange light, and under it crumpled bodies lay scattered in the most horrific scene. I now know what happened to the baby. Agha Siraj Durrani, a PPP parliamentarian, was watching the access to my truck. When the man tried to hand the baby up, Agha Siraj told him to get lost. The man then went to a police vehicle to the left of the truck, which also refused to take the baby.

"As the man tried to hand the baby to the second police vehicle, the first police vehicle warned: 'Don't take the baby, don't take the baby, and don't let the baby up on the truck'. Both these police vehicles were exactly parallel to where I was sitting inside the truck. As the man scuffled with the police to hand the baby over, the first explosion took place. Everyone in that police van was killed, as were those around it. Within 50 seconds, a 15-kilogram car bomb was detonated, scattering pellets, shrapnel and burning pieces of metal."

Why did fire brigades wash the crime scene?

Nonetheless, suicide bomber or baby bomb, the intent of those who wanted to kill Bhutto was to ensure the concealment of the role of the shooter. All explosions yield a variety of clues to the type of explosives used and the trigger devices employed, forensic evidence considered vital to establish the possible identity of groups involved in the crime. But, inexplicably, hours after Bhutto was assassinated, the administration pressed in fire brigades to wash the spot where the suicide bomber had wreaked havoc, consequently spawning theories about the possible role of the establishment in the assassination. One might wonder at the great hurry in hosing down the crime scene the same evening instead of preserving it in accordance with the standard procedure of international criminal investigations.

According to a senior PPP leader and a former interior minister in Bhutto cabinet Barrister Aitzaz Ahsan, destruction of evidence is itself a very serious crime. "When a murder takes place even in the remotest village in this country, the crime scene is preserved for days until it is thoroughly examined, measured and mapped. Footprints are carefully preserved for days in cases of theft and housebreak. Then the second question: why was the crime scene washed after such horrendous crimes? If you keep in mind the significance of the telltale cell-phone chip in the investigations into the December 2003 suicide attack on Musharraf, it is perhaps easy to discern why".

According to Aitzaz, after the twin but aborted suicide attempts on General Pervez Musharraf on 24 December 2003, just beyond Chaklala Bridge in Rawalpindi, the crime scene was sealed by the investigators for several days and not even a fly was allowed inside the cordoned area. Nothing was touched or moved except by experts. The area was minutely fine-combed. Finally one telling piece of evidence was found: "a cell phone chip. The miniscule find was crucial which eventually led to the identification of the perpetrators of the crime who were arrested, tried by a military court and sentenced. That one chip did it all".

Another significant question is: how were 21 dead bodies buried [of those killed in the Liaqat Bagh tragedy] without a single autopsy? That is not possible even in the most ordinary murder case. There has to be a postmortem report. That is because the dead body is the surest piece of evidence. Who pressured the doctors to hand over as many as 21 dead bodies without autopsies? Again, interrogate the senior police officials present and get to the bottom of the mystery.

Then no serious effort was made to trace out the sharp shooters who might have killed Benazir Bhutto. Evidence of well-positioned sharpshooters may have been collected through different available means. According to Aitzaz, the shooters must have used cell phones. "Had all those who made calls via towers of cell phone companies linking the site at Liaqat Bagh with their mainframe been questioned by the investigators, the circle could have been narrowed. Suppose 5,000 calls were made during the hour before the assassination and the half hour thereafter through these cell phone towers. Each caller could be identified from company records. Each person, without exception, should then have been grilled narrowing the inquiry down to 20 to 30 suspect calls. But have the 10,000 persons, each caller and recipient, been questioned? Not to anyone's knowledge. The evidence of recall and memory may have been irretrievably lost or degraded by now. Besides the tell-tale chips lost to the drains of the garrison town of Rawalpindi, this would be the best evidence which must have been lost by now".

Chilling images of a sharp shooter firing at Bhutto

That the Musharraf regime had been tying itself in knots over the assassination case is beyond any doubt. First, on December 28, barely 24 hours after the murder, Interior Ministry spokesman Brigadier (retd) Javed Iqbal Cheema claimed that Benazir Bhutto died because her head had been smashed against the lever of her vehicle's sunshade. This could as well have become the official version of the murder. However, much to the Musharraf regime's discomfiture, several privately-run television channels released on 29 December 2007 chilling images of a sharp shooter firing at Bhutto a few seconds before the deadly explosion took place. It was only then that the Musharraf administration sought the Scotland Yard's assistance in the investigation that, in any case, eventually endorsed the official government version.

The PPP then approached the United Nations, seeking the setting up of a high-level International Commission to thoroughly investigate the Bhutto murder and to bring the perpetrators, organisers, financiers and sponsors of the murder plot to justice. The demand, raised in a letter signed by Co-Chairman of the PPP Asif Ali Zardari, was sent directly to the United Nations Secretary General on 16 January 2008. On 19 January 2008, only two days after the PPP had approached the United Nations for the Bhutto murder probe, the Pakistani authorities detained a teenager, allegedly part of a five-man terrorist squad which had been assigned to kill Benazir Bhutto at Liaqat Bagh.

Arrested from the Dera Ismail Khan district of the North Western Frontier Province, the 15-year-old Aitzaz Shah confessed to his involvement in the murder plot the very next day, on 20 February 2008. But his confession was rejected by the Pakistan Peoples Party spokesman Farhatullah Babar as a "cock and bull story" intended to reduce pressure on Musharraf, adding that the so-called confession was obtained under coercion. The arrested youth, who has already been declared a juvenile by the court, said exactly the kind of things the Pakistani authorities wanted to hear, backing up conclusions that seem to have been reached within hours of the killing.

Bhutto talks about her murderers

Since her assassination, Benazir Bhutto's old e-mails and interviews are being circulated among the public. In these she points the finger at some high-level officials in the establishment as her would-be killers. Addressing his first press conference after the murder, Bhutto's widower, Asif Zardari, made public her 20 October 2007 email to Wolf Blitzer of the *CNN* which mentioned the name of her would-be assassin. 'The said e-mail should be treated as Bhutto's dying declaration. She talks about her murderers from her grave and it is up to the world to listen to the echoes', he said. Bhutto wrote to Wolf Blitzer in her e-mail: 'If it is God's will, nothing will happen to me. But if anything happened to me, I would hold Pervez Musharraf responsible'. Blitzer received the e-mail on October 26 from Mark Siegel, a friend and long-time Washington spokesman for Benazir. That was eight days after she narrowly escaped an attempt on her life in Karachi. Bhutto wrote to Wolf: 'I have been made to feel insecure by Musharraf's minions'.

Benazir Bhutto had pointed out in her mail that she had not received the requested improvements to her security and was being prevented from using private cars or vehicles equipped with tinted windows. Bhutto added that she had also not been provided with signal jammers to prevent remote controlled bombs or with police mobile outriders to cover her vehicle on all sides. According to Mark Siegel, Benazir Bhutto had asked permission to bring in trained security personnel from abroad. In fact, she and her husband repeatedly tried to get visas for such protection but the Pakistan government denied them again and again. A US-based security agency Blackwater and a London-based firm Armor Group, which guards UK diplomats in the Middle East, were not allowed to protect Benazir Bhutto. She urged Musharraf to improve her security after the Karachi suicide bomb attack, besides requesting American and British diplomats to pressurize Musharraf in providing adequate security to her. But Musharraf never listened.

The Bhutto-Musharraf-tiff

Benazir Bhutto's security concerns and General Musharraf's refusal to address them have also been highlighted by a Pulitzer Prize winning US journalist Ron Suskind, in his book titled "The Way of the World: A Story of Truth and Hope in an Age of Extremism". Published in August 2008, the book is full of disclosures, with its fair portion about Musharraf-Benazir conversation including General Musharraf's quote "You should understand something, your security is based on the state of our relationship". The writer disclosed that the US intelligence agencies had taped Bhutto's phone calls, prior to her arrival in Pakistan, in a bid to play under-the-table, cut-throat games more effectively. About those bugging Bhutto, Suskind writes on Page 293 of the book: -"What they'll overlook is the context and her tone in the many calls they eavesdrop on – overlook the fact that she's scared and preparing for the possibility of imminent death".

The book disclosed details of Bhutto's meeting with Senator John Kerry requesting for her security and his reply that "United States is generally hesitant to ensure the protection of anyone who is not a designated leader". In a subsequent interview on August 15, 2008, Suskind quoted Bhutto as having told him: "I've got two enemies who have been in an unholy alliance for many years now – dictatorial power and messianic radicalism, and I have no protection. Why? Because Dick Cheney won't make the phone call! Why? Explain it to me, the idea that they assured me Cheney would make the call to Musharraf simply to say, 'You're the dictator, make sure she is protected. She has to make it to election-day. If she doesn't, we're going to hold you responsible.' Narrating Musharraf's message to Bhutto that her safety "is based on the state of our relationship", Suskind said: "It was all but like a Mafia threat. And this is something that the US, frankly, deep down understands, too. They let this process unfold. And ultimately, folks around Bhutto now are saying that she was abandoned by America".

Did Dick Cheney order her murder?

In a related development, a well-known American investigative journalist Seymour Hersh claimed in a 12 May 2009 interview that a special death squad had assassinated Benazir Bhutto on the orders of former US vice-president Dick Cheney. In an interview to an Arab television channel, the Washington-based Hersh, who writes for the

New Yorker magazine and a few other prominent media outlets, also claimed that the former vice-president had been running an "executive assassination ring" throughout the Bush years. The cell reported directly to Cheney. Hersh indicated that the same unit killed Bhutto because in an interview with *Al-Jazeera* TV on 2 November 2007, she had said she believed that *Al-Qaeda* leader Osama bin Laden was already dead. She said she believed that Sheikh Ahmed Omar Saeed, an *Al-Qaeda* linked activist imprisoned in Pakistan for killing US journalist Daniel Pearl had murdered Osama bin Laden. But the interviewer, veteran British journalist David Frost, deleted her claim from the interview, Hersh said.

The controversial American journalist believed Ms Bhutto was assassinated because the US leadership did not want Laden to be declared dead. The Bush administration wanted to keep Osama bin Laden alive to justify the presence of US army in Afghanistan to combat the Taliban, Seymour Hersh said. The Pulitzer prize-winning journalist claimed that the same assassination squad, led by General McChrystal, also killed former Lebanese Prime Minister Rafique Al Hariri as well as the army chief of that country. Rafique Hariri and the Lebanese army chief were allegedly murdered for not safeguarding American interests and refusing to allow US to set-up military bases in Lebanon.

Earlier, on 10 March 2009, Seymour Hersh told a seminar at University of Minnesota that the unit Cheney headed was very deeply involved in extra-legal operations. "Congress has no oversight of it. It is an executive assassination wing, essentially. And it's been going on and on and on. And just today in the Times there is a story saying that its leader, a three-star admiral named McRaven, ordered a stop to certain activities because there were so many collateral deaths. It's been going under President Bush's authority. They've been going into countries, not talking to the ambassador or the CIA station chief, and finding people on a list and executing them and leaving. That's been going on, in the name of all of us."

Soon after Seymour Hersh's Minnesota speech, *CNN*'s Wolf Blitzer asked Dick Cheney's former National Security Adviser John Hannah about Hersh's claim: "Is there a list of terrorists, suspected terrorists out there who can be assassinated?" Hannah said while responding: "There is clearly a group of people that go through a very extremely well-vetted process, inter-agency process ... that have committed acts of war against the United States, who are at war with the United States, or are suspected of planning operations of war against the United States, whom authority is given to the troops in the field and in certain war theatres to capture or kill those individuals. That is certainly true".

When Wolf Blitzer asked was that totally constitutional and legal to go out and find these guys and to hit them, John Hannah said: "There is no question that in a theatre of war, when we are at war, and we know – there is no doubt, we are still at war against *Al-Qaeda* in Iraq, *Al-Qaeda* in Afghanistan and on that Pakistani border, that our troops have the authority to go after and capture and kill the enemy, including the leadership of the enemy".

Murder co-conspired by Bush-Mush regimes?

So would it be too wild to speculate that Benazir Bhutto's murder was co-conspired by the then Pakistani and the American administration? On his part, when asked at a media briefing in Islamabad on 1 January 2008, if he had blood on his hands, General Musharraf said the question was "below my dignity" but he wanted to give a public answer in any case. 'I am not a feudal and I am not a tribal. I have been brought up in a very educated and civilized family with beliefs and values and which believes in character. My family is not a family which believes in killing people, assassinating, intriguing. That is all that I want to say,' he said.

A day later, on 3 January 2008, Musharraf admitted for the first time that Bhutto may have been shot by a gunman, but said Bhutto alone bore responsibility for her death. Musharraf said in an interview on the CBS news' Sixty Minutes show that he had personally told Benazir that she was under threat and that under the circumstances she should not have done the things that she did on that fateful day in December. She should not have stood up in her car as she left a rally. "For standing up outside the car, I think it was she to blame alone – nobody else. Responsibility is hers". He said: "I had asked her not to come before the election, and that we will arrange – then she could come after the election, which she had agreed. But then she decided to come all of a sudden. She did not stick to her agreements with me to an extent. Now that changed a little. It upset me a little".

Musharraf's logic apart (Responsibility is hers), the fact remains that Benazir Bhutto must have had many powerful enemies in the Pakistani military and intelligence establishment as well as the militant organisations, who first wanted to stop her homecoming and her subsequent political comeback, and later wished her to be eliminated physically. By her own estimate, no fewer than four different jehadi organisations backed by certain powerful elements in the Pakistani military and intelligence establishments wanted her dead within hours of her homecoming. Furthermore, Bhutto was convinced of Musharraf's involvement.

What Bhutto herself told the author?

On 13 November 2007, hardly a few weeks before her murder, Benazir Bhutto told me in an interview in Lahore, the capital of Punjab, that the Karachi suicide attack could not have been possible without General Musharraf's blessings. In her off-the-record conversation with me at the residence of Senator Latif Khosa (now the Attorney General of Pakistan) a few hours before being put under house arrest by the Musharraf regime [in a bid to prevent her from leading a long March on Islamabad against the Musharraf regime], Bhutto said she knew fully well even before returning home that an attempt would be made on her life.

'I have come to know following investigations by my own sources that the October 18 attack was masterminded by some highly placed officials in the Pakistani security and intelligence establishments. My enemies in the establishment had first engaged an *Al-Qaeda* linked militant leader who in turn hired one Maulvi Abdul Rehman Otho alias Abdul Rehman Sindhi to execute the Karachi attack,' Bhutto disclosed. She said the information she acquired showed that some local militants were hired by the higher-ups in the Pakistani intelligence establishment to carry out the Karachi attack. 'I have come to know that three local militants were hired to carry out the bombing and one Maulvi Abdul Rehman Otho alias Abdul Rehman Sindhi [an *Al-Qaeda* linked *Lashkar-e-Jhangvi* militant from Dadu district of the Sindh province] was entrusted with the task of executing the entire operation.'

Benazir Bhutto said according to her sources, Abdul Rehman Sindhi (who was reportedly arrested in June 2004 from Khuda Ki Basti area in Kotri near Hyderabad district of Sindh for his alleged involvement in the February 2002 car bombing outside the US Cultural Centre building in Karachi) was mysteriously released by the Pakistan authorities shortly before her homecoming, citing lack of evidence.

'You can name Musharraf as my assassin'

Benazir Bhutto said that while realising her mistake after the Karachi suicide bomb attack, she had already written another letter to someone important, naming her would-be assassins. Asked if she has named Pervez Musharraf in that letter and to whom, the letter was addressed, Bhutto smiled and said: 'Mind one thing, all those elements in the Pakistani establishment who stand to lose power and influence in the post-election set up are after me, including the General. I can't give you more details at this stage. However, you can name Pervez Musharraf as my assassin if I am killed.'

The PPP leader said she was in London when she first learnt of a conspiracy to assassinate her upon her homecoming. 'Having come to know of the plot, I instantly wrote a letter to Musharraf, naming three persons in the establishment possibly conspiring to kill me, seeking appropriate action against them. However, it could not occur to me at that time that I was actually committing a blunder and in a way signing my own death warrant by not naming my number one enemy as one of my possible assassins. It later dawned upon me that Musharraf could have possibly exploited the said letter to his advantage and orchestrated my physical elimination.' Bhutto further said that the inquest into the Karachi bombing had already been wrapped up under instructions from the Musharraf administration since she had accused one of the General's close aides of involvement in that attack.

A week before my 13 November 2007 conversation with Benazir Bhutto, a high-level meeting presided by Musharraf in Islamabad had already dismissed her accusations as childish. According to Pakistani media reports, the participants of the meeting were informed that the suicide attack on Bhutto bore the hallmarks of *Al-Qaeda*, arguing that she had incurred the wrath of militants because of her support for the military operation against the Red Mosque fanatics in Islamabad in July 2007 and for declaring that she would allow the International Atomic Energy Agency (IAEA) to question the father of the Pakistani nuclear programme, Dr A.Q. Khan, pertaining to his proliferation activities. Days before her return to Pakistan, Bhutto told *The Guardian* on 15 October 2007 she felt the real danger to her life came from well-placed fundamentalist elements in the Pakistani establishment who were opposed to her return.

On 19 October 2007, a day after the Karachi bomb attack, Benazir Bhutto disclosed at a press conference that she had informed Musharraf in a confidential letter, written on 16 October 2007 that three senior government officials were planning to assassinate her upon her return. 'However, I had further made it clear to General Musharraf that I won't blame Taliban or *Al-Qaeda* if I am attacked, but I will name my enemies in the Pakistani establishment,' she told journalists. In an interview with French magazine, *Paris-Match* the same day, Bhutto said: 'I know exactly who wants to kill me. They are dignitaries of General Zia who are behind extremism and fanaticism.'

Although Benazir did not publicly name the three persons, PPP circles later told the media that they were Director General Intelligence Bureau, Brig (retd) Ejaz Hussain Shah, Chief Minister Punjab Chaudhry Pervez Elahi and Sindh Chief Minister Arbab Ghulam Rahim. While concluding the letter, Bhutto reportedly asserted that her life was in danger, particularly from Ejaz Shah. Incidentally, it was Ejaz Hussain Shah who had arranged the surrender of Sheikh Ahmed Omar Saeed, the killer of US journalist Daniel Pearl, in February 2005 in Lahore. Then, Ejaz Shah was the home secretary of Punjab. Shah knew that Omar's family well as both of them belong to the Nankana Sahib area of the Punjab province. However, the actual relationship between Ejaz Shah and Omar Saeed was one of a handler and his agent – both coming from the ISI.

In an interview with the *Daily Times* on 13 August 2007, Benazir Bhutto said, 'Brigadier Ejaz Shah and the ISI recruited Sheikh Ahmed

Omar Saeed, who killed American journalist Danny Pearl. So I would feel very uncomfortable making the Intelligence Bureau, which has more than 100,000 people underneath it, being run by a man (Ejaz Shah, the DG IB) who worked so closely with militants and extremists.' On 3 November 2007, two weeks after she returned home, Bhutto, in an interview with Sir David Frost on the TV programme *Frost over the World*, referred to "three individuals who wanted to kill her, one of them a very key figure in security who she claimed had dealings with Omar Saeed Sheikh."

Asked in an interview on NBC television on 20 October 2007 whether it was not risky to name a close friend of Musharraf as being someone who's plotting against her, Bhutto said: 'Well, at that time I did not know whether there would be an assassination attempt that I would survive. And I wanted to leave on record the suspects. I also didn't know that he was a friend of Musharraf. But I asked myself that even if I knew that he was a friend and I thought of him as a suspect, would I have not written? No, I would have written.'

On 28 December 2007, twenty-four hours after Benazir was assassinated, *Asia Times Online*, a Hong Kong-based web newspaper, reported that *Al-Qaeda* has claimed responsibility for her killing, adding that the death squad consisted of the Punjabi associates of the underground anti-*Shia* militant group *Lashkar-e-Jhangvi* (LeJ), operating under *Al-Qaeda* orders. 'We terminated the most precious American asset who had vowed to defeat the *mujahideen*,' according to Mustafa Abu al-Yazid, an important *Al-Qaeda* commander for Afghanistan operations as well as an *Al-Qaeda* spokesperson. 'This is our first major victory against those (Benazir and Musharraf) who have been siding with infidels (the West) in the fight against *Al-Qaeda...*'

Interestingly, the responsibility claim by *Al-Qaeda* confirmed Bhutto's own findings that the Karachi assassination bid was executed by an *Al-Qaeda* linked LeJ operative Abdul Rehman Sindhi – whom Benazir Bhutto had named in our conversation in November. According to her information, Abdul Rehman Sindhi had sought asylum in Afghanistan during the Taliban regime and obtained training in militancy before returning to Pakistan after the fall of the Taliban regime.

She was about to expose an ISI operation to rig general elections

Just hours before she was killed Benazir Bhutto was apparently trying to expose a suspected ISI operation to rig the 8 January 2008 general elections in favour of the Musharraf-backed Pakistan Muslim League (PML-Quaid-e-Azam). Benazir Bhutto was collecting information about a rigging cell allegedly established at a safe house of the Inter Services Intelligence in Islamabad which. Bhutto was informed by one of her close confidants on 25 December 2007 in an e-mail message sent at her e-mail address – *sazdubai@emirates.net.ae* – that the Musharraf regime had set-up a cell to engineer the 2008 elections. Bhutto was further informed that the cell headed by one Brigadier (retd) Riazullah Khan Chib was working in tandem with the Intelligence Bureau Director General Brig (retd) Ejaz Hussain Shah.

The information she received said the so-called "Election Monitoring Cell" would ensure that stamped ballot papers in over one hundred constituencies of Punjab and Sindh were all set to be polled on January 8 in favour of the "Queue" League candidates. The information further said that the provincial headquarters of the ISI and IB would ensure that the ballots were polled in a smooth manner at the ghost polling stations in the district headquarters of Punjab and Sindh and counted in the final count before the official election result was handed over to the successful candidates by the presiding officers. 'All this is being done because of the fact that Musharraf simply can't afford a hostile parliament as a result of the 2008 polls,' the information passed on to Bhutto said.

In her reply which Bhutto sent from her blackberry the same day she wrote: 'I was told that the ISI and the MI have been asked not to meddle. But I will double check.' In her second message to the same confidant a day later on 27 December at 1:12 p.m. – five hours before her assassination – Bhutto wrote: " 'I need the address of the safe house [in Islamabad] as well as the phone numbers of the concerned. Plz [please] try and obtain ASAP [as soon as possible]. Mbb" [Ms Benazir Bhutto], Sent from my BlackBerry® wireless device'. The confidant wrote back at 3:06pm the same day: 'I have re-checked the information with the same source which earlier said the ISI and the MI have been asked not to meddle. The source claims Brig Riazullah Khan Chib retired from the ISI a few months ago but was re-employed, since he belongs to the arm of the Artillery and is considered close to Musharraf who too comes from the same wing of the army. The source says Chib's cover job is somewhere else but he is actually supervising a special election cell which is working in tandem with the chief of the Intelligence Bureau. I have further been told that Brigadiers Ejaz Hussain Shah and Riazullah Chib are close friends because of their having served in Punjab as the provincial heads of the ISI and the Punjab Regional Director of the Anti-Narcotics Force (ANF) respectively in the past. Both are considered to be loyalists of Chaudhry Shujaat Hussain, the president of the PML-Q.'

Information passed on to Benazir Bhutto further stated: 'The rigging cell/safe house in question is located on *Shahra-e-Dastoor*, close to the Pakistan House Bus Stop in Sector G-5 of Islamabad. It is a double storey building, without inscribing any address as is the case with most of the safe houses. The cell consists of some retired and serving military and intelligence officers, which will show its magic on the election-day. The message was sent to Benazir Bhutto hardly three hours before her assassination.

Notably, the day she was assassinated, Bhutto was due to meet two senior American politicians to show them a confidential report, compiled on the basis of information ascertained by Bhutto's own contacts within the Pakistani security and intelligence services, alleging that the Musharraf administration was using some of the $10 billion in US military aid that Pakistan had received since 2001 to rig the elections. Patrick Kennedy, a Democratic congressman, and Arlen Specter, a Republican member of the US Senate's sub-committee on foreign operations, were scheduled to have a dinner meeting with Benazir Bhutto on 27 December during which they were to be provided this report.

According to a 1 January 2008 report, published in British daily *The Times*, Asif Ali Zardari had confirmed the existence of the report, its basic contents and Benazir Bhutto's plans to meet the American lawmakers. Asked if such a report was in his possession, he said:

'Something to that effect.' Asked if the report contained some evidence that the ISI was using US funds to rig the elections, he said: 'Possibly so. The confidential report could have been one of several motives for killing her. It was a general combination of all of these things. The fact that she's on the ground exposing everybody, I guess, would have been one reason.'

Zardari blames Musharraf cronies for the murder

Significantly, on 30 December 2007, two days after Benazir Bhutto's murder, a visibly furious Asif Zardari had accused [at a press conference in Naudero] the PML-Q leadership of his wife's murder besides describing the party as "*Qatil* League" (the killer League)). Hitting back in the same tone the same evening (31 December 2007), the Punjab Chief Minister Chaudhry Pervez Elahi had charged Zardari with Bhutto's murder, saying, "Who has benefited the most from the assassination? Zardari, and only Zardari. Check the authenticity of Benazir's will. Find out the amount for which she was insured." Zardari had already been elected as the co-chairman of the PPP by that time.

On 18 October 2008, on the first anniversary of the terrorist attack made on Bhutto's procession, the Karachi police had finally lodged a second FIR of the Karsaz attacks on the basis of her letter, naming three persons as those who could be involved in her assassination. The national newspapers reported on 20 October 2008 that those named in the second were Chaudhry Pervez Elahi, Ejaz Shah and Hameed Gul. Confirming the lodging of the second FIR, Sindh Chief Minister Qaim Ali Shah said Ms Bhutto's own attempts to lodge a second FIR of the Karsaz tragedy were foiled by the PML-Q government.

Bhutto had forwarded a written request to the SHO Bahadurabad police station for registration of an FIR on her behalf, maintaining that the FIR (183/2007 under almost all the same sections) was originally lodged on behalf of the state against "some unidentified persons", without naming those she had named in her letter to Pervez Musharraf. But the police did not lodge the case saying it was not possible to file two FIRs of a single incident.

However, a year later, a second FIR (213/2008) of the Karsaz tragedy was lodged by Bahadurabad police station under Sections 324 (attempt to commit *Qatl-e-Amd*), 302 (Qatl-e-Amd), 427/34 (mischief causing damage to the amount of fifty rupees) of Pakistan Penal Code and Sections 3 (punishment for causing explosion likely to endanger life or property) and 4 (punishment for attempt to cause explosion or for making or keeping explosive with intent to endanger life or property) of the Explosive Substances Act, 1908, after the Sindh government declared the findings of the previous Investigation team irrelevant.

Sindh Home Minister Dr Zulfiqar Mirza subsequently told newsmen in Karachi that the fresh FIR was registered in line with the court orders, suggesting conversion of Bhutto's letter into an FIR. "In Benazir Bhutto's request, she had mentioned a letter she wrote to Musharraf two days before her 18 October 2008 return to Pakistan in which she said her life could be harmed by three persons," Zulfiqar Mirza said and added that the new police team led by Deputy Inspector General Investigation Sindh Ghulam Qadir would take into account every possible aspect during the course of investigations as the previous team had only established that the Karsaz blasts were suicide attacks.

On 20 October 2008, Sindh Chief Minister Qaim Ali Shah declared while talking to newsmen in Karachi that the three persons nominated by Benazir Bhutto would be arrested soon for interrogations. However, hardly ten days later, on 1 November 2008, Chaudhry Pervaiz Elahi claimed in an exclusive interview with *The News* that the Presidency had stopped the Sindh government from implicating him in the Benazir murder case. Perez Elahi revealed that following the registration of a second FIR in the Karsaz case, he and his first cousin Chaudhry Shujaat Hussain went to see Asif Zardari's close aide, Dr Qayyum Soomro, who had delivered their message to the President.

"After our meeting with Dr Soomro during which we protested on the issue, [Sindh Home Minister] Dr Zulfiqar Mirza was told by the presidency not to talk about the case any more". Elahi's claim eventually proved credible given the fact that after the initial outburst against the PML-Q leaders, not only Dr Zulfiqar Mirza and Sindh chief Minister Qaim Ali Shah fell silent but the rest of the PPP leaders also adopted a mysterious mum.

United Nations Commission of Inquiry

Even after a lapse of two years since her tragic murder, the Bhutto murder case is yet to be solved. Despite the installation of a PPP government in Islamabad and the elevation Asif Zardari as the President of the country, the decision makers in the government seem reluctant to initiate proceedings against any of the suspects, be it Musharraf or the PML-Q leadership, who had been named by Benazir herself as her would-be assassins. Zardari keeps insisting that only the United Nations Inquiry Commission could carry out a credible investigation of the assassination. The UN Secretary General Ban Ki-moon had constituted in April 2009 a UN Commission of Inquiry into the facts and circumstances of Benazir Bhutto's murder, led by Chile's Permanent Representative to United Nations Heraldo Munoz. On 19 June 2009, Ban Ki-moon announced that the three-member UN Commission would commence its six-month mandate on 1 July 2009.

The United Nations spokesman subsequently made it clear in an official statement: "In accordance with the agreed terms of reference, the Commission's mandate will be to inquire into the facts and circumstances of the murder. The duty of determining criminal responsibility of the perpetrators of the murder remains with the Pakistani authorities. The Commission will submit its report to the secretary-general within six months of the commencement of its activities". To a question regarding the mandate of the Commission, the spokesperson said the narrow mandate had been cleared by the Pakistani government. But many of Benazir's associates were of the view that an internal effort to unravel the Bhutto murder mystery by the PPP government would produce more answers that the UN team could provide.

Zardari says she died by a bullet and not by the bomb

On 27 December 2008, while speaking on the first anniversary of her wife's death, President Asif Zardari claimed that he knew the killers of Benazir Bhutto and that he would reveal their identity at the right time. Commenting on his statement, English daily *The News*, stated in its 30 December 2008 editorial titled 'Mystery murderers': "This is mystifying. If Mr Zardari is indeed able to answer the question as to who killed Benazir Bhutto, there seems to be no plausible reason why he should keep up the suspense. Almost every citizen wishes to know the answer. The investigation has stalled despite the fact that her PPP is the senior partner in the governing coalition, and her husband, Zardari, wields enormous influence as the Party's leader. All kinds of questions have been raised from various quarters as the first death anniversary of Benazir was observed. Many doubts, many suspicions remain. These have in fact grown. Zardari must take note of prevailing sentiment. If the president can indeed name the killers, now is the time to do so when the government is in a position to bring them to justice and thus act to avenge a murder that shook nearly everyone in the country regardless of political affiliation".

On 6 July 2009, President Asif Zardari blamed his predecessor Musharraf for the murder of Benazir Bhutto, claiming that she died by a bullet and not by the bomb that a Scotland Yard report identified as the cause. "I wish Musharraf had looked after my wife as I can look after myself," President Zardari told British newspaper *The Telegraph* in an interview.

On 17 July 2009, the United Nations Inquiry Commission formally initiated its investigation into the Bhutto murder on Pakistani soil by meeting security officials and discussing with them Islamabad's own probe into the gory act of terrorism. The UN team also called on President Asif Zardari besides holding separate meetings with Interior Minister Rehman Malik and Foreign Minister Shah Mehmood Qureshi. Briefing the newsmen about the meeting, the President's Spokesman Farhatullah Babar said that at the outset, President welcomed the team and thanked the UN and its Secretary General Ban Ki Moon for setting up the Commission. The President reiterated the rationale behind the decision of the government to request a UN probe and said the mission was faced with a "challenging and onerous" task.

"We approached the United Nations because first of all we wanted transparent and aboveboard investigations so that there are no accusations of bias. We also wanted to unearth any conspiracy to balkanise Pakistan and let the world know how a democratic leader heroically laid down her life to foil the designs against the country and thereby to honour her internationally," Farhatullah Babar quoted the President as saying to the members of the UN team. The President said that the Parliament and all provincial assemblies had adopted unanimous resolutions demanding a UN probe. The UN had also passed resolutions condemning the assassination and the need to expose the organisers, perpetrator and financiers of the crime and it was befitting that the world body formed its own fact-finding Commission, the President said.

President Zardari further said the conspirators planned to postpone elections indefinitely and provoke the PPP into taking to the streets on that fateful day to hasten the process of balkanisation. However, the PPP took the sagacious decision to seek revenge in a different way as the party's new Chairman Bilawal Bhutto Zardari declared "democracy is the best revenge," the President had added. "We have also carried out our own investigations and the findings will be made available to the UN investigators", Babar quoted President Zardari as saying during his meeting with UN team members.

While addressing a news conference in Islamabad on 18 July 2009, Munoz, the head of a three member UN team vowed to bring out the truth about the Bhutto murder case, but not without making it clear that it will not seek to name culprits. "The Commission of Inquiry would ensure that its final report clearly establishes the truth regarding the facts and circumstances of the assassination of Benazir Bhutto. But if you think that there will be smoking guns in terms of names, our job is not that. Our mandate is to look into the facts and circumstances of the assassination of former prime minister and the mandate does not include a criminal investigation", he added.

When asked if the Commission would summon former President General (retd) Pervez Musharraf and other persons named by Benazir Bhutto in her emails as persons who could assassinate her, Heraldo Munoz said: "The Commission cannot summon anyone legally because it would be a voluntary process. We would greatly appreciate the voluntary involvement and engagement of all Pakistanis in this effort. We cannot be fully successful without the cooperation of the people of Pakistan. And I need to stress at this point the key part that the Pakistani media can play in helping the Commission".

A costly non-probe

The press conference by the head of the UN Inquiry Commission invited the wrath of the Pakistani media, with many national newspapers stating in their editorial notes that the murder investigation which would cost $4 million would be a waste of time and money as the Commission will only investigate the circumstances leading to the assassination and not fix responsibility. One such editorial note by daily *Dawn* on 20 July 2009, titled "A costly non-probe", stated: The futility of asking the United Nations to investigate Benazir Bhutto's murder has now become obvious, with the probe team chief saying it would fix no 'criminal liability.' Then what is the probe all about?"

After all, the editorial note said, the aim of every investigation into an act of crime is to find out who committed it and give justice to the guilty. As he defined it at his press conference, the UN Commission chief Heraldo Munoz said that the mandate of his mission was limited to determining the facts and circumstances of the murder and that the mandate does not include a criminal investigation. This means we have asked the UN to conduct a costly non-probe that in the end is programmed to prove nothing. We are also reminded of the investigation by Scotland Yard, whose finding limited itself to determining the cause of Ms Bhutto's death. Again, the all-important question – who killed Benazir Bhutto? – remained unanswered".

The daily *Dawn* editorial went on to state: "The Muslim world's first woman prime minister was killed at a time when the PPP was not in power. The party's demand that the UN should investigate the Pakistani icon's murder was indicative of its lack of trust in the Musharraf government. However, even after it came to power after the February 2008 election, the PPP still had a resolution passed by the National Assembly asking the world body to investigate what indeed was a crime that had stunned the world. One could understand the UN investigating the Rafiq Hariri murder case. He was anti-Syrian, and Damascus had troops and influence in Lebanon.

A situation like this did not exist in Pakistan on 27 December 2007. Before the assassins struck, Benazir had written a letter to Musharraf naming the persons she thought wanted to assassinate her. Indeed given her lineage and gender, she had reason to suspect that, with the elections approaching, the powerful lobby well-entrenched in the Pakistani establishment since General Zia-ul Haq's days could eliminate her. Benazir's murder was a crime against a Pakistani citizen committed on Pakistani soil. For that reason, there is no alternative to a high-level investigation by Pakistan itself."

In a strange move on 17 August 2009, the government requested the Rawalpindi anti-terrorism court hearing the Benazir Bhutto murder case to postpone the further proceedings and transfer the case to the Federal Investigation Agency (FIA) so as to enable it to arrive at a definitive conclusion. On 22 August 2009, the anti-terrorism court judge accepted the petition. On 25 August 2009, the government formed a high-level team to re-investigate the murder. The Special Investigation Group of FIA was assigned the task to fix criminal liability on the assassins and planners of the gun-and-bomb attack on Bhutto. It was announced that the SIG's investigation will be parallel to the probe being carried out by the United Nations Commission. "The main reason for the fresh probe is that the inquiry report to be prepared by the UN Commission cannot be presented before any court of law as desired by the UN. The government requires a separate investigation report for a proper trial against the criminals in the court", a senior FIA official said, adding that the UN's report would have no legal standing and it could not be used for prosecution.

Zardari concedes Musharraf was given a safe exit

On 15 September 2009, President Asif Zardari conceded at a dinner meeting with senior newsmen that foreign powers with interest in the South Asian region had guaranteed a safe exit to his predecessor, and he too had been party to the deal that was struck at the time of Musharraf's resignation in 2008. A belated denial issued by the presidential spokesman two days after Zardari's meeting with the media people claimed that his remarks have been distorted and misrepresented. However, many journalists who had attended the presidential dinner-meeting insisted that President Zardari did talk about the safe exit deal in detail as per which Musharraf was to play golf in his post-presidential life.

In November 2009, General (retd) Pervez Musharraf finally appeared before the UN inquiry Commission, taking a U-turn on his earlier stance that any outside agency has no legal ground to question him. Following his refusal to be interviewed, the UN Commission had actually warned Musharraf his name would be passed on to the UN Secretary General as one of those who are not cooperating with the Commission. As the Commission formally asked the Pakistan government to arrange a meeting of the UN investigators with Musharraf, the latter changed his rigid stance, saying he has no objection to meeting the UN Commission but will not record his statement. While being interviewed by the Commission in Philadelphia on 27 October 2009, Musharraf refuted reports of his involvement in the Bhutto murder, adding that the people who had been involved in multiple suicide attempts on his life in Rawalpindi in December 2003 were involved in the assassination of the slain PPP chairperson.

On 10 December 2009, the Lahore High Court decided to proceed ex-parte against Pervez Musharraf on a petition seeking registration of a criminal case against him and others for allegedly plotting the assassination of Benazir Bhutto. Justice Khawaja Imtiaz Ahmed of the Rawalpindi bench of the Lahore High Court took the decision after a special messenger reported that a man at Pervez Musharraf's farmhouse in Islamabad had refused to receive the court notice which required a response to the petition filed by Chaudhry Mahmood Aslam, the former protocol officer of Benazir Bhutto. The LHC further decided to proceed ex-parte against former Punjab chief minister Chaudhry Pervaiz Elahi, former interior minister Gen (retd) Hamid Nawaz and former spokesman for the Ministry of Interior Brig (retd) Javed Iqbal Cheema for not replying to court notices.

On 14 December 2008, UN Secretary General Ban Ki-moon announced that he was extending the mandate of the UN Commission investigating the Bhutto murder by another three months as sought by its head who wanted more time to complete its work. The Commission was mandated to submit its report to the

UN secretary general by 31 December 2009.

On the second death anniversary of Benazir Bhutto, daily *Dawn* stated on 27 December 2009 in a story titled "BB murder probe: investigators groping in dark" that two parallel investigations being conducted by the UN Investigation Commission and Federal Investigation Agency (FIA) on her assassination remain clueless even after a lapse of two years. The report stated: "The PPP government has so far failed to unveil faces behind the murder of its leader, including killers, perpetrators, abettors, financiers and the mastermind of the attack, even though it has all kinds of resources at its command. Unfortunately, the entire nation is in the dark on the issue as no one from the government side has so far come up with any concrete statement about the progress made in the investigations".

The same day, on 27 December 2009, daily *The News* stated in its report titled "Benazir's murder trail goes cold", that one would have thought that heavens would be moved by her party after assuming power to unmask her killers. However, two years after her assassination, the report said, the elusive killers are still at large and the murder case seems to have been thrown into cold storage. "In fact, the entire responsibility of unearthing the killers has been put on the UN sponsored probe, even though the UN investigators have already stated that finding the killers does not even fall in their scope of responsibilities".

On 31 December 2009, the Pakistani media reported that the country's top military leadership including Army Chief General Ashfaq Kayani and the ISI chief Lt Gen Ahmed Shuja Pasha have declined a request by the UN Commission to question the *khaki* top brass in the Bhutto murder. English daily *The Nation* reported while quoting *Online News Agency* that through a letter to the government of Pakistan, the head of the UN Commission Heraldo Munoz had sought access to the Army Chief General Ashfaq Pervez Kayani (who had been the ISI chief at the time of Benazir's assassination), ISI chief Ahmed Shuja Pasha, the former director general of the ISI Lt Gen Nadeem Taj and the former director general of the Military Intelligence Maj Gen Nadeem Ijaz. While Lt Gen Nadeem Taj was serving as director general of the ISI at the time of Benazir Bhutto's murder, Maj Gen Nadeem Ijaz was the director general of the MI.

On 7 January 2010, Interior Minister Rehman Malik said in Islamabad, as reported by English daily *The Nation* that the Pakistan Army has nothing to do with the murder of Benazir and the UN Inquiry Commission would never be allowed to questions the country's military top brass.

On 18 February 2010, the UN Commission questioned the former director general of the Intelligence Bureau (IB) Brig (retd) Ejaz Hussain Shah, mainly on two counts – firstly, what arrangements he had made being the person officially responsible for protecting Bhutto and secondly, why did she name him in a letter as someone who could hurt her.

Almost a week later, President Asif Ali Zardari, being the supreme commander of the armed forces, finally allowed the UN Commission to interview Army Chief General Ashfaq Kayani, the ISI chief Lt Gen Ahmed Shuja Pasha and others in connection with the Bhutto murder. Talking to local journalists in Islamabad on 24 February 2010, the presidential spokesman Farhatullah Babar quoted Zardari as saying that the nation awaited the findings of the commission and wanted to know the motive behind the assassination. "The stature of Ms Bhutto called for an independent, transparent and above-board investigation so that no accusation of bias of any kind could be made by any circle. The terms of reference of the UN Commission clearly stated that it can interview anyone, including the military leadership", the president was further quoted as having said.

On 26 February 2010, Pakistani English daily *The News* reported that only the head of the UN Commission called on the Army chief and no one else was accompanying him. "It has already been agreed that only the head of the UN Commission would call on the military leadership. In fact the Army leadership had made a request to the government for meeting the UN team. The military leadership had made the request to ensure the outcome of the investigations must not remain inconclusive and that all the facts are brought to the front. It is not correct to say that anyone from the government directed the military top brass to meet the UN Commission," said the news report while quoting unnamed military sources.

REFERENCES

1. Press Conference, Abdul Majeed, Rawalpindi Central Investigation Department, July 2007.
2. Benazir Bhutto, *Reconciliation: Islam, Democracy, and the West*, Simon & Schuster, 2008.
3. Asif Ali Zardari, Press Conference, December 2007.
4. Ron Suskind, The Way of the World: A Story of Truth and Hope in an Age of Extremism, August 2008.
5. Interview, Ron Suskind, 15 August, 2008.
6. Seymour Hersh, Interview, 12 May 2009.
7. Seymour Hersh, Seminar Address at University of Minnesota, 10 March 2009.
8. Pervez Musharraf, Media Briefing, 1 January 2008.
9. Benazir Bhutto, Interview, *Daily News & Analysis*, 13 November 2007.
10. Benazir Bhutto, Interview, *Daily Times*, 13 August 2007.
11. Benazir Bhutto, Interview with Sir David Frost for Frost over the World, 3 November 2007.
12. Benazir Bhutto, Interview for *NBC*, 20 October 2007.
13. Report, *Asia Times Online*, 28 December 2007.
14. Report, *The Times*, 1 January 2008.
15. Mystery Murders, Editorial, *The News*, 30 December 2008.
16. Asif Zardari, Interview, *The Telegraph*, 6 July 2009.
17. A Costly Non-Probe, Editorial, *Daily Dawn*, 20 July 2009.
18. Munoz, United Nations Organisations, News Conference, 17 July 2009.
19. Report, *Daily Dawn*, 27 December 2009.
20. Report, Daily *The News*, 27 December 2009.
21. Report, *The Nation*, 31 December 2009.
22. Statement, *The Nation*, 7 January 2010.
23. Report, *The News*, 26 February 2010.

CHAPTER 18

Baitullah Mehsud – A scapegoat to hush up Bhutto murder

Benazir Bhutto had named jehadi kingpin Qari Saifullah Akhtar as a key suspect in the 18 October 2007 attempt to kill her at Karachi but she wanted General Pervez Musharraf to be named as her assassin in the event of her murder. Instead, the Musharraf regime was quick to name Baitullah Mehsud, the *ameer* of the *Tehrik-e-Taliban-e-Pakistan* (TTP) or the Pakistani Taliban Movement and one of the most important neo-Taliban militant commanders in the South Waziristan region, as the mastermind of the 27 December 2007 suicide attack in Rawalpindi that killed Ms Bhutto.

Baitullah Mehsud was an obscure figure on the Pakistani tribal scene until late 2004, when he filled the vacuum left by another tribal jehadi leader, Commander Nek Mohammad, to become the new hero of tribal youth who used to view with contempt the American occupation of Afghanistan and Iraq and were opposed to Islamabad's siding with Washington in the war against terror. Nek Mohammad d in June 2004 in South Waziristan in a laser-guided missile attack, carried out by the Afghanistan-based US Allied Forces. By 2006, Baitullah's growing influence in South Waziristan led terrorism analysts to label him as the unofficial *ameer* of South Waziristan.

Before his August 2009 death in an American drone attack, the shadowy Taliban commander, whose vertiginous rise to infamy landed him on 2008's *TIME* 100 List, had literally transformed the badlands of the South Waziristan Agency on the Pak-Afghan tribal belt into *Al-Qaeda's* most important redoubt. Baitullah was bound to be killed because his meteoric rise from a comparatively little-known figure in South Waziristan to the head of a full-fledged Taliban movement in the Pakistani tribal areas was no more a local trouble confined to Pakistan, but was also creating numerous problems for the US-led Allied Forces in Afghanistan. Before being killed, Baitullah used to control much of South Waziristan where Islamic militancy has given birth to a new generation of jehadi leadership in the aftermath of the 9/11 terror attacks and the subsequent invasion of Afghanistan by the US-led forces.

In the 7 April 2009 issue of *TIME* Magazine, Alex Altman had described the TTP chief in these words: "Baitullah Mehsud is a natural leader: cagey, dogged and charismatic, with an apparent knack for uniting disparate jehadi factions around a common cause. But instead of channeling those talents toward building an empire, Baitullah is trying to bring one to its knees". The 16 June 2009 issue of *TIME* said about him: "No one has contributed to Pakistan's slide into chaos over recent years more than Baitullah Mehsud. From his base in the wilds of South Waziristan, the leader of the Pakistan Taliban has overseen the killing of over 1,200 civilians and several hundreds of soldiers through brutal means, including suicide bombings, kidnappings and beheadings. He nearly routed the Pakistani Army from the country's beleaguered North West Frontier Province, establishing himself as an icon of global jehad – not unlike his idol, Mullah Mohammad Omar".

'I did not kill Bhutto'

Among the atrocities attributed to Baitullah Mehsud also includes the brazen assassination of Pakistan's twice-elected Prime Minister Benazir Bhutto on 27 December 2007. Baitullah denied involvement in the murder, but even if he was innocent of that crime, there was no shortage of reasons the *TIME* magazine dubbed him "an icon of global jehad". He had first been accused of masterminding the Bhutto murder by the Pakistani Interior Ministry Spokesman, Brig (retd) Javed Iqbal Cheema and afterward by Musharraf. In his 28 December 2007 press conference, a day after the murder, Cheema claimed that the suicide bomber, who blew himself up near Benazir's bullet proof vehicle, was an *Al-Qaeda* operative hailing from the Baitullah group. In his televised address five days after the murder on 2 January 2007, Pervez Musharraf asked Scotland Yard to help the Pakistani investigators in identifying the culprits. Yet, in the mind of the General, it was obviously clear who is to be blamed.

At his 28 December 2007 news conference, Brig (retd) Cheema said: "We just have an intelligence intercept that was recorded this morning in which Baitullah Mehsud congratulated his people for carrying out the cowardly act [of Benazir Bhutto's assassination]. He was quick to distribute among the media persons the English and Urdu transcriptions of recorded conversation which he claimed had taken place between two persons Baitullah Mehsud and one Maulvi Sahib. The following is the English transcription of the conversation which Cheema said took place in Pushto:

Baitullah Mehsud congratulates Maulvi Sahib, who explains that the attack was carried out by three of their own operatives.

Maulvi Sahib: Congratulations, I just got back during the night.

Baitullah Mehsud: Congratulations to you, were they our men?

Maulvi Sahib: Yes they were ours.

Baitullah Mehsud: Who were they?

Maulvi Sahib: There was Saeed, there was Bilal from Badar and Ikramullah.

Baitullah Mehsud: The three of them did it?

Maulvi Sahib: Ikramullah and Bilal did it.

Baitullah Mehsud: Then congratulations.

But despite repeated demands by the newsmen attending the press conference, neither the original tape was provided nor was it proven that the recorded voice was that of Baitullah. On 29 December 2007, a day after Brig Cheema's press conference, PPP spokesman Farhatullah Babar refuted the Musharraf regime's claim. He told newsmen that after the 28 October 2007 suicide attack in Karachi, Benazir had received a message from Baitullah: "Identify your enemy, I am not your foe, I have nothing to do with you or against you or with the assassination attempt on you on 18 October". The top PPP leadership trusted the message, Babar said, adding that the message was conveyed by Baitullah Mehsud through two different reliable emissaries. He said Mehsud had conveyed to Benazir that his activities were limited to South Waziristan and were of a defensive nature. "I neither have the resources to fight outside Waziristan nor I have any plans to target you" Baitullah said.

A day after the assassination attempt during her welcome procession, Bhutto had stated during a press conference in Karachi that people like Baitullah Mehsud were mere pawns and what worried her was the threat from within the Musharraf regime. On his part, Baitullah too was quick to issue denials. His spokesman, Maulvi Omar, said on 29 December, a day after the Interior Ministry spokesman's press conference: "Why on earth would we kill Benazir Bhutto? We had no enmity with her and more importantly, she had done no wrong to us... By blaming us for the murder of Benazir Bhutto, Musharraf is attempting to portray the tribal areas as centers of terrorists so as to earn dollars from his Western masters. We are equally grieved by the tragic death of Benazir Bhutto and extend our sympathies to her family as well as the Pakistan People's Party workers...."

Maulvi Omar said that Commander Baitullah Mehsud, after learning about the allegations against him and sensing gravity of those charges, had convened an emergency meeting of the *Tehrik-e-Taliban Pakistan's Shura* (council) at a secret location somewhere between South and North Waziristan. "Addressing the participants, he made it clear that harming a woman was against the teachings of Islam and *Shariah* as well as the centuries-old rich traditions of the Pakhtun tribal people. Commander Baitullah accused the Pakistani intelligence agencies for the murder of Benazir Bhutto and said the modus operandi and precision of the Rawalpindi strike clearly indicated that the grisly murder, carried out by using a skilled sniper first, to be followed by a suicide bomber, was committed by some highly trained professional hands".

But the Musharraf administration was adamant to prove that the assassination was masterminded by none other than Baitullah Mehsud. Reacting to Baitullah's statement, the Interior Ministry spokesman reiterated on 30 December 2007 that the TTP chief had threatened to kill Benazir Bhutto upon her return in October 2007, and was also behind the first attempt on her life in Karachi the same month which killed over 140 and wounded 500. Brig. Cheema quoted Baitullah as having threatened on 6 October 2007 to launch suicide attacks against Benazir Bhutto, saying his bombers were waiting in the wings to welcome her when she would return. My men will welcome Bhutto upon her return. We don't accept Musharraf and Benazir because they only protect the Americans and see things through US glasses. They are only acceptable if they wear the Pakistani glasses", Cheema had quoted Baitullah as having stated.

On 31 December, Baitullah strongly reacted to Cheema's accusations and rejected any type of involvement in the 18 October suicide attack, saying he had neither issued any such statement nor could he think of ordering an attack that would kill innocent civilians in such a large number. Two months later, on 1 March 2008, Baitullah was declared a proclaimed offender with an arrest warrant issued for him by an anti-terrorist court in the garrison town of Rawalpindi. The haste with which the Musharraf regime proceeded against Baitullah to establish him as Bhutto's killer, and that too without any solid evidence, gave an impression as if he was being made a scapegoat in the hush-up of one of the most high-profile murder cases in the recent history of South Asia.

In the shadowy world of the numerous jehadi organisations, rebel elements of the Pakistani military and intelligence establishment and rival politicians who used to hate Benazir, Baitullah Mehsud had thus been registered more clearly in the public eye. He was a Pashtun from the Broomikhel branch of the Shabikhel sub-tribe of Mehsuds. Son of the late Muhammad Haroon, Baitullah was born in 1974 in Bannu, an NWFP district at the gateway to Waziristan. His ancestral village of Shaga is located in South Waziristan, one of the seven tribal agencies in the ethnic Pashtun belt straddling the Pakistani border with Afghanistan. While geographically, the whole of Waziristan is a single unit, it was divided into two separate agencies – North Waziristan Agency and South Waziristan Agency – mainly for administrative convenience.

This apparently inhospitable terrain with high and difficult hills and deep and rugged defiles is home to over 700,000 tribal people, of which the Mehsud tribe makes up around 60 percent of the population, followed by the rival Wazir tribe which comprises approximately 35 percent. Islamic extremists, both homegrown and foreign, have long been present in the Waziristan tribal region, primarily due to the past acquiescence and support of the Pakistani military establishment and the American governments, which used to support the *mujahideen* to fight against the Soviet occupation forces in Afghanistan in the 1980s. Since the Pakistani tribal areas are the natural geo-strategic gateway to Afghanistan, the South Waziristan agency was a particularly important supply route for the *mujahideen*, helped by the fact that the same tribe lives on both sides of the Pak-Afghan border.

The first non-Malik tribal chief

According to a 2008 research paper on Baitullah Mehsud, published by the Long War Journal, since the tribal pattern in the FATA is radically different from the settled districts in the NWFP, the tribal style of living is dissimilar as much as they are governed by the local customs and traditions, observed by their forefathers through centuries. "Despite the fact that there is a federal government representative in each tribal agency, the real local governing power comes from the tribal leaders. The tribal Malik is the chief of a tribe with manifold responsibilities – he is a spokesman, guardian of tribal interests, and head of the tribal elders who enjoys immense powers of the jirga (the council of elders). The Malik has considerable administrative and political influence within his tribal jurisdiction and with the provincial and federal governments".

According to the Long War Journal, prior to Baitullah Mehsud's rise to power in South Waziristan, it was unheard of for someone other than a Malik to become a leader of such prominence in a tribal area. "The FATA tribesmen, though diverse in many ways, share some common defining characteristics: they fiercely value their independence to the point of obsession; all foreign elements are by default considered suspicious (including Pakistani forces); and they would rather fight to the bitter end than lay down their arms in combat zones. Yet, at the same time, as history shows, they are prone to compromises if there are tangible dividends available that do not impact upon their traditional lifestyle. From the outside, the Pashtun man is a delightfully confusing mix of contradictions. He can be a life long friend and a deadly enemy, a paradox of honesty and a shameless cheat, a jovial person who would watch Pashto movies, while taking a break to say his prayers".

"After the fall of the Taliban regime in Afghanistan in late 2001, thousands of the Pakistani, Afghan, and foreign militants fleeing from the US-led Allied forces gathered in Waziristan due to the naturally porous borders. The largest number of them chose South Waziristan as their new destination from where they could keep waging their battle against the US-led Allied Forces in the neighbouring Afghanistan. And their most prominent militant commander today is none other than Baitullah Mehsud who currently leads his tribe against the foreign invaders in accordance with the Pashtun traditions. Therefore, his enemies include not only the United States and the other NATO Allies in the ongoing war on terror, but the Pakistan Army as well", the Long War Journal report added.

The rise and rise of Baitullah

Educated till the age of 12 in a *deeni madrassa*, Commander Baitullah Mehsud was barely literate. According to his close associates, as a young *madrassa* student, he was greatly inspired by the Taliban ideology of Mullah Omar and frequently went to Afghanistan as a volunteer to join in the Taliban drive for enforcement of the Islamic *Shariah* there. By the time of his sudden death, Baitullah had grown from strength to strength to emerge as a powerful Taliban commander in his own right, diligently pursuing Mullah Omar's jehadi agenda on the Pakistani side of the Afghan border. He pledged himself to Mullah Omar in March 2005 in the presence of five key Taliban commanders and used to be a staunch follower of the fugitive Taliban *ameer*. Baitullah used to shun the media and refused to be photographed, just like Mullah Omar. Like Omar's Taliban militia, the private army of Baitullah too had hundreds of foreign fighters, mostly Uzbeks, who used to impose *Shariah* in the Pakistani tribal areas with a view to prevent "vice" and promotes "virtue".

Baitullah Mehsud also used local clerics and illegal FM radio channels to enforce his writ in Waziristan. Like Mullah Omar, his followers also enforced an extreme form of Islamic Laws in his territory. Women were made to observe a strict form of *purdah* and men were forbidden to shave their beards. Watching movies and playing music were declared to be the law of the land. Like the Afghan Taliban, Baitullah was also notorious for having ordered the murder of several adulterers by stoning. There are few Pakistani courts in the tribal region and the people of Waziristan seldom used them when Baitullah was alive. They used to approach him to settle their disputes and differences. Interestingly, he had a signature and grisly method of dealing with people he deemed disloyal. He first used to send the offender 1,000 rupees, a reel of thread, a needle, and a note instructing the person to have a *kafan* (burial shroud) made within 24 hours. When the time was up, the person was killed.

The Pakistani authorities accused Baitullah Mehsud of receiving money from *Al-Qaeda* and the Taliban to run the affairs of his parallel state in South Waziristan. His name hit international media headlines due to his role in spearheading, with the help of his suicide bombers, a bloody insurgency across Pakistan against the security forces, which are hunting fugitive *Al-Qaeda* and Taliban militants in the tribal areas. However, many in Pakistani intelligence establishment believe it was the peacemaking policies of the Musharraf regime that actually led to the rise of Baitullah Mehsud as a powerful Taliban leader to reckon with. For several years, there had been a consistent pattern of negotiations going on between Baitullah and the Pakistan authorities: there was a military operation, then negotiations, followed by a cease-fire. Then the cease-fire was violated by the TTP men and the intervening period was ostensibly used by the private army of Baitullah Mehsud to strengthen his position militarily.

To tell the truth, Baitullah was the same person with whom the Pakistan Army had signed a peace agreement in February 2005 despite the fact that he had been a wanted terrorist even at that time. But the pressure to negotiate with Baitullah instead of proceeding against him came from the then provincial government of the NWFP, a coalition of right-wing religious parties (*Muttahida Majlis-e-Amal* or MMA), which had a soft corner for the Taliban and was opposed to the presence of the US troops in Afghanistan. An embattled Musharraf, whose rule was being challenged by the opposition parties at that time, both as president and the army chief, agreed to hold peace talks with the Pakistani Taliban fighters in Waziristan and signed a peace agreement with them in exchange for support of the MMA legislators in the Parliament to pass the controversial 17th Amendment to the Constitution of Pakistan that eventually allowed him to continue as a president in military uniform for the next three years.

On 7 February 2005, about 1000 people, including the locals and the government and the military officials, including then Corps Commander Peshawar Lt Gen Safdar Hussain, attended the signing ceremony of the peace deal with Baitullah Mehsud near the Sararogha Fort some 80 kilometers from the Wana in South Waziristan. Speaking on the occasion, Baitullah said the peace agreement was in the interest of the tribal regions as well as in the interest of the government of Pakistan, since hostile forces like India and the Russian-backed former Northern Alliance fighters were benefiting from the lack of unity between the government and the tribesmen.

Declared a soldier of peace by the Army

The signing ceremony ended with the Corps Commander declaring Baitullah "a soldier of peace" and the militants raising slogans of *Allah-o-Akbar* (God is great) and *Death to America*. As part of the Sararogha peace agreement, Baitullah had pledged not to provide any assistance to *Al-Qaeda* and Taliban militants and not to launch attacks against Pakistani security forces. He also gave his word to the military authorities that his Mehsud tribe would not protect Abdullah Mehsud, a former Guantanamo Bay inmate and an anti-US Pakistani Taliban commander, wanted by the Pakistani authorities.

Noor Alam alias Abdullah Mehsud, a former Guantanamo Bay inmate who had become a most wanted jehadi commander resisting the Pakistani security forces in the South Waziristan region following his release from the US-run detention centre at Cuba, eventually blew himself up with a hand grenade in the wee hours of 24 July 2007 after the Pakistani security forces closed in on his Zhob hideout in Baluchistan and asked him to surrender. Abdullah Mehsud, 32, was one of seven Guantanamo detainees publicly identified by US Defence Department as having returned to the fight against the US-led Allied Forces in Afghanistan following their release. The death of Abdullah Mehsud, who was wanted for the abduction of two Chinese engineers working in Pakistan in 2004, was a crucial element in catapulting Baitullah Mehsud to the top leadership slot in South Waziristan and its vicinity.

As the deal between the military and the militants gave Baitullah a free hand to recruit and motivate more youngsters, the strength of his private army in South Waziristan reportedly went up from around 1000 to about 20,000 within weeks, enabling him to virtually establish an independent zone South Waziristan region. Within a year of the so-called peace agreement, Baitullah's private army gunned down over 120 pro-government tribal leaders of his area on charges of spying for the American and Pakistani agencies. But his biggest success came on 30 August 2007 when his private army captured 200 soldiers of the Pakistan Army in South Waziristan. Demanding the withdrawal of the security forces and the release of his comrades in exchange for freeing the soldiers, Baitullah had threatened to put the arrested soldiers on trial for violating the peace agreement the army had signed with him in February 2005 by launching a military operation in his area.

"Just as the government side has put my people on trial and sentenced them to imprisonments, I will put the Pakistani army soldiers on trial. I have my own courts which will try the soldiers for violating the peace pact," Baitullah Mehsud was quoted as saying on 5 September 2007 by his spokesman. As three abducted soldiers were beheaded in the next three days, Musharraf ordered the release of 25 hardcore Taliban militants who were already under trial on terrorism charges. The remaining *khaki* hostages were released in the first week of November 2007.

By this time, Musharraf had invoked a state of emergency in the country and sacked almost 50 judges of the superior courts including the Chief Justice of the Supreme Court. Interestingly, Musharraf's emergency charge sheet accused the superior judiciary of having released several hard core Islamic extremists and terrorists and suicide bombers, who had been arrested and were being interrogated by the agencies. "Militants across the country were, thus, encouraged while the law enforcement agencies were subdued," Musharraf said in his proclamation order, under which he justified a fresh military action

hons

in South Waziristan. Also, it may be recalled that the 25 Baitullah associates released by the Musharraf regime were trained suicide bombers and one of them was even under indictment at an anti-terrorist court for participating in a suicide bombing. However, the fact remains that it was actually the refusal of the army to release Baitullah's five associates which prompted a series of suicide attacks against the Pakistani security forces, compelling the Musharraf regime to hot back in South Waziristan.

The birth of the TTP

Baitullah Mehsud's military might further multiplied on 12 December 2007 when a council of 40 senior militant leaders commanding a pooled force of 40,000 gathered in Peshawar and decided to come together under a single banner, the *Tehrik-e-Taliban Pakistan (TTP)*. Baitullah was appointed the TTP *ameer*, Maulana Hafiz Gul Bahadur of North Waziristan the senior *naib ameer* (senior vice chief) and Maulana Faqir Muhammad of the Bajaur Agency was appointed the third in command.

The council meeting not only had representation from all seven tribal agencies of FATA, but also from the settled districts of NWFP, including Swat, Bannu, Tank, Lakki Marwat, Dera Ismail Khan, Kohistan, Buner and Malakand. A subsequent statement by Baitullah's spokesman Maulvi Omar on 13 December 2007 said the sole objective behind the launching of the TTP is to unite the Pakistani Taliban and set-up a centralised organisation against the NATO forces in Afghanistan, besides waging a defensive jehad against the security forces. The consolidation of the disparate "local Taliban" movement was seen as a logical step in the Pakistani Taliban's insurgency drive in northwestern Pakistan. Before that, the Pakistani Taliban, while allied with *Al-Qaeda* and the Afghan Taliban, had been operating as local groups.

However, the creation of a unified Taliban movement on the Pakistani side of Pak-Afghan border enhanced their coordination to carry out both military and political operations with their jehadi companions coming from Afghanistan. The launching of the TTP showed Baitullah's ability to organize and command large numbers of Islamic fighters, fend off the Pakistani military in South Waziristan, take the fight to the neighboring agencies and districts of the Pak-Afghan border areas, and organize a nationwide suicide bombing campaign against Pakistani security forces.

In his first ever television interview conducted by an *Al-Jazeera* correspondent, Ahmed Zaidan, at an unknown location and aired on 28 January 2008, Baitullah said: "The main objective of the coalition of militants is waging a defensive jehad. The Pakistan army is deploying its soldiers under orders from George Bush. The army is bombarding our houses and fighting with us. Therefore we have formed this coalition to guarantee the safety of civilians and this war which the army launched in the tribal areas is an American war. We no more feel sad about the Pakistani soldiers' deaths. They are actually implementing the orders of the West and the United States and they are destroying our houses. And I do pray that Allah will guide them back to the right path because they are Muslims and this is an Islamic country. But when the army soldiers come to this area to kill us, we will definitely be killing them."

During the 25-minute interview, Baitullah declared: "Our main aim is to finish Britain and United States and to crush the pride of the non-Muslims. We pray to God to give us the ability to destroy the White House, New York and London. And we have trust in God. Very soon, we will be witnessing jehad's miracles". While taking on Musharraf, Baitullah said: "Musharraf is no more than a slave to Bush and the non-believers. Musharraf is no more than a slave to his masters. He started attacking mosques, killing women, children, and the elderly inside the mosques. What was pushing him to do all this was his will to satisfy Bush. But now we are saying Musharraf has committed crimes against Muslims and he has destroyed mosques and our response will be much harder than his actions. We will be teaching him a lesson which history will write in gold and God willing, Musharraf will be in severe pain. And all those who assisted him will also be in pain".

Almost three years after the signing of the Sararogha peace agreement with the Pakistani military authorities, Baitullah's private army captured the British-era Sararogha Fort [on 16 January 2008]. The historic Fort, which was being manned by the paramilitary Frontier Corps, was demolished by Baitullah's men and the Pakistani soldiers present inside were either killed or taken prisoner. Skirmishes continued for next few weeks till the February 2008 general elections. However, soon after taking oath as Prime Minister, Syed Yousaf Raza Gilani declared that his government was ready to talk to all those people who give up arms and are ready to embrace peace. "Let me make it clear that our government will prefer negotiating with the militants as a strategy to counter the rising terrorism and extremism and to ensure peace and stability", he had said.

Subsequent peace talks led to another truce on 15 May 2008 between the military and the Taliban militants led by Baitullah. According to the proposed draft of the peace pact, in return for withdrawal of army troops from three strategic positions in the border area under Baitullah Mehsud's sway, the *Tehrik-e-Taliban Pakistan* would refrain from resorting to violence and provocative acts. The withdrawal of the Pakistani troops from the troubled tribal areas, a key demand of the militants, was accepted by the military which ultimately paved the way for the two sides to exchange prisoners – 24 suspected militants and 12 security personnel – on 15 May 2008.

The 15-point proposed draft of the peace accord contained clauses under which the Mehsud tribe gave an undertaking that the government functionaries and the security forces would not be targeted at all; their equipment and property would not be damaged; no military or government functionary would be kidnapped; all roads would be opened to the Frontier Corps in accordance with the old practice and there would be no restriction on their movement. Mehsud tribes were also required to ensure that no terrorist activity takes place anywhere in Pakistan, including the tribal regions.

Baitullah Mehsud consequently directed his TTP militants to stop violence in the tribal areas of South Waziristan to bring peace to the region. A pamphlet titled "*Eilan-e- Umoomi*" (general announcement) issued to the activists of the *Tehrik-e-Taliban*, said: "Directives are hereby issued to all the workers of the *Tehrik* from their *ameer* Baitullah Mehsud that a strict ban has been imposed on provocative activities in Waziristan for the sake of peace. Obeying this order is compulsory for all his followers and its violators would be simply hanged upside down and punished publicly".

'Yes, I am helping the Taliban in jehad against US'

As the two sides were contemplating to sign the peace deal, Baitullah addressed a press conference on 24 May 2008, admitting that he has been sending fighters to battle the US troops in Afghanistan. Addressing reporters invited to a hideout in the mountainous South Waziristan region, Baitullah Mehsud said the holy war would continue until the US-led forces are made to withdraw from Afghanistan. "Yes, we are helping the Taliban in the jehad against United States of America," Baitullah said, holding an AK-47 as he sat in a disused school building in Kotkai, a Waziristan village. "We send our people to fight against the Americans and God willing; we will evict them from Afghanistan the same way the Soviet forces were driven out from there". Mehsud denied that he was sheltering Osama, but said he would like to meet him. "If Osama needs protection in our areas, we will feel proud to shelter him," he responded to a query.

Baitullah Mehsud's admission of sending Taliban fighters to Afghanistan led to enormous American pressure on Pakistan government to scrap the peace deal. A NATO spokesman went to the extent of threatening retaliatory strikes if the Taliban militants kept entering Afghanistan from Pakistan to attack its forces in Afghanistan. This compelled the Pakistani military authorities not to withdraw troops from the tribal area under Baitullah's control, as had been agreed in the proposed peace deal. Baitullah, therefore, announced the suspension of further talks with the federal government, saying the American pressure had forced the authorities not to honour the peace accord. On 27 June 2008, Baitullah declared: "If the security forces' operations continue, people will see Sindh and Punjab turn into furnace."

"Let me make it clear that regardless of the situation in the tribal areas, the holy war against Americans in Afghanistan would continue and the Taliban militants would resort to waging a jehad against the Pakistan Army as well if it continued helping the Americans launch attacks inside tribal areas. Allah on 480 occasions in the Holy Koran extols Muslims to wage jehad and we only fulfil the orders of God. Only jehad can bring peace to the world and we will continue our jehad until the foreign troops are thrown out of Afghanistan. Then we will attack them in America and Britain until they either accept Islam or agree to pay *jizya* (a form of tax which the non-Muslims living in an Islamic state used to pay in the past)," Baitullah Mehsud concluded.

However, on 1 December 2008, in the wake of the 26/11 Mumbai terror attacks and the ensuing war of words between India and Pakistan, a spokesman of the Pakistan Army termed Baitullah Mehsud as a "patriotic" Pakistani. At a news briefing in Islamabad, the spokesman said all the main militant groups fighting in the Federally Administered Tribal Areas (FATA) of Pakistan have contacted the government after the Mumbai bombings and have offered a ceasefire if the Pakistan Army also stops its operations in the tribal belt. "We have no big issues with the Pakistani militants in FATA. We have only a few misunderstandings with Baitullah Mehsud which could be removed through dialogue", the Army spokesman added.

'Ready to fight against India under Pakistan Army's command'

On 23 December 2008, Baitullah Mehsud warned the Indian authorities that he has provided suicide jackets as well as explosives-laden vehicles to hundreds of his would-be bombers who have been deployed on the Indo-Pak border alongside the country's armed forces to counter a possible aggression by the enemy forces. Talking to English daily *The News* on phone from an undisclosed location, Baitullah even declared that the Taliban were ready to fight under the command of the Pakistan Army. "Thousands of our well-armed militants as well as suicide bombers are ready to fight alongside the army if a war is imposed on Pakistan. Our *mujahideen* would be in the vanguard if fighting broke out with India. Our fighters will fall on the enemy like thunder," he declared.

With the departure of Bush and Obama becoming the new American President, the US State Department announced on 26 March 2009 a $5 million head money for information leading to Baitullah. He subsequently became the only Pakistani fugitive with a head-money separately announced by the Pakistan government and

American administration. The $5 million FBI head money announced by the FBI for Baitullah placed him just below Mullah Omar in terms of his importance to the Taliban movement in Afghanistan and Pakistan. The reward for Mullah Omar is $10 million and that for Osama bin Laden and Dr Ayman Al Zawahiri $25 million each. International media reports said that the US move was largely aimed at dissuading Baitullah's 25000-plus private army to join hands with the Taliban militia of Afghanistan headed by Mullah Omar who intended to launch a major spring offensive against the Afghanistan-based NATO forces.

The Obama administration's efforts to hunt down Baitullah Mehsud and other important Taliban commanders were believed to be motivated by US intelligence reports that the Taliban leaders have chalked out a three-pronged strategy for the spring offensive – cutting off the NATO supply lines running from Pakistan to Afghanistan, recruiting fresh volunteers and the creation of a strategic corridor running from Pakistan all the way to the Afghan capital Kabul. The US bounty was announced a few weeks after the Taliban militants active in North and South Waziristan decided to join hands as per the advice of Mullah Omar to stop attacking the Pakistani security forces and to join hands to fight out the NATO forces in Afghanistan. They had subsequently formed in February 2009 a new alliance – *Shura Ittehadul Mujahideen* (Council for Unity of Holy Warriors) – in the twin tribal agencies after burying the hatchet.

The alliance leadership declared the *ameer* of the Afghan Taliban Mullah Omar as their supreme leader and *Al-Qaeda* chief Osama bin Laden as their role model. According to an announcement by the Pakistani Taliban, the new alliance would comprise the groups led by central chief of the *Tehrik-e-Taliban Pakistan*, Baitullah Mehsud and two pro-government key commanders – Maulvi Nazir from South Waziristan and Hafiz Gul Bahadur from North Waziristan. The three met at an undisclosed location and decided to resolve their differences to foil the external forces designs to divide the multiple Taliban groups based in Pakistan. "As Jews, Christians and Hindu infidels stand united against the Muslims under the leadership of the US, the *Mujahideen* have set aside internal differences and joined hands, the Taliban announcement said and added: "The alliance has been directed by Mullah Omar to devise a new strategy to counter the occupation forces in Afghanistan".

'My fighters will target the White House'

On 1 April 2009, hardly four days after the US State Department had announced the bounty for Baitullah; the fugitive TTP chief broke his silence and claimed responsibility for a series of terrorist attacks inside Pakistan besides threatening that his militants would soon attack the Americans in their own country to teach them a lesson by targeting the White House. On 4 April 2009, he again claimed responsibility for a 3 April attack on a US immigration center in New York in which 14 people were killed. "I accept responsibility. They were my men. I gave them orders in reaction to American drone attacks", Mehsud told Reuters by phone. But an FBI spokesman, refuted Baitullah's claim, saying: "Based on the evidence, we can firmly discount his claim since the shooter was an abnormal Vietnamese who eventually committed suicide".

However, there was a consensus in the American and the Pakistan intelligence circles that Baitullah could be using his rhetoric in an attempt to steer the more nationalist jehadis in Pakistan and Afghanistan towards his transnational agenda and that he should be hunted down. Yet, Mark Hosenball of the *NEWSWEEK* magazine claimed in his investigative story on 5 April 2009 titled "Mehsud's pals in high places" that Baitullah has been dodging death because he has friends in high places. "He has a curious gift for escape. On several occasions over the past couple of years, security forces in Pakistan launched operations to kill or capture him, and each time he vanished without incident... Officials in both Washington and Islamabad suspect that Mehsud has contacts inside the ISI (Inter Services Intelligence), Pakistan's inscrutable and sprawling agency. Mehsud's contacts, the theory goes, are tipping him off before the Pakistani security forces can pounce".

A few days later, on 8 April 2009, Richard Holbrooke, the US special envoy for Afghanistan and Pakistan, described Baitullah Mehsud as a "terrible man" and a great danger to Pakistan and Afghanistan. Addressing a joint press conference with Admiral Mike Mullen, the chairman of US Joint Chiefs of Staff, Holbrook said:

"His (Baitullah's) threats against the US are not backed up but he is bad as any bad actor can be".

Pak-US resolve to hunt down Baitullah

These remarks were followed by a reported understanding between Islamabad and Washington to stage "coordinated military operations" in South Waziristan to kill Baitullah. On the other hand, Baitullah retaliated and stepped up his suicide bomb attacks all over Pakistan, especially targeting the Punjab province. In a deadly attack on 27 May 2009, following heavy exchange of fire between the TTP terrorists and the Pakistani security forces, a human bomb riding a wagon ripped through the provincial ISI headquarters in Lahore, killing 35 people and injuring over 300. A few days later, on 9 June 2009, yet another suicide bomber riding an explosive-laden truck struck Peshawar's five-star Pearl Continental Hotel, adjoining the residence of the corps commander Peshawar, and that too following an exchange of heavy fire between the attackers and the security personnel.

The Pakistan government, therefore, announced on 15 June 2009 the launching of a decisive military offensive against Baitullah by declaring him Pakistan's public enemy number one. Officially announcing the operation, Governor of the NWFP Owais Ghani described Baitullah Mehsud as "the root cause of all evils", adding that his nexus with *Al-Qaeda* has brought enormous death and destruction to Pakistan. The very next day, the Pakistani military spokesman said Baitullah and his network of fighters and suicide bombers have wreaked havoc on Pakistan, while his tribal areas have served as a major safe haven for *Al-Qaeda*, Islamic Movement of Uzbekistan, and a host of Punjabi and Kashmiri terror groups. He announced that the Pakistani forces were about to launch a massive operation against him in South Waziristan.

"The Army has received requisite orders from the government and necessary steps are being taken by the military to launch the Operation *Rah-e-Nijat* (the way of salvation)," Major General Athar Abbas said in Islamabad on 16 June 2009. The same day, the Pakistani Army Chief General Ashfaq Pervez Kayani said that the head of the Taliban in Pakistan must be eliminated. "Baitullah

Mehsud has a hand in virtually every major terrorist attack in Pakistan and he is not fighting for Islam", he said. It was, perhaps, the first significant indication from the army leadership that the military establishment – long derided for avoiding taking the chief of Pakistani Taliban head-on – had had enough.

However, the military operation suffered an early set back with the 23 June 2009 assassination of Qari Zainuddin Mehsud, another Pakistani Taliban commander and the arch rival of Baitullah. Zainuddin was poised to join the Pakistan army's Waziristan fight against the Taliban by leading his own militia to take down Baitullah. Although Zainuddin too had a ruthless past, he had already parted ways with Baitullah and accused him for a string of suicide bomb attacks that killed thousands of innocent Pakistanis. Zainuddin was seen by the Pakistani military authorities as a key to a successful army offensive in South Waziristan given the fact that like Baitullah, he too was a native Mehsud and had been challenging Baitullah's leadership to stage a coup against him. It was for the first time in recent years that the Pakistani military authorities had succeeded in creating divisions within the Mehsud tribe, after which the Operation *Rah-e-Nijat* was launched in South Waziristan.

Zainuddin's murder was followed by an Asia Times Online (AToL) news report, titled "Pakistan targets its most wanted man", saying Baitullah was armed and financed by Arab militants who fled to the Pakistani tribal areas after the US-led forces invaded Afghanistan. "Crucially, he hooked up with the fugitive chief of the Islamic Movement of Uzbekistan, Qari Tahir Yuldashev, who had a profound influence on Baitullah Mehsud, inculcating in him anti-state ideology and hard line training. Baitullah was placed in charge of over 2,500 Uzbek fighters who formed the backbone of a militia that soon established a reign of terror in the area. Having been given this start, the shrewd Baitullah emerged as one of the most important warlord in the Pakistani tribal areas, giving him a status almost at par with Taliban leader Mullah Omar".

The Asia Times report added that among the stated objectives of Baitullah group are resistance against the Pakistani army, enforcement of *Shariah* law and jehad against foreign forces in Afghanistan. "Baitullah Mehsud opened his arms to the scattered leadership of *Al-*

Qaeda, the Punjabi fighters and any Islamic militant wanted by the Pakistani security agencies. He drove out tribal elders from his area and then used his Mehsud clan members for robberies, kidnappings and acts of terrorism from his backyard to the port city of Karachi. And it is the epicenter of this militant network that the Pakistani security forces now want to destroy and from the perspective of the United States, the *Al-Qaeda* element that is a part of it".

Baitullah Killed by a US drone

On 27 June 2009, the Pakistan government announced revising the head money for Baitullah and increased the amount up to a whopping 50 million rupees. Thereafter, battle lines were clearly drawn between the military and the militants led by the most wanted TTP chief. A marked man by the American and the Pakistan security forces, his mountainous demesne in South Waziristan thus became under intense missile attacks by the Pakistani fighter planes and the US drones, in a desperate bid to hunt him down and curb the tsunami of terrorism engulfing Pakistan. Almost a month later, in the wee hours of 5 August 2009, the ruthless, unforgiving and vindictive Baitullah Mehsud, a friend-turned-foe of the Pakistani military establishment, was finally killed in an American drone strike in the Zangarha area of South Waziristan along with his wife and bodyguards.

Although the authorities failed to retrieve his dead body, the government circles insisted that the TTP chief was targeted by a drone while he was getting a leg massage on the roof of his father-in-law's house where he had gone to see his second wife. Mehsud died on the spot, with his torso totally damaged except for his head. Pakistani Interior Minister Rehman Malik also claimed on 8 August 2009 that Baitullah had been killed in the 5 August 2009 drone strike and laid to rest in the village of Narghasi the same day along with his wife and father-in-law.

According to an 8 August 2009 *CNN* report, on the night of the drone attack, US surveillance in Pakistan spied a man on the roof of Baitullah Mehsud's father-in-law, Ikramuddin's residence in South Waziristan. The description was of a short, stocky man who was following the physical description of Mehsud, *CNN* said, citing US intelligence officials. A woman was massaging the man's leg and the Central Intelligence Agency knew Mehsud had diabetes, experienced pain in his legs, and often sought relief in that way, the report said. Officials already had authorisation from President Obama to strike Mehsud if they thought they had a clear shot. "That's when the CIA decided to move in," the *CNN* network reported.

According to a 9 August 2009 news report filed by Christina Lamb and carried by *The Sunday Times*, it might have been the desire for a son that had led to the Taliban leader's demise. The report said: "The 35-year-old had four daughters by his first wife but, in the tribal lands of Waziristan, it is only the birth of a boy that is greeted by rifle fire and jubilation. In November 2008, Mehsud took a second wife, the daughter of an influential local cleric. He was spending the night with her at her father's house in the village of Zangarha when the missiles hit. Initial reports suggested only Mehsud's wife and two of his fighters had been killed. But suspicions were raised when a large funeral was held the next day in the village of Narghasi under local tradition bodies must be buried by sunrise the following day".

The Sunday Times report further said: "It was around 1am on Wednesday and Pakistan's most wanted man had taken the risk of spending the night at the house of his father-in-law. A diabetic Baitullah had been feeling poorly in the scorching summer heat of South Waziristan and the local doctor called round to give him a glucose drip. As he lay on a couch on the roof tended by his new wife, somewhere high up in the clear starry sky a distant unmanned US plane was hovering, invisible to the naked eye. Its cameras locked in on him, a command was given thousands of miles away in the Nevada desert, and two Hellfire missiles tore into the mud-walled structure. A Pakistani intelligence officer based in the Makeen town of South Waziristan later confirmed that Mehsud was killed in the US drone attack".

While hunting down Baitullah had been a top priority of the Pakistani security forces for quite some time due to an unending spate of deadly suicide attacks unleashed by his human bombs, it is largely believed he actually became a prime target of the American drones hardly a few months before his death after he had threatened that his militants would soon attack the Americans in their own country to teach them a lesson, especially by targeting the White House. He was killed by an American predator barely four months after the FBI had declared him the most wanted *Al-Qaeda*-linked Pakistani terrorist and announced [on 26 March 2009] a five million dollars bounty.

Interestingly, a few weeks before his death, Baitullah had been described by the Pakistani media as an agent of the United States and India, wreaking havoc in Pakistan to fulfil the American aim of establishing the hegemony of India in South Asia and to facilitate the elimination of Pakistan's nuclear arsenal. Some Pakistani military officials had even complained that the Americans had failed to target Baitullah Mehsud with their drones despite them having supplied precise intelligence information about his location thrice. The reason they gave was that the TTP chief had been more focused against the Pakistani security forces in his militancy rather than fully directing his militants against the Allied Forces in Afghanistan.

Hence, going by the Pakistani military establishment's thesis, the Americans initially were not too keen to take on Baitullah Mehsud. However, the situation changed after the launching of the military operation in the Swat district of the NWFP when it became obvious to the American policy-makers that the mighty Pakistani establishment was now serious to thwart the increasing *Talibanisation* of Pakistan. They had perhaps also realised that Baitullah had developed strong ties with the fugitive Taliban *ameer* Mullah Omar and providing sanctuaries to his fighters on the Pakistani side of the Pak-Afghan border. The US reaction to Baitullah's presumed death was a testimony to the fact that the Americans were quite serious to hunt him down and hence chasing him vigilantly.

Commenting on Baitullah's death, the White House spokesman Robert Gibbs described him as a murderous thug, followed by US President Barack Obama's declaration on 20 August 2009: "We in fact took out Baitullah Mehsud. His death was made possible due to an intensive US operation and sustained pressure on the Taliban and *Al-Qaeda* miscreants along the restive Pak-Afghan border. You've got the Pakistan Army for the first time fighting in a very aggressive way and that's how we took out Mehsud, the top Taliban leader in Pakistan who was also one of Osama bin Laden's key allies," Obama told a radio talk show host in a live broadcast from the White House.

Hakeemullah Mehsud, the new TTP *ameer*

On 19 August 2009, Maulana Faqeer Mohammad, a close aide of Baitullah, claimed having taken over Mehsud's position as the acting chief of the TTP. (Faqeer was killed by the Pakistan Army six months later in the Pindyali Yehsil areas of the Mohmand Agency on 5 March 2010). Faqeer spoke to the *BBC* over the telephone, strongly denying reports about his commander's death, and adding that Baitullah is ill and underground for that reason. On 22 August 2009, the Pakistani Taliban appointed their new chief, selecting a top commander considered quite close to Baitullah. The announcement came from none other than Maulvi Faqeer Mohammad, who told the *Associated Press* that a 42-member Taliban council, or *shura*, appointed a new head because Baitullah Mehsud was ill. "I do confirm that a *shura* has elected Hakeemullah Mehsud as the new chief of the Pakistani Taliban, and it was a unanimous decision", he added.

Hakeemullah used to command the TTP militants in Orakzai, Khyber and Kurram Agencies of the Federally Administered Tribal Areas. While he has 8,000 warriors under his command, Baitullah had 30,000. The 42-member *shura* met in Orakzai agency, the stronghold of Hakeemullah, indicating that he was able to establish himself as the most powerful commander with an outreach matched by no one else within the TTP. He is reported to have dominance in three tribal agencies of the Federally Administered Tribal Areas of Pakistan, Orakzai, Kurram and Khyber, somewhat akin to what Baitullah had. Subsequent media reports said the selections of 28-year-old Hakeemullah could herald an increase in terrorist attacks as the group tries to prove it is still intact and operational.

On 22 August 2009, the *BBC* reported the possible involvement of Baitullah Mehsud's in-laws in giving away his position to his enemies, adding that the Pakistani Taliban had arrested Baitullah's father-in-law Maulana Ikramuddin, his son Ziauddin, brother Saadullah and a nephew for their role in helping the Americans track him down. On 23 August 2009, *Daily Times* reported that a paid agent, possibly a relative of Baitullah, had helped signal his whereabouts to the Central Intelligence Agency (CIA), thereby taking out Baitullah. While quoting official sources, the newspaper said agents pin-pointed the TTP chief's position and the CIA took him out through a drone attack.

"Baitullah Mehsud was simply not spotted through the powerful lens fixed on the drone. Rather the complete set of procedures laid down for such missions was followed. A belt wrapped above an agent's waist carries two electronic chips. The agent is supposed to push the first chip when he finds himself close to the target to intimate the satellite, which transfers the data to the control-room. The second chip is pushed only when the target is present and the agent has moved to a safer place. That is what when the drone is positioned and Hellfire missiles are fired", the report explained.

Another English daily *Dawn* reported on 23 August 2009 that Baitullah's in-laws are being tried on charge of spying for the 'enemies' and ditching Baitullah. The report said that Saadullah, the brother of Maulana Ikramuddin, a paramedic who lived nearby, had been called to provide medical treatment for Mehsud's stomach problem on 5 August 2009 when he was hit by a US drone. The missile targeted the house shortly after Saadullah had left, arousing the Taliban's suspicion that he had passed on information with the consent of Ikramullah. A few hours after these reports were published, Pakistani Interior Minister Rehman Malik said [on 23 August 2009] that the TTP militants have killed Baitullah's father-in-law and some other relatives who had been arrested a few days ago on spying charges.

On 25 August 2009, 20 days after the 5 August 2009 American drone strike, Hakeemullah Mehsud finally conceded to the *BBC* in a telephonic interview that Baitullah Mehsud had died a couple of days ago since he could not succumb to his injuries that he had suffered in the drone hit. He said Baitullah died only on 23 August 2009 after remaining in coma for 18 days.

On 30 September 2009, a brief video showing the dead body of Baitullah was released by the *BBC*. The video of less than two minutes duration showed the bodies of Mehsud and his wife moments after they were hit by missiles fired by a US drone. The video, which was shot with a mobile phone, was received by the Urdu service of the *BBC* and the clipping showed Mehsud's body lying on a plain surface and covered with a white cloth. His injuries were not visible and it showed only a few cuts on the right side of his face. The silent video featured a few people sitting near Mehsud's body. The *BBC* quoted Taliban operatives as saying that the video of Baitullah Mehsud's body was made a few hours after the attack that killed him.

Baitullah Mehsud's death came as the most serious blow the Pakistani Taliban had suffered since they first emerged on the national horizons in 2003-04. But the strategic goals of the TTP have not undergone any radical change under its new *ameer* Hakeemullah Mehsud, who is notorious for his ruthless efficiency in staging bloody terrorist attacks. According to a *Daily Times* editorial of 24 August 2009, Hakeemullah represents the typical breed of long-haired and bearded killers that one sees everywhere in the video coverage of their tribal hideouts. "He comes across as a rash strutting fighter who would rather kill than sit down and talk; and not give ground when invited to talks. Above all, he is violently sectarian and, together with Qari Hussain Mehsud, the most savage of warriors with expertise in producing suicide-bombers. The new TTP chief is infamous for his slack allegiance to any Islamic ethic. His leadership will give encouragement to the criminal aspects of the TTP from Peshawar to Karachi".

And these estimates have apparently proved true keeping in view the increase in the number of suicide attacks in the NWFP, the Punjab and Islamabad especially after Hakeemullah Mehsud assumed the TTP's command. In fact, his selection as the TTP head following Baitullah's death had alarmed those who knew him, had met him or followed his career as a militant commander. They were concerned that Hakeemullah was a far more dangerous and unpredictable man than Baitullah. However, the force behind the suicide bombings and the more spectacular attacks by groups of militants on military and police installations could be Qari Hussain, a cousin of Hakeemullah who has been given a free hand to plan and execute attacks now that Hakeemullah is the TTP boss.

TTP bounced back with a vengeance

A series of *fidayeen* attacks on important military installations across Pakistan, including the one targeting the heavily-guarded General Headquarters (GHQ) of the Army in Rawalpindi on 10

October 2009 were enough to belie claims being made by the Pakistani authorities that the TTP was breathing its last after the death of Baitullah Mehsud. These attacks showed that the TTP was bouncing back with a vengeance to establish the authority of Hakeemullah Mehsud as the new terror king of Pakistan. Hakeemullah is the same person who had taken hostage over 300 security forces personnel in South Waziristan in August 2007, compelling the Musharraf regime to release 25 hardened militants who were being tried on terrorism charges. Yet, stepping into Baitullah's shoes was not easy for Hakeemullah because of the fact that his predecessor had become a mythical personality among his followers due the importance that the US and its allies had given to him.

The rise of Hakeemullah Mehsud

Despite his comparatively young age, the battle-hardened Hakeemullah was unanimously elected the new TTP chief due to a unique combination of characteristics – his proximity with Baitullah, extraordinary military skills, personal charisma and proven leadership abilities. Hakeemullah actually shot to fame in 2007 under the name Zulfiqar Mehsud following several ruthless commando raids carried out by the TTP fighters under his command against the Pakistani security forces in South Waziristan. But his biggest success came on August 2007 when his men captured 300 soldiers of the Pakistan Army in South Waziristan. The bizarre abduction added to Hakeemullah's stature, prompting Baitullah Mehsud to reward him by elevating him as the chief operational commander for three important regions – Khyber, Kurram and Orakzai agencies. Since then, Hakeemullah's star was constantly on the rise.

Born in the Kotkai village of Sarwaki subdivision in South Waziristan Agency in 1980 as Jamshed Mehsud, Hakeemullah belongs to the Eshangai branch of Mehsud tribe and also known in the TTP circles with the name of Zulfiqar Mehsud. Incidentally Hakeemullah and his jehadi mentor both had been studying at a *Deobandi* religious seminary or *madrassa* in Hangu district of the NWFP, though Baitullah had been quite senior to him. However, Hakeemullah dropped out a few years later without graduating as a

Mullah. Later on, Hakeemullah joined hands with his fellow tribesmen to become a jehadi fighter, initially serving Baitullah as a bodyguard and then becoming his trusted driver. He soon gained fame in the Taliban circles for his expertise in combat – someone who knew a lot about weapons and machines and can drive even an armoured-plated Humvee that his men had captured during a raid on a convoy of American vehicles in the Khyber Agency.

Interestingly, Hakeemullah also nicknamed as Guddu, is often compared in the TTP circles with another Taliban commander, Nek Mohammad, who is often referred to in the FATA areas as the founder of the Pakistani Taliban movement. The TTP circles say the comparison of Nek with Hakeemullah sits well because of their striking resemblance in many ways, especially their shoulder-length hair, youthful appearance, jehadi passion, love for weapons, their shooting and driving skills as well as their extremely adventurous streaks. Hakeemullah is also known for having imposed *Shariah* in Orakzai Agency in December 2008 as well as levying *Jazia* (a tax non-Muslims population used to pay to their Muslims rulers in the past) on members of Sikh and Hindu communities living in Orakzai and Khyber agencies of the FATA. However, above all, Hakeemullah is believed to be extremely sectarian and has a violently anti-*Shia* agenda which he has been pursuing in the Khyber, Kurram and Orakzai agencies, together with his first cousin Commander Qari Hussain Mehsud.

According to Zahir Shah Sherazi, a staffer of daily *Dawn*, who had been part of a group of Pakistani television journalists that had traveled to Hakeemullah-controlled part of the Orakzai tribal agency in November 2008, it was not difficult to immediately notice in him the ambition and desire to be in the leadership role. In fact, the trip arranged by Hakeemullah's men was largely designed to introduce the 'young turk' of the Taliban movement to the media and to air his views on religion and politics and his ambition to take the movement beyond FATA to mainland Pakistan.

"It was a journey a few of us will forget. Although quite photogenic, and unlike most other militant leaders, smartly dressed, his cold looks and wry smile left little doubt that he may not think twice before killing anyone. Yet he was intelligent enough to grasp the significance and power of the media and tried to make the maximum of the presence of the television teams to express his views on issues ranging from the situation in Afghanistan, to TTP's links with Mullah Omar and his Taliban movement, to Pakistan's political scene. At the same time, Hakeemullah also wanted to present himself as a modern man, who not only had the desire to 'conquer' rest of the tribal territories, but also someone who knew a lot about guns and machines. So, while at one point he sought the cameramen's indulgence while showing off by speeding around in an armoured-plated Humvee that his men had captured during a raid on a convoy of American vehicles in the Khyber Agency, an hour later he invited the journalists to participate in a gun-shooting competition", said Shirazi.

According to Syed Shoaib Hasan, another Pakistani journalist, who works for the *BBC* and had met Hakeemullah twice in 2007 and 2008, despite his pleasant demeanour and cheeky smile, danger radiates from the man. "When we met on that autumn day in 2007, Hakeemullah took us for a drive. To demonstrate his skill with the vehicle, he drove like a man possessed, manoeuvring around razor sharp bends at impossible speeds. He finished the demonstration by braking inches short of a several hundred foot drop. While the rest of us sat in stunned silence, he just laughed chillingly and stuck the car in reverse to smoothly continue the journey".

Compared with Baitullah Mehsud, who was described as an introvert and media-shy person, Hakeemullah is known as an outgoing person and is media-savvy. Unlike Baitullah, his successor likes his smiling face being captured on television cameras. At the same time, Hakeemullah is said to be more ambitious than his predecessor and has expansionist designs unlike his mentor who largely kept his jehadi fighters to the South Waziristan region. Having lived under the shadow of Baitullah for almost five years, Hakeemullah started spreading his wings in 2008 by carrying out some deadly ambushes on the Pakistani security forces and the NATO supply trucks in Khyber Agency and looting of goods and food destined for NATO troops stationed in Afghanistan.

Hakeemullah is the person who had claimed responsibility for destroying over 600 NATO vehicles destined for Afghanistan in terrorist attacks targeting freight terminals on the outskirts of Peshawar. Like his predecessor, the new TTP chief's anti-American views, his soft corner for *Al-Qaeda* and his admiration for the fugitive Taliban *ameer* Mullah Omar are well known, keeping in view his media conversation in the past. Talking to a select group of Pakistani journalists in November 2008 in the Orakzai tribal agency, Hakeemullah had openly praised the Osama-led terrorist organisation, by saying: "We are *Al-Qaeda*'s friends since we, the Taliban and the Arab fighters both have shown our allegiance to *Ameerul Momineen* Mullah Omar of Afghanistan".

As Hakeemullah Mehsud reappeared on 7 October 2009 in South Waziristan to dispel the rumours of his death, he told a select group of journalists that an army of suicide bombers is waiting in the wings. He maintained that the TTP had become stronger, not weaker, in the post-Baitullah period and has resumed its campaign of suicide bombings across Pakistan after waiting for a while for the government to change course, stop military operations and refuse to work for the American agenda in the region.

South Waziristan military operation

It was hardly three days after his press talk that the audacious *fidayeen* attack on the General Headquarters of the Pakistan Army was launched by the TTP militants [on 10 October 2009], thus prompting the military authorities to finally launch a massive military operation in South Waziristan – Operation *Rah-e-Nijat* (Path to Salvation). Over 30,000 Pakistani troops, backed by military jets and helicopter gunships, had been deployed in the TTP stronghold. The rapid pace speed at which the troops were able to seize major towns and villages of South Waziristan and thus securing main supply routes in the embattled tribal region took many an analyst by surprise.

The swift gains by Pakistani troops in South Waziristan might not ensure eradication of terror networks in the region because the Taliban themselves have declared that they have withdrawn from the area as a strategic retreat to save their men and ammunition and continue to fight from remote valleys and neighbouring tribal districts. Although tough resistance was expected from thousands of well-trained Taliban fighters, the army operation, to the surprise of the military leadership, relatively proved easy. Fighting small rearguard actions, the Taliban fighters simply deserted their bunkers and posts in the major towns, leaving space for the troops to occupy.

Is Hakeemullah dead or alive?

In the early hours of 14 January 2010, two missiles fired from a US drone struck a compound in the Shaktoi area of South Waziristan, where Hakeemullah was believed to be sleeping. Unnamed officials speculated that the TTP chief was among the 18 persons killed in the predator attack. But on 16 January, the TTP released an audiotape carrying the voice of Hakeemullah, who said: "Today, on the 16th of January 2010, I am saying it again - I am alive, I am OK, I am not injured ... when the drone strike took place, I was not present in the area at that time".

Almost two weeks later, on 31 January 2010, the state-run Pakistan Television (PTV) claimed that having escaped a US drone strike on 14 January 2010, Hakeemullah Mehsud was eventually caught up in another predator attack on 17 January in Shaktoi, a village close to the border with North Waziristan. The PTV claimed that Mehsud was injured in the attack and died three days later of his injuries. However, the TTP rejected reports about Hakeemullah's death, amid American and Pakistani media reports that American intelligence was 90% sure that he was dead. While the TTP did release a videotape of Hakeemullah being interviewed [on 28 February], American terrorism experts questioned when the tape was made, as Mehsud did not provide details on current events. As of 10 March 2010, it was still unclear whether he was dead or alive.

Hakeemullah's profile was actually raised raised after he had appeared in a farewell video with a suicide bomber who finally killed seven CIA employees in Afghanistan on 31 December 2009. It was the deadliest single day for the American intelligence agency since eight CIA officers were killed in the 1983 bombing of the American Embassy in Beirut. Interestingly, a spokesman for the *Tehrik-e-Taliban Pakistan* had claimed responsibility for targeting the CIA base in Khost was responsible for carrying out US drone strikes and covert operations in Afghanistan and Pakistan. The TTP spokesman said in his 1 January 2010 responsibility claim that the TTP had managed to infiltrate the CIA base with the suicide bomber who was disguised as a soldier of the Afghan National Army.

Analysts say the *Tehrik-e-Taliban Pakistan* may experience a certain drop in its capabilities if reports of Hakeemullah's death in a missile strike are accurate, but this does not mean the group will be incapable of recovering, and it may in fact decide to increase the number of attacks it stages, as it did after finding its footing following Baitullah's death.

REFERENCES

1. Alex Altman, *TIME Magazine*, 7 April 2009.
2. Brigadier Cheema, Press Conference, 28 December.
3. Syed Manzar Abbas Zaidi, Research Paper, *Long War Journal*, July 2008.
4. Baitullah Mehsud, Interview with Ahmed Zaidan, *Al-Jazeera* Correspondent, 28 January 2008.
5. Pakistan targets its most wanted man, News Report, *Asia Times Online*, 25 June 2009
6. Christina Lamb, *The Sunday Times*, 9 August 2009.
7. Report, *CNN*, 8 August 2009.
8. Report, *BBC*, 22 August 2009.
9. Report, *Daily Times*, 23 August 2009.
10. Report, *Daily Dawn*, 23 August 2009.
11. Editorial, *Daily Times*, 24 August 2009.
12. Telephonic Interview, *BBC*, Hakimullah Mehsud, 25 August 2009.
13. Audiotape, Hakeemullah Mehsud, 16 January 2010.
14. Report, Pakistan Television, 31 January 2010.
15. Statement, TTP Spokesman, 1 January 2010.

CHAPTER 19

Saifullah Akhtar: Intelligence Tool Tasked to Kill Bhutto?

The mysterious assassination of Benazir Bhutto took a new turn in the second week of February 2008 when Qari Saifullah Akhtar, the *ameer* of the pro-Taliban *Harkatul Jehadul Islami* (HUJI) or the Movement of Islamic Holy War, was named by the slain PPP leader in her posthumous book as a principal suspect in the 18 October 2007 attempt to kill her in Karachi, a few hours after her homecoming from self-exile.

Shortly before being assassinated, Benazir Bhutto was putting the final touches to her hard-hitting memoirs entitled, *Reconciliation: Islam, Democracy and the West*, published by Simon & Schuster six weeks after her death. In the book she has made some shocking allegations from the grave, stating that Qari Saifullah had been involved in the Karachi attack.

For almost 10 hours on October 18, the people of Karachi choked the streets, cheering Benazir on her return home. As her cavalcade threaded its way through an enraptured throng towards the mausoleum of Mohammad Ali Jinnah, where she was to address a public rally, a visibly emotional Bhutto stood atop an especially fortified, bullet-proof truck, waving proudly to her followers. At 12:09 a.m. on October 19, the cavalcade had reached the Karsaz Bridge, still 10 km away from the destination. But Benazir was not to be seen – 19 minutes earlier, she had gone down to use the makeshift washroom built in the lower deck of the truck.

It was then that someone apparently tossed a hand grenade on to the right side of Benazir's truck, hoping the explosion would break the three rings of security cordon around it. The outer ring was of policemen, the inner two of the *Janisar* Force of the PPP. Her personal guards valiantly held their ground. In the ensuing confusion, a suicide bomber tried to break the security cordon to get close to the truck from the left. Challenged by the security men, he detonated himself. The carnival mood soon turned funereal – human flesh and limbs flew around, people wailed in agony and grief; the final toll was a chilling figure of over 140.

The explosion was powerful enough to rip off a door of her truck; what saved Benazir was that she wasn't atop the truck at that fatal moment. Subsequent investigations revealed prior knowledge of the security architecture around Benazir. Not only was the attack three-pronged, the masterminds chose a suicide bomber to evade the jamming devices fitted into two vehicles immediately in front and behind her truck. The jammers could have prevented any explosion triggered by a remote-controlled device, as had happened during one of the two attempts on Musharraf's life in December 2003 in Rawalpindi.

The nature of the explosives used in the Karachi attack indicated highly intricate planning. Investigations revealed that the suicide bomber, a 21-year old bearded youth, whose head was recovered from the scene of the carnage, had strapped himself with 15-20 kg of an explosive mix of C4 and Trinitrotoluene explosives. C4 explosive is rated as the best quality military plastic explosive that detonates with tremendous velocity. The other ingredient – Trinitrotoluene or TNT – has the capacity to shatter concrete structures. Investigators were of the view that the TNT explosive was meant to pierce through the bullet-proof casing of the PPP leader's vehicle, with the C4 inflicting damage over a wide area. However, fortunately for Benazir, two police jeeps accompanying her welcome procession bore the brunt of the explosion.

So, who were the people having access to such devastating and rarely available explosives and being aware of the obstacles they would encounter in targeting Bhutto? In her book, Benazir stated, "It was

Qari [Saifullah Akhtar] to whom the intelligence officials in Lahore had turned to for help before my homecoming on 18 October 2007". Although no one is sure if there was a link between the release of Qari and the murder of Bhutto, PPP circles ask why an *Al-Qaeda* linked dreaded terrorist having known links with the Taliban militia was set free by the Musharraf regime after three years in imprisonment, shortly before Benazir's homecoming. The clandestine release, months before Bhutto's return, therefore, evoked suspicions among PPP circles of a nexus between Qari Saifullah Akhtar and the Musharraf regime.

Benazir Bhutto writes in her book: "I was informed of a meeting that had taken place in Lahore where the bomb blasts were planned. However, a bomb maker was needed for the bombs. Enter Qari Saifullah [Akhtar], a wanted jehadi terrorist who had tried to overthrow my second government in the 1990s. He had been extradited by the United Arab Emirates and was languishing in the Karachi Central Jail. According to my sources, the officials in Lahore had turned to Qari for help. His liaison with elements in the government was a radical who was asked to make the bombs and he himself asked for a *fatwa* (edict) making it legitimate to oblige. He got one".

On 26 February 2008, exactly two weeks after Benazir Bhutto's revelations, the Musharraf administration arrested Qari Saifullah Akhtar for the purpose of interrogations, although there were many in the establishment circles who believed that Qari has actually been taken into protective custody by his spy masters. As a matter of fact, the HUJI *ameer* is generally considered to be a handy tool of the Pakistani intelligence establishment who is used and dumped whenever required by the all-powerful spy master. Qari was seized by the security agencies along with his three sons (Asif Ali, Abdul Rehman and Mureed Ahmad) in Ferozwala, near Lahore. He was grilled by a joint interrogation team comprising of operatives from the Punjab Police, Inter Services Intelligence and the Special Investigation Group of the Federal Investigation Agency.

During interrogations, Qari Saifullah claimed that he had already adopted the path of Sufism since his May 2007 release and was living for the past few months in the secluded *khanqah* (memorial) of a renowned Sufi-*cum*-militant of the 18th century, Syed Ahmad Shaheed (b.1786 d.1831). Although Syed Ahmed's tomb is situated in Balakot, his followers have established a khanqah in his name near the Sagian Bridge in the Ferozwala area, close to Lahore, from where he was seized. Qari told his interrogators that upon his release, he went to *Masjid-ul-Huda* lane in Hamza Town, Lahore to meet his *Pir* (mentor), Syed Nafees Shah, also a follower of Syed Ahmed Shaheed, who ordered him to stay in the Ferozwala *khanqah* and work for the spiritual guidance of the people.

Qari Saifullah described himself as a staunch follower of Syed Ahmed Shaheed and Ahmed Shah Abdali who fought and laid down their lives for the creation of an Islamic state. He conceded that his failed 'Operation *Khilafat*' (Operation Caliphate) of 1995 to topple Bhutto's second government with the help of his like-minded army men, was meant to bring in the *Khilafat* (Caliphate) system in Pakistan and to enforce Islamic *Shariah* in accordance with the teachings of Syed Ahmed Shaheed. Qari Saifullah also told his interrogators that his *Pir* Syed Nafees Shah had declared him '*Khalifa*' (Caliphate) in his place, shortly before his 5 February 2008 death and he was duty bound to fulfil his mission of converting Pakistan into a pure Islamic state, to be ruled by a Khalifa who has the traits of both Syed Ahmed Shaheed and Ahmad Shah Abdali.

Ironically, his arrest actually established the fact for the first time that despite all the charges leveled against him Qari Saifullah had been released much before Benazir Bhutto's return home. Born on 8 January 1959 in South Waziristan, Qari Saifullah is a graduate of the *Jamia Binoria* in Karachi, the infamous religious seminary of the sub-continent which has the privilege of having produced several known pro-Taliban *Deobandi* kingpins like the *Harkatul Mujahideen* chief Maulana Fazalur Rehman Khalil and the *Jaish-e-Mohammad* chief Maulana Masood Azhar. He was arrested and extradited from the United Arab Emirates on 7 August 2004 on charges of plotting twin suicide attacks on Musharraf in Rawalpindi in December 2003.

However, instead of trying to prosecute and convict him after his arrest, the Pakistani intelligence agencies chose to keep him under detention for the next two years and nine months, without even filing any criminal charges against him, giving credence to reports of his being a handy tool of the Pakistani intelligence establishment who is used and dumped whenever required. His 'unprovoked' arrest was challenged in the Supreme Court of Pakistan in the first week of January 2005. On 18 January 2005 the Supreme Court dismissed the petition against Qari's arrest and directed the petitioner to first move the High Court by filing a habeas corpus writ petition. A Supreme Court bench of Justice Hamid Ali Mirza and Justice Falak Sher ruled that the arrest in this case was not a matter of public importance and hence a constitutional petition could not be filed directly in the Supreme Court under Article 184(3) of the Constitution.

However, following Benazir Bhutto's murder, it emerged that Saifullah Akhtar was quietly released by the intelligence establishment as one of the missing persons being sought by a Supreme Court bench headed by Chief Justice Iftikhar Mohammad Chaudhry. Before that, on 5 May 2007, the federal government told the Supreme Court that Qari Saifullah Akhtar was not in the custody of the state agencies. The concise report presented by the National Crisis Management cell to the Court revealed: "He is engaged in jehadi activities somewhere in Punjab," thus denying that he was under detention. Two weeks later, on 21 May 2007, Qari Saifullah suddenly reached his hometown in Mandi Bahauddin of the Punjab province. The *Daily Times* reported on 22 May 2007 that Qari Saifullah was actually released by an intelligence agency earlier that morning when he was thrown out of an official car in a deserted area near the Chakwal district of Punjab.

The release was subsequently brought to the notice of the apex court on 26 May 2007 by the Ministry of Interior. Hashmat Habib, the counsel for Qari Saifullah Akhtar, having confirmed the release of his client, told the Court that while setting him free, the intelligence officials had told his client that had they not picked him up, there was a strong possibility of the American Federal Bureau of Investigation (FBI) taking him away for interrogations because of his alleged *Al-Qaeda* and Taliban links.

At the time of his August 2004 dramatic arrest and subsequent extradition from the United Arab Emirates, the Pakistani authorities described the development as a major blow to the *Al-Qaeda* sponsored terrorist network and its local affiliates in Pakistan. The then Information Minister Sheikh Rasheed Ahmed went to the extent of painting him as a close aide of Osama bin Laden and Mullah Omar, and the operational head of *Al-Qaeda* in Pakistan. "We confirm that we have arrested Qari Saifullah Akhtar. He was on our wanted list for a long time", he had stated during a news conference.

The timing of Qari Saifullah's arrest and repatriation to Pakistan was significant given the fact that it happened only after the arrest of a Pakistani computer engineer Naeem Noor Khan alias Abu Talha from Gujarat on 12 July 2004 along with Ahmed Khalfan Ghailani, a key suspect in the August 1998 bombings of US embassies in Kenya and Tanzania. Naeem had been creating websites and secret e-mail codes for *Al-Qaeda* operatives to communicate with each other. International media reports after Naeem Noor's arrest said Pakistani agencies recruited him as a double agent and were thus able to communicate with *Al-Qaeda* through him. Because of this premature disclosure, the noose around *Al-Qaeda* in the United Kingdom had to be quickly tightened. The homecoming of Qari Saifullah Akhtar was, therefore, connected with the revelations made by Ahmed Khalfan in Gujarat.

On 4 March 2008, hardly a few days after Qari Saifullah was rearrested, two suicide bombers blew themselves up at the Navy War College building on the Mall Road in Lahore, killing eight Navy employees. A war-related course was in progress in a lecture room adjacent to the parking lot of the college when the human bombs forcibly made their way into the building and blew themselves up. Six days later, on 11 March, terrorists once again struck Lahore by using suicide bombers – the first batch targeted the Federal Investigations Agency (FIA) headquarters on the busy Temple Road, and a few minutes later a second batch targeted a safe house of the FIA in the Model Town area, killing 36 people, mostly FIA officials. Subsequent investigations by Pakistani agencies indicated that all the three attacks were carried out by the *Harkatul Jehadul Islami* as a reaction to the arrest of Qari Saifullah Akhtar. As a matter of fact, six of the HUJI activists, arrested after the 4 March Naval War College suicide attack, were then being interrogated.

On 20 March 2008, almost three weeks after his 26 February

arrest, Qari Saifullah was produced before an Anti-Terrorism Court in Karachi for his involvement in the October 2007 attacks on Benazir's welcome procession in Karachi. Justice Khawaja Naveed Ahmed subsequently granted 12 days' remand to the Karachi police till 29 March 2008 so that Qari could be grilled thoroughly. On 20 March 2008, Hashmat Habib, the counsel of Saifullah, told the media in Karachi that he had sued the printer, publisher and beneficiaries of Benazir Bhutto's book for falsely accusing his client of being involved in the Karachi bombing and thus damaging his reputation. "I have moved the suit under Section 8 of Defamation Ordinance 2002 ... seeking damages of $200 million".

Six days later, on 26 March, Justice Khawaja Naveed Ahmed ordered the release of Qari Saifullah on bail after the investigation officer reported to the court that no evidence had been found to link him with any terrorist activity. Investigation officer Nawaz Ranjha submitted a report to the court stating that during initial investigations he did not get enough evidence to file a charge sheet against Qari. "The suspect was interrogated during the 12-day period given by the court but he denied involvement in the blasts. Under Section 497 of the Criminal Procedure Code, when a person accused of a non-bailable offence is arrested without warrant by an officer-in-charge of a police station, he may be released on bail when he is brought before a court, but he shall not be so released if there are reasonable grounds to believe that he is guilty of an offence punishable with death or imprisonment for life or imprisonment for 10 years", the report submitted to the court.

Although the judge accepted the report and ordered Qari Saifullah's release on bail, the jehadi kingpin was rearrested under the Maintenance of Public Order (MPO) and shifted to a Karachi safe house. Two months later, on 8 June 2008, Qari Saifullah was released by the Sindh Home Department when the term for his detention expired. "He is a free person. There is no case against him anywhere in Pakistan", Saifullah's lawyer told the media. However, there were many in the establishment who believed the release might have been facilitated by the agencies in an apparent bid to stop the deadly wave of suicide bombings, let loose by the followers of Saifullah.

Though Qari Saifullah's role in the October 18 Karachi suicide attack could not be explored further due to the lack of interest shown by the PPP government, his previous involvement in a failed coup plot of 1995 had projected him as one of the most deadly militants who, from the intelligence establishment's viewpoint, had gone astray. The group of the potential plotters busted by the Military Intelligence at that time included four serving army officers, headed by Major General Zaheerul Islam Abbasi, with Brig Mustansar Billa having been described as the ideologue of the religiously motivated army men. They were accused of plotting to first take over the General Headquarters (GHQ) of the Pakistan Army in Rawalpindi during the Corps Commanders Conference and later overthrow the Benazir government to eventually enforce their own brand of Islamic *Shariah* in Pakistan.

They were charged by a Field General Court Martial (FGCM) with conspiring to assassinate military commanders with the help of a group of Kashmiri militants belonging to the *Harkatul Jehadul Islami* (HUJI) who were to be provided with military uniforms, and equipped with arms and ammunition by Qari Saifullah to carry out the covert operation. However, once the FGCM formerly started, Qari Saifullah's name was dropped from the list of accused when he decided to turn approver against his *khaki* co-conspirators. Those conducting the court martial proceedings had admitted at one stage that without the testimony of Saifullah, it would have been extremely difficult to convict the accused *khakis*. However, after the dismissal of the second Bhutto government in 1996, Qari Saifullah Akhtar was released; he went to Afghanistan and was inducted into the cabinet of the Taliban *ameer* Mullah Mohammad Omar as his advisor on political affairs.

Once in Afghanistan, the militants of Qari's HUJI were called 'Punjabi' Taliban and offered employment, something that other jehadi organisations could not get out of Mullah Omar. Interestingly, the HUJI had membership among the Taliban, too, as three Taliban ministers and 22 judges belonged to the group. The *Harkat* militants are known to have supported Mullah Mohammad Omar in difficult times. According to international media reports, at least 300 HUJI militants lost their lives while fighting the Northern Alliance troops, prompting Mullah Omar to give *Harkat* the permission to build six more training camps in Kandahar, Kabul and Khost, where the Taliban army also used to receive military training. Before the 9/11 attacks and the subsequent invasion of Afghanistan, the HUJI had branch offices in 40 districts across Pakistan. While funds were collected from these grass root offices and from foreign sources, the *Harkat* had accounts in two branches of the Allied Bank in Islamabad.

Qari Saifullah Akhtar was one of the few jehadi leaders who had escaped with Mullah Mohammad Omar after the US-led Allied Forces invaded Afghanistan in October 2001. He first took shelter in the South Waziristan Agency; then moved to Peshawar and eventually fled to Saudi Arabia, from where he decided to move to the UAE. Three years later, on 6 August 2004, he was arrested by the UAE authorities and deported to Pakistan after revelations during investigations of the December 2003 twin suicide attacks on Pervez Musharraf that he had been executing terrorist operations in Pakistan with the help of his right hand man, Amjad Hussain Farooqi.

The intelligence agencies had concluded that the twin Rawalpindi attacks were masterminded by Amjad Farooqi, a key operative of HUJI, who was later killed in Nawab Shah, Sindh on 26 September 2004, almost 50 days after his mentor's arrest and the subsequent information he had provided to his interrogators. Investigations revealed that one of the suicide bombers, Khalique Ahmed alias Hazir Sultan, belonged to the HUJI while the other, Jameel Suddhan, belonged to the *Jaish-e-Mohammad.* Khalique Ahmed, 42, a resident of the Panjsher valley in Afghanistan, was camped in South Waziristan Agency before being moved to Rawalpindi to carry out the 2003 suicide attack.

It further transpired that the *Harkat* and the *Jaish* were components of a five-member 'Brigade 313', which was launched in 2001 after the fall of the Taliban regime in Afghanistan. Three other components of the Brigade 313 were the *Lashkar-e-Jhangvi* (LeJ), the *Jaish-e-Mohammad* (JeM) and the *Lashkar-e-Toiba* (LeT). The Brigade leaders had pledged to target some key Pakistani leaders who in their opinion were damaging the cause of jehad and protecting the US interests in Pakistan. The arrest of Qari Saifullah Akhtar marked a serious blow to the *Al-Qaeda* sponsored terrorist network and its local affiliates in Pakistan, which had been making desperate attempts to physically eliminate Musharraf who they believed was acting as an American agent.

According to the South Asia Terrorism Portal (SATP), HUJI is a Pakistan-based jehadi group with affiliates in India and Bangladesh. An SATP report claims that the HUJI is closely linked to the Inter Services Intelligence, the Taliban and *Al-Qaeda.* "The group receives patronage and support from Pakistan's Inter Services Intelligence and is also linked with several Islamist groups operating in India, including the *Lashkar-e-Toiba* and the *Jaish-e-Mohammad.* While the exact formation date of the group is not known, its origin is traced to the Soviet-Afghan war. Qari Saifullah Akhtar along with two of his associates, Maulana Irshad Ahmed and Maulana Abdus Samad Sial, all seminary students from Karachi in Pakistan, were instrumental in laying the foundation of a group, *Jamiat Ansarul Afghaneen* (the Party of the Friends of Afghan People), sometime in 1980".

"Towards the end of its Afghanistan engagement, the *Jamiat* rechristened itself as HUJI and reoriented its strategy to fight for the cause of fellow Muslims in the Indian State of Jammu and Kashmir. The *Harkat* continued to exist after the Soviet withdrawal from Afghanistan in 1989 by merging with another Pakistani militant group known as the *Harkatul Mujahideen,* to form the *Harkatul Ansar* which subsequently began terrorist operations in Kashmir. In order to avoid the ramifications of the US designation of *Harkatul Ansar* as a Foreign Terrorist Organisation in 1997, it renamed itself as *Harkatul Mujahideen*".

Following the 8 May 2002 suicide bomb attack outside Karachi Sheraton Hotel that killed 11 French engineers working in the port city on a submarine project, Khaled Ahmed, a well-known intellectual and writer, wrote in *The Friday Times* an article about the birth and the growth of HUJI. The article, entitled '*The Biggest Militia We Know Nothing About*' stated: "The *Harkat* is the only militia which boasts international linkages. It is active in Arakan in Burma, and Bangladesh, with well-organised seminaries in Karachi, and Chechnya, Sinkiang, Uzbekistan and Tajikistan. The latest trend is to recall the Pakistani fighters stationed abroad and encourage the local fighters to take over the operations. Its fund-raising is largely from Pakistan, but an additional source is its activity of selling weapons to other militias. Its acceptance among the Taliban was owed to its early allegiance to a leader of the Afghan war, Maulvi Nabi Muhammadi and his *Harkate Inqlabe Islami* whose fighters became a part of the Taliban forces in large numbers."

"According to *Al-Irshad*, the journal of the *Harkatul Jehadul Islami*, which is published from Islamabad, a *Deobandi* group led by Maulana Irshad Ahmad was established in 1979. Looking for the right Afghan outfit in exile to join in Peshawar, Maulana Irshad Ahmad adjudged Maulvi Nabi Muhammadi as the true *Deobandi* and decided to join him in 1980. *Harkate Inqlabe Islami* was set-up by Maulana Nasrullah Mansoor and was taken over by Nabi Muhammadi after his martyrdom. Eclipsed in Pakistan, Maulana Irshad fought in Afghanistan against the Soviets till he was killed in battle in Shirana in 1985. His place was taken by Qari Saifullah Akhtar, which was not liked by some of the *Harkat* leaders, including Maulana Fazlur Rehman Khalil who then set-up his own *Harkatul Mujahideen*".

"According to some sources, the *Harkatul Mujahideen* was a new name given to *Harkatul Ansar* after it was declared terrorist by the United States. Other sources claim it was *Harkatul Jehadul Islami* that had earlier merged with the *Harkatul Ansar*. The HUJI relations with Maulana Fazlur Rehman Khalil remained good, but as Maulana Masood Azhar separated from *Harkatul Mujahideen* and set-up his own *Jaish-e-Mohammad*, *Harkatul Jehadul Islami* opposed the *Jaish-e-Mohammad* in its journal *Sada-e-Mujahid* or the Voice of the Soldier (May 2000) and hinted that 'you-know-who' had showered *Jaish* with funds. The *Jaish* was supported by Mufti Nizamuddin Shamzai of the *Binori Mosque* in Karachi and was given a brand new camp in Balakot, Azad Kashmir, by the ISI".

Following the August 2004 arrest of Saifullah, *Daily Times* wrote an editorial on 9 August 2004, entitled 'Significance of Qari Saifullah Akhtar's arrest': "Qari Saifullah Akhtar is a crucial figure in Mufti Nizamuddin Shamzai's efforts to get Osama bin Laden and Mullah Omar together as partners-in-jehad... From its base in Afghanistan, the *Harkat* launched its campaigns inside Uzbekistan, Tajikistan and Chechnya. It finally became the biggest jehadi militia based in Kandahar located in the middle of the Taliban-Al-Qaeda strategic merger. The *Harkat* called itself 'the second line of defence' for all Muslim states and was active in Burma, Bangladesh and Sinkiang. Due to their common origin in *Jamia Binoria, Harkatul Jehadul Islami* and *Harkatul Mujahideen* were merged in 1993 for the sake of 'better performance' in Kashmir. The new organisation was called *Harkatul Ansar*. . . ."

Who is Commander Ilyas Kashmiri?

While the Pakistan chapter of the *Harkatul Jehadul Islami* is led by Qari Saifullah Akhtar, its Azad Kashmir chapter is autonomous and headed by Commander Ilyas Kashmiri, a veteran of the Kashmir jehad who has spent several years in an Indian jail. Born in Bimbur (old Mirpur) in the Samhani Valley of Pakistan-administered Kashmir on 10 February 1964, Ilyas Kashmiri passed the first year of a mass communication degree at Allama Iqbal Open University, Islamabad. He did not continue due to his heavy involvement in jehadi activities. The Kashmir Freedom Movement was his first exposure in the field of militancy, then the *Harkatul Jehadul Islami* and ultimately his legendary 313 Brigade. This grew into the most powerful group in South Asia and its network is strongly knitted in Afghanistan, Pakistan, Kashmir, India, Nepal and Bangladesh. Little is documented of Ilyas' life, and what has been reported is often contradictory. However, he is invariably described by the Pakistani intelligence agencies as the most effective, dangerous and successful guerrilla leader in the world.

According to several international media reports, Ilyas had conducted several major military operations in India, including the *al-Hadid* operation in New Delhi, to get some of his jehadi comrades released. His group of 25 people included Sheikh Omar Saeed (the abductor of US reporter Daniel Pearl in Karachi in 2002) as his deputy. The group abducted several foreigners, including American, Israeli and British tourists and took them to Ghaziabad near New Delhi. They then demanded that the Indian authorities release their colleagues, but instead they attacked the hideout. Sheikh Omar was injured and arrested. (He was later released in a swap for the passengers of a hijacked Indian aircraft). Ilyas escaped unhurt. On 25 February 2000, the Indian army killed 14 civilians in Lonjot village in Pakistan-administered Kashmir after commandos had crossed the Line of Control (LoC) that separates the two Kashmirs. They returned to the Indian side with abducted Pakistani girls, and threw the severed heads of three of them at Pakistani soldiers.

The very next day, Ilyas conducted a guerilla operation against the Indian army in Nakyal sector after crossing the LoC with 25 fighters of 313 Brigade. They kidnapped an Indian army officer who was later beheaded – his head was paraded in the bazaars of Kotli back in Pakistani territory. However, the most significant operation of Ilyas was in Aknor cantonment in Indian-administered Kashmir against the Indian armed forces following the massacre of Muslims in the Indian city of Gujarat in 2002. In cleverly planned attacks involving 313 Brigade divided into two groups, Indian generals, brigadiers and other senior officials were lured to the scene of the first attack. Two generals were injured (the Pakistan army could not injure a single Indian general in three wars) and several brigadiers and colonels were killed. This was one of the most telling setbacks for India in the long-running Kashmiri insurgency. But despite what some reports claim, Kashmiri was never a part of the Special Services Group, nor even of the army.

Ilyas Kashmiri was arrested by the Pakistani authorities after the December 2003 twin suicide attacks on President General Musharraf's presidential cavalcade in Rawalpindi, but released a few weeks later due to lack of evidence. He later shifted his base to the North Waziristan region on the Pak-Afghan tribal belt and joined hands with the *ameer* of the *Tehrik-e-Taliban Pakistan* (TTP), Commander Baitullah Mehsud. Having switched from the freedom struggle in *Jammu & Kashmir* to the Taliban-led resistance against the NATO forces in Afghanistan, Ilyas Kashmiri established a training camp in the Razmak area of North Waziristan and shifted most of his warriors from his Kotli training camp in Azad Kashmir.

The Azad Kashmir chapter of the *Harkatul Jehadul Islami* went into Kashmir in 1991 but was at first opposed by the *Wahabi* elements there because of its refusal to criticize the grand *Deobandi* congregation of *Tableeghi Jamaat* (the party of preachers) and its quietist posture. As days passed, the HUJI warriors led by Ilyas were recognised as Afghans. It finally had more martyrs in the jehad of

Jammu & Kashmir than any other militia. Its resolve and organisation were recognised when foreigners were seen fighting side by side with its Punjabi warriors. However, the HUJI activities in Jammu & Kashmir have declined since 9/11, especially after Ilyas shifted his base to North Waziristan.

In May 2009, Ilyas Kashmiri was accused of plotting the assassination of Army Chief General Ashfaq Pervez Kayani, in collusion with *Al-Qaeda*. A Hong Kong-based web newspaper, Asia Time Online (AToL), claimed on 23 May 2009 that an *Al-Qaeda*-linked cell of militants led by Kashmiri guerrilla commander Ilyas Kashmiri had completed all plans for the assassination of General Kayani, in 2008. However, when the matter was sent to the top *Al-Qaeda* hierarchy for a final approval, it immediately ordered the murder plot to be shelved, fearing that the backlash from such an incident would damage their overall objective – to win the war in Afghanistan.

The AToL report claimed by quoting a top *Al-Qaeda* ideologue on condition of anonymity that Army Chief General Ashfaq Kayani's daily visits to a gym in 2008 were tracked by an *Al-Qaeda* cell in Pakistan, which noted a security breach that left him vulnerable to a suicide bomber as he stepped out of his car. "A plan was drawn up to take him out, and a team, picked from Brigade 313's *Jundul Fida* group, was selected. But the assassination plot was abandoned as the *Al-Qaeda* leadership felt at the time that had the murder attempt been carried out, Pakistan could turn into a battle ground between Pakistani security forces and militants – and the chief beneficiary would be none other than India and the United States."

The AToL story quoted the senior *Al-Qaeda* ideologue as saying: "There is a *shariah* [Islamic law] under which his (General Kayani) murder could have been justified. But then there is a *hikmat* [strategy] under which his murder could have been a serious blunder. [Had he been killed], the Pakistan army could have launched an all-out war in the tribal areas, and we could have retaliated with equal strength. In that process, Pakistan would have become a battleground and enemies like India and the United States would have received the chance to intervene. Although in our files Pakistan does not exist, we of course don't want the enemies of Islam to take advantage of any situation".

The AToL report, filed by its Pakistan bureau chief, further stated that once the murder plot was shelved, the *Al-Qaeda* cells were advised to work on a much broader strategy to defeat the Western forces stationed in Afghanistan. "They were told that any *Al-Qaeda* action against Pakistan, India and Iran was not aimed at destabilizing these countries, but to deter them from supporting the US-led war against terror in a bid to create a balance in favor of the anti-Western resistance". The report then quoted the unnamed *Al-Qaeda* ideologue as saying that the Osama-led organisation doesn't mean any hostility against the state of Pakistan or its state institutions.

"This message was passed on by *Al-Qaeda* leaders when they met a top Taliban delegation in the North Waziristan agency on the border with Afghanistan a few weeks ago. The delegation was headed by Mullah Abdul Ghani Baradar and he conveyed Taliban leader Mullah Omar's message that *Al-Qaeda* hostilities against the Pakistani security forces should be avoided. The delegation even warned *Al-Qaeda* in a muffled way that if hostilities against Pakistan and the Pakistani security forces were not stopped, it would be seen as damaging the cause of Islam. *Al-Qaeda* repeated that its goal was to make the Pakistani security forces neutral in the war on terror. The overall object is to win the war in Afghanistan. To this end, *Al-Qaeda* will continue to engage the security forces in the Swat area. The simple reason is that *Al-Qaeda* fears that the military, under US pressure, has plans in place to move into North and South Waziristan, where *Al-Qaeda* and the Taliban have key resources vital to their ongoing struggle in Afghanistan. So it is better to keep the military pinned down in Swat", the AToL report concluded.

Interestingly, hardly two weeks before Ilyas was accused of conspiring to kill General Kayani, he was named in a charge sheet filed by the Islamabad police in the November 2008 gruesome murder of Major General (retd) Amir Faisal Alvi, the former General Officer Commanding (GOC) of the Pakistan Army's Special Services Group (SSG). The 12-page charge sheet which was submitted in an anti-terrorism court on 12 May 2009 stated that the former SSG commanding officer was killed to avenge the role he had played in the fight against Taliban linked militants in the tribal areas of

Pakistan. The charge-sheet prepared by the Koral police station said three people involved in the murder and already arrested included Major (retd) Haroon Rasheed, a resident of Azad Kashmir; Mohammad Nawaz Khan of Peshawar and Ashfaq Ahmed of Okara. It said the murder of Major General Alvi was carried out on the instructions of Commander Ilyas Kashmiri who had also provided funds and weapons.

The charge sheet pointed out that Ilyas Kashmiri had already been named by the intelligence agencies for involvement in the October 2008 kidnapping for ransom of Satish Anand, a Karachi-based renowned film producer and distributor and the uncle of Juhi Chawla, a well known Bollywood actress. After Satish Anand was finally recovered in April 2009 and the kidnappers arrested, it transpired during interrogations that one of them – Major Haroon Rasheed alias Abu Khattab – was a former Pakistani Army officer and involved in the murder of General Alvi. According to the murder charge sheet, the three accused – Haroon, Ashfaq and Nawaz followed Alvi when he left his residence in Bharia Town in Rawalpindi for his private office in Islamabad and killed him and his driver near the PWD Colony.

In September 2009, some international media reports claimed while citing US intelligence sources that Ilyas Kashmiri has been killed in North Waziristan in an US drone attack along with Nazimuddin Zalalov alias Yahyo, a top *Al-Qaeda* leader belonging to the *Islamic Jehad of Uzbekistan*. These reports said that both died in two separate drone attacks conducted on 7 September and 14 September 2009 respectively by the Afghanistan-based American drones in the Machikhel and Khushali Toori Khel villages of the Mir Ali sub division of North Waziristan. And Ilyas Kashmiri died after the predator targeted a car carrying five suspected militants in Khushali Toori Khel village.

However, hardly three weeks after his reported death, Ilyas Kashmiri re-surfaced and gave an interview to a Pakistani journalist to show that he was alive and ticking. In his 13 October 2009 interview with *Asia Times Online* (AToL), he promised retribution against the United States and its proxies besides giving his views on what the upcoming battle will look like, what its targets will be, and how it will impact the West in relation to the destabilisation of a Muslim state such as Pakistan.

On 9 December 2009, English daily *The News* reported that the US intelligence sleuths stationed in Pakistan are trying to ascertain whether Abdur Rehman Hashim Syed, alias Pasha, a retired major of the Pakistan Army who had been named by the FBI as a key link between the 26/11 Mumbai terror attack suspect David Coleman Headley and his *Lashkar-e-Toiba* handlers, is the brother-in-law of Qari Saifullah Akhtar. Abdur Rehman was charged in a Chicago court by the American Federal Bureau of Investigations (FBI) on charges of conspiring terrorist attacks in association with David Headley, a US national of Pakistani-origin, who is already in the FBI's custody.

The report said the American intelligence sleuths are trying to determine if Abdur Rehman Hashim Syed is the same person who had filed a petition in the Supreme Court of Pakistan on 12 October 2004, challenging the arrest of Qari Saifullah Akhtar and seeking his production in the apex court. The petitioner had also sought a court order to prevent a possible deportation of Qari Saifullah Akhtar, his brother-in-law, to another country. But the petition was thrown out on 18 January 2005 and the petitioner was instructed to move the High Court by filing a habeas corpus writ petition.

According to the 42-page FBI charge sheet, Abdur Rehman coordinated with Commander Ilyas Kashmiri and Tahawwur Hussain Rana, an operative of the *Lashkar-e-Toiba*, to commit terrorist acts involving murder and maiming outside the US, and conspired within and outside the US to provide material support to that conspiracy. David Headley, already arrested on 3 October 2009, had been charged with criminal conspiracy in the Mumbai terror attacks and having links with Abdur Rehman who liaised between him and terror groups including LeT and HUJI. The charges filed in the federal court in Chicago said Headley, 49, conducted extensive surveillance of targets in Mumbai for over two years preceding 26/11, and supplied pictures and videotapes of targets to the ten attackers. He was charged with six counts of conspiracy to bomb public places in India, murder and maim persons in India and Denmark, provide material support to foreign terrorist plots, provide material support to the LeT, and six counts of aiding and abetting the murder of US citizens in India.

As far as Major (retd) Abdur Rehman was concerned, he had been charged with participating in planning a terrorist attack in Denmark, and coordinating with Headley in his surveillance of the intended targets. Rehman alias Pasha, referred to as individual A in FBI documents, corresponded with Headley beginning late 2008 by email or telephone in coded language regarding the "Micky Mouse Project" – their plot to attack the facilities of a Danish newspaper. After traveling to Copenhagen, Headley visited Pakistan wherein Rehman took him to the Federally Administered Tribal Areas to solicit Ilyas Kashmiri's participation in the plot. Following his return from Pakistan, David Headley communicated with the LeT leader. The FBI had released transcripts of a series of telephone calls between Headley and Rehman on reports of Ilyas Kashmiri's death in an American drone attack in South Waziristan which eventually proved faulty.

On 6 January 2010, English daily *The News* reported that the US authorities have sought from Pakistan an immediate arrest and extradition of Ilyas Kashmiri for allegedly planning [in tandem with the *Tehrik-e-Taliban Pakistan*) a suicide attack on the Central Intelligence Agency (CIA) Forward Operating Base of Chapman in Khost, Afghanistan, bordering North Waziristan, on 31 December 2009, that killed seven CIA officers and injured six others. On 1 January 2010, a TTP spokesman claimed responsibility for the CIA base attack in Khost.

On 11 January 2010, English daily *The News* reported that investigations into the rising incidents of suicide bombings in the Pakistani-administered Azad Kashmir (AK) have indicated the involvement of *Lashkar-e-Zil* (LeZ) or Shadow Army – a loose alliance of *Al-Qaeda-* and Taliban-linked anti-US militant groups active in Pakistan and Afghanistan. The report said there are clear indications that the 6 January 2010 suicide attack targeting a military installation in Sudhnoti district of Azad Kashmir, which killed four soldiers of the Pakistan Army and the 31 December 2009 suicide attack on the Forward Operating Base of the US Central Intelligence Agency in Khost, Afghanistan, killing seven CIA officers, were masterminded by *Lashkar-e-Zil.* Instead of indulging in traditional warfare, the report said, the LeZ has distinguished itself by carrying out unusual guerilla operations.

The report added: "While the LeZ is mainly active in Pakistani tribal areas of North and South Waziristan, Bajaur, Peshawar, Khyber, and Swat in the NWFP, it has already carried out several deadly bombings against the US-led Allied Forces in the Afghan provinces of Khost, Kabul, Kandahar, Nuristan, Nangahar, Wardak, Paktika, Ghazni and Kunar, killing dozens. The *Lashkar-e-Zil* mainly consists of *Tehrik-e-Taliban Pakistan* (TTP) led by Commander Hakeemullah Mehsud, the Azad Kashmir chapter of the *Harkatul Jehadul Islami* (HUJI) led by Commander Ilyas Kashmiri, and the *Lashkar-e-Jhangvi* (LeJ) led by Qari Zafar, the Afghan Taliban militia led by its *ameer* Mullah Omar, the *Hizb-e-Islami Afghanistan* (HeI) led by Commander Gulbaddin Hekmatyar and the Haqqani militant network led by Jalaluddin Haqqani. While the LeZ seeks guidance from Dr Ayman Zawahiri, the second-in-command of Osama bin Laden, the chief of the HUJI (Azad Kashmir chapter) Ilyas Kashmiri happens to be its chief operational commander, currently based in North Waziristan, which borders Khost".

In the third week of February 2010, on the heels of the much-awaited Indo-Pakistan secretary-level talks, the Indian authorities sought intelligence sharing from Pakistan on the possible whereabouts of Ilyas Kashmiri for having threatened to target international sporting events being hosted by India. The Indian authorities had also sought from Pakistan credible information about his possible links with some other jehadi groups, especially *Lashkar-e-Toiba* which was accused of involvement in the 15 February 2010 bomb blast at the German Bakery in Indian city of Pune, which killed 10 people including two foreigners. The attack came hardly 24 hours after India and Pakistan agreed to resume their stalled foreign-secretary-level talks in Delhi from 25 February 2010.

A few hours after the Pune bombing, an email message sent to a Hong Kong-based web newspaper by Ilyas Kashmiri implied the involvement of his 313 Brigade, believed to be an operational arm of *Al-Qaeda* and pursuing its jehadi agenda in Pakistan while working in tandem with several other militant groups. Diplomatic circles in

Islamabad were of the view that some Pakistan-based pro-Kashmir jehadi groups had accelerated their terrorist activities to sabotage the Indo-Pak confidence-building process and scuttle the ice-breaking secretary-level talks between the two countries. Therefore, they opined that Ilyas Kashmiri's threat to target the upcoming international sporting events being held in India was timed to derail the resumption of the Indo-Pak peace talks.

The text of the email message sent by Ilyas Kashmiri on 15 February 2010 read: "We warn the international community not to send their people to 2010 Hockey World Cup, Indian Premier League and Commonwealth Games [to be held in New Delhi later this year]. Nor should their people visit India – if they do, they will be responsible for the consequences. We, the *mujahideen* of 313 Brigade, vow to continue attacks all across India until the Indian Army leaves Jammu & Kashmir and gives the Kashmiris their right of self-determination. We assure the Muslims of the subcontinent we will never forget the massacre of the Muslims in Gujarat and the demolition of the *Babri Masjid*. The entire Muslim community is one body and we will avenge all the injustices and tyranny. We once again warn the Indian rulers to compensate for all its injustices. Otherwise, they will see our next action".

REFERENCES

1. Benazir Bhutto, *Reconciliation: Islam, Democracy and the West*, Simon & Schuster, 2008.
2. Khaled Ahmed, The Biggest Militia we know Nothing About, *The Friday Times*.
3. Significance of Qari Saifullah Akhtar's arrest, *Daily Times*, 9 August 2004.
4. News Report, *Asia Time Online*, 23 May 2009.
6. Report, *The News*, 9 December 2009.
7. Report, *The News*, 6 January 2010.
8. Report, *The News*, 11 January 2010.

CHAPTER 20

The *Harkatul Mujahideen*: With Known Osama Links

Known as the only jehadi linchpin from Pakistan with a record of closeness to *Al-Qaeda* chief Osama bin Laden, Maulana Fazlur Rehman Khalil is a founding member of the *Harkatul Ansar* (HUA). Believed to be a *Wahabi* member of Osama's International Islamic Front (IIF) for "Jehad Against the Crusaders and the Jewish People" and a co-signatory of bin Laden's first *fatwa* issued in 1998 calling for attacks against the United States, Maulana Fazlur Rehman Khalil was in the *Al-Qaeda* training camps when they were hit by US cruise missiles in Khost and Jalalabad in August 1998.

Formed in 1993, *Harkatul Ansar* was renamed *Harkatul Mujahideen* (HUM or the Movement of the Holy Warriors) after the US State Department designated the HUA as a Foreign Terrorist Organisation in October 1997 and then re-named as the *Jamiatul Ansar* (JUA) after the Musharraf regime banned the HUM in January 2002, under American pressure. The leadership of the *Jamiatul Ansar* represents the *Deobandi* School of Islamic thought, whose members are fanatic *Sunni* Muslims who distinguish themselves from other *Sunni* Muslims by describing themselves as *Ansar*, the term given by Prophet Mohammad to actual Muslim residents of Medina in Saudi Arabia. With a pan-Islamic ideology, the group struggles to achieve secession of Jammu & Kashmir from India through militant means and its eventual merger with Pakistan.

The HUM has enjoyed a long career in the ISI-sponsored Afghan and Kashmir jehads. Besides being wanted by the Indian Central Bureau of Investigations (CBI) for his alleged involvement in terrorist activities in Jammu & Kashmir, Maulana Fazlur Rehman Khalil is also being sought by the American Federal Bureau of Investigation (FBI) for his alleged links with the *Al-Qaeda*. Following the August 1998 US attacks on *Al-Qaeda* training camps in eastern Afghanistan, Maulana Khalil had vowed at a press conference in Islamabad that the harm done to the members of his jehadi group by the US missile strikes won't go unanswered. On their part, Americans still take quite seriously his 1998 public warning at the news conference: "For each of us killed or wounded in the cowardly US attack, at least 100 Americans will be killed. I may not be alive, but you will remember my words."

Hardly a year after these strikes, Maulana Fazlur Rehman Khalil was chosen by one of the architects of the Kargil operation, Lt Gen Mohammad Aziz Khan to take part in the daring raid into the Indian territory. After Commander Bakht Zameen Khan of the *Al-Badr* captured some Kargil peaks, Khalil fought side-by-side with the Pakistan army and the *Al-Badr* fighters and remained part and parcel of the entire military strategies. This wasn't the first time Maulana Khalil was fighting alongside the Pakistan Army. He was a veteran of the Afghan war against the Soviets and acclaimed by his Afghan colleagues for his heroic role in the conquest of Khost city in 1991. Khost was the first Afghan city to fall to the Afghan *Mujahideen* after the withdrawal of the Soviets from Afghanistan in 1989, following which the central communist government in Kabul fell like a house of cards. After the 9/11 attacks, Khalil sent several thousand fighters to Afghanistan well in advance of the US-led attack on the country, and personally commanded the forces.

The HUM was born out of the *Harkatul Jehadul Islami* (HUJI) that was launched in 1980 as part of the Pakistani jehadi network involved in fighting Russian troops in Afghanistan. Two Pakistani *Deobandi* religious bodies – *Jamiat Ulema-e-Islam* (JUI) and the *Tableeghi Jamaat* (TJ) established HUJI primarily to run relief camps for the Afghan *mujahideen*. As the war intensified, the Pakistani ISI, contracted by the American CIA, approached the HUJI leadership, especially its founding *ameer*, Maulana Irshad Ahmed, offering their services for recruitment and training of the militants who wanted to take part in the Afghan jehad against the Russian occupation forces.

The HUJI then developed links with an Afghan resistance group, the *Hizb-e-Islami* (Yunus Khalis faction). The jehadi activities of HUJI finally began when its *ameer* Maulana Irshad Ahmed, along with Maulana Fazlur Rehman Khalil, Qari Saifullah Akhtar and Maulana Abdus Samad Siyal, went to Afghanistan on 25 February 1980, to participate in the Afghan jehad along with the forces of Ahmed Shah Masood and Prof Burhanuddin Rabbani. A power struggle erupted in the group after the June 1985 death of Maulana Irshad Ahmed during the Afghan jehad. Maulana Fazlur Rahman Khalil, the group's commander-in-chief, split with the new *ameer*, Qari Saifullah Akhtar, and decided to form the HUM while retaining its links with the *Hizb-e-Islami*.

Maulana Fazlur Rehman Khalil, a resident of Dera Ismail Khan and a staunch follower of Maulana Mufti Mahmood, the founder of the *Jamiat Ulema-e-Islam*, became the first *ameer* of the HUM while Maulana Masood Alvi was appointed its central commander. Though Qari Saifullah Akhtar stayed on to lead the *Harkatul Jehadul Islami*, it soon split once again, with Maulana Masood Kashmiri launching a third splinter group, the *Jamiatul Mujahideen* [which is different from the *Jamiatul Mujahideen* splinter group of the *Hizbul Mujahideen*].

Having parted ways with the HUJI, the *Harkatul Mujahideen* started sending volunteers into Afghanistan on its own. Money, largely from Pakistan, Afghanistan and Saudi Arabia helped recruit and train over 6,000 volunteers from Pakistan, Algeria, Egypt, Tunisia, Jordan, Saudi Arabia, India, Bangladesh, Myanmar and the Philippines. The initial batch of the HUM volunteers was trained in the use of arms, ammunition and explosives at training camps in the Pakhtia province of Afghanistan being run by Afghan leader, Jalaluddin Haqqani, who belonged to the *Hizb-e-Islami* (Maulvi Yunus Khalis group) but later joined hands with the Taliban.

Soon, however, the HUM set-up its own training camps in the Afghan territory just across the Miran Shah in the Pak-Afghan tribal belt of Waziristan. Some of the best fighters of the Afghan war came from these camps. Impressed by their motivation and prowess, the US Central Intelligence Agency supplied them with Stinger missiles and trained them in their use to bring down Soviet planes and helicopters. After the withdrawal of the Soviet troops, HUM started focusing on the Kashmir jehad and worked in competition with the HUJI led by Qari Saifullah Akhtar. The first batch of the HUM volunteers entered Jammu & Kashmir in 1991 under Sajjad Shahid's leadership, who was the first military commander of the outfit in Kashmir. The *Harkat* started its operations soon afterwards in J&K to promote its radical pan-Islamic agenda.

In 1993, two leading *Deobandi ulemas* of Pakistan – Maulana Samiul Haq, the *ameer* of the *Jamiat Ulema-e-Islam* and Hafiz Yusuf Ludhianvi, the *ameer* of the *Sunni Tehrik* – asked the leadership of the three splinter factions of the HUJI to reunite in the larger interest of the Kashmir jehad. The three groups – *Harkatul Jehadul Islami, Harkatul Mujahideen* and *Jamiatul Mujahideen* – finally merged on 13 October 1993, to form what came to be known as *Harkatul Ansar.* Maulana Khalil was appointed *ameer* while Maulana Shahadat Ullah was made the chief commander of the group. The reunion led to intensification of jehad in Jammu & Kashmir and the group soon carved a place for itself on the Kashmiri landscape through some major operations in the Valley.

While the *Harkatul Ansar* was successfully launched in Pakistan, the merger of three factions in Jammu & Kashmir was to be finalised by the then *Harkatul Ansar* general secretary Maulana Masood Azhar who had gone to Srinagar for the purpose of reunification. On 10 February 1994, Masood Azhar had convened a meeting of the HUJI, the HUM and the JUM leaders at Matigund, Anantnag district, to finalise the merger. While returning from the meeting, Masood Azhar and Sajjad Afghani, respectively the secretary general and the military chief of the *Harkatul Ansar,* were arrested in Srinagar, thus ending the move to reunite the three HUJI factions.

A few months later in April 1994, an unknown jehadi outfit, *Al-Faran,* kidnapped two British tourists from the Kashmir valley to use them as a bargaining chip for the release of Maulana Masood Azhar and Sajjad Afghani. It later transpired that *Al-Faran* was actually launched by two *Harkatul Ansar* commanders, Abdul Hameed Turki and Mohammad Sikandar. The kidnappings drew so much international criticism that for the first time in American history, two Kashmiri militant outfits – *Harkatul Ansar* and *Al-Faran* – were placed on the US State Department's list of terrorist outfits.

On 1 October 1997, US Secretary of State Madeleine Albright notified to the American Congress a list of 30 international terrorist organisations which the US government had decided to bring under the purview of the Anti-Terrorism and Effective Death Penalty Act, 1996, that made it an offence for any citizen or resident of the US to provide funds or other assistance to such organisations. The Act also empowered the American administration to deny visas to members of such organisations and prohibit their representatives from operating from US territory. The *Harkatul Ansar* was one such organisation so notified. The terror tag split the *Harkatul Ansar* into two factions.

The HUJI faction blamed Maulana Fazlur Rehman Khalil for masterminding the kidnapping since the two commanders who had set up *Al-Faran* belonged to his group. Under tremendous pressure, Maulana Khalil simply disowned *Al-Faran* and dubbed it as a creation of the Indian Research & Analysis Wing (RAW). Sikandar and Hameed were killed soon afterwards, making it easy for Khalil to detach himself from *Al-Faran*. But the issue finally led to a split in the *Harkatul Ansar*, with both the groups reverting to their previous identities. Interestingly, however, both the jehadi outfits kept enjoying exemplary relations with the Taliban regime that had allowed them to run their respective training camps in Afghanistan.

That the *Harkatul Mujahideen* had been associated with Osama bin Laden was prove on 20 August 1998, when American bombing on Afghanistan destroyed two *Harkat* training camps and killed 21 of its activists. Two days later, speaking at a news conference in Islamabad on 22 August 1998, Maulana Fazlur Rahman Khalil denied that Osama was indulging in terrorism and accused the US of killing 50 innocent civilians in Afghanistan. He said the camps bombed by the US in the Afghan territory were actually set-up by the CIA during the Afghan war to fight the Russian occupation forces and were now being used by the HUM for imparting Islamic education to Afghan students.

At yet another press conference on 25 August 1998 at Peshawar, Maulana Fazlur Rehman Khalil gave more details. He said nine HUM members died in the American attack and two Tajiks and four Arabs, were also killed. According to him, the US Cruise missiles destroyed four mosques, partially damaged another and burnt 200 copies of the Holy Koran kept in the camps. He then warned: "The United States has proved itself to be the world's biggest terrorist by carrying out terrorist attacks on Afghanistan and Sudan. I want to convey to the American leadership that we will take revenge for these attacks." In another warning to the US on 1 September 1998, Maulana Khalil said: "The Americans have struck us with Tomahawk Cruise missiles at only two places, but we will hit back at them everywhere in the world, wherever we find them. We have started a holy war against the US and they will hardly find a tree to take shelter beneath."

On 29 September 2001, hardly three weeks after the 9/11 attacks, the Pakistan government banned *Harkatul Mujahideen*, following the US State Department's decision to freeze all its assets along with those of 26 other organisations and individuals in connection with a worldwide campaign against the possible sources of terrorism. Although the ban compelled the *Harkatul Mujahideen* leadership to rename the group as the *Jamiatul Ansar*, it went on to use the cover up name of the *Harkatul Mujahideen Al-alami* in a bid to keep functioning uninterrupted. The *Al-alami* came into the limelight in June 2002 when the Karachi Rangers arrested five extremists in connection with the suicide bomb blast outside the American Consulate in Karachi on 14 June 2002. Three were named.

The three accused confessed having planned to blow up General Musharraf's cavalcade in Karachi on 26 April 2002 by exploding a Suzuki car loaded with deadly explosives. They told their interrogators they had parked a Suzuki high-roof vehicle full of explosives near the Falak Naz Centre on *Shahrah-e-Faisal*. But the remote controlled device developed a technical fault at the eleventh hour and did not work. The Suzuki vehicle was later used for the suicide bombing attack on the American Consulate in Karachi. Two of the three persons arrested were produced at the press conference addressed by DG Sindh Rangers on 8 July 2002. They included Mohammad

Imran Bhai, *ameer* of *Harkatul Mujahideen Al-alami* and Mohammad Hanif, *naib ameer* (assistant chief) of the group as well as the in charge of its *askari* (military) wing.

As Muhammad Imran Bhai, a bearded resident of Karachi, was produced before a Karachi court a few days later, he told reporters present inside the courtroom: "I am a member of the *Harkatul Mujahideen*. The *Harkatul Mujahideen Al-alami* is the product of the Rangers and the security agencies. I am working for the *Harkatul Mujahideen* and let me tell you that there is no split in the *Harkat*." Despite identifying Imran and Hanif as *Harkatul Mujahideen Al-alami* leaders, the Pakistani authorities had nothing to produce on the organisation in terms of literature or any propaganda material. Therefore, the conclusion drawn by the Pakistani agencies was that the *Al-alami* was nothing more than a cover up name for the *Harkatul Mujahideen*.

As of today, American intelligence agencies believe the *Harkatul Mujahideen* still retains links, like most jehadi groups, with the Taliban remnants and *Al-Qaeda* operatives hiding on the Pak-Afghan border. They recall Maulana Khalil's taking hundreds of his men to Afghanistan in 2001 after the US-Allied Forces invaded the country. The *Harkat* chief returned home safely in January 2002 and lived for the next six months in an Islamabad sanctuary, with no constraints until August 2002 when he was suddenly placed under house arrest. Pakistani intelligence circles say he was taken into protective custody only after US intelligence sleuths stationed in Islamabad had sought his custody to debrief him. The Pakistani authorities, however, refused to oblige. Maulana Khalil was released a few months later.

On 20 December 2004, Pakistani English newspaper *Daily Times* reported that the agencies had released Maulana Fazlur Rehman Khalil. Hardly a few weeks later, he resigned as the *ameer* of the *Jamiatul Ansar* (formerly known as *Harkatul Mujahideen*) because of pressure from intelligence quarters which in turn were under intense pressure from the Americans. A *Daily Times* report stated the same day that Khalil submitted his resignation at a meeting of the executive committee of the organisation and asked the committee to elect a new chief. Maulana Badar Munir from Karachi was subsequently elected the new *ameer* of the organisation.

However, Maulana Khalil's name again hit the international media headlines following the 5 June 2005 arrest of a pair of Pakistani-Americans by the Federal Bureau of Investigation from the sleepy little farming town of Lodi, California. Hamid Hayat, 23, and his father, Umar Hayat, 47, were later charged with lying to the authorities regarding their connection with jehadi training camps. But the formal FBI affidavit contained the bombshell piece of information that the jehadi training camps were not in the notorious tribal areas, but right outside the city of Rawalpindi, which also hosts the Pakistan army headquarters. Hamid and Umer told the FBI they had received training in terrorism at a military training camp being run by Maulana Khalil, who maintains a jehadi facility at Dhamial area in the garrison town of Rawalpindi. They said Hamid Hayat had been given a first-class tour of all the inner workings of terrorist camps and had seen hundreds of attendees from various parts of the world.

Assistant US Attorney Steven Lapham subsequently told a federal jury that Hamid Hayat, a US citizen, traveled repeatedly to Pakistan where he "learned to kill Americans" while attending a terrorist camp for six months in 2003 and 2004. The fresh disclosures revived the interest of the American intelligence sleuths in interviewing Khalil. But the Pakistani agencies again moved swiftly and took him into their custody. He was once again released in the first week of July 2005. Khalil subsequently restricted himself to his Islamabad headquarters. But almost eight months later, on 29 March 2006, he was abducted in Islamabad as soon as he left his *madrassa*-cum-office headquarters, tortured and thrown onto the Fateh Jang road in the Rawalpindi city by unidentified people.

Khalil's name resurfaced during the Pakistan Army's Operation Silence at *Lal Masjid*. The Musharraf regime decided to rope in the defunct HUM chief as negotiator as he was considered close to the fanatic clerics running the Mosque. Khalil's close associates say the fact that many hardcore militants belonging to several leading jehadi groups active in Indian Kashmir were holed up inside the *Lal Masjid*, prompted him to step in as a mediator in a last ditch effort to save the lives of his jehadi associates. However, after Khalil conducted crucial parleys with some close associates of Musharraf, the talks somehow broke down and the Pakistan Army subsequently launched a military operation that killed Maulana Rasheed Ghazi and hundreds more. Maulana Fazlur Rehman Khalil's name once again resurfaced in October 2009 when some key leaders of several jehadi and sectarian groups were flown to Rawalpindi through special chartered flights to hold talks with a group of TTP militants who had taken hostage over 40 people at the General Headquarters of the Pakistan Army after having stormed the GHQ building on 10 October 2009. And one of them was Khalil who summoned from the federal capital Islamabad to negotiate with the hostage takers. But the talks eventually failed and led to a military operation on 11 October 2009. Since then, Fazlur Rehman Khalil remains underground.

REFERENCES

1. Press Conference, Maulana Fazlur Rahman Khalil, 22 August 1998.
2. Press Conference, Maulana Fazlur Rahman Khalil, 25 August 1998.
3. Report, *Daily Times*, 20 December 2004.

CHAPTER 21

Pakistan's Sectarian War Getting Bloodier

Celebrating liberal democracy during his speech to the Constituent Assembly on 11 August 1947, the father of the nation and the founder of Pakistan Mohammad Ali Jinnah famously declared, "You may belong to any religion or caste or creed ... that has nothing to do with the business of the state. You are free, free to go to your temples; you are free to go to your mosques or to any other places of worship in this state of Pakistan". However, six decades later, a secular Jinnah's vision of a democratic Pakistan has been eclipsed by a rising spiral of sectarian violence that has assumed menacing dimensions and resulted in the killing of thousands of Pakistanis.

Pakistan, the country with the second largest Muslim population in the world, has seen serious bloody *Shia-Sunni* sectarian violence in recent times, although the conflict actually began to escalate 20 years ago, when Pakistanis watched two epic struggles take place in neighboring states of Afghanistan and Iran. Almost 77% of Pakistan's population is *Sunni*, while 20% is *Shia*, but the latter minority forms perhaps the second-largest *Shia* population of all Muslim countries, larger than the *Shia* majority in Iraq. Differences between the *Sunni* majority and *Shia* minority of Pakistan go back to a schism following the death of the Holy Prophet Mohammad (Peace Be Upon Him).

However, in the past two decades, those differences have been manifested in frequent violence wrought by *Sunni* and *Shia* extremists, making the ongoing sectarian war bloody and deadly. Officially released figures indicate that over 4,000 people were killed and more than 6,000 injured in 1100 plus incidents of sectarian terror that took place between January 1999 and January 2010, with no end in sight. Since the overall direction of the Pakistani military establishment is towards an Islamic ideological state, some of the militant groups whom the establishment used to support are often found involved in bloody acts of sectarian violence.

From the security perspective, sectarianism in Pakistan is rooted in a complex web of social, political and economic factors, local as well as external. The role of Saudi Arabia, Iran, Libya, Iraq, Afghanistan and the United States in supporting and sustaining the sectarian networks and *madrassas* throughout the last three decades has been widely acknowledged and investigated. The wide mandate of these sectarian groups to fight their enemies and their involvement in many other illegal activities makes it difficult to separate sectarianism from the wider conflict typology in Pakistan. In most analyses, the blaming finger for creating conditions for sectarianism to flourish is, however, pointed towards the nexus of the state, the army and secret services and rightly so.

It is generally believed that official support for the Pakistani militant groups fighting in the state of Jammu & Kashmir and Afghanistan has indirectly promoted sectarian violence in the country. Originally a product of the Pakistani military and intelligence establishment to beef up its security *vis-à-vis* India, most of the Pakistan-based militant or jehadi groups now evidently threaten the country's internal security. The linkages between the militants active in Jammu & Kashmir or Afghanistan and those within Pakistan are not surprising since the sectarians share the same *madrassas*, training camps, and operatives. Therefore, by facilitating the actions of irregulars in the Kashmir valley, Pakistan actually promotes sectarian jehad and terrorism back home.

The origins of sectarian violence in Pakistan can be traced back to the days of Afghan jehad against the Soviet occupation troops. With dollars coming from the US Central Intelligence Agency, Islamabad sponsored a huge number of militant groups and religious seminaries inside Pakistan. At that time, Washington needed Islamists to wage the so-called jehad against the Soviet occupation troops in Afghanistan, while Islamabad needed them to bring in billions of American dollars. Hence, both turned a blind eye to their radical ideology and methods. The drawbacks to this became obvious once the Soviet forces were defeated and made to leave Kabul. While radical Islamists in Afghanistan formed the Taliban, their brethren in Pakistan turned their attention towards Jammu & Kashmir or to sectarian opponents inside Pakistan.

Each act of sectarian killing in the country began a cycle of revenge attacks, with the civilian governments failing to curb the menace, either because they wanted the militants to fight Pakistan's corner in Jammu & Kashmir or because they lacked the will and the strength to do so. However, a stage came when external factors other than Jammu & Kashmir started giving rise to the menace of sectarianism in Pakistan, with the *Sunni*-dominated Saudi Arabia and the *Shia*-dominated Iran sponsoring rival *Sunni* and *Shia* groups. When General Pervez Musharraf seized power in 1999, he faced a formidable foe: well-armed, well-trained and well-financed sectarian groups with a huge resource pool of recruits in thousands of Pakistani religious *madrassas.*

Dealing with such a foe was not going to be easy for an unelected military ruler. But his task was made somewhat easier by the 9/11 terror attacks in the US and the worldwide backlash against extremist Islam. Islamabad's decision to cut support for the Kashmiri militants also boosted its drive against sectarianism. Before that, many sectarian organisations had emerged in the country, which were being tolerated because of their links with groups fighting in Jammu & Kashmir. Once Islamabad decided to put the Kashmir issue on the back burner under American pressure, for the sake of better ties with New Delhi, it no longer had to put up with the jehadi groups operating in the Kashmir valley. The first clear sign of a shift in the Pakistani government's attitude came in a televised speech by Musharraf to the nation on 12 January 2002, a few months after the 9/11 terror attacks. While announcing a massive campaign to eradicate the sectarian menace, Musharraf had banned two major sectarian organisations, the *Sipah-e-Sahaba Pakistan* (SSP) and the *Tehreek-e-*

Jaafria Pakistan (TJP), besides putting the *Sunni Tehrik* on notice. Six months later [on 14 August 2002] he banned two other sectarian outfits – *Sipah-e-Mohammad Pakistan* (SMP) and *Lashkar-e-Jhangvi* (LeJ). However, the genie of sectarian violence refused to be bottled.

Although the *Sunni-Shia* conflict is centuries old, its more modern and virulent manifestation in Pakistan can be traced to Imam Khomeini's successful revolution in Iran and the subsequent setting up of a *Shia* state. In response, extremist *Sunni* groups began to espouse the transformation of Pakistan into a *Sunni* state where the *Shias* were to be deemed a non-Muslim minority. The military regime of Zia fostered the growth of sectarianism in a number of ways. It created among the *Shia* community a perception that his government was moving rapidly towards the establishment of a *Sunni Hanafi* state in which the Islamisation of laws was seen to reflect the Islam of the dominant community.

The 1980 siege of the government Secretariat building in Islamabad by tens of thousands of *Shias* protesting against the *Zakat* and *Ushar* ordinance was a clear indication of their apprehensions about General Zia's Islamisation project. The selective backing of the largely *Sunni-Deobandi* Afghan *mujahideen* organisations resisting the Soviet occupation troops in Afghanistan also corresponded to a sectarian pattern of preferences that reinforced perceptions on both sides of the divide.

By the end of the Zia rule, the consequences of his policies were fairly obvious. Over the last decade, there has been a major escalation in sectarian tension, the number of sectarian killings and armed sectarian groups. Among those groups that have gained particular prominence are the anti-*Sunni Sipah-e-Mohammad Pakistan* (SMP), which is an offshoot of the *Tehrik-Nifaz-e-Fiqah-e-Jaafria* (TNFJ), the main religio-political party of the *Shia* sect in Pakistan, which later was renamed as *Tehrik-e-Jaafria Pakistan* (TFP); and the anti-*Shia Anjuman Sipah-e-Sahaba*, later to become the SSP, an offshoot of the *Jamiat-e-Ulema-e-Islam* (JUI), a leading religio-political *Sunni Deobandi* party. The LeJ, considered to be the most violent sectarian organisation, is a further offshoot of the SSP. The Pakistani intelligence agencies believe most of the JUI-linked *Sunni* sectarian organisations, especially the LeJ and the SSP, are also linked to *Al-Qaeda* and the Taliban.

The pattern and scale of the ongoing bloody sectarian violence in Pakistan indicates some key features. The contending groups are well organised and well armed and their ability to maintain their effectiveness and to elude law enforcement agencies is due to an extensive support network that includes *madrassas*, political parties, bases in Afghanistan and financial support from foreign countries. With the Saudi-linked *Sunni* sectarian groups targeting their rival *Shia* groups in Pakistan and the Iran-backed *Shias* coordinating reprisals across Pakistan against their *Sunni* opponents, a proxy war between Iran and Saudi Arabia is being fought on Pakistani soil, with groups in Afghanistan weighing in as well.

Since the 9/11 terror attacks in the United States and the ensuing invasion of Afghanistan and Iraq, the pro-Taliban *Deobandi* extremists are targeting *Shias* in Karachi, Peshawar, Quetta, Hazara and elsewhere. But one may ask why? The answer is very simple. The *Deobandis* believe that the Iran-backed *Shias* supported the US to invade Afghanistan in October 2001 which led to the fall of the Taliban regime there. They argue that Iran had supported the Northern Alliance to capture Afghanistan and the Hazara *Shias* were instrumental in the killing of thousands of the Taliban in Afghanistan after its invasion by the US-led Allied Forces. The *Deobandis* further point out that the *Shias* supported the Americans to invade Iraq besides ditching the *Sunnis* in Faluja where Muqtada Sadar was neutralised by Iran.

To tell the truth, the present *Shia-Sunni* strife is strongly intertwined with that in Afghanistan. The anti-*Shia* Taliban regime in Afghanistan had helped anti-*Shia* Pakistani organisations and *vice versa*. Subsequently, the leadership of the *Lashkar-e-Jhangvi* and *Sipah-e-Sahaba Pakistan*, sent thousands of its volunteers to fight with the extreme *Deobandi* Taliban regime and in return the Taliban gave sanctuary to their leaders in the Afghan capital, Kabul. According to celebrated Pakistani journalist Ahmed Rashid, over 80,000 Pakistani militants have trained and fought with the Taliban since 1994 that now form a hardcore militia of Islamic activists, ever ready to carry out a similar Taliban-style Islamic revolution in Pakistan.

Therefore, the *Shia-Sunni* strife inside Afghanistan has mainly been a function of the puritanical *Sunni* Taliban's clashes with *Shia* Afghans, primarily the Hazara ethnic group.

Even though most of the violence branded as sectarian in Pakistan after 9/11 is violence between *Deobandis* and *Shias*, the sectarian terrain is much wider. The sectarian problem facing Pakistan is different from the many other Muslim societies with sectarian tendencies. Though sectarianism in the Pakistani context often refers to the conflict between the majority *Sunni* and minority *Shia* traditions, the definition is misleading given the fact that these two sects are not homogenous; they have their own sub-sects, local variants and different schools of thought which are rivals to each other. Not only different sects like *Sunni* and *Shia*, but also different schools of thought, like *Barelvis* and *Deobandis* and *Wahabis* are in opposition to each other. For instance, the country reeled under its biggest-ever sectarian blow on 12 April 2006 when a grand *Barelvi* congregation of the *Sunni Tehrik*, celebrating the birthday of Prophet Mohammad (PBUH) was targeted at Nishtar Park in Karachi by a suicide bomber, killing 57, including the top leadership of the group.

The deadly Karachi bombing remains unsolved officially despite the fact that the country's intelligence agencies had then concluded that the hard line *Sunni* sectarian outfit, the *Lashkar-e-Jhangvi*, was responsible for the bombing that wiped out the entire leadership of the *Sunni Tehrik*. The agencies were of the view that one of the worst suicide attacks was actually the outcome of a growing intra-sectarian tussle between two major *Sunni* groups – the pro-Taliban *Deobandis* and the anti-Taliban *Barelvis*. The *Sunni Tehrik* is considered to be the only *Barelvi* outfit that departed from the sect's predominantly moderate posture and eventually became militant like most of the *Deobandi* and *Ahl-e-Hadith* groups.

The *Sunni Tehrik* was actually set-up in 1990 to counter the growing *Deobandi* and *Ahl-e-Hadith* dominance in Karachi, by Maulana Salim Qadri, a member of *Dawat-e-Islami* (Green Turbans) who was himself shot down on 18 May 2001 at Chandni Chowk in Karachi. A *Lashkar-e-Jhangvi* activist Mohammad Faisal alias Pehlwan was eventually sentenced to death by a Karachi Anti Terrorism Court for the murder. Therefore, one can say the divide between different

Sunni sub-sects in Pakistan is equally large as the divide with *Shias* and looking at the problem of sectarianism only as a *Shia-Sunni* problem is too simplistic.

In a similar incident of sectarian terrorism on 27 March 2009, 76 persons were killed and over 125 injured in a suicide attack at a *Shia* mosque on the Peshawar-Torkham Highway in the Jamrud Sub-division of the Khyber Agency during the Friday congregation. The bombing reduced the single-storey roadside mosque to rubble. In yet another incident of bombing targeting a *Shia* procession in Karachi, December 28, 2009 [which was taken out in connection with the death anniversary of Muslim Caliphate Imam Hussain], at least 43 people were killed and 62 others injured.

While the official determination of those responsible for the two attacks carried out in 2009 is still awaited, both the incidents seems to be a continuation of the abhorrent tactic of sectarian terrorist groups targeting places of worship. While the strategy of targeting mosques is now increasingly being used by a melange of militant groups across Pakistan, this is a method that has been applied with lethal effect for years by sectarian jehadis. In fact, between 2002 and 2009, sectarian jehadis targeted mosques on at least 50 occasions across the country.

According to a well known Pakistani writer Khaled Ahmed, Pakistanis are in a state of denial about the menace of sectarianism in their country, yet the reality is that thousands of Pakistani *Shias* have died in sectarian violence. Speaking at an Asia Program event co-sponsored by the Middle East Program in Washington on 2 May 2007, Khaled argued that Pakistan is not a truly sectarian country; *Sunnis* and *Shia* largely don't hate each other and most of the internecine violence is restricted to portions of cities like Karachi and Quetta and in the provinces of Punjab and NWFP. Why, then, does a non-sectarian nation suffer sectarian strife? The answer, said Khaled, is that Pakistan has become a relocated battlefield for the *Sunni-Shia* violence of the Middle East.

"Prior to the 1979 Iranian Revolution, the Pakistani *Shia* minority was unresponsive to Iran's radical *Shia* ideology. Instead, many Pakistani *Shia* clerics studied in the Iraqi *Shia* city of Najaf and developed views at variance with those of Iran's revolutionary leader,

Ayatollah Khomeini. Yet Iran's *Shia*-led revolution kindled a sectarian fervour that eventually spread to Pakistan. The Pakistani *Shia*s, therefore, began training at the Iranian holy city of Qom. The Pakistani authorities used jehadi militias in their proxy wars and the seminaries that trained the jehadis began apostatizing through issuing of *fatwas* or edicts", said Khaled adding that sectarianism had increased in Pakistan under Musharraf, because he was unable to control Pakistan's 'ungovernable spaces,' into which non-Pakistani sectarian-minded groups are entering and which may comprise as much as 60 percent of the total Pakistani territory.

As a matter of fact, Pakistan is the only country – now aside from Iraq – where most of the suicide bombings (66%) are based on sectarian hatred. The hate literature and cassettes from the two sides – easily available across the country – clearly violate the law of the land but seldom invite sanction. Offences such as murder and destruction of property do get a state response but it lacks the will to take the difficult steps necessary to deal with the phenomenon. A narrow law and order approach, with a police force unequipped to deal with highly motivated, well trained and well organised militants, has obviously not had much of an impact, particularly when the militants have state-of-the-art weapons. The increasing militarisation and brutalisation of the conflict shows that there are virtually no sanctuaries left – neither home, nor mosque or the hospital. And being innocent is not the issue. Just 'being' is enough – being *Shia* or *Sunni, Barelvi* or *Deobandi.*

REFERENCE

1.   Khaled Ahmed, Speaking at Middle East Program in Washington, 2 May 2007.

CHAPTER 22

Sipah-e-Sahaba Pakistan – The Sunni Sectarian Army

The *Sipah-e-Sahaba Pakistan* (SSP) – or the Corps of the Prophet Mohammad's Companions – is a violently anti-*Shia* *Sunni* sectarian group responsible for targeting the *Shia* minority in Pakistan and is described by many as the mother of almost all the *Deobandi* jehadi organisations in Pakistan. The ultra-fanatic sectarian organisation had emerged in central Punjab in the mid-1980s as a response to the Iranian Revolution, seeking proclamation of Pakistan as a *Sunni* state. Earlier known as *Anjuman-e-Sipah-e-Sahaba*, the *Sipah-e-Sahaba Pakistan* belongs to the *Deobandi* school of thought and has ideological affinity with the Taliban. It aims at restoring the Caliphate system and has declared the country's *Shia* minority to be non-Muslim.

Allegedly involved in spreading sectarian violence across Pakistan, with the *Shia* and Iranian interests in Pakistan as its prime targets, the SSP is actually an offshoot of the *Jamiat Ulema-e-Islam* (JUI), a *Sunni Deobandi* religio-political party, which had played an active role in the electoral politics of Pakistan since its inception. Maulana Haq Nawaz Jhangvi, Maulana Ziaur Rehman Farooqi, Maulana Esar-ul-Haq Qasmi and Maulana Azam Tariq established the SSP, initially as *Anjuman-e-Sipah-e-Sahaba Pakistan* (ASSP), in September 1985 in an environment of increasing sectarian hostility in Punjab. The SSP founder Maulana Haq Nawaz Jhangvi, who was a prayer leader at a *Sunni*-run Jhang mosque, was a product of *madrassa* education and was known for his anti-*Shia* oratory. Maulana Haq Nawaz Jhangvi was groomed during the 1974 anti-Ahmedi agitation (against the country's minority *Qadiani* community) like many other leaders of the SSP and later rose to become the vice chairman of the *Jamiat Ulema-e-Islam*. Jhangvi remained associated with the JUI till 1989 when he finally discarded it because of a completely different line of struggle. Maulana Jhangvi was militant in nature and had an anti-*Shia* hardline agenda, compared with the JUI, which claimed to be a non-partisan and non-sectarian religio-political party.

The *Anjuman-e-Sipah-e-Sahaba* was then renamed *Sipah-e-Sahaba Pakistan*, with Jhang city of Punjab being made its base which has very high numbers of landholdings by the *Shia* landlords and the people working for them are primarily *Sunnis*. The SSP cadres soon resorted to violent means to achieve their goals and made public their intentions to make Pakistan a *Sunni* state. While fervently believing in hostility towards *Shias*, the SSP declared that the *Shias* were non-Muslims. While the *Shia* activists were following the developing trend closely and making themselves ready to counter the SSP jargon, the *Tehrik-e-Nifaz-e-Fiqah-e-Jaafria* (TNFJ) or *Movement for Enforcement of Jaafria* (Religious Law) chief Allama Arif Hussain Al Hussaini was assassinated in August 1988, serving a severe blow to the *Shias* in Pakistan. The TNFJ was renamed as *Tehrik-e-Jaafria Pakistan* (TJP) and then renamed as the *Tehreek-e-Islami Pakistan* (TIP).

Soon afterwards, it was Maulana Haq Nawaz Jhangvi's turn, who too was killed on 23 February 1990, within a year of Allama Arif Hussaini's murder. Maulana Ziaur Rehman Farooqi subsequently took over the SSP command but he too was assassinated in a powerful bomb explosion inside the Lahore Sessions Court building on 19 January 1997. Maulana Azam Tariq succeeded Maulana Ziaur Rehman Farooqi before being killed in October 2003 by his *Shia* opponents. The next in line was the SSP patron-in-chief, Allama Ali Sher Haideri, who was shot dead in the Khairpur district of Sindh on 17 August 2009.

Hardly four days before Ali Sher Haideri's murder, Interior Minister Rehman Malik had stated in the National Assembly [on

12 August 2009] that there was no doubt that the *Sipah-e-Sahaba Pakistan* had been involved in several recent acts of terrorist in the country. Speaking on a point of order in the National Assembly the same day, a parliamentarian from Jhang Sheikh Waqas Akram said on 12 August 2009 that the SSP is once active once again in his area which could result in a re-emergence of the frantic sectarian violence. He asked who has allowed the SSP to stage a comeback?

A subsequent editorial carried by *Daily Times* on 13 August 2009 titled 'Threat from Jhang' answered the pertinent query in these words: "Clearly, lack of action on the part of the Punjab government and its law-enforcement institutions is a major factor. The lower courts are scared of convicting SSP men and it is now the foreign press that is reporting news about the imminent release of the most dreaded killer of SSP, Akram Lahori, because 'there is no evidence against him'. There is little real reporting from the districts where the terrorists exploit a weak writ of the state to intimidate local journalists. MNA Akram has pointed to a very specific case. He said that all the 200 SSP activists arrested in Jhang – after a judge took a *suo moto* notice of an incident of violence – had been released one by one; and that he had learned during a visit to the Gojra city of Punjab that members of the same group had attacked the Christians in Gojra, burning seven of them alive. He has further asked another pertinent question: Why was a leader of SSP allowed to address his arrested group activists in jail and to go around the country despite the fact that SSP was a banned organisation? His words were: "Don't leave us at the mercy of these *Maulvis*".

The *Daily Times* further added: "In a bid to address these questions, Interior Minister Rehman Malik maintained that it was actually a provincial subject and the Punjab government should be held answerable. However, down in Punjab, the feudal politicians had decided not to crib openly about the armed *Maulvis*, from the point of view of their own security. Why are the South Punjabis sceptical about standing up to the old jehadis-turned-terrorists? The answer is quite near the surface if you talk to them. It is the centre and the agencies at the centre – who have handled these elements as 'assets' of the state in the past – that send down signals that no one dare ignore. How can Rehman Malik control these agencies? The last time he tried to bring one under his wings [Inter Services Intelligence], he nearly lost his job".

Almost six months later, on 23 February 2010, Sheikh Waqas Akram accused the Punjab government [of Chief Minister Shehbaz Sharif] of patronising the SSP to garner the support of the banned organisation in a bye-election on a vacant provincial assembly seat. He said Punjab Law Minister Rana Sanaullah had accompanied the SSP leader Maulana Mohammad Ahmed Ludhianvi in his official vehicle during his visit to Jhang on 21 February 2010. Speaking on the point of order in National Assembly, Waqas said Rana Sanaullah had visited Jhang in connection with a bye-election in PP-82. "By doing so, the Punjab government is giving a message to the people of Jhang that they should not vote for liberal and enlightened candidates".

A subsequent editorial published by daily *Dawn* on 25 February 2010 stated: "Unfortunately, a statement by the Punjab law minister gives an indication of just what kind of impact the impassioned pleas from the National Assembly are having on the provincial leadership. The minister explains his recent Jhang hobnobbing by arguing that he is fully within his rights to woo voters, whatever group they may belong to. Simple reasoning which, if anything, adds to the prevailing sense of insecurity. The National Assembly members are quite right in demanding that the federal government play a more active role in curbing extremism".

Daily Times stated in its 1 March 2010 editorial: "It is a matter of extreme concern that a provincial law minister has been seen pandering to a banned organisation's senior leader. Rana Sanaullah either forgot his own designation during his recent visit to Jhang or was suffering from amnesia when he took *Sipah-e-Sahaba Pakistan* leader Maulana Mohammad Ahmed Ludhianvi on a ride in his car. He also visited the banned organisation's madrassa. Is it not ironic that the law minister gave full protocol to a sectarian outfit's leader, an organisation that has officially been banned by the government? Thus it was all but inevitable that there was an uproar over Rana Sanaullah giving official patronage to Ludhianvi in the National Assembly".

On 6 March 2010, English daily *The News* reported: "Governor

Punjab Salman Taseer has written a letter to Punjab Chief Minister Shehbaz Sharif, expressing his deep concern over the provincial government's act of releasing two convicted terrorists of the SSP, ahead of the bye-election in PP-82 (Jhang) to garner their support". The report said that Talib Qiamat and Siddiqui Jopoo, who had been arrested in 1992, were released under a deal to get votes of the SSP in Jhang to win the bye-election.

The letter by Governor Punjab further said: "What is worse is that the activities of the Punjab Law Minister clearly flout the provisions of the Anti Terrorism Act 1997." Quoting from the anti terrorism law 1997, the letter said, the Section 11-F says: "(1) A person is guilty of an offence if he belongs or professes to belong to a proscribed organisation; (2) a person guilty of an offence shall be liable to conviction to a term not exceeding six months of imprisonment; (3) a person commits offence if he solicits or invites support for a proscribed organisation or addresses a meeting which he knows is to support a proscribed organisation, further the activities of a proscribed organisation or to be addressed by a person who belongs or professes to belong to proscribed organisation; (4) a person commits an offence if he addresses a meeting or delivers a sermon to a religious gathering by any means whether verbal, written, electronic, digital or otherwise and the purpose of his address or sermon is to encourage support for a proscribed organisation or to further its activities. I am of the firm opinion that canvassing by Rana Sanaullah has further endangered the already fragile sectarian peace in and around the sensitive district Jhang".

The SSP was one of the five militant and sectarian outfits that were banned by President General Pervez Musharraf on 12 January 2002 for their involvement in terrorist activities in Pakistan. After being banned, the SSP chief, Maulana Azam Tariq, had renamed it as *Millat-e-Islamia Pakistan (MIP)*, saying that his party believed in political struggle through parliament with the ultimate aim of constitutionally turning Pakistan into a *Sunni* state, just as Iran is constitutionally a *Shia* state. He was shot dead in Islamabad on 6 October 2003 while going to the Parliament building to attend the National Assembly session. The 42-year-old SSP leader had escaped two prior assassination attempts in the mid-1990s by suspected rival

Shia militants. Considered to be pro-Taliban, Azam Tariq had won a National Assembly seat in the 2002 general elections from the *Sunni*-dominated Jhang district while contesting as an independent candidate. Maulana Azam Tariq had been a frequent visitor to Afghanistan during the Taliban rule, and was an ardent supporter of banning music, television and cinema in all of Pakistan. In December 1999, he had pledged to send 500,000 jehadi activists to Indian-occupied Jammu & Kashmir to carry out terrorist actions.

In the aftermath of the 9/11 terror attacks and the subsequent invasion of Afghanistan by the US-led forces, Maulana Azam Tariq had joined hands with the Afghan Jehad Council, an alliance of the country's anti-US and pro-Taliban religio-political parties opposed to the American occupation of the neighbouring Muslim state. The SSP had vigorously opposed the Pak-US alliance that was formed in the aftermath of the 9/11 attacks as the coalition targeted the Taliban regime in Afghanistan, a major supporter of the pro-*Sunni* terrorist outfits in Pakistan.

The SSP had joined the *Jamaat-e-Islami Pakistan* (JI), Maulana Fazlur Rehman faction of the *Jamiat Ulema-e-Islam* (JUI-F), Samiul Haq faction of the *Jamiat Ulema-e-Islam* (JUI-S) and the *Jamiat Ahl-e-Hadith* (JAH), maintaining that the US-led invasion of Afghanistan was not a war against Taliban but against Islam, and for that reason it was essential for the Muslims to declare jehad against the US-led forces in Afghanistan. Under his leadership, the SSP was linked with two pro-*Deobandi* jehadi organisations – *Harkatul Mujahideen* (HuM) led by Maulana Fazlur Rehman Khalil and *Jaish-e-Mohammad* (JeM) led by Maulana Masood Azhar.

Many Pakistani analysts believe that the origin of the SSP actually lies in the feudal set-up of Punjab and the religio-political developments in the 1970s and 1980s. As a matter of fact, the political and economic power in central Punjab was a privilege of large landowners, mostly *Shias*, a minority as compared to the majority *Sunni* sect. The urban Punjab in contrast, was a non-feudalised middle-class society, largely from the *Sunni* sect. The socio-economic rationale for the SSP's origin is explained largely from the economic profile of Jhang district, the home town of Jhangvi and the home base of the SSP.

Located in a region that divides central from southern Punjab province, Jhang still has a significantly high proportion of large land holdings, leaving feudalism comparatively undisturbed. Most large landlords in Jhang, who are *Shias*, dominate both society and politics in the region. But, over the years, the area has developed as a central market town, gradually increasing the power of traders, shopkeepers and transport operators in the region. Seeking a political voice and role, this class, largely from the *Sunni* sect, has been challenging the traditional feudal hold.

However, the most serious political challenge to the control of feudal interests in Jhang had been articulated in the form of violent sectarianism, with the formation of the SSP. As in most areas affected by violence, a major contradiction has already risen in Jhang. While a sizeable proportion of the Jhang traders and shopkeepers continue to fund the SSP, most do not believe in the violence associated with the party, rather it is now a matter of buying security from the SSP henchmen. Nevertheless, there is a decline in their support for the SSP over recent years as a result of the economic consequences of sectarian strife.

Writer Hassan Abbas maintains in his book titled '*Pakistan's drift into extremism, Allah, the Army and America's war on terror*', (published in 2004) that extremists among *Sunnis*, especially belonging to the *Deobandi* and *Ahl-e-Hadith* groups had been from the very beginning uncomfortable with the *Shia* minority for theological differences. However, sectarian violence until then was rare. "But the 1979 Iranian revolution changed the character and magnitude of sectarian politics in Pakistan. It emboldened Pakistani *Shias* who in turn became politicised and started asserting for their rights. The zealous emissaries of the Iranian revolutionary regime started financing their outfit *Tehrik-e-Nifaz-e-Fiqah-e-Jaafria* (TNFJ) and providing scholarships for Pakistani students to study in Iranian religious seminaries".

For the military regime of President General Zia though, he writes, the problematic issue was *Shia* activism leading to a strong reaction to his attempts to impose *Hanafi* Islam (a branch of the *Sunni* sect). "For this, he winked at the hardliners among the *Sunni* religious groups to establish a front to squeeze the *Shias*. It was in this context that Maulana Haq Nawaz Jhangvi was selected by the intelligence community to do the needful. The adherents of the *Deobandi* school of thought were worried by *Shia* activism for religious reasons anyhow. The state patronage came as an additional incentive. Consequently, in a well-designed effort, *Shia* assertiveness was projected as their disloyalty to Pakistan and its Islamic ideology. It was only a matter of a few months that Saudi funds started pouring in making the project feasible".

For Saudi Arabia, Hassan Abbas further states, "the Iranian revolution was quite scary for its ideals were conflicting with that of a *Wahabi* monarchy. More so, with an approximately ten percent *Shia* population, the royal family of Saudi Arabia was concerned about the expansion of *Shia* activism in any Muslim country. Hence, it was more than willing to curb such trends in Pakistan by making financial investment to bolster its *Wahabi* agenda".

As far as its organisational set-up is concerned, the *Sipah-e-Sahaba* reportedly maintains its headquarters in the two largest *Deobandi madrassas* of Punjab – *Jamiat-ul-Uloom Eidgah* in Bahawalnagar city, and *Darul Uloom Deoband Faqirwali* in the Fort Abbas subdivision. However, all organisational controls are exercised from regional headquarters located in the *Jamia Faruqiya*, Jia Moosa, Shahdara near Lahore while the international units are controlled by the *Madrassa Mahmoodiya* in Jhang. The SSP networks in Multan, Jhang, Quetta, Hyderabad and Peshawar are under Maulana Abdul Ghafoor, Rana Ayub, Hafiz Qasim Siddique, Maulana Farooq Azad and Maulana Darwesh respectively. The tentacles of the organisation are widespread, as the SSP has paid considerable attention to setting up district level units. The organisation boasted over 300 district-level units before being banned by the Musharraf regime in 2002.

Although rooted in Punjab province, the SSP is considered to be a truly national and increasingly international phenomenon. With 20 branches in foreign countries including Saudi Arabia, Bangladesh, Canada, the United States, the United Kingdom, Japan, etc., the SSP claims to be the largest and most pervasive *Sunni* supremacist organisation in the world. Going by media reports, the organisation has tens of thousands of active supporters and boasts up to 6,000 trained and professional cadres, many of whom are actively involved in sectarian violence. The SSP extremists operate in two ways: target killings of prominent *Shia* leaders and attacking worshippers through bomb blasts in mosques operated by opposing sects. The SSP leadership accuses Iran of sponsoring the *Shia* extremist organisations in Pakistan. Therefore, when any major *Sunni* leader is assassinated in the country, the Iranians in Pakistan are allegedly targeted by the SSP for retribution. For instance, the Iranian Consul General in Lahore, Sadiq Ganji, was killed in December 1990 in what was reported to be a retribution for the February 1990 killing of the SSP founder Maulana Haq Nawaz Jhangvi.

The SSP leadership chose to lie low after General Pervez Musharraf's military coup of November 1999, lending credence to the hypothesis that the SSP, like other sectarian and ethnic groups, indulges in violence only when the state guarantees an environment of neutrality and even tacit support to this violence. As the Musharraf regime took a hard-line stance against internal violence in Pakistan, the SSP decided to keep a low profile for the time being. But following Afghanistan's invasion by the US-led Allied Forces, Azam Tariq warned to fight alongside the Taliban militia. In an interview with the *BBC*, he had openly praised the former Taliban rulers of Afghanistan and endorsed attacks on the *Shias* in Pakistan. He was locked up in October 2001 as the Allied Forces rained bombs on the Taliban-ruled Afghanistan, followed by several violent rallies taken out by the SSP in various parts of Punjab. However, when the 2002 general elections were held almost a year later by the Musharraf regime, Azam Tariq campaigned from behind the bars and won a National Assembly seat from Jhang.

On 7 April 2006, in a strange move, the Musharraf regime allowed the outlawed SSP to hold a massive rally in Islamabad during which its leaders vowed to establish a global caliphate, beginning with Pakistan. In a rally attended by thousands of activists of the banned group to commemorate the birth of the Prophet Mohammad, SSP leaders called for an Islamic theocracy in Pakistan. "The concept of a nation state is an obstacle in the establishment of an Islamic Caliphate. We will start the establishment of Caliphate in Pakistan and then will do so across the world", said Major General (retd) Zaheerul Islam Abbasi, who was arrested in 1995 and court-martialed for trying to topple the government of former Prime Minister Benazir

Bhutto. The participants of the rally were sold video compact discs of the beheadings of US soldiers in Iraq, and jehadi activities in Afghanistan. One of the organisers thanked the Islamabad administration for allowing the rally, which was reportedly held under floodlights in a bus depot, with hundreds of riot police watching.

A section of the national press even reported after the rally that the Musharraf regime has almost decided to allow the reincarnation of the SSP to function as a political party and take part in the 2007 general elections. The media reports said that the decision was taken in a meeting of officials from the Interior Ministry's National Crisis Management Cell and other law enforcement agencies and the SSP leaders. The government officials reportedly asked the SSP leaders to maintain a low profile and not to incite sectarian hatred. However, the country's *Shia* leadership belonging to the *Tehreek-e-Islami Pakistan* strongly resented the relaxation granted to the SSP by the government, saying it would only lead to massacres of *Shias*, like in the past.

The fact, however, remains that the SSP never ceased to operate after being banned on 12 January 2002 and it only changed its name. Its terror structure was never dismantled; its offices remained open and it continued to publish its monthly magazine. The SSP has continued to supply manpower to its anti-*Shia* armed wing, *Lashkar-e-Jhangvi*, which is now accused of having direct links with the *Al-Qaeda* network. But all these activities did damage the standing of the SSP in Jhang. Maulana Mohammad Ahmad Ludhianvi, the sitting chief of the *Sipah-e-Sahaba Pakistan*, contested the 2007 general elections from Jhang, saying he wanted to fight for the reinstatement of his group if he wins a seat in the Pakistani National Assembly. However, he was defeated by a margin of 5,000 votes despite getting over 35,000 votes.

The shocking defeat of Maulana Mohammad Ahmad Ludhianvi came as a major blow to the SSP given the fact that his predecessor – Maulana Azam Tariq – had been elected to the National Assembly from the same seat in the 1990, 1993 and 2002 general elections. In the 1997 general elections, Azam Tariq had opted to run for a Punjab assembly seat and had won. The 1990 election was a particularly big success when Azam Tariq had defeated the government-backed candidate Sheikh Yusuf by a big margin. In the 2002 elections, he was elected as a member of the National Assembly despite the fact that he was under detention. As things stand, the anti-*Shia* movement in Pakistan has two faces. One is the *Millat-e-Islamia Pakistan*, earlier called *Sipah-e-Sahaba Pakistan*, which believes in political struggle through parliament with the ultimate aim of constitutionally turning Pakistan into a *Sunni* state. The other face of the anti-*Shia* movement is the *Lashkar-e-Jhangvi* (LeJ), which subscribes to the policy of eradication of the 'infidel' *Shias.*

The 1993 World Trade Centre Bombing, Ramzi Yusuf and SSP

The *Sipah-e-Sahaba Pakistan* (SSP) has often been linked to Ramzi Ahmed Yusuf, the key accused in the New York World Trade Centre bombing of February 1993. He was arrested from an Islamabad guesthouse on 7 February 1995 and was handed over to the United States. Exploring Ramzi Yusuf's links with a Pakistani sectarian outfit, *Sipah-e-Sahaba*, a 27 March 1995 news report in Pakistan's English daily, *The News* stated: "The Pakistani investigators are now sure of Ramzi Yusuf's ties with the *Sipah-e-Sahaba*, which flourished mostly in the military training camps inside Afghanistan designated for Arabs and Pakistanis. Orthodox *Sunni* religious schools in Pakistan serve as feeders for these military training camps".

The report stated: "Pakistani investigators have identified a 24-year-old religious fanatic Abdul Shakoor residing in Lyari in Karachi, as an important Pakistani associate of Ramzi Yusuf. Abdul Shakoor had intimate contacts with Ramzi and was responsible for the 20 June 1994 massive bomb explosion at the shrine of Imam Ali Reza in Mashhad. The Iranian government had earlier held the rebel *Mujahideen Khalq* group responsible for the explosion. Some analysts suspect Ramzi Yusuf's connection with *Mujahideen Khalq* because of his Iraqi background".

The News report added: "Independent reports suggested that in *Moharram* (first month of the Islamic calendar) last year (1994), Ramzi Yusuf traveled to Iran via Turbat in Baluchistan. Abdul Muqeem, another long-time resident of Karachi and identified as a brother of Ramzi, had also spoken about Ramzi's involvement in the Mashhad bomb blast. Ramzi is understood to have strong connections in the Pakistani and Iranian sides of Baluchistan. Last year (1994), Ramzi's associates in Karachi were given the task to murder Maulana Salim Qadri, the chief of the *Sunni Tehrik*, an organisation of moderate *Sunnis* from the *Barelvi* school of thought. Besides Abdul Shakoor, investigators believed that Abdul Wahab, owner of Junaid Bakery in the Lyari area of Karachi and the unit in charge of the *Sipah-e-Sahaba* in Chakiwarah, neighbourhood of Karachi, was another close aide of Ramzi."

The report said Ramzi also ran a network of Saudi nationals committed to destabilising the royal family in that country. "There is no evidence available to suggest that the *Sipah-e-Sahaba* was in any way aware of Ramzi's anti-kingdom operations inside Saudi Arabia. A nationwide hunt is currently on to trace Munir Madni, a suspected Saudi national and a resident of Bahadurabad in Karachi. Evidence confirmed that Ramzi, through Munir Madni, had established a front import-export company that used to get a gift of *Aabe Zam Zam* (holy water) from Saudi Arabia worth many millions of rupees. At one point last year (1994), the same front company generated about Rs. 7 million by selling the holy water. The money was later used by Ramzi to finance Saudi extremist groups. Official investigation has also revealed that dozens of Saudis committed to jehad all over the world are visiting the military training camps inside Afghanistan. These training camps are ideal places to rub shoulders with persons like Ramzi Yusuf whose colleagues in Pakistan and Afghanistan were still busy in fuelling unrest in the kingdom".

A July 2002 report by South Asia Analysis Group stated, "In 1996, cadres of the *Sipah-e-Sahaba, Lashkar-e-Jhangvi, Lashkar-e-Toiba* and *Harkatul Mujahideen* encouraged by the ISI (Inter Services Intelligence), entered Afghanistan in numbers of thousands to help the Taliban in its successful assault on Jalalabad and Kabul. After the capture of Kabul by the Taliban militia in September 1996, they stayed behind in Afghanistan to help the Taliban in its fight against the Northern Alliance. It was the SSP/LeJ elements, which had joined the Taliban and later carried out the brutal massacre of the *Shias* in the Hazara belt".

The report added: "When bin Laden moved over to Afghanistan from Sudan in 1996, he did not have to create a new terrorist infrastructure to help him in his operations against the United States and Israel. A well-motivated and well-trained infrastructure already existed on the ground consisting of trained Arabs as well as Pakistanis and he took over their leadership. After he formed his International Islamic Front for Jehad against America and Israel in 1998, the Pakistani organisations – the HuM, the LeT, the JeM and the SSP/LJ – joined it and fought against the Northern Alliance and then against the international coalition led by the US. Subsequently, after the collapse of the Taliban, this infrastructure moved over to Pakistan, along with the surviving leaders and cadres".

Though Ramzi's nationality remains disputed, it is believed that he was a native of the Baluchistan area of Pakistan, a wild lawless border region with deep and broad ties to the former Taliban regime. His uncle and partner-in-crime, Khalid Sheikh Mohammad, is also believed to hail from Baluchistan. Following his 1995 arrest from Pakistan, a spokesman of the Foreign Ministry in Islamabad denied that Ramzi Ahmed Yusuf was a Pakistani national and asserted that his papers showed that he is an Iraqi national. This gave rise to the question: whether Ramzi and his associates might have organised the 1993 New York World Trade Centre explosion, which coincided with the second anniversary of the end of the 1991 Gulf War.

While the Pakistani and American agencies failed to collect any credible evidence to prove or refute this suspicion, an American researcher Ms. Laurie Mylorie, then affiliated with the Foreign Policy Research Institute of Philadelphia, made a detailed investigation into Ramzi Yusuf's nationality and a paper based on the results of her research was carried by a US journal 'The National Interest' in its issue for Winter 1995/96. While enquiries into his real nationality after his arrest established that he was a Yemeni-Baluchi from Pakistan, she came to the following conclusions on his possible links with Iraq:

(i) On 1 September 1992, Ramzi arrived in the US with an Iraqi passport under the name Ramzi Ahmed Yusuf without a US visa. He was granted temporary asylum pending an enquiry.

(ii) On 9 November 1992, he reported to the Jersey City Police that his name was Abdul Basit Mahmud Abdul Karim, a Pakistani national born and brought up in Kuwait, and that he had lost his passport. His report was recorded.

(iii) Between 3 December and 27 December 1992, Ramzi made a number of phone calls to Baluchistan, several of which were conference calls to key numbers, a geographical plotting of which suggested they were related to his probable escape route through Pakistani and Iranian Baluchistan across the Arabian Sea to Oman, after which the telephone trail ended.

(iv) On 31 December 1992, he went to the Pakistani Consulate in New York and submitted a copy of the report recorded by the Jersey City Police about the loss of his passport along with the copies of his lost passport to show that he was a Pakistani national – Abdul Basit Mahmud Abdul Karim and applied for a new passport. The Consulate issued to him a temporary passport under this name with which he escaped from the US after the explosion.

(v) The Kuwait government's archives did have the papers and finger-prints of one Abdul Basit Karim, a Pakistani national born in Kuwait, but without copies of his passport. The archives contained a note that Abdul Basit and his family had left Kuwait for Baluchistan via Iraq and Iran on 26 August 1990.

(vi) After finding out that Ramzi had fled the US after the explosion as Abdul Basit, a Pakistani national, the US Immigration sent his finger prints to the Kuwaiti authorities who confirmed that they tallied with the finger prints in their records.

(vii) Thereafter, the American authorities presumed that Ramzi's real name was Abdul Basit; that he entered the US as Ramzi Ahmed Yusuf, an Iraqi national and fled after the World Trade Centre explosion as Abdul Basit, a Pakistani national. For some reasons, which remained unclear, they chose to prosecute him as Ramzi Yusuf and not as Abdul Basit.

According to the FBI investigations, Ramzi Yusuf was out of the US before the smoke had cleared from the World Trade Centre's halls. He escaped to Pakistan hours after the bombing where he first visited his family and then decided to stay at a guest house in Islamabad. Ramzi then reacquainted himself with his uncle, Khalid Sheikh Mohammad and organised several attempted terrorist acts, some of which succeeded. In a meeting with Khalid Sheikh Mohammad and Abdul Hakim Murad, an old friend of Ramzi, the three discussed airplanes and pilot training. After a few months, say the FBI findings, all three were dispatched to Manila, Philippines, under orders from Osama bin Laden to begin plotting direct strikes on the United States.

As with many elements of Ramzi's life, it remains a mystery exactly when did he first join forces with the *Al-Qaeda*. There is some evidence that the first WTC bombing might have been assisted or facilitated by Laden, but there is a lot more evidence that Ramzi's Manila cell was an *Al-Qaeda* shop, financed by bin Laden's brother-in-law, Mohammed Jamal Khalifa. There is a school of thought in the American intelligence community that believes that Ramzi might have been working for Iraq instead of *Al-Qaeda*, particularly since the first WTC bombing took place on the anniversary of the liberation of Kuwait by allied forces in the first Gulf War. However, most theories closely tying Ramzi to the government of Iraq tend to involve an amount of misdirection and the connections have thus never been proven.

According to US intelligence reports, with funds flowing from *Al-Qaeda*, Ramzi Yusuf sat down with Khalid Sheikh and together they devised what would have been the biggest and most devastating terrorist act in history. And they came within two weeks of pulling it off. Project Bojinka (a Serbo-Croatian word for explosion) was the devious brainchild of these sessions. The plan was ruthless. In Phase One of Bojinka, a minimum of five *Al-Qaeda* operatives would work in concert to destroy 11 US-bound airliners over the Pacific almost simultaneously starting on 21 January 1995. The terrorists would board planes bound for the US with stopovers all across Asia. They would plant bombs timed to explode on the second leg of the flight, then get off during the layover and repeat the process for another plane.

The FBI findings said that the plan was elegant and highly coordinated, as all the five operatives would have escaped to Pakistan unharmed. If the plan had succeeded, it would have killed an estimated 4,000 people and completely shut down all air travel around the world for days or even weeks. The bombs were ingenious constructions, using Casio digital watches as timers and virtually undetectable liquid nitroglycerin as the explosive. Ramzi tested the device on a flight from Manila to Tokyo on 11 December 1994. He built his bomb in the lavatory and left it under his seat when he disembarked in Philippines. It exploded on the way to Japan, killing the businessman unfortunate enough to have taken over Ramzi's seat. The plane managed to land successfully thanks to a heroic effort by the pilots. Ramzi subsequently resolved to increase the potency of the explosive.

On 5 January 1995, one of Ramzi's compatriots started a small chemical fire in the apartment where the bomb supplies were being mixed. The conspirators fled, leaving documents and a laptop computer behind. Watching smoke pour out the apartment window, Ramzi calmly sent Abdul Murad back to retrieve the computer after the fire department left, but the police were already on their way and Murad was arrested. Yusuf left the country a day or two later and Khalid Sheikh (the mastermind of the 9/11 terrorist attacks already under detention in US) was not far behind. Murad, left at the mercy of the Philippines police, began a lengthy confession under torture. During the course of his confession, he laid out Phase Two of Bojinka. Murad told his interrogators that he had been selected for the great honour of martyrdom. Murad, who was trained as a pilot in the United States, had been instructed to hijack a commercial airliner and crash it into a US landmark. Possible targets included the World Trade Center, the Pentagon and CIA headquarters.

Ramzi Yusuf and Khalid Sheikh subsequently fled to Pakistan. One month later, the FBI operatives tracked Ramzi Yusuf down and arrested him. The joint team of FBI agents and Pakistani intelligence officials, which arrested Ramzi from Islamabad was so busy patting themselves on the back that they completely ignored Khalid Sheikh, who was sleeping in the room next door. Yusuf was flown back to the United States and into New York, where an outstanding indictment for the WTC 1993 bombing awaited him. As the story goes, as soon as Ramzi's plane landed, an FBI agent pointed out the World Trade Centre towers to the terrorist, and commented, "They are still standing". Ramzi Yusuf reportedly responded, "They wouldn't be if I had enough money and explosives."

Ramzi Yusuf was convicted in a New York courtroom for both the WTC bombing and the Bojinka plot, and sentenced to life in prison without parole. Judged a high escape risk, he was sent to serve his sentence at the Supermax prison in Colorado. Ramzi might have been locked away but on 11 September 2001 he still managed to take one last shot at his favourite target, and this time he succeeded. An *Al-Qaeda* operation believed to be led by Ramzi Yusuf's uncle Khalid Sheikh Mohammad finally made the Bojinka plan a reality, hijacking four jets and crashing three of them into their targets: the World Trade Centre towers and the Pentagon. With a body count around 3,000, it was only a little less mayhem than would have been caused by Ramzi Yusuf's first draft of the plan. And the twin towers did come down this time.

REFERENCES

1. Hassan Abbas, *Pakistan's Drift into Extremism, Allah, Army and America's war on terror,* Pentagon Press, 2004.
2. Report, *The News,* 27 March 1995.
3. Report, *South Asia Analysis Group,* July 2002.
4. Laurie Mylorie, Foreign Policy Research Institute of Philadelphia, *The National Interest,* Winter 1995/96.
5. *Daily Times,* Editorial, 13 August 2009.
6. Daily *Dawn,* Editorial, 25 February 2010.
7. *Daily Times,* Editorial, 1 March 2010.
8. Report, *The News,* 6 March 2010.

CHAPTER 23

Lashkar-e-Jhangvi – The Lethal anti-Shia Army

Most of the major terrorist attacks carried out in Pakistan since 9/11 appear to have a common grandmother – the *Lashkar-e-Jhangvi* (LeJ) or the Army of Jhangvi – an anti-*Shia Sunni-Deobandi* sectarian turned anti-America jehadi organisation which is currently the group of choice for hard-core Pakistani militants who are adamant to pursue their ambitious jehadi agenda.

Launched in 1996 as a *Sunni* sectarian group, the *Lashkar* today has deep links with *Al-Qaeda* and the Taliban and is considered to be the most violent terrorist organisation operating in Pakistan with the help of its lethal suicide squad. As with most *Sunni* sectarian and militant groups, almost the entire LeJ leadership is made up of people who have fought in Afghanistan and most of its cadre strength has been drawn from the numerous *Sunni madrassas* in Pakistan. Besides receiving sanctuary from the Taliban in Afghanistan for their terrorist activities in Pakistan, the LeJ operatives used to fight alongside the Taliban militants. Being part of the broader *Deoband* movement, the LeJ secured considerable assistance from other *Deobandi* outfits. The LeJ also has an effectual working relationship with other *Deobandi* religio-political and terrorist organisations at a personal level, if not at the organisational level. Also, Pakistani intelligence findings show that *Al-Qaeda* has been involved with training of the LeJ members, and that the *Lashkar* militants also fought alongside the Taliban against the Northern Alliance troops in Afghanistan.

The LeJ was launched by a break away faction of the *Sunni* extremists of the *Sipah-e-Sahaba Pakistan* (SSP), who walked out of the outfit, accusing its parent organisation of deviating from the ideals of its co-founder, Maulana Haq Nawaz Jhangvi, who was assassinated by his *Shia* rivals in February 1990. After Jhangvi's assassination, those of his followers especially Riaz Basra, who wanted to continue his mission through violent means, started leaving the *Sipah-e-Sahaba*, forming their own groups under different names. In the process, six splinter groups came into being including *Jhangvi Tigers, Al Haq Tigers, Tanzeemul Haq, Al-Farooq, Al-Badr Federation* and *Allah-O-Akbar*. While *Al-Badr Federation* was created in Karachi, the other five groups were established in the Jhang, Faisalabad, Sargodha, Sumandari and Chiniot areas of Punjab province.

When the central secretary information of the SSP, Riaz Basra, finally decided to form the *Lashkar-e-Jhangvi* in 1996, the leaders of the already existing *Jhangvi Tigers, Al-Haq Tigers* and *Allah-o-Akbar*, decided to merge their groups into his LeJ. While parting ways with the SSP, Basra, who believed in the use of force to further *Jhangvi's* mission, alleged that the SSP leadership has abandoned the path of Maulana Haq Nawaz Jhangvi, which was not acceptable to him. However, there are those in Pakistani intelligence circles who insist that the LeJ was launched with the consent of the SSP leadership, giving it the militant role.

Riaz Basra was appointed the '*Salar-e-Aaala*' (Chief Commander) of the LeJ, with 12 *salars* (sub-commanders) under his command. A well-entrenched LeJ network was established for an uninterrupted supply of arms and ammunition from Afghanistan to Punjab and from there to Karachi in Sindh. Although the trained LeJ operatives never crossed the figure of 800, yet they proved themselves to be the deadliest of all. In January 1997, a deadly bomb blast at the Sessions Court in Lahore left 30 people dead, including the SSP chief Ziaur Rehman Farooqi along with 22 policemen and a journalist. As a swift reaction, the Iranian Cultural Centre in Lahore was attacked and set on fire by a group of violent SSP activists, while seven people were shot dead in Multan district of Punjab including the Iranian diplomat Muhammad Ali Rahimi the same month. In September 1997, five personnel of the Iranian armed forces who were in Pakistan for training purposes were killed in Rawalpindi near Islamabad.

Subsequent investigations revealed the involvement of SSP-linked *Lashkar-e-Jhangvi* militants in the murder of the Iranian cadets. The investigators noted that both the SSP and the LeJ enjoy an easy access to sophisticated arms and ammunitions and that their well-armed henchmen have the ability to use them even against the law enforcement agencies. However, the public stance of the SSP and the LeJ leadership is that they are not at all organisationally linked. But the fact remains that the two organisations are working in tandem with each other to advance their cause. Their cadres come from the same *madrassas* as also a similar social milieu and the SSP leadership has never criticised the LeJ because the two organisations share the same sectarian belief system and worldview. The two also have a similar charter of demands, which includes turning Pakistan into a *Sunni* state.

Both the *Sunni* sectarian outfits have consistently resorted to violence and killings to press their demands, though the SSP has been attempting to adopt a political path at the same time. Although Maulana Azam Tariq, the late chief of the SSP, repeatedly dissociated himself publicly from the terrorist activities of the LeJ, the Pakistani agencies indicated that the two outfits are closely linked to each other. For instance, when LeJ terrorist Sheikh Haq Nawaz Jhangvi was due to be hanged in February 2001 for terrorist offences, Maulana Azam Tariq, instead of dissociating himself from the terrorist, led a campaign for the remission of his sentence and also offered blood money to Iran. However, Sheikh Haq Nawaz Jhangvi was hanged in the Mianwali Central Jail for killing an Iranian diplomat in Lahore.

It was during the second tenure of Prime Minister Nawaz Sharif that his younger brother as well as Punjab Chief Minister Shahbaz Sharif's government had moved against the SSP and the LeJ militants, killing 36 of them in fake police encounters, and that too within a short span of one year. During his last days as Prime Minister, Nawaz Sharif, whose own life was under threat from the SSP and the LeJ and who had already survived an assassination attempt by them in Lahore, went public in naming Afghanistan as the country providing shelter and training to the SSP and LeJ hit men.

Before that, on 3 January 1999, the Riaz Basra-led LeJ had attempted to blow up a bridge on the Lahore-Raiwind road, close to Nawaz Sharif's farm house, shortly before he was due to pass by. Hardly few minutes before the Prime Minister's convoy was to pass, two policemen on a routine patrol stopped their van under the bridge and got out to pee. Their driver pressed the button to talk on his radio. As the van was parked only a few yards from the bridge, the rudimentary device switched on prematurely and detonated the explosives hidden under the bridge. The blast was so powerful that the two-span bridge went awry, killing one person. Before this incident, the LeJ had offered through a press release a reward of Rs. 135 million for anyone who would undertake the killing of Nawaz Sharif and his younger brother, the Punjab Chief Minister Shahbaz Sharif.

The *Lashkar-e-Jhangvi* uses terror tactics as part of its grand strategy to force the state into accepting its narrow interpretations of the *Sunni* sectarian doctrines as official doctrines. Besides targeting American interests in Pakistan, the victims of its terror tactics have been leaders and workers of rival *Shia* outfits, bureaucrats, policemen and worshippers. As the *Lashkar* hit men indulged in terrorism, they used to shoot their targets from moving motorbikes. Later on, they started using timed devices and graduated to throwing hand grenades and mowing down targets with machine guns. Another terror technique used by the LeJ hit men is a combination of hand grenades to kill and create panic, automatic fire to strike those stampeding to safety and suicide detonations to finish-off themselves and the rest.

According to Pakistani intelligence circles, a standard *Lashkar-e-Jhangvi* cell is made up of two or three young men while the number can exceed up to seven in exceptional cases. The cell often disbands after a terrorist operation and regroups at another location. The cell members are drawn from a pool of young men trained in Afghanistan who are scattered all over Pakistan. The country's premier intelligence agency, with long-standing and murky links to jehadi groups, planted informers in the Afghanistan-based LeJ training camps who reported back on consignments that were dispatched from Afghanistan. However, fresh boys without criminal records were difficult to trace once they crossed back into Pakistan. Terrorist attacks carried out by the fresh LeJ batches simply left the Pakistani security agencies helpless to prevent further attacks.

After the fall of the Taliban regime in Afghanistan, the LeJ militants preferred to take their chances with the Pakistani authorities – even risk liquidation – instead of falling into the hands of Northern Alliance commanders. And the ISI lost what little control it had over the LeJ when new internationalist militants took over. The LeJ leadership recruits hit men and operatives with care, looking for strong religious conviction and steady nerves. The trained martyrs, called the armoured corps of jehad, return to their homes and jobs to live normally until summoned. While they wait, they are under strict orders to shun beards and traditional clothes, to maintain a neat and inconspicuous appearance, to have their documents (real ones issued under fake names) in order and to carry them at all times and to do nothing illegal or out of the ordinary.

Terrorism experts say the *Lashkar* has become media-savvy and times daylight terror attacks to catch the evening news. They believe the planners of the terror attacks watch Hollywood films for ideas. And that is how they thought of disguising the late LeJ chief, Riaz Basra, putting his leg in a cast and wheeling him into former Prime Minister Nawaz Sharif's Lahore residence in 1998 as part of a scheme to show that the LeT hit men could infiltrate anywhere. Another idea came from a famous Bollywood movie: the LeJ organised a fake wedding procession in Multan district of Punjab in 1997, with a bridegroom on a white horse accompanied by musicians, singers and dancers. A cameraman kept recording the event. As the noisy convoy passed the heavily guarded Iranian Cultural Center, hit men climbed over the back wall and shot dead the Center's *Shia* Iranian director and six others. Fireworks set-off by the wedding guests camouflaged the gunfire.

In October 2000, the LeJ split into two factions with one group headed by Riaz Basra and the other by the chief of the group's *Majlis-e-Shoora* (Supreme Council), Qari Abdul Hai alias Qari Asadullah alias Talha. Qari Hai was Basra's lieutenant and ran his training camp in Sarobi, Afghanistan, until the two leaders fell out and formed their own respective factions. While the majority of Hai's supporters were Karachi-based, Basra's cadres had their roots in Punjab. The issue leading to the split was serious difference between the two over resumption of the ethnic strife, which had receded into a relative lull after General Musharraf's 1999 military coup. While Basra wanted to resume attacks against *Shia* targets, Qari Hai opposed the plan terming it suicidal for the organisation, saying that with a military regime in power, any armed activity would invite stern action against the *Lashkar*.

On 14 August 2001, General Musharraf, in the face of growing public criticism of his failure to control anti-*Shia* violence, announced the banning of the *Lashkar-e-Jhangvi*. Five months later, on 15 January 2002, Musharraf banned the *Sipah-e-Sahaba Pakistan* (SSP). Soon afterwards, the military regime had rounded up a large number of LeJ and SSP activists. However, despite being outlawed almost seven years ago, both the groups continue to carry out their terrorist activities across Pakistan. Since 2002, the *Lashkar-e-Jhangvi* has allegedly provided services for carrying out large-scale suicide attacks.

A suicide operation in March 2002 in an Islamabad church in the well-guarded sensitive diplomatic enclave killed five Christians, including two American nationals. In May 2002, 11 French engineers who were mistaken for being Americans were blown up in Karachi and 12 Pakistanis were killed in yet another suicide attack on American diplomats in the port city of Karachi on 14 June 2002. At least five of the 10 terrorists who had been identified belonged to the LeJ cadres. It was also the first occasion that police identified LeJ as being involved in all the three incidents. One of the photographed men, Asif Ramzi, was already wanted in the Daniel Pearl murder case, with a three million head money. According to investigators, the *Al-Qaeda* network worked in close coordination with the LeJ cadres to plan both the car bomb attacks in Karachi.

On 30 January 2003, the US State Department added the *Lashkar-e-Jhangvi* to its List of Foreign Terrorist Organisations and to those outfits covered under an Executive Order. Making the announcement on his boss Colin Powell's behalf, the US State Department spokesman Richard Boucher said that the terrorist group has already claimed responsibility for the 1997 killing of four American oil workers in Karachi. "They have ties to *Al-Qaeda* and the Taliban, in addition to receiving sanctuary in Afghanistan for their activities in Pakistan. Moreover, the group was involved in the kidnapping and subsequent murder of American journalist Daniel Pearl", Boucher had added.

As far as the LeJ's leadership and command and control structure is concerned, Muhammad Ajmal alias Akram Lahori is its last known *Salar-e-Aala* (Commander-in-Chief). Lahori was originally with the *Sipah-e-Sahaba Pakistan*, which he had joined in 1990. Subsequently, in 1996, he along with Malik Ishaq and Riaz Basra founded the LeJ and launched terrorist activities in Punjab. Lahori, who had established a training camp in the Sarobi area of Afghanistan after securing support from the erstwhile Taliban regime, succeeded Basra, who was killed on 14 May 2002 in the Mailsi areas of Multan in a fake police encounter. Riaz Basra was involved in over 300 acts of terrorism including attacks on Iranian missions, killing of an Iranian diplomat Sadiq Ganji and targeting government officials.

Riaz Basra was arrested and tried by a special court for Iranian diplomat Sadiq Ganji's killing, but he had escaped during trial in 1994 from police custody while being produced in court. He was chief of the Khalid bin Waleed unit of the Afghan militants training camps in Afghanistan. Lahori is himself in police custody after his arrest in Orangi Town, Karachi, on 17 June 2004. Before being arrested, he was carrying Rs. 5 million head-money announced by the Sindh government and another Rs. 5 million announced by the Punjab government. So far, it is not clear if Lahori has passed on the mantle to any one else, or continues to head the outfit from his prison cell.

The newspaper files of 2 July 2002, stated while quoting senior police officials that Akram Lahori was involved in 38 cases of sectarian killings in Sindh. These included the killing of Ehteshamuddin Haider (brother of former Federal Interior Minister Lt. Gen. (retd) Moinuddin Haider) and Pakistan State Oil Managing Director Shoukat Raza Mirza. Besides, he was involved in the murder of Iranian cadets in Rawalpindi. Lahori confessed during interrogation that he was involved in 30 cases of sectarian killings in Punjab, including those of 24 persons who were attending a *Majlis* or a religious congregation in Mominpura, Lahore. He also revealed that his group had planned to kill former Interior Minister Moinuddin

Haider, but had to murder his brother due to tight security measures.

Pakistani intelligence sources even claim that the *Lashkar* has prepared women suicide bombers to attack several *Shia* places of worship in Karachi. A suspected mastermind of bomb blasts at two *Shia* mosques in Quetta had disclosed to the Karachi police during interrogation that the *Lashkar* had brainwashed a few girls aged between 16 and 20 years to carry out suicide missions. Daily *Dawn* of 1 July 2004 quoted a Karachi police officer Manzoor Mughal as saying that Gul Hasan, an arrested accused, had disclosed that the girls, persuaded by *Lashkar-e-Jhangvi* to explode themselves in the women section of Karachi mosques, would be wearing veils or school uniform and carrying handbags. According to intelligence reports, Aziza, a citizen of Uzbekistan and the widow of Ubaidullah, who was an active member of the Islamic Movement of Uzbekistan, had been imparting training to female suicide bombers at a base in Pakistan's tribal area. Ubaidullah was killed during a military operation in South Waziristan in January 2004. Aziza actually wanted to avenge her husband's killing.

Those involved in tracking down the *Jhangvi's* terror network in Karachi say the group might be working in the provincial capital of Sindh as the delta force of *Al-Qaeda*. Delta force is a special *Al-Qaeda* unit that was trained under *Al-Qaeda* leader Khalid Sheikh Mohammad before his 2003 arrest from Rawalpindi and is tasked with specific high profile targets. Investigations into the attack on the Karachi Corps Commander in June 2006 gave broad hints that it was an operation jointly planned and carried out by the *Lashkar-e-Jhangvi* henchmen and their *Al-Qaeda* associates – Dawood Badini and Mosabir Aruchi. Intelligence circles did not rule out their involvement in the abduction and the murder planning of an American journalist Daniel Pearl who was beheaded in Karachi in 2002.

The FBI has already identified Khalid Sheikh as the person who slaughtered Pearl with his own hands. According to the Pakistani investigators, Dawood Badini and Mosabir Aruchi – are related to Ramzi Yusuf, who has already been convicted in the 1993 bombing of the World Trade Centre in New York. Dawood Badini is reportedly a brother-in-law of Ramzi Yusuf and is wanted in a 2003 Quetta mosque bomb attack that killed more than 40 people. Badini's sister is married to Ramzi Yusuf. The other man arrested, Mosabir Aruchi, is a nephew of Khalid Sheikh, Ramzi's uncle, which makes Aruchi and Yusuf cousins.

While the *Lashkar-e-Jhangvi* obviously takes some directions from the *Al-Qaeda*, the group stays admirably focused on its home turf and its stated goal of radicalising Pakistan. The stakes in that battle are far from parochial. In addition to its nuclear arsenal, Pakistan is a key strategic ally of the US in its War on Terror. Most terrorism experts agree that the *Lashkar-e-Jhangvi* operatives are the most highly trained and equally vicious killers the world of terror has to offer. Media reports quoting intelligence sources say the *Lashkar* has finally moved to centre stage and the past claims by Pakistani agencies of its demise after the capture of the LeJ chief Akram Lahori have proved to be wide off the mark. These reports say the LeJ has already started a recruitment drive and is forming new cells at the district and provincial levels.

According to media reports, a Most Wanted LeJ terrorist Matiur Rehman had been tasked with reorganising the group's terror cells and suicide squads across Pakistan. An expert in bomb making, Matiur Rehman has links with *Al-Qaeda* and is believed to be using drug money coming from the Taliban to fund the recruitment drive and reorganisation of the lethal *Lashkar-e-Jhangvi*. The 33-year-old Matiur comes from Bahawalpur and his head carries a bounty of Rs. 10 million. As the evidence of the Pakistani link in the August 2006 transatlantic bombing plot mounted, British media had reported that Matiur was one of the prime suspects in the scheme. ABC News' Alexis Debat did the lion's share of the investigation of Matiur. Just one day prior to the uncovering of the London Airline Plot, Debat described Matiur as "The Man Who Is Planning the Next Attack on America".

In March 2006, Debat explained Rehman's role as the liaison between *Al-Qaeda* and the Pakistani jehadi community, saying he was the new chief of *Al-Qaeda*'s military committee. He was of the view that the LeJ is emerging as the Trojan horse of *Al-Qaeda* to carry out operations on behalf of the Osama-led terrorist group in areas where it faces difficulty in operating directly. US intelligence sleuths stationed in Pakistan describe Matiur Rehman as an emerging *Al-Qaeda* figure, who helped train thousands of fellow Pakistani militants at training camps during the late 1990s. They portray him as extremely dangerous due to his role as a crucial interface between the brains of *Al-Qaeda* and its muscle, which is mainly composed these days of militants belonging to several Pakistani jehadi groups. The Most Wanted Matiur Rehman is still at large.

A 6 January 2007 *Daily Times* editorial explored the *Al-Qaeda* links of the *Lashkar-e-Jhangvi* in these words: "According to Pakistani security agencies, three incidents of terrorism in Karachi in 2006 – the blast at the US Consulate [on 3 March, killing diplomat David Foy], the Nishtar Park massacre [on 11 April which eliminated the entire leadership of the *Sunni Tehrik*] and the 14 July murder of *Shia* leader Allama Hasan Turabi – were all carried out by the sectarian militia *Lashkar-e-Jhangvi* and were planned in the South Waziristan tribal agency under the tutelage of *Al-Qaeda*. The new combination is *Lashkar-e-Jhangvi*, Wana and *Al-Qaeda* and the LeJ is the blanket term now used for all manners of jehad in which all the *Deobandi-Ahl-e-Hadith* militants have made common cause. All three incidents were staged through the device of suicide-bombings which is clearly the Arab signature in the violence spreading in Pakistan....

"All three terror incidents had been traced to the Wana area of Waziristan: one ostensibly committed for *Al-Qaeda* and two for the local sectarians. In fact the entire conglomerate of jehadi militias has accepted a common sectarian banner now, and this has come in the wake of *Al-Qaeda*'s own transformation from an intellectually fashioned anti-American organisation into an intra-Islamic exterminator of the *Shia*. Analysts in Pakistan believe this has been done through the mental somersault of equating the *Shias* – the government in Iraq plus, strangely, Iran – as allies of the United States!"

The editorial further stated: "To understand what is going on we have to go back to the late 1980s when *Al-Qaeda* was formed in Peshawar in the midst of a gathering sectarian storm in Pakistan. Because this wave was orchestrated by Saudi Arabia, *Al-Qaeda* tried to keep away from it. But later, starting with the return of Osama Bin Laden and other *Al-Qaeda* elements to Jalalabad from Sudan after

1996, the terror group had to accept a kind of coexistence with the sectarian militias which were taking training in its camps. That is why whenever Pakistan demanded the return of the *Lashkar-e-Jhangvi* killers from the 'friendly' Taliban government, a deaf ear was turned to it, and the *Lashkar* terrorists continued to live in *Al-Qaeda* camps outside Kabul. . .

"There were times when *Al-Qaeda* was actually helped by Iran, especially during the tenure of Abu Musab Zarqawi as head of a training camp in Herat from where he infiltrated into Kurdistan through Iranian territory. However, after 2003, there was a cleavage of opinion inside *Al-Qaeda*. Zarqawi spearheaded the new trend of viewing the *Shia* of Iraq – and Iran itself – as the beneficiaries of the American invasion. At first Zawahiri resisted this trend and *Al-Qaeda* officially advised him in Iraq to stay away from *Shia*-killing, but later the prospect of a grand *Sunni* Arab consensus against Iran became irresistible and Zarqawi was hailed as a martyr when he finally died in Iraq.

"Now *Lashkar-e-Jhangvi* is supposed to have planned a fresh targeting of the *Shia* community in the Pakistani cities where they are found in large numbers: Lahore, Rawalpindi, Gujranwala, Multan, Khanewal, Layya, Bhakkar, Jhang, Sargodha, Rahimyar Khan, Karachi, Dera Ismail Khan, Bannu, Kohat, Parachinar, Hangu, Hyderabad, Nawabshah, Mirpur Khas and Quetta. This is certainly a new challenge for the government in charge of facing up to sectarian violence in the country. Both the mainstream parties – the PPP-P and the PML-N – faced it when they were in government but failed because of the exclusive handling of jehad by the intelligence agencies...."

A 24 May 2009 investigative news report in daily *Dawn*, titled "South Punjab sees Taliban connection as stigma", stated that South Punjab has grabbed the attention of the Western media and their governments over the past few months because of the alleged involvement of the Punjabi Taliban – a blanket term for members of the banned sectarian and jehadi groups like *Lashkar-e-Jhangvi, Sipah-e-Sahaba Pakistan, Jaish-e-Mohammad* and *Harkatul Jehadul Islami*, arrested in Punjab and the federal capital after a spate of terror attacks. The story said the links of the arrested operatives of outlawed sectarian and jehadi groups from the impoverished South Punjab with the Baitullah Mehsud-led *Tehrik-e-Taliban Pakistan* and other militant groups in the Federally Administered Tribal Areas (FATA) of Pakistan and the North West Front Province (NWFP) are also a cause of grave concern in the powerful western capitals, as well as for the rulers in Islamabad.

The *Dawn* report stated: "The Americans are worried because the purported liaison between the banned sectarian organisations (for whom southern Punjab serves as catchments) and the *Tehrik-e-Taliban* in parts of the NWFP threatens the stability of the country. The NWFP government is anxious because it believes that fresh recruits for militant groups challenging its writ are coming mostly from the southern districts of Punjab – D.G. Khan, Bahawalpur, Bahawalnagar, Muzaffargarh, etc. The 5 April 2009 arrest of two Seraiki-speaking men linked with the killing of 27 people in a suicide attack at the Johar Ali Imambargah in Dera Ghazi Khan has already led to the formation of convenient theories that the militant Taliban groups have already forged a strong alliance with outfits in the southern Punjab. Investigators believe the local militants provide logistical support and, in certain cases, human resource, to the Taliban for carrying out their terror operations in Punjab. The police claim that Qari Mohammad Ismaeel, who had masterminded the D.G. Khan bombing, and Ghulam Mustafa Kaisrani, who had facilitated the Pashtun bomber, belonged to SSP/LeJ, now operating as *Ahle Sunnat Wal Jamaat*, and had close links with TTP in South Waziristan has reinforced this belief."

The report further added: "Even before the arrest of Ismaeel and Kaisrani, the investigators had found evidence of close collaboration between the *Tehrik-e-Taliban Pakistan* and the Punjabi militants, especially those belonging to *Lashkar-e-Jhangvi*, in several other terrorist incidents – the September 2008 Marriott bombing in Islamabad, the March 2009 attack on the Sri Lankan cricketers in Lahore and the siege of Manawan police training academy in Lahore the same month. Most militants involved in the terrorist acts in the recent months have been identified as being from southern Punjab. The alleged nexus between the Punjabi Taliban and Pashtun militant groups has also led to a convenient theory that the militants in the southern Punjab are regrouping to take over some southern districts like D.G. Khan or Muzaffargarh just as they have done in Swat....

"The fears of militants consolidating their ranks in south Punjab don't stem only from the recent evidence of their links with the TTP or their involvement in recent terrorist acts. The leadership and activists of the banned groups, particularly the LeJ and SSP, with a strong base in Punjab have a history of close relationship with the Afghan Taliban as well as militants in Fata. The LeJ, for example, is said to be more active in Dera Ismail Khan these days and SSP president Qari Hussain Mehsud is said to be acting as a deputy of Baitullah Mehsud there. Likewise, other leading names like Saifullah Akhtar, Maulana Jabbar and Commander Ilyas Kashmiri are sitting pretty in the tribal areas. Whenever they faced pressure in Punjab, they took shelter either in the tribal areas or in Afghanistan. Riaz Basra, a slain leader of the LeJ, for example, was given shelter in Kabul by the then Taliban regime for years before he returned home to be killed in a police encounter....

"Punjab militants, possibly in the hundreds, fled to FATA when the government of Pervez Musharraf hunted down *Lashkar-e-Jhangvi* and *Jaish-e-Mohammad* operatives after two attempts on his life. These militants are reported to have fought alongside a group of Pakhtun Taliban led by Maulvi Nazir to flush out Uzbek and Chechen fighters from Waziristan a few years ago. It is difficult to say how many Punjabi militants fled to the Pakistani tribal areas, but their presence there is significantly large. Just as militants from Punjab fled to Waziristan via Dera Ghazi Khan, there is no dearth of people who are worried about the influx of the TTP activists into Punjab province as they feel the heat of the military operation in Swat and the tribal areas."

On 15 July 2009, English daily *The News* reported that the main objective of the 3 March 2008 attack on the Sri Lankan cricket team in Lahore was to hijack the bus carrying the players and pressurize the Pakistan government into releasing the arrested terrorists of the *Lashkar-e-Jhangvi* including Akram Lahore and Malik Ishaq. Citing an investigation report submitted by the Ministry of Interior to the National Standing Committee on Sports, the story stated that the main accused, Muhammad Zubair, son of Mahboob Hussain

Mukhlis (alias Nek Mohammad) , was motivated by one Saifullah to wage jehad, by narrating sufferings of the *Lal Masjid* students and quoting verses from the Holy Koran. "The *Lashkar-e-Jhanghvi* terrorists had actually planned attacking the visiting Sri Lankan cricketers on 1 March 2009, but missed the target as they arrived at the Liberty Chowk minutes after the bus carrying the team had already left".

On 7 August 2009, the *New York Times* reported that one Fida Hussein Ghalvi who had testified 12 years ago against Malik Ishaq – a founding member of the *Lashkar-e-Jhangvi* [already charged with 70 murders, including the killing 12 of Ghalvi's family members] – fears an imminent release of the terrorist leader, thus adding horror to Ghalvi's life of grief, already reduced to the limits of his house in Multan. The newspaper said Ghalvi still gets threats from followers of Ishaq – who, maddeningly, has never had a conviction that stuck, although Punjab police records show a dizzying tally of murders against his name. "When Ishaq was arrested in 1997, he unleashed his broad network against his opponents, killing witnesses, threatening judges and intimidating police, leading nearly all of the prosecutions against him to collapse eventually," said *New York Times*. "Now, with the cases against him mostly exhausted, Ishaq (50) – a 'jehadi hero' – could be out on bail as early as this month. That prospect terrifies Ghalvi," the NYT added while quoting his as having said: "My life is totally constrained. I can't even go to funerals. What have I gotten from 13 years of struggle except grief?"

On 24 February 2010, the acting *ameer* of the *Lashkar-e-Jhangvi* Commander Qari Zafar was killed in an American predator strike in Miramshah, the headquarters of North Waziristan. The death of Qari also confirmed the *Al-Qaeda* connection of the *Lashkar-e-Jhangvi* which had been working in tandem with the *Tehrik-e-Taliban Pakistan* ever since the latter's formation in 2007 to let loose a reign of terror in almost every nook and corner of Pakistan. The drone had actually targeted a house in Peerano Killay near Miramshah, killing nine Punjabi Taliban, including Qari Zafar, who was working in coordination with the TTP's key militant commander, Qari Hussain Mehsud, better known as Ustad-e-Fidayeen (Teacher of suicide bombers).

Both Qari Zafar and Hussain Mehsud had last appeared before a small group of journalists on 5 October 2009 at an unspecified place in South Waziristan when the TTP chief Hakeemullah Mehsud, thought to have been killed during infighting, had addressed a press conference to refute media reports of his death. Speaking on the occasion, Hakeemullah said militant commanders like Qari Zafar had formally joined hands with the TTP and hundreds of their suicide bombers were waiting for their turn to hit targets in Pakistan and Afghanistan. Consequently, a series of deadly *fidayeen* attacks was carried out in Lahore, Rawalpindi and Islamabad, including the October 10, 2009 assault on the General headquarters (GHQ) of the Pakistan Army in the garrison town of Rawalpindi.

Subsequent investigations by the Pakistani authorities revealed that these stunning commando style terror attacks were jointly coordinated by Qari Zafar and Qari Hussain, while the latter also happens to be a first cousin of Hakeemullah Mehsud. Hence, the death of Qari Zafar in a drone attack came as a huge relief for the security agencies. Actually hailing from Karachi, Qari Zafar had become a member of *Al-Qaeda*'s hardline *Takfiri* group and was enjoying the protection of the TTP. Qari Zafar was arrested for questioning in connection with the 2 March 2006 car bomb attack outside the US consulate building in Karachi. The bombing killed three Pakistani citizens as well as an American diplomat David Foy, thus making the Federal Bureau of Investigations FBI to announce an award of $5 millions on his head.

However, Zafar escaped from the custody of the agencies in Lahore in 2007 and was operating from Waziristan till his death. He was also the alleged mastermind of the September 2008 suicide truck bombing of the Marriot Hotel in Islamabad. His involvement in the attack was established from phone numbers found on the mobile phones of some of those arrested in Punjab. Zafar's role in the Marriott Hotel blast was not only for planning the attack but also, arranging for the procurement of massive quantity of explosives [with the help of his LeJ followers] and even the vehicles used in the attack. Qari Zafar had been leading the LeJ as its acting *ameer* ever since the arrest of Muhammad Ajmal alias Akram Lahori, the *Salar-e-Aala* or *ameer*. Lahori was indicted on 20 February 2010 by an anti-terrorism court in Karachi in a 2002 sectarian killing case.

On 8 March 2010, a suicide bomber rammed his explosive laden vehicle into the Special Investigation Unit (SIU) building of the Punjab Police in the Model Town area of Lahore, killing 15 people besides injuring 77 others. Subsequent investigations showed the attack was carried out by the Punjab chapter of the *Tehrik-e-Taliban Pakistan* to avenge the killing of Qari Zafar. While confirming Qari Zafar's death in a statement faxed to local journalists on 25 February 2010, a *Lashkar-e-Jhangvi* spokesman had described him as a martyr and pledged to avenge his death. "The mujahideen will soon take revenge from the Pakistan government for his killing by resorting to suicide bombings anywhere in the country", the LeJ spokesman had added.

REFERENCES

1. Alexis Debat, The Man Who Is Planning the Next Attack on America, *ABC News.*
2. Editorial, *Daily Times,* 6 January 2007.
3. News Report, South Punjab sees Taliban connection as stigma, *Dawn,* 24 March 2009.
4. *Daily The News,* Editorial, 15 July 2009.
5. *New York Times,* 7 August 2009.

CHAPTER 24

The Militant Face of the *Tableeghi Jamaat*

The *Tableeghi Jamaat* (TJ) or the Party of Preachers, is a non-militant organisation of practising Muslims which claims to have never indulged in any militant or political activities as a matter of principle. The *Tableeghi Jamaat* is also translated as the "Society for Spreading Faith".

The TJ leadership says it is actually an Islamic missionary and revival movement that had been founded in British India as a response to Christian evangelists working among the poor and poorly educated Muslims in British India. The group primarily came into existence to spread the message of the Holy Koran with two main objectives: to ensure that Muslims strengthen their faith and to carry out humanitarian work. It was founded in British India in the late 1920s by a *Deobandi* cleric Maulana Muhammad Ilyas Kandhalawi (1885-1944) in the Mewat province of India. '*Tableegh*' in Arabic means 'to deliver (the message)' and the *Tableeghi Jamaat* (or the Proselytising Group) claims to revive this duty, which they consider as a primary responsibility of the Muslims.

However, concerns are being raised lately by the international media about how much the so-called Islamic missionary organisation has been infiltrated by jehadi elements which might be using the apparently non-violent TJ platform as a cover to promote their violent jehadi agenda across the globe.

The *Tableeghi Jamaat* grew out of the *Deobandi* School of Islamic Thought which emerged under British rule in the Delhi region of northern India. In pre-colonial India, Islamic scholars learned informally, by traveling with their teachers. But in the 19th century, inspired by European educational practices, Muslim clerics in India established geographically fixed institutions, known as *deeni madrassas* or religious seminaries, with sequential curriculum, organised classes, and paid faculty. The *madrassas* were actually founded by specialists in the '*hadith*' – the narratives that constitute the sayings and practices of Prophet Mohammad (PBUH), which guide all aspects of moral behaviour in Islam. The *Deobandi* Muslims emerged from the *madrassas* as a movement centered on the *Ulema* (Islamic scholars or clerics).

Deobandis considered themselves reformists, proscribing adherence to a pristine text (the Koran) as a solution to worldly powerlessness. They opposed various contemporary Islamic practices, including excessive rituals at tombs, elaborate lifestyle celebrations and *Shia*-influenced practices. Following British repression of Indian Muslims during the Mutiny of 1857, the *Deobandi* leadership adopted an avowedly apolitical stance. But as the Indian nationalist movement rose after World War I, the movement grew politically, supporting the Indian National Congress against the British.

However, a *Deobandi* scholar and the founder of the *Tableeghi Jamaat* Maulana Muhammad Ilyas Kandhalawi intended the group to be an antidote to Hindu conversion efforts that actually targeted Muslim peasants. The members of the *Tableeghi Jamaat* took the dissemination of Islamic teachings out of the *deeni madrassa* or religious seminaries, de-emphasising the importance of clerics and encouraging lay Muslims to undertake proselytising missions. *Tableeghis* also clung to the original *Deobandi* rejection of any explicit political program and to remaining apolitical.

After Maulana Mohammad Ilyas died in 1944, his son, Maulana Muhammad Yusuf (1917–95) took over the TJ and expanded its reach. The movement grew after the partition of India, regaining importance during the 11-year military rule of Pakistan's fourth dictator President General Zia-ul Haq, who had ambitions of making Pakistan an Islamic state under *Shariah*. Under his encouragement,

Maulana Yusuf and his successor Maulana Inamul Hassan began targeting non-Muslims, too. This coincided with the establishment of a synergistic relationship between Saudi *Wahabis* and South Asian *Deobandis*, which eventually led to the Saudi financing of the TJ.

The *Tableeghi* pilgrims are trained missionaries who have dedicated much of their lives to spread Islam across the globe: they are part of the reason for the explosive growth of Islamic religious fervour and conversion. The TJ movement, which has spread to 150 countries, has over one million members worldwide and its headquarters for South Asia are located in India. Despite its huge size and tremendous value, the *Jamaat* remains largely unknown outside the Muslim community, even to many scholars of Islam. This is no coincidence. The *Tableeghi Jamaat* officials work to remain outside of both media and governmental notice. They usually limit their preaching and missionary activities to within the Muslim community itself, since its main aim is to bring spiritual awakening to the Muslims of the world.

The *Tableeghi Jamaat's* lack of a formal bureaucratic structure makes its growth hard to quantify. But in recent years, millions of adherents have congregated annually at three-day TJ congregations in the Raiwind area of Lahore district [in Pakistani Punjab], said to be the second largest gathering of Muslims anywhere in the world after the Hajj in Saudi Arabia. And it was at the Raiwind session in 2007 that the ISI connection with the Pakistan branch of the TJ became concretised by the presence of four former director generals of the all powerful Inter Services Intelligence – Lt Gen (retd) Hameed Gul, Lt Gen (retd) Javed Nasir, Lt Gen (retd) Naseem Rana and Lt Gen Mahmood Ahmed.

As the media highlighted their presence at the Raiwind annual congregation, the organisers maintained that the participation of the four former ISI chiefs was an integral part of the *ijtema* for years now, and all of them had been attending the event since the days they were in uniform. "Their presence in the *ijtema* and their speeches, especially that by Lt Gen (retd) Hameed Gul helped motivate and inspire others to attend the congregation," a spokesman of the TJ said in a press statement. However, there are those who maintain that the presence of ex ISI chiefs in the TJ congregation showed the exact picture of a well-designed, well-controlled and well-managed strategy to organise Islamic combatants who are ready to wage jehad in the name of Allah against infidels, who are painted at the *ijtema* as enemies of Islam.

Since Pakistani law treats the *Tableeghi Jamaat* as a humanitarian group and not as a religio-political party, there is no ban on government servants, members of the armed forces and the nuclear and missile scientific community joining the party [even as members] to work for it. As a result, many Pakistani government servants, military officers and scientists devote at least part of their annual leave to do voluntary work for the *Tableeghi Jamaat*. Interestingly, after his appointment as the DG ISI by Prime Minister Sharif, Lt Gen Nasir continued to act as adviser to the TJ and, after his removal from the ISI under US pressure in 1993, took over as the full-time leader of the TJ.

During Lt Gen Javed Nasir's tenure as the DG ISI, the Mumbai serial blasts were carried out in 1993 and plans chalked out for the revival of Islam in the Central Asian States, Chechnya and Dagestan in Russia and Xinjiang in China with the help of the TJ workers and funds from Saudi Arabia. Similarly, Lt Gen Hameed Gul and Lt Gen Mahmood Ahmed, who served under the commands of two military dictators, General Zia and General Musharraf, had been quite vocal supporters of the Afghan *mujahideen* who later formed the Taliban militia in Afghanistan. Hameed and Mahmood were removed from their slots prematurely and sent home because of their extremist views and unblemished support for the jehadi elements.

Hardly two months before the 7 July 2005 terror attacks in London, a study paper prepared by Daniel Friedman of the Centre for Policing Terrorism, noted: While the *Tableeghi Jamaat* is nonviolent, the zealotry of its recruits has proven easy for violent groups to manipulate. The research paper titled '*Tableeghi Jamaat* Dossier' and published in May 2005, stated: "The TJ stresses traditional Islamic practices linked to worship, dress and behavior as a path to personal improvement. Thus, it easily attracts troubled, vulnerable young men and instills them with extreme religious conviction. While the *Jamaat* claims to be non-violent, the zealotry of its recruits might be proving easy for violent jehadi groups to manipulate. Its missionary work, moreover, demands the TJ members to travel throughout the world, including Pakistan and Western countries. Thus, there is every chance of some militant groups using it as a cover to travel".

The research paper also stated: "The *Tableeghi Jamaat* assembles radical recruits and deposits them in places where they can be gathered by terrorist groups. Some of these recruits have taken part in Afghan jehad; others have returned to the US with violent intentions. *Tableeghi Jamaat* does not just aid terrorists by preparing recruits ideologically. Terrorist organisations and their members can't move at will in Western countries, particularly since 11 September 2001. They are, to a degree, stuck in place. By physically assembling groups of radicalized Muslim men and depositing them in Pakistan, the *Tableeghi Jamaat* performs a valuable logistical service for militant groups, facilitating these groups' recruiting process. The defeat of the Taliban and destruction of *Al-Qaeda* training camps in Afghanistan, have also eliminated a major source of terrorist training, but with TJ still sending recruits to Pakistan, where violent groups await to recruit them, they remain likely to create ripe, susceptible young men for terrorist jehadi organisations".

The study report further stated: "Western intelligence agencies even believe the TJ has radicalised to the point where it has emerged as a driving force of Islamic extremism and a major recruiting agency for the jehadi causes world wide. Many terrorists seem to view the *Jamaat's* lack of transparency, peaceful reputation, and international network as an ideal vehicle for moving innocuously around the world. For example, Lyman Faris and members of 'Lackawana Six' (a group of alleged terrorists, raised in a Yemeni community outside Buffalo, New York) pretended to be TJ members in order to facilitate trips to meet with terrorists. Indeed, Islamic terrorists have infiltrated the group. Without an effort by the *Tableeghi Jamaat* leadership to stop them, it is probable that terrorist groups will continue to exploit TJ in one way or the other".

In 1995, the study paper noted, the members of the *Tableeghi Jamaat* were accused of plotting a coup against the relatively secular Prime Minister Benazir Bhutto. "Whether members of the Taxila group represent a sub-section or a breakaway faction of *Tableeghi*

Jamaat is disputable. But in either case, they demonstrate the potential of TJ members to embrace overtly political or violent means. The coup plot against Bhutto was supported by members of *Harkatul Mujahideen* (HUM), a Pakistani militant organisation. Pakistani news sources claim that almost all founding members of the HUM were former *Tableeghi* members. HUM members have been quoted professing a close association with the *Tableeghi Jamaat*, though *Tableeghi* does not reciprocate the claim".

Similarly, an investigative report by a Pakistani English daily *The News* on 13 February 1995, brought to light for the first time the nexus between the *Tableeghi Jamaat*, the *Harkatul Mujahideen* and their clandestine role in supporting Islamic extremist movements in different countries. The report quoted unidentified office-bearers of the *Harkat* as saying, "Ours is basically a *Sunni* organisation close to *Deobandi* school of thought. Our people are mostly impressed by the *Tableeghi Jamaat*. Most of our workers do come from the *Tableeghi Jamaat*. We regularly go to its annual meeting at Raiwind in Lahore. Ours is a truly international network of genuine jehadi Muslims."

The story quoted the HuM office-bearers as claiming that among the foreign volunteers trained by them in their training camps in Pakistan and Afghanistan, were sixteen African-American Muslims from various cities of the US and that funds for their activities mostly came from Muslim businessmen of Pakistan, Saudi Arabia, Egypt and the UK. It has already been reported in the US media that the Lackawanna Six, a group of six Yemeni-Americans arrested by the FBI in the US after the 9/11 attacks in its search for sleeper agents (an agent who can be used at any time but may not be tasked for up to a decade or more) were found to have links with TJ. They had all visited the TJ headquarters in Raiwind before the 9/11 attacks.

The group gained notoriety in 2001, following the news that John Walker Lindh, the American Taliban, first entered Pakistan through the encouragement of a *Tableeghi Jamaat* missionary. Subsequently, a number of other alleged terrorists have been linked to the TJ. The list includes Omar Padilla, currently held as an enemy combatant for planning to detonate a radiological device in the United States; Richard Reid, who attempted to ignite a shoe bomb on a flight from Paris to Miami in 2001, and a group of seven Muslims in Portland,

Oregon accused of attempting to join the Taliban to fight against the US.

Following the July 2005 London bombings, international media reported that Shehzad Tanweer, one of the human bombs who had been a British national of Pakistani origin, used to attend the *Tableeghi Jamaat* meetings at a number of London mosques. According to these reports, bands of *Tableeghi* missionaries recruit mostly young men at mosques, Islamic centers and college campuses and then invite them to join the group for a few days or weeks on the road. The TJ was also accused of making recruitments in the United States through *Jamaatul Furqa*, a violent organisation led by Pakistani Sheikh Mubarik Ali Gilani, with whom American journalist Daniel Pearl had fixed a meeting in Karachi the day he was abducted. Daniel Pearl wanted to interview him regarding a suspected connection between Gilani and Richard Reid. The Gilani-Pearl meeting was fixed by Sheikh Ahmed Omar Saeed, who has already been convicted by a Pakistani court for the abduction and murder of Pearl. Gilani was questioned by Pakistani authorities after the murder but subsequently released.

Likewise, according to US intelligence findings, as reported in Western media, among the foreign nationals who fought in Afghanistan against the Northern Alliance troops and US-led Allied Forces as members of Pakistan-based jehadi outfits, were American Muslims (mostly Afro-Americans), nationals of the West European countries, Thai, Malaysians, Singaporeans who projected themselves as Malays from Malaysia and Indonesians. These reports claimed that *Harkatul Mujahideen, Lashkar-e-Toiba* and *Harkatul Jehadul Islami* teams had visited these countries as preachers and recruited them all. The reports added that Osama bin Laden too had used HuM, LeT and HJI teams going abroad under the garb of TJ preachers to communicate instructions to his network of non-Arab organisations in different countries. In the 1990s, many members of the *Harkatul Mujahideen* traveled to the southern Philippines as preachers and trained the cadres of the Abu Sayyaf and the Moro Islamic Liberation Front, and participated in their operations against the Philippine security forces.

However, in an unprecedented move on 29 April 2009, the top

leadership of the *Tableeghi Jamaat,* groaning under suspicions being expressed by international media about the possible involvement of the TJ in terrorist activities, denounced enforcement of *Shariah* at gunpoint, religious extremism, militancy and terrorism. Leaders of the *Jamaat,* who scrupulously avoid speaking on controversial issues, also called for promoting inter-faith harmony, tolerance, human rights, social justice and peace. Speaking at the concluding session of a three-day annual congregation in Islamabad, Haji Abdul Wahab, the *ameer* of the Pakistan chapter of the *Tableeghi Jamaat,* said: "*Shariah* cannot be enforced at gunpoint. Had that been the case, Allah Almighty would have sent fierce angels to protect prophets and enforce their faiths". The 90-year-old scholar, who left his job as session's judge in pre-partition India and joined the TJ, then cited the example of Prophet Mohammad (PBUH), saying the Prophet never used force. "Instead he spread the word of God only by peaceful means".

Haji Abdul Wahab also condemned extremism and militancy in the name of Islam, a reference to the growing tendency of *Talibanisation* and demands for the enforcement of *Shariah* in Swat and other areas in NWFP. However, a 23 June 2009 news report, published by Pakistan's leading English daily *Dawn,* negated the TJ claims of being a purely religious organisation rather than one with a political agenda.

Titled "Efforts on for patch-up between Darra Taliban, Adezai *Lashkar*", the *Dawn* report stated: "Some invisible forces are out to narrow the differences and broker an understanding between the Darra Adam Khel-based Taliban and leaders of the *Qaumi Lashkar* of Adezai on the outskirts of Peshawar – the Taliban conditions included that their men would freely move in parts of Peshawar and would take action against those found involved in un-Islamic activities and the *Lashkar* would not object to their actions. Secondly, the Taliban want the *Lashkar* not to create hurdles while they recruit new members. Another condition of the Taliban is that the *Lashkar* will not support the security forces in case of any clash between the Taliban and law enforcing agencies".

It added: "Apparently, two rounds of negotiations have already been held and members of the *Tableeghi Jamaat* were active to broker an understanding between the Taliban and the *Lashkar.* Such reports, if true, question the sincerity of the army's efforts and rob its actions and claims of credibility. It is difficult to believe that even while the army is engaged in fighting and dying in Swat another arm of government is negotiating deals with the same blood thirsty foe of murderers, kidnappers and drug peddlers."

The report also belied the claims of the *Tableeghi Jamaat* that it is a purely non-violent preaching organisation which is not involved in any objectionable activity anywhere across the globe. While commenting on the daily *Dawn* news report, Zafar Hilaly, a former Pakistani diplomat, wrote in an article in Pakistan's English daily *The News* [on 24 June 2009]: "I recall being summoned to the Yemeni Foreign Office in 1988 and being asked by the authorities why the *Tableeghi Jamaat* has chosen Yemen to spread the word of Islam. In the words of a high-ranking Yemeni foreign office official: "Excellency, Islam is our religion, we gave it to you, please don't try and teach us the real Islam. Ask them to go somewhere else. Or do they have some other agenda?"

REFERENCES

1. Daniel Friedman, *Tableeghi Jamaat* Dossier, Centre for Policing Terrorism, May 2005.
2. Report, *The News,* 13 February 1995.
3. Report, Efforts on for patch up between Darra Taliban, *Adezai Lashkar,* 23 June 2009.
4. Zafar Hilaly, *The News,* 24 June 2009.

CHAPTER 25

The Islamisation of Pakistani Cricket

The Pakistani cricket team that was once known as a hot band of happy-go-lucky stars has gone through a total transformation in the last decade, slowly turning into a coterie of preachers who seem to be more interested in preaching Islam than concentrating on the game.

Long before the Islamists discovered their frightening zeal, Pakistani cricketers were considered a paragon of modern Muslims: they played flamboyantly, partied hard and didn't flaunt their religion publicly. They were the playboys of their times – polished, educated and dashing; they had their one-night stands, clubbed and tippled; as great exponents of reverse swing as they were ardent admirers of fine legs. They had the lifestyle only stars have – in any country, of any sport, of any religious persuasion.

During the 70s and 80s, Islam and the Pakistani cricket team were strangers to each other. The main hallmark of the cricket team at that time was professionalism as most of the cricketers used to play county cricket in England and because of their frequent interaction with British society, their grooming would show off well in their behaviour. The 3-4 months in a year that the Pakistani cricket stars such as Imran Khan, Majid Khan, Asif Iqbal, Sarfraz Nawaz, Javed Miandad, Zaheer Abbas, Mohsin Khan, Rameez Raja, etc. used to spend in England playing county cricket, would make them adopt the lifestyle of any other English cricketer: liquor, night clubs, girlfriends and every thing else that comes with the package.

However, those days of cricketing casualness are now a memory, as are so many aspects of the secular life in Mohammad Ali Jinnah's Pakistan who wanted his country to be secular and liberal. The Pakistani cricketers have never pursued their religious beliefs as devoutly as they do now-a-days. '*Bismillah*' (In the name of Allah) or '*Inshallah*' (God willing) stud their every utterance, whether they are on the field or elsewhere. The team members huddle together to pray on the ground during pre-match preparations; the 'Islamic beard' is sported as an advertisement of their faith; batsmen have known to cramp because they fast and play during the holy month of Ramadan.

This religiosity has come about because a clutch of the Pakistani cricket stars – Inzimamul Haq, Mohammad Yousaf, Saqlain Mushtaq, Shahid Afridi, Shoaib Malik, Yasser Hameed and Mushtaq Ahmed (bowling coach) – became members of the *Tableeghi Jamaat* (TJ), or the party of preachers, participating in public gatherings organised to propagate Islam and stressing upon the virtue of an 'authentic Islamic lifestyle'.

The extent to which the Pakistani cricket team had been Islamised at the time of the 2007 World Cup could be gauged from the fact the *Tableeghi Jamaat* (TJ) had literally invaded the dressing room of the team – *tableeghis* with long beards and moustaches could be seen praying with players and reciting the Holy Koran for the team's success (never mind that it has been performing poorly). As *Tableeghi Jamaat's* membership makes it incumbent upon a person to preach, most of the *Tableeghi* cricketers, especially the team captain, Inzimamul Haq, often used to conduct preaching tours across Pakistan.

By that time, Inzimam's penchant to mix Islam with cricket had already sparked accusations that he used to favour *Tableeghi* players over those who were either secular or preferred to confine religion to their private lives. The non-*Tableeghi* group in the Pakistani team at that time was led by Younas Khan, then vice-captain and now the captain and included Shoaib Akhtar, Mohammad Asif, Danish Kaneria, Imran Nazir, Abdul Razzaq, etc. This divide often shadowed differences between players even on the playground.

Inzimam's religious passion could be gauged from the fact that on tours abroad, one of the hotel rooms was always declared a prayer room, where the *Tableeghi* players would offer prayers and discuss religious issues. A former television personality and now a member of the *Tableeghi Jamaat*, Naeem Butt, was usually allowed to accompany the Pakistani team and stay in the same hotel, obviously on the insistence of the skipper Inzimam. Naeem Butt would arrange interacting sessions between the cricketers and office-bearers of the *Tableeghi Jamaat* chapter of the host country.

The conspicuous Islamisation of the Pakistani cricket team even prompted the then patron-in-chief of the Pakistan Cricket Board (PCB) President Pervez Musharraf to advise the PCB chairman at that time Dr Naseem Ashraf to ask the players to strike a balance between religion and cricket. The chairman subsequently warned the *Tableeghi* cricketers at a press conference, asking them to stop exhibiting their religious beliefs in public. In Naseem Ashraf's own words: "I had discussed the matter in detail with Inzimam, making it clear to him that religion is purely a private affair and there should not be any pressure on those team players who don't pray regularly. He assured me that there won't be any pressure at all on any of the players to do anything they don't want to do".

After the Pakistan cricket team's disastrous first round exit from the 2007 World Cup Cricket in the wake of a humiliating defeat at the hands of an immature Irish team, P J Mir, the then media manager of the PCB had confessed that it was an overkill of piety, the team's over-indulgence in Islamic rituals, preaching and lack of focus on the game that actually failed the Pakistani cricket team and led to its fall from grace. He claimed that the Pakistani cricketers were more focused on preaching Islam than playing the 2007 World Cup in the West Indies.

"Other teams were also present in the West Indies but the Pakistani players were more enthusiastic about converting non-Muslims than playing cricket. To be frank, I was not in a position to disclose this fact before. But I have now informed the Performance Evaluation Committee that most of the players had no focus on cricket and their fixation was on preaching, which affected their preparations", he told reporters at a press conference in Lahore after the World Cup. "The boys were up against the most challenging task to prove their skills in the prestigious World Cup tournament, but I am sorry to say they had no drive for the game and were much more active in preaching and praying", said the ex-media manager.

When reminded that Inzimam had dismissed such speculations, P J Mir said that it would not have been an issue with him or anybody had it been done within reasonable limits. "I have video footage which will prove me right and I will hand over those tapes to the PCB chairman," he said. Mir added that the players, led by Inzimam, made a public show of their prayers instead of praying privately and in the process compromised with their primary duty of playing cricket. He cited incidents to highlight his point and added that some players even made it a point to pray in the gallery of the aircraft on flights rather than privately in their seats.

The Performance Evaluation Committee was constituted by the PCB to look into the causes of the team's humiliating first round exit from the World Cup, which it had won twice in the past. Inzimam, who had to step down as captain and subsequently retired from international cricket after the World Cup, had been criticized for using the cricket team platform for religious activities. The team's foreign coach from South Africa, Bob Woolmer, too had complained to the PCB that he found it frustrating to see many players taking part in religious activities after matches when he wanted to discuss cricket with them. He had attributed the decline in the performance of the Pakistani cricket team in recent years to the growing influence of the *Tableeghi Jamaat* on many of the team members and their consequent indifference to training as they believed they could perform better and win the game by praying.

Imparting credibility to this perception was former PCB chief Shahryar Khan, who had revealed in an interview after the 2007 World Cup fiasco that Woolmer had been voicing his frustration at the religious obligations of his players. Shahryar claimed that Woolmer found it difficult to communicate with his side during match intervals because they would use the time to pray. "Bob told me before the World Cup that he was very frustrated because the team was always at prayer at lunchtime, tea and after play", he told

Sportsweek on *BBC Radio Five Live*. He was not able to get through to them on cricketing issues. Bob felt frustrated about that and asked me what to do. I told him, "Please Bob, you are an outsider and foreigner. So do not interfere with anything religiously-inclined because it will be counter-productive." Eventually, he learned to live with it.

And now the important question – how has the flamboyant cricket team of the past become a *Tableeghi Jamaat* redoubt? The Islamisation of the team, in a way, has been in tandem with the political and social transformation of Pakistani society. The transformation began with the 1977 ouster of a moderate Zulfikar Ali Bhutto government and the confiscation of power by General Zia-ul Haq, an Islamic fundamentalist. That was also the time moderate cricket stars of the 70s started leaving the scene, allowing the Islamic factor to gradually seep into the team. In the early days of the transformation, the Pakistani players didn't flaunt their religion. But the person who made religion trendy in cricket was none other than Imran Khan, as famous for his cricketing feats as he was for his romantic dalliances.

His 'awakening' following retirement from cricket, and his public, even strident, endorsement of Islam provided a justification for those wanting to wear their religion on their sleeves – if even Imran Khan could be unabashed about Islam, why shouldn't they, so went the logic. It was just the boost for Islamists nurturing the hope of luring cricketers to their cause. Among these Islamists was Maulana Tariq Jameel, who, like Inzimam, was a Multani, and a close associate of Maulana Abdul Wahab, the *ameer* of the *Tableeghi Jamaat's* Pakistan chapter. He began to concertedly target the cricket team once he had converted opening batsman Saeed Anwar to the cause of the TJ.

The stylish left-handed opener, and a computer engineer by training, became a born-again Muslim in 2001 after the tragic death of his infant daughter. The traumatic experience prompted Saeed Anwar to find solace in religion; he joined the TJ. His primary task: work on present and former cricketers to join the TJ and spread the message of Islam. About his *Tableeghi Jamaat* experience, Anwar says: "There is only one aim in my life – follow Allah Almighty's path and prepare for the Day of Judgment. I am a different Saeed Anwar today; the material world to me is meaningless. I have turned to Allah for solace and am committed to spread the religion to all parts of the world. ... Islam is a moderate religion and I am not a fanatic or a jehadi".

Thereafter, religion became a badge the Pakistani cricketers were willing to wear publicly, particularly Inzimam, whose shy and retiring personality acquired an assertive edge under the influence of Maulana Tariq Jameel. Perhaps religion provided Inzimam an anchor in the glamorous and corporate world that cricket has become. With the skipper under its sway, *Tableeghi Jamaat* now had an open field, winning over players in a number that the team could be said to be divided between the TJ and non-TJ groups. However, Inzimam denies that the religious activities of the team members used to affect their performance, and insists that the preaching sessions of the cricketers with Islamic scholars developed unity within the team. But there are many who allege that most team members had grown beards as a show of allegiance to their captain and to boost their chances of being in the Pakistani squad.

There is the peculiar case of star batsman Mohammad Yousaf, who converted from Christianity and seemingly never shaved thereafter. Despite repeated denials, many Pakistanis feel Yousaf Youhana converted to boost his chance of becoming captain in the future. He, however, ascribes his conversion to the influence of the *Tableeghi Jamaat* preachers at their sessions in Raiwind, Lahore. "My conversion is because of a change of heart and not a calculated move. Danish Kaneria, another team player, is a Hindu and there is no problem. I have already played for Pakistan for ten long years and there has been no problem. I didn't do this to be captain. Islam is the true religion because it says that life after death is the real life; the better you prepare for it, the better your present life will be."

Interestingly, however, his transformation was not only confined to his faith, but extended to a change in name, appearance, behaviour – and even performance on the field. A string of tall scores imparts credence to those who say Allah favours those who turn to Him. Residing in a posh Lahore locality, and having bought a Mercedes, Mohammad Yousaf credits benediction from above for the change in his fortune. And he is going to repay his debts to Allah. How?

"After I retire, I plan to serve God by devoting myself to preaching Islam to all those out there who have not been exposed to the real face of the religion".

However, the non-*Tableeghi* members of the cricket team pooh-pooh the notion of religious fervour helping players perform better and point out the irony of Saeed Anwar, Mushtaq Ahmad, Saqlain Mushtaq and Shahid Afridi, all members of the *Tableeghi Jamaat*, who lost their form once they took to sporting beards. But Pakistan's English-speaking opening batsman Salman Butt pleads to the positive impact Islam has had on the team. As for religion-linked cricketing performance, Butt explains: "A lot of people work hard, but only those get to their destination who are lucky and have the help of God. We believe if we pray five times a day and go in the way of God, we will get help. That is our firm belief. It puts all of us in a very good spirit, and has made us disciplined – a definite change in the Pakistan team".

The non-TJ group, though, has a litany of complaints: a stifling atmosphere, charges of bias, mutual suspicion; that mixing religion with cricket is no way of playing the game. Former cricketer-turned-*Tableeghi* Agha Zahid says the TJ recruits sporting stars, as also showbiz personalities, because "if they change their lifestyles, then others who idolise them would follow their examples". But at the same time, there are those in Pakistani society who insist that the issue is not about being religious but the manner in which it is flaunted, thereby threatening some and pressuring others to follow suit. They argue that for a society driven by religious passions that often shrinks the secular space, cricketer-turned-preachers could become the antithetical forces arrayed against a so-called agenda of enlightened moderation. This shrinking of the secular space is perhaps already happening in the cricket team. But for those persevering in the way of Allah Almighty, these are minor matters.

CHAPTER 26

The Axis of Evil – of ISI, *Al-Qaeda* and Taliban Links

Once upon a time, long before the 9/11 terrorist attacks occurred, prompting the United States to launch its war against terror, India used to be the only country accusing the Pakistani Inter Services Intelligence (ISI) of fomenting terrorism and hatching diabolic plots of death and destruction in its neighbourhood. Pakistan used to dismiss these allegations outright, arguing that India saw in the ISI a convenient, external bogey for its own inability to address its domestic discontent.

The world accepted this logic. Or, it ignored the ISI chicanery, as the problem was confined to the Indo-Pak subcontinent. Nonetheless, this perception has changed drastically, considering the fusillade of charges from around the world against the ISI since the 9/11 attacks. There has been a growing flurry of reports appearing in the Western media since 9/11, exploring the hidden links of the Pakistani military and intelligence establishment with *Al-Qaeda* and the Taliban. Despite being a crucial US ally in the war on terrorism since 2001, the ISI remains in the eye of a worldwide media storm following the detection of a series of deadly international terror plots in America, England, Afghanistan, Iran, China and India, with their foot prints traced back to Pakistan.

The moments during which the ISI has not been the focus of attention in the past quarter of a century have been very rare indeed.

Often described by critics as a state within the Pakistani state, the ISI was set-up by the country's military establishment as the intelligence wing of the army a year after Pakistan came into being in 1947. The agency was established within the Pakistan Army to supplement the existing Military Intelligence [MI] as a means to address the lack of inter-service intelligence cooperation which had proven so disastrous for Pakistan in the 1947 Indo-Pak war. However, the Soviet invasion of Afghanistan in December 1979 transformed the ISI. The Reagan administration's decision to support the Afghan forces against the Soviet forces placed Pakistan on the frontline as the base from which the CIA would mount its campaign.

The crucial development for the ISI was the Reagan administration's decision to use the ISI [through its CIA] as the instrument of support for the Afghan fighters. But the ISI, which already had deep inroads into Afghanistan, had laid down some strict conditions, which the CIA accepted, the most important being that the ISI would be controlling almost all aspects of how the guerrilla war against the Soviet forces was to be fought and supported. The other conditions included that the ISI would retain control over contacts with the Afghan fighters; that movements of weapons within Pakistan and their disbursement to Afghans would be handled exclusively by the ISI, which would also be handling all the training activities of the Afghan militants.

The subsequent role the ISI played in the Afghan jehad ultimately changed it into a classic overgrown covert operations security agency that has a specific world view and has got a role in foreign policy as well as in domestic politics and which is not at all accountable to the civilian government. Since then, the goings on behind ISI's headquarters, located behind high walls on *Khayban-e-Suharwady* avenue in the heart of the federal capital Islamabad and its operational offices in the adjoining garrison town of Rawalpindi, have dominated Pakistani domestic and foreign policies – especially those related to Afghanistan and India.

As the Taliban militia led by Mullah Mohammad Omar took Kabul in 1996 Pakistan was the first and one of only three countries to have offered diplomatic recognition to the new regime. Afterwards, the Taliban continued to benefit from ISI's support, including military training, through all their excesses, through 11 September 2001, and up to the present time. The proximity between the ISI and the Taliban, and the intimacy between the Taliban and *Al-Qaeda* necessarily raises the issue of the nature of relations between the ISI and *Al-Qaeda*. It is generally believed that the link between the ISI and *Al-Qaeda* chief Osama bin Laden goes back to almost 25 years ago. The wealthy Saudi national with strong links to the Saudi royal family and Saudi intelligence had good contacts with the ISI. Osama had emerged as a significant foreign fighter for the ISI during the CIA-sponsored Afghan jehad.

By most accounts, *Al-Qaeda* was formed in August 1988 as a means of continuing the jehad against the global enemies of Islam, with many of the foundational meetings taking place in Pakistan as the Russian occupation forces started withdrawing from Afghanistan. Osama used to enjoy the protection of the ISI, which sought to co-opt him two projects: the overthrow of Najibullah in Kabul and the dismissal of Benazir Bhutto's government in Islamabad, both of whom were seen as the enemies of Islam by the ISI. Due to Osama's four year long absence from Afghanistan [between 1992 and 1996 after the withdrawal of the Soviet troops], he had no direct role in the rise of the Taliban, and was unfamiliar with them when he returned to Afghanistan in May 1996. It is said that Osama's initial meetings with Mullah Omar were actually facilitated by the ISI which were successful enough to see him move to Kandahar as the winter of 1996 closed in.

With the backing of the ISI and the Taliban regime, Osama reportedly began to expand the activities of *Al-Qaeda* for global jehad. Focused on its regional agenda – fomenting trouble in Indian-administered Jammu & Kashmir and strengthening the Taliban regime in Afghanistan, the ISI leadership colluded with Osama to establish further training camps inside Afghanistan, and to facilitate the spread of *Al-Qaeda*'s influence in existing camps on both sides of the border, in order to host, indoctrinate and train foreign fighters who could reinforce pro-Kashmir jehadi groups like the *Lashkar-e-Toiba*, support the Taliban regime, and promote a pro-Pakistan Islamist agenda from Chechnya, through Uzbekistan, to China. The additional supporters of Osama were Saudi Arabia and the United

Arab Emirates. The then director general of the ISI Lt Gen *Hameed Gul*, who was a typical fundamentalist having deeply Islamist and anti-Western views, was the chief supporter of the Taliban regime and Osama bin Laden.

The ISI's support to the Taliban regime and the *Al-Qaeda* chief continued even after General Pervez Musharraf staged a military coup in October 1999 and became the most-trusted American ally in the war on terror, launched in the wake of 9/11. This was primarily because the degree of overlap between the pan-Islamist agenda of the country's military establishment, being exercised through the ISI, was quite deep and extensive. Hours after the 9/11 terror attacks that shook the entire world, the Musharraf regime had to agree to share desperately needed information about the Taliban network with the Central Intelligence Agency (CIA). Since then, the ISI has been working as the eyes and ears of the US-led covert action to seize Osama from the Taliban, with hundreds of its agents and their assets continuing to operate across Afghanistan.

Having joined the US-led war on terror as an important ally, General Musharraf kept claiming that Pakistan was playing a key role in nipping the evils of *Al-Qaeda* and Taliban in the bud. However, the international community remained skeptical of his claims and kept showing concern that the ISI has not abandoned its strategic objective of rebuilding its lost influence in Afghanistan. As the gravity of the conflict in Afghanistan has risen, the notorious ISI is again at the centre of the controversy, amid allegations being leveled by the United States, Britain and Afghanistan that it was helping the revival of the Taliban-led resistance movement in Afghanistan. While intense international counter-terrorism efforts strive to track down and stop plots originating out of Pakistan, the sheer number of such conspiracies continues to pose a serious threat.

The Taliban and *Al-Qaeda*-linked Pakistani militant groups, intertwined with Islamic elements in state institutions like the ISI, are playing a dangerous double game, amid allegations by Western intelligence agencies that the ISI keeps pursuing its pre-9/11 agenda despite claims to the contrary. The Pakistani denials apart, the fact remains that the ISI has expanded into a state within a state under President General Zia-ul Haq to run the Afghan jehad. The ISI's original mandate is to provide strategic intelligence, including external threat perceptions and covert operations, to the prime minister, the three armed forces and to the Joint Services Headquarters. However, its internal security wing does cover internal security matters, including providing security clearance for armed forces personnel work on counter-intelligence to undermine the intelligence assets of adversarial countries deployed within Pakistan.

The policy-makers who had conceived and helped set up the ISI would not have even imagined how this organisation would, one day, go beyond its mandated functions and literally become self-directed in its decisions and actions, prejudicial to the interests of the country. While Musharraf was still holding both the coveted slots of the president as well as the army chief, New Delhi accused Pakistan of planning the July 2006 Mumbai train bombings, claiming to have solid proof that could link the ISI to the massacre. In August 2006, President Karzai held the ISI responsible for backing the resurgent Taliban in his country besides providing sanctuary to Osama bin Laden and Mullah Omar. In September 2006, the Afghanistan-based NATO commanders demanded that their governments get tough with Pakistan over ISI's covert support for the Taliban. By the time, Musharraf had reached London after concluding his unofficial visit to the US which was meant for the launching of his book – *In the Line of Fire*. As he landed in England, Musharraf had to confront a hostile British media in the wake of a British Ministry of Defence's think-tank report, leaked by the *BBC* and saying that the ISI was indirectly supporting extremism in Afghanistan, Iraq and Britain.

"The Army's dual role in combating terrorism and promoting six-party religious alliance – the *Muttahida Majlis-e-Amal* at the same time, besides supporting the Taliban through the ISI is coming under closer and closer international scrutiny. Indirectly, Pakistan has been supporting terrorism and extremism through the ISI, whether in London on 7/7 (the 7 July 2005 suicide bombings on London's transport network) or in Afghanistan or Iraq," said the report. The *BBC* report, written by a senior military official linked to Britain's foreign intelligence service, MI6, and part of a fact-finding mission to Pakistan in June 2006, had proposed using military links between British and Pakistani armed forces to persuade Musharraf to step down as leader of the country, which is on the edge of chaos, accept fair elections, withdraw the Army from civilian life and dismantle the ISI.

Stunned, Musharraf's riposte was typical: "I would like to tell the British Ministry of Defence spokesman that the Ministry itself should be dismantled before the ISI is dismantled. You will be brought down to your knees if Pakistan doesn't co-operate with you. That is all I would like to say. If we were not with you, you would not manage anything. Let that be clear. And if the ISI is not with you, you will fail. Let that be very clear also. Remember my words: if the ISI is not with you and Pakistan is not with you, you will lose in Afghanistan. From 1979 to 1989, we fought the Soviet Union for you. We won the Cold War for you. The Pakistan Army and the ISI had played a part in training tens of thousands of Muslim fighters to resist the Soviets. But it was the West's decision to leave Pakistan high and dry after the Soviet withdrawal that had paved the way for the creation of radicalized Taliban and *Al-Qaeda* from the remnants of Afghan *mujahideen*", said Musharraf in a subsequent interview.

Yet, the fact remains that Pakistan's close links with the Taliban and ISI's past role as the key sponsor of the Islamist hardliners prior to Islamabad's decision to join hands with the US in the aftermath of the 9/11 is a matter of record. "Pakistan, not Iraq, was a patron of terrorism and had closer ties with Osama bin Laden and *Al-Qaeda* leading up to the 9/11 attacks. The Taliban's ability to provide the *Al-Qaeda* chief a haven in the face of international pressure and the United Nations sanctions was significantly facilitated by Pakistani support. Pakistan broke of with the Taliban only after 9/11, even though it knew the Afghan militia was hiding Osama bin Laden", the June 2004 interim report by the US National Commission on the 9/11 Terrorist Attacks had stated.

The report said Pakistan benefited from the Taliban-*Al-Qaeda* relationship, as Osama bin Laden's camps trained and equipped fighters for Pakistan's ongoing struggle in Jammu & Kashmir. "The Taliban faction that seized Kabul was itself supported by Pakistan", said the 12-page US National Commission report, and added that even when headquartered in Sudan, *Al-Qaeda* had been using Pakistan and Afghanistan as regional bases and training centers, supporting Islamic insurgencies in Tajikistan, Kashmir and Chechnya.

"The training at *Al-Qaeda* and associated camps was multi-faceted in nature. A worldwide jehad needed terrorists who could bomb embassies or hijack airliners, but it also needed foot soldiers for the Taliban in its war against the Northern Alliance, and guerrillas who could shoot down Russian helicopters in Chechnya or ambush Indian units in Kashmir. Thus, most recruits received training that was primarily geared towards conventional warfare. Terrorist training was provided mostly to the best and most ardent recruits. The quality of the training provided at *Al-Qaeda* and other jehadi camps was quite good. There was coordination with regard to curriculum and great emphasis on ideological and religious indoctrination. Instruction underscored that the US and Israel were evil, and that the rulers of Arab countries were illegitimate", the report stated.

In his 4 April 2004 investigative report titled '*9-11 and the smoking gun*', carried by Asia Times Online, a well known journalist and analyst Pepe Escobar wrote: "If the 9-11 Commission is really looking for a smoking gun, it should look no further than Lt Gen Mahmood Ahmad, then director of the Pakistani Inter Services Intelligence who was in Washington when the 9/11 attacks occurred. He arrived in the US on 4 September 2001, a whole week before the attacks. He had meetings at the State Department after the 9/11 attacks. But he also had a regular visit of consultations with his US counterparts at the CIA and the Pentagon during the week prior to the 9/11 attacks. What was the nature of these routine pre-9/11 consultations? Were they in any way related to the subsequent post-9/11 consultations pertaining to Pakistan's decision to cooperate with US? Was the planning of war being discussed between Pakistani and US officials?"

The report added: "On 9 September 2001, while Lt Gen Mahmood was in the US, Commander Ahmad Shah Masood was assassinated in Afghanistan. The Northern Alliance had informed the Bush administration that the ISI was allegedly implicated in the assassination. The Bush administration consciously took the decision in the post-9/11 consultations with Mahmood Ahmad to directly cooperate with the ISI despite its links to Osama and the Taliban and its alleged role in the assassination of Ahmed Masood, which coincidentally occurred two days before the terrorist attacks. Meanwhile, senior Pentagon and US State Department officials had been rushed to Islamabad to put the finishing touches on US war planes. Prior to the onslaught of the bombing of major cities in Afghanistan (7 October 2001), Lt Gen Mahmood Ahmed was sacked from his position as head of the ISI".

Interestingly, a few days before being sacked, Lt Gen Mahmood, in his talks with the CIA chief in Washington, had defended the Taliban *ameer* Mullah Omar describing him as a pious humanitarian, not a man of violence. Months before surrendering to American arm-twisting, the Musharraf regime had been vehemently defending its support for the Taliban regime, for it was providing Pakistan strategic depth. It was the same Mahmood who tried to convince the American administration positively about the Taliban when Thomas Pickering, Deputy Secretary of State in the Clinton administration, had warned Pakistan against the consequences of being in bed with the Taliban. Astonishingly, within the course of a week after 9/11, the Musharraf regime took an about-turn and the notorious spy agency that had been deeply involved with the Taliban, was guiding the US-led Allied Forces into Afghanistan.

According to a research paper published by the US-based Pakistan Security Research Unit, at present, there is arguably no more important intelligence organisation than Pakistan's Directorate of Inter Service Intelligence (ISI), which remains an enigma after decades of close co-operation. "Is it the indispensable ally of the West as the Pakistani President insists? Or is it something else: an organisation that foments terrorism, that operates against Western interests, and that functions as an obstacle to, rather than the means for, progress in the War on Terrorism? Of course, this is to pose a slightly false dichotomy: the ISI need not be a trusted ally to remain important to the West. The real question is whether there is sufficient overlap between Western interests and the activities of the ISI to merit the trust and the investment of the West, primarily the US, makes in the ISI indirectly through the support of the military government of President General Musharraf and directly to the organisation itself?"

The January 2008 study report prepared by Shaun Gregory and

titled '*The ISI and the War on Terrorism*', further stated: For Pakistan and the ISI, the consequences of the 9/11 attacks were almost incalculable. "Pakistan was co-opted by the US as a necessary if uncertain partner for the war on terrorism and as an indispensable forward base for the overthrow of the Taliban which – once the Taliban refused to hand the *Al-Qaeda* leadership over – became a sine qua non for the destruction of *Al-Qaeda*. The military government of Pervez Musharraf was given no choice other than to assist the United States and was offered lavish rewards of aid, debt write-off and the lifting of Pressler's sanctions and the additional restrictions imposed after the Pakistan nuclear tests in 1998".

The researcher added: "In almost all other respects, the consequences of the 9/11 attacks have been catastrophic for Pakistan. The ISI and the Pakistan Army were asked to hunt down *Al-Qaeda* operatives in Pakistan and help hunt them down in Afghanistan. The way the ISI responded has been shaped by two sets of tensions: the first the tensions between the need for Musharraf to demonstrate fidelity to the US in the pursuit of *Al-Qaeda* and Musharraf's sensitivity to the widespread support for *Al-Qaeda* and Taliban across Pakistan, a support evinced by a large proportion of the people, by Islamist political parties, and by elements within the Pakistan Army and ISI. The second, the tensions between the US objectives in relation to *Al-Qaeda* and in terms of the region more broadly, and Pakistani objectives in the region as a whole. These tensions explain the ambiguity of ISI actions since 9/11".

The study paper went on stating: Notwithstanding these complexities, there is no question that the ISI was essential to the US and the West in the early phase of the War on Terrorism. "The ISI helped the United States arrest many hundreds of suspected *Al-Qaeda* and Taliban members, amongst them many leading *Al-Qaeda* figures. The ISI has also been of some help to the West in unraveling some of the details of international terrorist operations or in helping foil international terrorist operations, a large number of which actually have had their roots in Pakistan. Of particular importance in this respect have been the investigations into the 9/11 attacks, and into the 7/7 London bombings, and the ISI's role in foiling the alleged summer 2006 plot to simultaneously blow up airliners leaving

London's Heathrow airport for the United States. However, law enforcement and intelligence service critics in the US and UK point to systematic problems with the ISI's role in these operations, in particular that the ISI tends to act on US and/or UK intelligence but not to be proactive in bringing its own intelligence to the West; the ISI is unhelpful in relation to specific investigations – notably of 7/7 – where the trail in Pakistan seems to have gone cold; the ISI has restricted or denied the US/UK access to many terrorists as well as to many of its own operatives and assets; the ISI manipulates intelligence for its own internal and geopolitical reasons, and misdirects American and British intelligence services".

Shaun Gregory believed that the crucial point was not that the ISI is aiding *Al-Qaeda* directly – though some of its operatives may be – but rather Pakistan's geopolitical interests, and the ISI's promotion of pan-Islamist jehad, making it an unreliable ally for the West. In addition, he stated, the ISI's support for *Sunni* Islamism in Pakistan adds another layer of complexity to the West's problems in Pakistan. Concluding his thesis, Gregory stated that as ISI successes against *Al-Qaeda* have declined since 2003 and the hunt for its fugitive leadership has petered out, and the number of *Al-Qaeda* aided operations emanating from Pakistan continues to rise, the ambiguous role being played by the ISI in the war on terror has become a mounting problem for the West. Therefore, he added, a Western rethink of its intelligence strategy in Pakistan is now urgently overdue."

Hussain Haqqani, Pakistan's Ambassador to Washington, wrote in one of his articles in 2007, that instead of just protecting Pakistan from enemies identified by a lawful government, which is what an intelligence or security service is supposed to do, the ISI defines what is or is not good for Pakistan. "The ISI is convinced that India is Pakistan's eternal enemy, Kashmir can be won by weakening Indian resolve to hold on to it through unconventional warfare and Afghanistan should be the backyard of Pakistan in every way. Instead of implementing the state policy, the ISI virtually makes its own policies for the state. Historically, the intelligence agencies that have grown so large, so powerful and so unaccountable, as the ISI, finally cause problems for the state they control. Instead of the ISI controlling Pakistan, the Pakistanis should be controlling the ISI. Otherwise, covert terrorist operations abroad will continue to undermine Pakistani democracy and keep the country engaged in conflicts with Afghanistan and India".

However, General Musharraf, who used to support ISI actions tooth and nail, kept denying during his days in power that the agency was anyway involved in spreading terrorism. "Some dissidents, rogue elements, retired people who were in the forefront in the ISI during the period of Afghan jehad between 1979 and 1989, might have links somewhere here and there. But we are monitoring them closely and will get hold of them if at all that happens", he had stated in a 2006 interview with NBC television.

Nevertheless, independent analysts in Pakistan were never ready to buy his thesis. "It is dishonest to argue that the ISI is run by rogue elements, and its boss, Director General ISI, and his boss, the Army Chief [General Pervez Musharraf], don't know what is going on at the lower level. While this can't be ruled out in particular instances here or there, there is no way that some rogue elements can actually make or break ISI policy which is made by the national security establishment headed by none other than President General Musharraf himself", so read an October 2006 *Daily Times* editorial.

Constitutionally, the ISI is accountable to the prime minister, yet most officers in the ISI are from the army, so that is where their loyalties and interests lie. Until the end of 2007, as the army chief and the President, General Musharraf used to exercise firm control over the intelligence agency. However, with a new President (Asif Zardari) and a new Prime Minister (Yousaf Raza Gilani) calling the shots, effort is being made by the elected civilian leadership of the country to assume control of the ISI. It was on 27 July 2008 that ahead of his official trip to the US, Prime Minister Yousaf Raza Gilani attempted to place the shadowy ISI under civilian control, in a bid to deflect mounting criticism over its role in the failed war on terror in neighbouring Afghanistan.

As Prime Minister Gilani left Islamabad for Washington, the Cabinet Division issued a notification to clip the ISI wings by placing it under the administrative control of the interior ministry. A subsequent statement by Asif Zardari, then PPP chairman, said the move was aimed at establishing civilian rule in the country besides saving both the army and the ISI from getting a bad name. The attempt to bring the ISI under the government control was apparently motivated by intense pressure from Washington to rein in the rogue elements in the agency. But the bid was short-lived. Hardly a few hours after the issuance of the Cabinet Division notification, the army leadership forced the prime minister to withdraw the orders.

During his subsequent meeting with Pakistani Prime Minister Gilani on 29 July 2008 in Washington, President Bush expressed his concern and annoyance over the role of the ISI, saying it has established deep ties with the *Al-Qaeda* and Taliban militants operating in the Pakistani tribal areas. The national media reported that although Bush was in a good mood when he met the Pakistani prime minister, he was blunt about expressing US reluctance to share intelligence information with Pakistan. Quoting Pakistani Defence Minister Chaudhry Ahmed Mukhtar, *The News* reported on 31 July 2008 that President Bush expressed grave concern that certain elements in the ISI were leaking information to Islamic terrorists before they could be hit by the American or Pakistani forces. "President Bush also asked who is controlling the ISI," the defence minister said, indicating that Bush was probably aware of the fiasco created by the failed attempt on the part of the civilian government to take control of the ISI.

The day Prime Minister Gilani was meeting with the US President, the *New York Times* reported on 29 July 2009 that a senior CIA official visited Pakistan in July and confronted Pakistani officials with evidence of ties between Pakistani intelligence service and militants in the tribal areas. Citing defence and intelligence sources, the paper said the trip by CIA Deputy Director Stephen Kappes demonstrated a harder line being taken against Pakistani ties to those responsible for the surge of violence in Afghanistan, including a fugitive Taliban leader Jalaluddin Haqqani. It was a very pointed message saying, "Look, we know there's a connection, not just with Jalaluddin Haqqani but also with the other bad guys and the ISI, and we think you could do more and we want you to do more about it," the *New York Times* quoted a senior US official as having said.

Reacting sharply to the US accusation against the ISI, Musharraf, who was still the President, once again came to its rescue, saying any attempt to target the spy agency will weaken Pakistan as it is the first line of defence. Addressing businessmen in Karachi on 3 August 2008, he said conspiracies against the ISI were actually aimed at defaming Pakistan. "ISI is a patriotic institution, which is working for the stability of the country", *The News* quoted the president as saying.

But whatever people like Musharraf think and say about the ISI, Pakistan remains under intense international pressure to tame its premier intelligence agency. While announcing its new Af-Pak strategy for the Pak-Afghan region on 27 March 2009, the new US President Barack Obama undertook an ambitious plan for Pakistan which entailed political restructuring as well as changing perceptions. The political restructuring involves bringing the notorious ISI effectively, and not just technically, under the civilian government's control. And to achieve the said goal, the Americans are seeking to change the Pakistan military establishment's perception of India as an enemy. As a replacement, they are offering a new enemy: the *Al-Qaeda* and Taliban-linked jehadis operating along the Pak-Afghan border.

On 28 March 2009, a day after President Obama announced his Af-Pak strategy, the US military said it has evidence elements within the ISI continue to provide support to the Taliban, which has to end. Chairman Joint Chiefs of Staff, Admiral Mike Mullen, said in a *CNN* interview that the ISI had links with militants on both the Pakistani borders with neighbouring Afghanistan and India. "There are certainly indications that's the case. Fundamentally that's one of the things that has to change".

In yet another interview the same day (28 March 2009), the head of the US Central Command, General David Petraeus, said that some of the militant groups had been established by the ISI and their links continued. He said there was evidence that in the fairly recent past, the ISI had tipped-off Taliban and *Al-Qaeda* linked militants when their positions were in danger. "It's a topic that is of enormous importance, because if there are links and if those continue and if it undermines the operations [against militants], obviously that would be very damaging to the kind of trust that we need to build", said

Petraeus in a PBS interview.

The next day, on 29 March, 2009, Richard Holbrooke, the special American envoy to South Asia said of all issues, investigating the Inter Services Intelligence was the most important. "The issue's very disturbing," Holbrooke told PBS in an interview when asked if the ISI was assisting *Al-Qaeda* and Taliban-linked extremists. "We cannot succeed if the two intelligence agencies (the CIA and ISI) are at each others' throat or don't trust each other and if the kind of collusion you referred to is factual", Holbrooke said.

On 21 November 2009, English daily *The News* reported that serious differences have cropped up between Pakistan's premier intelligence agency ISI and US Central Intelligence Agency (CIA) over the latter's dismal role in countering terrorism in Pakistan. According to the story, the differences between the two strategic partners in war against terror cropped up when ISI Chief Lt. Gen. Ahmed Shujja Pasha in a meeting expressed his disappointment to his US counterpart, the CIA chief spymaster Leon Panetta, over the US failure to help Pakistan in counter-terrorism efforts. "General Pasha was critical to the CIA's counter-terrorism strategy in Afghanistan and its failure to provide concrete actionable information to Pakistan in containing flow of Indian aid to terror networks operating from Afghanistan to destabilize Pakistan".

On 4 March 2010, *New York Times* reported that former Pakistani army officers are continuing to train Taliban fighters and have helped the militant outfit to stage a remarkable comeback since 2006. "The army trainers of the Taliban include some officers trained in prestigious US military academies, who now in public utterances remain vocal advocates of the outfit. These officers, some of whom have even risen high in Pakistan Army hierarchy, have no qualms that their trained fighters are battling their one time mentors, the paper reported saying their views reveal that the sympathies that have long run deep in the ranks of Pakistan's military and intelligence services", said the report.

The newspaper interviewed a retired army officer Colonel Imam, a former US trained officer in the ISI who sent insurgents into Afghanistan to fight the Soviet Union in the 80's and then to support the Taliban takeover of the country. By his own account, the NYT said the Colonel was so close to the Taliban supremo at large Mullah Mohammad Omar that he visited him days after the 9/11 attacks and left Kabul only when American bombing campaign began later in 2001. Colonel Imam, whose real name is Brig (retd) Sultan Amir, claimed that he has not returned to Afghanistan since and his parting advise to Omar was to fight on, but stick to guerrilla tactics. "Despite Pakistan's arrest of several high-level Afghan Taliban commanders, men like Colonel Imam sit at the centre of the questions that linger around what Pakistan's actual intentions are towards the Taliban", the American newspaper said.

Amidst all these development, there is a growing consensus in the international community that the time has come for the Pakistani establishment to bring the ISI squarely under the civilian government's control, mainly to ensure that the activities of the spy agency are brought within the framework of the overall strategy adopted by the elected government. Pakistan simply cannot afford a situation where its premier intelligence agency keeps operating at cross purposes with the aims and objectives of the elected government in Islamabad.

References

1. Report, *BBC*, June 2006.
2. Pepe Escobar, 9-11 and the Smoking Gun, *Asia Times Online*, 4 April 2004.
3. Shaun Gregory, The ISI and War on Terrorism, Pakistan Security Research Unit, January 2008.
4. Hussain Haqqani, Article, 2007.
5. Pervez Musharraf, Interview for *NBC TV*, 2006.
6. Editorial, *Daily Times, October 2006.*
7. Report, *New York Times*, 29 July 2009.
8. Pervez Musharraf, *The News*, 3 August 2008.
9. Mike Mullen, Interview to *CNN*, 28 March 2009.
10. Report, *The News*, 21 November 2009.
11. Report, *New York Times*, 4 March 2010

CHAPTER 27

Pervez Musharraf: The Fall of the Jehadi General

Almost eight years after the 9/11 terror attacks, Pakistan's cooperation in the US-led war on terrorism continues to be questioned by the international community, primarily because of the fact that the country's former military ruler and the once most trusted US ally President General Pervez Musharraf kept playing a double game during his eight-year stint in power by performing a balancing act on both the international and domestic fronts: cooperating with the West on one hand while going soft on the *Al-Qaeda* and Taliban-linked militants on the other, back home.

General (retd) Musharraf characterized himself as a moderate leader with liberal, progressive ideas, and used to express admiration for Kemal Ataturk, the secular founder of the Turkish Republic. For eight long years, he kept projecting himself as the sole saviour of Pakistan, insisting that he has been making frantic efforts to dismantle the *Al-Qaeda* and the Taliban-linked jehadi network from Pakistani soil. But all these claims were nothing more than mere sloganeering to appease the West and win over international support to prolong his autocratic rule. The hard fact remains that Musharraf hoodwinked the international community through a web of lies and deceit in the name of fighting terrorism, leaving the world a more dangerous place to live in today.

As an isolated Musharraf was forced to resign from the presidency

in the wake of the 2008 general elections, which routed his Pakistan
Muslim League-Quaid, it became obvious that the war on terror has
only created more terrorist groups in Pakistan, more dangerous, better
armed and networked before the 9/11 attacks. Musharraf had joined
hands with the United States against the Taliban regime in
Afghanistan in the aftermath of 9/11 after an ultimatum by President
George Bush. Musharraf agreed to give to the US three airbases for
Operation Enduring Freedom.

A day after the US Secretary of State Colin Powell and other
American officials met General Musharraf, he addressed the people
of Pakistan on the state-run television [on 19 September 2001] and
said Pakistan risked being endangered by an Indo-US alliance if it
did not cooperate with Washington. What Musharraf projected and
implied in his address was that Pakistan was under tremendous
pressure from the United States to act as he did. In other words, he
was saying that he would not proceed against the Taliban or *Al-Qaeda*
had he been given an option. Musharraf leaned heavily on Islamic
rhetoric and even invoked lessons from the early stages of Islamic
religious history as to how 'no-war pacts' with an enemy could be
entered into as a temporising measure by an Islamic state for the sake
of political or strategic expediency and could then be reneged later
on, to surprise and defeat the enemy.

However, for those who need a ready reckoning on Musharraf's
performance in the war on terror, one look at his record on handling
jehadi kingpins will suffice; not even a single chief of any of the major
banned jehadi organisations was either arrested or prosecuted during
his tenure, despite the fact that most of them had been wanted either
by the American Federal Bureau of Investigation (FBI) or the Indian
Central Bureau of Investigation (CBI) on terrorism charges. Banning
six top jehadi and sectarian organisations of Pakistan on terrorism
charges in two phases – on 5 January 2002 and 14 November 2003,
Musharraf had declared that no militant group or leader would be
allowed to indulge in terrorism to further its cause. However, after
the initial crackdown, all the five major jehadi groups were allowed
to resurface and regroup to run their respective militant networks as
openly as before, though with different names and identities.

When Musharraf was forced to quit the presidency in the wake of an impending impeachment motion by the newly-elected parliament, all the key jehadi leaders – Prof Hafiz Mohammad Saeed, the *ameer* of the *Jamaatul Daawa* (JuD), Maulana Masood Azhar, the *ameer* of the *Jaish-e-Mohammad* (JeM), Syed Salahuddin, the *ameer* of the *Hizbul Mujahideen* (HM), Maulana Fazlur Rehman Khalil, the *ameer* of the *Jamiatul Ansar (JuA)*, and Qari Saifullah Akhtar, the *ameer* of the *Harkatul Jehadul Islami* (HUJI), were on the loose and openly pursuing their jehadi agenda across Pakistan. The pattern of their handling by the Musharraf regime demonstrated that they were being kept on the leash, to keep the neighbouring states of India and Afghanistan under pressure, in accordance with its so-called geo-strategic agenda in the region.

That these militant groups could not have survived and achieved their present size without the backing of the Musharraf regime is beyond any iota of doubt. While the mighty military establishment working under Musharraf's command kept making overt noises about clamping down on these militant organisations, the fact remains that it was only playing to the gallery under international pressure. Although Islamabad's support had been critical in the arrest of over 700 *Al-Qaeda* and Taliban fugitives, the lack of political stability in Pakistan under Musharraf's autocratic rule bolstered the religious parties and their like-minded extremist elements in the country's military and intelligence establishments to carry on their covert support for the Taliban in Afghanistan and the jehadi groups active in Indian administered Jammu & Kashmir.

Was that Pervez Musharraf's typical military mindset; being a part of the Islamist Pakistan Army which still maintains *Jehad Fi Sabilallah* (Holy war in the name of Allah) as its motto or the fear of becoming irrelevant for the US which stopped him from dismantling the jehadi organisations and their infrastructure from Pakistani soil despite repeated sloganeering on the contrary? Many in Pakistan believe that it was a cross between the two. In September 2006, Musharraf had himself conceded what many in Pakistan already knew – that he was not at all a willing American ally in the war on terror but was compelled to join hands with Washington after the 9/11 terror attacks, primarily after being threatened by a high ranking American official that Pakistan could be bombed back to the Stone Age unless it cooperated with the United States against the Taliban regime in Afghanistan.

"My intelligence director (then ISI Chief Lt Gen Mahmood Ahmed) told me that Richard Armitage (then US Deputy Secretary of State) has warned, "Be prepared to be bombed. Be prepared to go back to the Stone Age", Musharraf disclosed in an interview with a US television channel on 22 September 2006. "I think it was a very rude remark. One has to think and take actions in the interests of the nation, and that was what I did," Musharraf said in an interview a couple of days before the New York launch of his much-trumpeted autobiography – *In the Line of Fire* – A Memoir." Pervez Musharraf, who had been a diehard supporter of the Taliban regime till 9/11, elaborates in his autobiography on how he had first weighed the option of fighting the United States before finally taking a foreign policy U-turn and dumping support for the Taliban.

"I war-gamed the United States as an adversary," he writes, saying he assessed whether Pakistan could withstand the onslaught. "The answer was no, we could not, on three counts: the Pakistani military would have been wiped out, its economy couldn't be sustained and the nation lacked the unity needed for such a confrontation," Musharraf writes in his book. Musharraf further adds that he was worried if Pakistan did not accede to US demands, the Bush administration would take up an Indian offer to provide bases. He foresaw India using the opportunity to either launch a limited offensive in the disputed Jammu & Kashmir region, or more probably New Delhi would work with the United States and the United Nations to turn the present disputed ceasefire line dividing Kashmir into a permanent border. He also feared that the US would seek to destroy Pakistan's nuclear weapons. Finally, Musharraf writes, he had to answer whether it was worth Pakistan destroying itself for the sake of the Taliban.

Musharraf's confession that he was not a willing ally in the war on terror helped the international community understand why his regime's policy in Afghanistan since 9/11 had been an ambiguous one of playing both sides of the fence, saying one thing but doing another, closing the militant training camps in one area of Pakistan and reopening them in another. A detailed examination of

Musharraf's military career, in the light of international media reports, before his 1999 coup and his post-coup policies on domestic and foreign fronts, draw an extremely conflicting and contradictory picture of the first commando president of Pakistan who claimed to have a liberal worldview and painted himself as a vocal advocate of enlightened moderation.

In the aftermath of 9/11 attacks, Musharraf affected a complete shift in Pakistan's Afghan policy that was actually devised by the mighty military establishment. Musharraf publicly ditched the Taliban and instantly became a 'trusted ally' of the United States in its global war against the Osama-led *Al-Qaeda* terrorists. However, the Western media's response to the General's U-turn on its Taliban policy was full of suspicion. In its 15 October 2001 editorial titled 'Pakistan's Double Game', the London-based *Guardian* stated: "The 180-degree turnabout in the Pakistani military regime's Afghan policy since 9/11 appears almost complete as Musharraf has withdrawn his diplomats from Kabul and is on the point of formally cutting ties with his former Taliban protégés. Islamabad says the evidence provided by the US implicating Osama and his *Al-Qaeda* gangsters now convince it. In point of fact, matters are somewhat more complicated. Far from admitting that his pro-Taliban policy was terribly misconceived, Musharraf (who vetoed a covert CIA-run operation to capture Osama bin Laden in 1999) still opposes Western backing for the Northern Alliance in Afghanistan.... He is still playing a double game".

In a 31 March 2002 report titled 'The myth of the good General Musharraf,' John Norris wrote in the *Guardian* that the Pakistani military ruler is telling the Western leaders exactly what they want to hear. He, however, pointed out that the West's new engagement with Pakistan was based on some dangerous misconceptions. In fact, said the *Guardian* report, Musharraf's image as a moderate leader fighting off a rogue ISI contrasts sharply with his past... "As Director General of Military Operations at Army Headquarters, General Musharraf oversaw ISI assistance to the Taliban. After 9/11, he had no choice in the face of the Western pressure but to reverse course on Afghanistan and to put a temporary halt to the jehad in Kashmir...."

In its 21 September 2003 editorial titled 'Pakistan, a Troubled Ally', the *New York Times* stated: "Musharraf managed to lift Pakistan's status in Washington from pariah to strategic partner by abruptly switching sides in Afghanistan and letting Washington use Pakistani bases to fight the Taliban. Yet, beneath the surface of Washington's new closeness with Islamabad, mutual suspicions continue to fester. Musharraf has failed to sever links with international terrorism. Pakistan's behaviour has fallen well short of what Americans are entitled to expect from an ally in the war on terrorism. Although it has cooperated in the arrest of some leaders of *Al-Qaeda*, Pakistan has never adequately sealed the Afghan border. That made it possible for key *Al-Qaeda* fugitives to escape and allow Pakistani recruits to join a reviving Taliban.... Fighting terrorism effectively requires allies untainted by terror"...

In its 9 July 2004 editorial titled 'Pakistan Without Illusions', the *New York Times* wrote: "General Musharraf is neither a convinced nor a convincing ally of the US in the struggle against radical Islamic terrorism, nuclear weapons proliferation and destructive dictatorship. Musharraf has done such a good job of repackaging himself as a vital American ally against radical Islamic terrorism that it is easy to forget how alarming Washington rightly found so many of his policies not very long ago. He crushed democracy, he was, at the least, recklessly indifferent to safeguards against the proliferation of nuclear weapons and backed the Taliban and the terrorist groups active in Indian-ruled areas of Kashmir. Musharraf publicly broke with the Taliban regime almost three years ago, but there has been inadequate progress on many of the other issues, and Pakistan has recently appeared to be backsliding on the Taliban".

According to Musharraf's close circles, he is always conscious to project himself as very liberal and modern. However, his critics say he is a conservative in his approach and liberal in his attitude only. His personal life to some extent bears this out, because he is known for his drinking and fondness for gambling. Unlike orthodox Muslims who consider dogs to be unclean, and therefore do not keep them as pets, Musharraf has several dogs. He is quoted to have said in an interview, "My dogs love me. And I love my dogs". Some of his first pictures after the 1999 coup were with his dogs, and his speeches were then peppered with terminologies such as 'doubling down' and 'tripling down' (drawn from blackjack).

In a 2005 article in the *Washington Post*, prominent journalist Pamela Constable wrote: "General Musharraf's personal life is distinctive in a number of ways. He is a *mohajir*, one whose family migrated from India in the 1940s, in an army dominated by clannish natives of what is now Pakistan. He enjoys Western music and occasionally drinks alcohol, even in his Islamic country. He speaks precise English, his son and one brother live in the US and his parents are naturalised American citizens – all of which augurs well for his stated desire to develop friendly relations with the US".

By 2006, the many layers of an enlightened Musharraf had gradually unfolded to a great extent, making the policy makers in Washington get to know the real face of their once most-trusted ally. Reacting sharply to allegations coming from Washington, London, Kabul and Delhi, that he was not a willing ally in the war on terror, a visibly perturbed Musharraf told in a harsh tone a gathering of over 200 senior military officers from 22 countries [who had gathered in Islamabad in October 2006 to discuss new tactics and strategy in their joint mission to combat rising terrorism]: "Our commitment and sincerity must not be doubted. We have suffered the maximum and we have contributed the maximum. Therefore, we will not accept that Pakistan is not doing enough in the war on terror. If anyone thinks I am bluffing or the ISI is bluffing, we should be out of the coalition. If the NATO forces think that the ISI is lying about its war against terrorism, Pakistan would rather disassociate itself from the alliance".

A subsequent 11 November 2007 report in the *San Francisco Chronicle*, titled "Friend or foe?" and filed by Adrian Levy and Catherine Scott-Clark, actually showed an extremely conflicting and contradictory picture of General Musharraf. The story said that while Washington hails Musharraf as an ally in the war on terror, critics make a case that the Pakistani leader is a terrorist, adding that the General had long-standing links with Islamic militant groups in Pakistan given the fact that he had been involved in preparing militants for waging jehad against the Russian forces in Afghanistan. The report said that extremist Islamist groups share a synergistic relationship with the dictatorship of Musharraf due to which he is unwilling to do anything to disturb that bond despite mounting pressures coming from the West.

The *San Francisco Chronicle* report added: "In Musharraf, the West has got the leader it has unreservedly championed for the last nine years, someone it fears it cannot do without, a weakness that Musharraf has manipulated since he signed up to the war on terror in the days after 9/11. It is an increasingly cantankerous and one-way pact that has enabled the growth in power of the most destabilizing factor behind Pakistan's implosion – the one Musharraf never referred to: the Pakistan military itself. Musharraf likes to be seen as a firefighter, and has portrayed himself as a bridgehead between the West and the badlands of Islamic South Asia, where our own spooks and soldiers are rarely able to tread. He has worked hard to finesse his special relationship with the White House, familiarly known inside Pakistan as "Mush and Bush", and it has paid off with Pakistan receiving billions of dollars in US aid".

On 4 December 2007, an research paper produced by the *Observer Research Foundation* (ORF) titled 'Musharraf: Curtain Call', stated: "Before Musharraf is forgotten as another footnote in history, he would be remembered as a military dictator in South Asia who promoted terrorist groups with religious pretext, scripted some of the worst human rights horror stories in the recent past, deepened chasms between communities not only in his country but in the neighbourhood and turned the region over to Western powers to play their own strategic games. For the people of Pakistan, it will be difficult to forgive a despotic ruler like General Musharraf."

The research paper said General Musharraf's worst legacy would be the band of religious extremists and terrorists who have been allowed to run riot across Pakistan, threatening not only life and property inside the country but also in Afghanistan, India and other parts of the world. "If the General had meant what he said, it would have been possible to rein in the jehadis, most of whom have been operating from Waziristan which was allowed to become a sanctuary as part of a strategy. It is naïve to believe that the General and his advisers were not aware of the pitfalls of allowing *Al-Qaeda* and the Taliban to regroup and recoup in Waziristan, a stretch of tribal land bordering Afghanistan where a see-saw battle is on between the Taliban (supported by *Al-Qaeda*) and the NATO forces".

The study report added: "The Pakistan Army views and uses the Taliban as a weapon to destabilise any regime in Kabul which is not friendly to Pakistan. In fact, India's considerable stake in the region is a bone of contention with General Musharraf's troops who consider Afghanistan as Pakistan's 'strategic depth'. In simpler terms, a strong foothold in Afghanistan is critical for Pakistan which considers itself a part of West Asia rather than South Asia dominated by India. What the General failed to factor in was that terrorist groups have a mind of their own. He should have learnt some lessons from recent history that terrorism often devours its creator or creators. The US is a case in point. It was the very set of jehadis created to oust the Soviets from Afghanistan in the early 1980s which executed a kamikaze attack on WTC. The flip flop in Waziristan has the potential of turning the area into an *Al-Qaeda* state. It has become a staging ground for global terrorists, spawning countless offshoots of extremist elements across the world. Pakistan is today home to several of them".

A subsequent book titled '*The General and Jehad,*' also published by the Observer Research Foundation, pointed out General Musharraf's duplicity in dealing with the menace of terrorism even after 9/11. The book highlighted Musharraf's policy of keeping the jehadi option alive as a strategic tool and exploiting the presence of Taliban and *Al-Qaeda* linked terrorists in Pakistan to project himself as a saviour of the country.

The book, authored by Wilson John stated: "Musharraf's projection of himself as a saviour of Pakistan is grossly misleading as terrorist and extremist groups have become more lethal and better networked in Pakistan and Afghanistan during the last eight years of his rule. No other country in the world has spawned and supported as many extremist and terrorist groups as Pakistan. Musharraf had claimed time and again he had been trying to put these jehadi groups in check and had launched several campaigns to rid Pakistan of Islamic terrorists. But nothing can be more misleading".

Therefore, many of his critics say Musharraf's persona could not have been more different from that of General Zia-ul Haq, the third military ruler of Pakistan whose father was a prayer leader. As General

Musharraf had spent some of his youth in Turkey, he had an admiration for Kemal Ataturk, and used to look positively on the role that the military plays in Turkish politics – which is clearly at odds with how the military has seen its own role in Pakistan. The combination of Kemalism and military rule differed significantly from General Zia's formula of combining Islamism with military rule. It appeared at face value that General Musharraf's response to the gradual melting away of the Zia days' infamous Mullah-Military-League alliance was to anchor the military rule in a completely different ideological foundation.

Despite his oft-repeated claims of being a secular and liberal leader, Musharraf eventually turned to rely on the orthodox religious parties to stay in power and to manage civilian-military ties. For self-preservation, Musharraf deliberately weakened the secular political structure, replacing it with a political environment which proved extremely conducive for religio-political militant organisations. Musharraf undermined the Pakistan Muslim League (PML) led by Nawaz Sharif and the Pakistan Peoples Party (PPP) led by Benazir Bhutto, to the advantage of a six-party religious alliance – *Muttahida Majlis-e-Amal* (MMA), and kept making efforts to wipe out support for both the mainstream political parties. Besides appeasing the MMA, often described by critics as the Mullah-Military Alliance, the Musharraf regime continued its linkages with the numerous religio-political militant groupings in pursuit of its geo-strategic agenda for Afghanistan and India.

The Taliban-friendly MMA had been running the provincial governments in the NWFP and *Baluchistan* bordering Afghanistan, following its success in the 2002 general elections. The MMA's government's policy in the NWFP to provide help to religious militancy, combined with Musharraf's strategy of benign indifference towards the Taliban and the Kashmiri militant organisations, led to a perfect jehadi storm. Enjoying substantial freedom under the MMA rule in the Frontier province, the militant groups in the Pak-Afghan tribal belt gained momentum and developed linkages with each other. Soon the Taliban, with its new allies, spread their tentacles from the Waziristan region to Swat and beyond. Besides, some of the militant organisations active in Jammu & Kashmir had by now joined up with these transnational jehad forces. Therefore, Musharraf's role in bringing about *Talibanisation* in Pakistan cannot be overlooked because it is a direct result of his legacy.

General (retd) Musharraf's self-centered policies eventually left Pakistan high and dry and ushered in an era of marked political instability after his exit. Eight years after his military take over, Musharraf, politically isolated, hated by his own people and no longer in command of the Pakistan Army, had to quit as Chief of Army Staff [on 28 November 2007], hardly 24 hours before he was to swear in for a much controversial third term as president. His stepping down as the army chief brought an end to his 46-year-long military career. "I will no longer command... but my heart and my mind will always be with you", he told his officers, trying to hold back his tears. He was certainly unhappy to hang up his uniform, which he had often described as his second skin.

On 16 August 2008, almost eight months after he had shed his uniform, Pervez Musharraf had to quit the office of the president too, in a bid to avoid an imminent impeachment by the newly elected Parliament which was about to vote him out for abrogating the Pakistani Constitution twice. His unceremonious exit from the political scene and the subsequent demand for his trial on treason charges was certainly a watershed that brought to an end a long period of personalised military rule. However, the mess he left behind is one that will not only haunt Pakistan in the times to come but the world as well besides making the world community even more worried about the future of Pakistan where *Al-Qaeda* and Taliban-linked terrorists are becoming stronger and audacious with each passing day.

REFERENCES

1. Pervez Musharraf, *In the Line of Fire – A Memoir*, Simon & Schuster.
2. Pakistan's Double Game, Editorial, *Guardian*, 15 October 2001.
3. John Norris, The myth of the good General Musharraf, *Guardian*, 31 March 2002.
4. Pakistan, a Troubled Ally, Editorial, *New York Times*, 21 September 2003.
5. Pakistan Without Illusions, Editorial, 9 July 2004, *New York Times*.
6. Pamela Constable, Article, *Washington Post*, 2005.

7. Adrian Levy and Catherine Scott-Clark, Friend or Foe?, *San Francisco Chronicle*, 11 November 2007.

8. Musharraf: Curtain Call, *Observer Research Foundation* (OBF), 4 December 2007.

9. Wilson John, *The General and Jehad*, Observer Research Foundation.

CHAPTER 28

Swat Operation – The End of Military-Militant Love Affair

Not too long ago, the picturesque Swat valley in the North West Frontier Province of Pakistan, with its rolling hills, gushing streams and scenic vistas, was described as Pakistan's Switzerland. Celebrated in the Hindu scriptures as *udyan* (garden), Swat is a strikingly scenic place where the Buddha once walked, cultures intersected, poets sang and mystics came in search of peace.

However, suicide bombings carried out by the human bombs dispatched to the valley by the *Tehrik-e-Nifaz-e-Shariat-e-Mohammadi (TNSM)* and the *Tehrik-e-Taliban Pakistan* (TTP) leadership and the subsequent erosion of the state authority eventually prompted the Pakistan Army in May 2009 to launch a decisive military operation against the jehadi mafia in the valley which had taken hostage the local populace. The previous three military operations launched by the Pakistan Army (Operation *Rah-e-Haq* I, II and III in October 2007, July 2008 and January 2009, respectively) had failed to contain the militants.

The process of *Talibanisation* in Swat actually started acquiring an evil ring in July 2006 when Maulana Fazlullah, the son-in-law of the TNSM chief Maulana Sufi Mohammad, and a hothead cleric-turned-Taliban commander, started broadcasting his *Wahabi* interpretation of the Koran and preaching extremist messages to people in the valley. Inspired by the *ameer* of the Afghan Taliban

Mullah Omar, Maulana Fazlullah, a diehard follower of TTP Chief Commander Baitullah Mehsud, soon became a local legend and acquired an army of volunteers in Swat. His private militia soon started enforcing Fazlullah's extremist brand of Islamic *Shariah* in the valley by burning girls' schools and CD shops and destroying the famous Buddha statues in the area, in a bid to turn their dream of installing an Islamic emirate into reality.

Things only got worse with the Islamabad-backed NWFP government being run by a secular liberal Awami National Party (ANP) striking 'peace deals', firstly with the father-in-law – Maulana Sufi Mohammad, and then with the son-in-law – Maulana Fazlullah. The result was quite obvious as the TNSM/TTP militants led by Maulana Fazlullah used these deals to their own advantage by extending their area of influence and strengthening themselves in the valley, ultimately forcing the government to order a massive military operation which turned Swat into a conflict zone. As things stand today, the road to the country's most scenic valley, which used to be an embodiment for breathtaking beauty, now invokes fear and lurking danger.

TNSM – The Black Turbaned Brigade

The *Tehrik-e-Nifaz-e-Shariat-e-Mohammadi* (TNSM) or the Movement for the Enforcement of Islamic Laws is a *Wahabi* militant organisation which was formally launched on 28 June 1989 by Maulana Sufi Mohammad after quitting the *Jamaat-e-Islami Pakistan*. The TNSM's goal has been quite clear since its creation – the implementation of a strict version of Islamic *Shariah* in the entire Malakand region, which includes the districts of Swat, Buner, and Upper and Lower Dir. Therefore, since its inception two decades ago, the TNSM has gradually emerged in the Malakand and Swat division of the North West Frontier Province (NWFP) and in the Bajaur Agency of the Federally Administered Tribal Areas (FATA) as a private militia to reckon with, finally compelling the government to order a massive military operation against the organisation in May 2009.

While Maulana Sufi Mohammad is the central *ameer* of the organisation, the Swat chapter of the TNSM is led by his fugitive son-in-law, Maulana Fazlullah, who is also the *ameer* of the *Tehrik-*

e-Taliban Pakistan, Swat. Sufi had chosen the black turban and black flag as the insignia of his pro-Taliban group, leading to their nickname, "The Black Turbaned Brigade". The TNSM was one of the five militant organisations proscribed by the Musharraf regime on 12 January 2002 under the Anti-Terrorism Act, 2000. In terms of sectarian linkages, Sufi is an ardent believer of the *Wahabi* school of thought and had been associated with some Saudi-sponsored groups from the Afghan war theater of 1980-88.

The TNSM motto is '*Shariah ya Shahadat*' (Islamic laws or martyrdom) which rejects all political and religio-political parties for they follow the western style of democracy. The members of the TNSM, whose leadership openly condones the use of force in jehad, are identified by their shoulder-length hair and camouflage vests over traditional *shalwar kameez* clothing, being the trade mark of Sufi Mohammad, which has become their identity. Ideologically, the TNSM is dedicated to transform Pakistan into a Taliban style Islamic state. In the words of Sufi Mohammad: "Those opposing the imposition of Islamic *Shariah* in Pakistan are *Wajibul Qatal* (worthy of death)."

The TNSM also rejects democracy as un-Islamic: "We want enforcement of Islamic judicial system in totality: judicial, political, economic, *jehad fi sabilallah* (holy war in the name of Allah Almighty), education and health. In my opinion, the life of the faithful will automatically be molded according to the Islamic system when the Islamic judicial system is enforced", Sufi Mohammad had declared in November 2001 shortly before being jailed in Pakistan on terrorism charges.

Who is Maulana Sufi Mohammad?

A Tajik by origin and the father of 13 sons and seven daughters, the 78-year-old TNSM *ameer* Maulana Sufi Mohammad was born in a village of Maidan, in the Lal Qila region of the NWFP's Dir district. He completed his religious education in 1959 from a religious seminary – *Darul Uloom Haqqania* – located in Saidu Sharif, headquarters of the Swat district in the NWFP. After receiving his *madrassa* degree, Sufi Mohammad returned to his native village and started preaching an extremist version of Islam in mosques and *madrassas*. Although he had been to a *Deobandi madrassa*, his long association with Arabs and Afghans during the days of the Afghan jehad against the Russian occupation forces brought him quite close to the strict *Wahabi* school of thought.

According to his close circles, Sufi was not a traditional religious scholar occupied with teaching Islamic duties to a local community. Instead, he was motivated towards establishment of a *Shariah*-based Islamic society where everything from daily life to governance and social services could be administered through the implementation of a strict version of Islam. He wanted to play a lead role in this regard, which led him to join *Jamaat-e-Islami* (JI), a hard-line Islamist party with great influence in the districts of Malakand, Swat and Dir. He remained an active member of the *Jamaat* for years and also participated in the CIA-sponsored Afghan jehad against the Soviet forces.

However, having returned from Afghanistan after the withdrawal of the Soviet forces, Sufi quit the *Jamaat-e-Islami* over sharp differences with his party's central leadership on the issue of electoral politics. He was of the view that there is no place for democracy in Islam and that any party or individual participating in the election process should be regarded as un-Islamic and non-Muslim. This was despite the fact that Sufi Mohammad did contest elections, winning a seat on the district council of Dir district on the *Jamaat-e-Islami* ticket and representing his Maidan constituency for a while. He then launched his own religious organisation in June 1989 – the *Tehrik-e-Nifaz-e-Shariat-e-Mohammadi*. In 1994, he led over 20,000 TNSM followers to block the Mingora-Peshawar road in the Malakand division for seven days by staging a sit-in. The protesters literally cut off the Swat district from the rest of Pakistan, demanding the enforcement of *Shariah* laws in the Malakand division with immediate effect.

Groaning under mounting pressure, the federal government formed a consultative committee to hold talks with the TNSM leadership but Sufi Mohammad and his associates refused to take part in any discussion, standing firm on their one-point agenda – the enforcement of *Shariah* in the strategically significant Malakand division that comprises one third of the NWFP province, and forms the northern part of Pakistan. It is spread over an area of nearly 30,000 square kilometers and has a population of 5.52 million. Malakand Division consists of seven districts – Malakand, Buner, Swat, Shangla, Upper Dir, Lower Dir and Chitral.

It borders Afghanistan's Badakshan and Nuristan Provinces in the north and northwest. In the southwest, Malakand Division shares a border with the Bajaur and Mohmand Agencies of Pakistan's Federally Administered Tribal Areas (FATA). In the east, Malakand Division shares a border in its Chitral and Swat districts with the strategically important Federally Administered Northern Areas (FANA) of Pakistan, which is contiguous with China's Uyghur-inhabited Xinjiang Province in the north. In the south, Malakand Division shares a border with Charsadda-Peshawar, Mardan and Swabi districts of the NWFP.

Acting under pressure, the NWFP government announced the proclamation of an ordinance, declaring the enforcement of *Shariah* in Malakand division. The ordinance was to remain in force for four months. After the expiry of this period, the members of the TNSM again came out on the roads, demanding that the ordinance should have been converted into an Act of the Parliament. However, the government took a firm stand this time and refused to bow to the TNSM pressure. Sufi's angry followers reacted strongly and occupied many of the government buildings including the local airport. This led to armed clashes between the TNSM activists and the law security forces. In the process, Badiuzaman Khan, a member of the NWFP Assembly belonging to the PPP, was taken hostage by Sufi's men who ultimately killed him.

As the security forces cordoned-off the TNSM headquarters to arrest Sufi, he announced to surrender himself and to cooperate with the government. Afterwards, Sufi, accompanied by the security forces personnel, visited all the TNSM centers in the area and asked his supporters to return to their homes. Subsequently, an agreement was signed between the government and the TNSM according to which the TNSM's demand for enforcement of *Shariah* was accepted. On 1 December 1994, Governor NWFP enforced *Nizam-e-Shariah* Regulation through an ordinance to set up the *Qazi* Courts for delivery of speedy justice. In Sufi's scheme of things, the *Qazis* were to enjoy a status higher than the deputy commissioner or the superintendent of police.

Two years later, in 1997, the TNSM activists led by Sufi Mohammad again resorted to agitation, forcing the then Pakistan Muslim League (PML) government, headed by Prime Minister Nawaz Sharif to introduce an amended *Nizam-e-Shariah* Regulation, making the already established *Qazi* courts more effective. The consequences were obvious. TNSM extended its writ outside the Malakand division to the adjacent districts of Hazara and Swat and in the Bajaur Agency. By that time, the Taliban movement led by Mullah Mohammad Omar had already surfaced in Afghanistan and was extending its writ by leaps and bounds after capturing Kandahar.

Within no time, Sufi Mohammad was able to establish strong ties with the Taliban regime, mainly because his group and the Taliban militia had the same religious vision and ideals. That was the time Mullah Omar started funding the TNSM to make sure that the organisational set-up of the group is extended to other parts of the NWFP and FATA.

Sufi's Shot to Prominence

Sufi Mohammad shot to prominence in the aftermath of the 9/11 attacks and the subsequent invasion of Afghanistan by the US-led Allied Forces. He not only issued a *fatwa* or edict ordering a jehad against the US-led forces, but openly recruited people from the Malakand division, before crossing the border into Afghanistan along with around 10,000 volunteers to fight the US troops. According to media reports of 27 October 2001, armed with Kalashnikovs, rocket launchers, missiles, anti-aircraft guns, hand grenades and swords, thousands of the TNSM cadres led by Sufi crossed the Pak-Afghan border. However, many of the inexperienced youngsters Sufi had taken to Afghanistan were killed and hundreds were trapped by various Afghan warlords, who then sold them back to their relatives in Pakistan for huge sums of money.

Upon his return home, Sufi was arrested by the Pakistani authorities and tried under the Anti Terrorism Act, 2000 by the assistant political agent of Kurram Agency in his capacity as additional district and sessions' judge. His speedy trial began on 30 March 2002 and he was sentenced only three weeks later [on 24 April 2002] to seven years imprisonment for inciting thousands of people to cross the Pak-Afghan border and for carrying explosive substances and lethal weapons. Sufi was sent to a Dera Ismail Khan jail in NWFP to complete his sentence after his refusal to contest his case in the court of law. Sufi was of the view that he did not believe in the existing laws which he believed were un-Islamic and that he would never appear in such secular courts.

In the aftermath of his jehadi misadventure, Sufi Mohammad lost much of his support in the Malakand division which was once his support base. As the Musharraf regime banned the TNSM and ordered crackdown against its activists, a majority of his supporters went underground. The TNSM had become almost dormant when Pakistan was struck by a devastating earthquake on 8 October 2005. However, contrary to many other banned militant groups that deemed it fit to resurface under new identities by renaming themselves, the TNSM activists decided against abandoning the original identity of the group.

In the process of helping out the quake affected people, the TNSM, now led by Maulana Fazlullah, the son-in-law of Sufi Mohammad, capitalised on the enormous human tragedy and used it as an opportunity to revive the organisation. As Fazlullah and his volunteers were in the forefront of humanitarian relief work, the popularity of the group once again shot up and the TNSM was able to re-establish its stronghold in the Malakand and Swat areas of the NWFP and in the Bajaur Agency of the FATA (Federally Administered Tribal Areas).

Almost a year later, in the early hours of 31 October 2006, over 80 people were killed in a US predator missile strike on a religious *madrassa* located at Chenagai village in the Bajaur Agency. The strike also killed Maulana Liaquat, a local cleric and incharge of the *madrassa*, besides being a key leader of the TNSM. Although the tribal elders alleged that the missile attack had been launched by the coalition troops stationed in Afghanistan through a predator, the Pakistani military authorities decided to claim responsibility for the attack, saying that it was carried out by the Pakistani forces in view of intelligence reports that the *madrassa* was being used by Taliban-linked militants to train suicide bombers who were being sent to Afghanistan.

A few hours after the October missile attack, Maulana Faqir Mohammad, a senior leader of the TNSM and the elder brother of Maulana Liaquat, announced to avenge the killings of the 'innocent' *madrassa* students by carrying out suicide bombings against the Pakistani security forces. Barely a week later, 45 Pakistan army recruits undergoing military training at the Punjab Regimental Centre Training School in Dargai, about 100 kilometers north of Peshawar, were killed and dozens injured in the early hours of 8 November 2006, as a suspected suicide bomber ran towards them and blew himself up in the middle of the parade ground. The investigators concluded that the attack was carried out by none other than the TNSM to avenge the *madrassa* attack.

The Sufi-Government Deal

Afterwards, there was a significant resurgence in TNSM activities, mostly targeting the security forces, finally compelling the government to sign a peace agreement with Sufi Mohammad on 20 April 2008 and release him from jail after six years of imprisonment. The government had maintained at that time that the deal was meant to restore normalcy to the Swat valley – a picturesque region in the NWFP that had been taken over by the TNSM, being backed by the *Tehrik-e-Taliban* Pakistan. The deal struck by the Awami National Party (ANP) – the only secular party of the NWFP running the government of the troubled province, brought Sufi back to help broker a deal between the government and the TNSM militants led by Maulana Fazlullah.

Under the six-point agreement, the TNSM founder renounced the use of force to achieve its goal of enforcement of Islamic laws in Swat and other parts of the Malakand region. He pledged to respect the institutions of the state, accept the government's right to establish its writ and keep distance from the elements involved in suicide attacks on security forces in Swat and elsewhere. In return, the government withdrew all the pending cases against Sufi, commuted his remaining prison term of four years and set him free unconditionally on 20 April 2008. Signed at the Chief Minister's

House, the six-point agreement stated:

> "Peaceful struggle for enforcement of *Shariat-e-Mohammadi* is the right of every Muslim and the TNSM renews the pledge to carry out that struggle; the TNSM renews the pledge to respect the state institutions so that the writ of the government is established and peace restored in NWFP; the TNSM has no links with those elements involved in attacking the armed forces and the police because soldiers, policemen and other government officials are our brothers and attacks on them are un-Islamic; the TNSM declares that motivation and mutual consultation are the means for enforcement of *Shariah*; all segments of society should extend cooperation to the government to restore peace and establishing the government writ so that people lead a peaceful life; and the TNSM will fully cooperate with the NWFP government, state institutions as well as local administration for restoration of a lasting peace and security of life and property of the people".

Speaking at a news conference soon after his release, Sufi Mohammad said: "We want peace and complete writ of the government. Those people who are bent upon lawlessness will be invited to restore peace through peaceful means, but if they do not refrain from militancy the government will have the right to take action against them. The government has taken the right decision and it will help in restoration of durable peace in the region". However, the critics of the deal maintained that it has legitimised the politics of a banned militant group. They argued that by providing amnesty to Sufi Mohammad and Maulana Fazlullah, many other militant groups were likely to use terror to blackmail the state into submission elsewhere also.

But interestingly enough, almost a week after his release, Sufi disowned his son-in-law, saying that he would not talk to Maulana Fazlullah for showing disobedience to him. However, there were those in the TNSM who said Sufi knew that he had to work hard to take back the initiative from his son-in-law, who had already established himself as the functional commander of the TNSM and strengthened his position by joining hands with Baitullah Mehsud-led *Tehrik-e-Taliban Pakistan*, an umbrella group of 40 militant groups of the Pakistani Taliban operating in South Waziristan, North Waziristan,

Bajaur, Darra Adamkhel and other tribal areas and districts of the NWFP. Therefore, Sufi Mohammad deemed it fit to simply disown Maulana Fazlullah, although some say that it was all planned.

Sufi's move forced the NWFP government to pursue Maulana Fazlullah independently, and eventually strike yet another peace deal [in Swat] with him almost a month later on 21 May 2008. However, the peace deal and the ensuing ceasefire between the military and the militants were finalized only after Sufi had agreed to be a guarantor on behalf of the Fazlullah-led militants. As per the agreement, the government had agreed to allow the implementation of *Shariah* in Malakand once violence had been stopped there.

Though it was not yet announced, a general amnesty for the militants was to cover Fazlullah and his top lieutenants. The government also gave in to the TNSM demand to give back the control of Fazlullah's headquarter in Mamdheray besides allowing him to resume operations of his FM radio station. An 11-member joint committee of government officials, provincial assembly members and TNSM representatives was formed to monitor and implement the accord, because of the worries that problems could arise with regard to the still undecided timeframe for withdrawal of over 20,000 Army troops from Swat valley.

Sufi Mohammad agreed to travel to Swat to discuss the peace move with Fazlullah and his followers. "We will open dialogue with the Taliban and ask them to lay down their weapons. We are hopeful they will not let us down. We will stay in Swat until peace is restored", said Sufi as he reached the valley.

The Fazlullah-Government Deal

The 15-point peace agreement between NWFP government and the Swat-based TNSM/TTP militants stated: "The Taliban of Swat will accept the writ of the provincial as well as central governments of Pakistan and will remain in the ambit of that; *Shariat-e-Mohammadi* will be implemented in Swat and the rest of the Malakand Division; the prisoners will be released after review of the cases; government machinery, law enforcement agencies, government officials, buildings and installations, police stations, policemen, police lines, army, Frontier Corps, Frontier Constabulary, bridges, roads, and electricity installations will not be attacked; there will be a complete ban on keeping private militias, there will be no suicide attacks, there will be no blasts in personal or governmental buildings, and there will be no remote-controlled bomb blasts; the Army withdrawal will be gradual, keeping in view the security situation in the area; non-local militants will be immediately handed over to the government and attacks on barber shops and markets visited by women should be stopped; the government will compensate the deserving people affected by the Swat operation, there will be no ban on health teams administering vaccination or drops to children against diseases like polio and there will be no ban on girls' education; there will be complete ban on display of arms and only arms having license would be allowed kidnapping and car lifting should be condemned and eliminated and all centres used for training militants and use of explosives must be eliminated; speeches will be allowed only on that FM radio which will have license, the local Taliban will cooperate with the government in investigations of cases against those involved in murders, dacoities and kidnapping; the government will be free to take action against thieves, dacoits, kidnappers and others involved in such crimes; and lastly the TNSM headquarters in Swat will be converted into an Islamic university, to be run by a board comprising representatives of the government and the Taliban".

The signing of the deal was severely criticized by liberal and progressive circles which had simply rejected clause No. 2 of the peace agreement – *Shariah*, or Islamic law, be enforced in Swat and the rest of Malakand region by amending the two similar ordinances promulgated in 1994 and 1997. The country's liberal circles had maintained that the enforcement of *Shariah* would place Swat outside the pale of Pakistani state law besides establishing a parallel judicial system. They also doubted Sufi's new role as a peace-broker and that too on behalf of his son-in-law, mainly in view of their long history of extremism and their strong links with the former Taliban regime of Afghanistan.

Even otherwise, it was also a known fact that all such peace deals in the past had miserably failed in bringing peace and stability to the region. Instead, the militant forces had used such deals to gain more power and strengthen themselves. These apprehensions became true hardly a month after the peace deal was signed, as Maulana Fazlullah announced on 18 June 2008 in Mingora that he was breaking the pact temporarily and setting a one-week deadline for the government to implement the agreement in letter and spirit. He said the government has only released 18 of the 50 Taliban prisoners despite giving a commitment that all of them would be set free. However, the government side was of the view that the prisoners were to be released according to a procedure after reviewing their cases, as had been mentioned in the peace accord.

As the five days deadline came to an end, Maulana Fazlullah announced that he had tasked his commanders to attack top government functionaries in NWFP if the government failed to demonstrate serious approach towards halting ongoing military operations against his Islamic militia and honouring the peace accord. In the aftermath of his statement, the peace accord virtually became ineffective, with the TNSM resuming their violent activities in the valley. On 26 July 2008, Fazlullah warned to target the security forces by using suicide bombers if the government re-launched military operation in Swat. He also announced that no more talks would be held with the government till further orders from Commander Baitullah Mehsud, the chief of the *Tehrik-e-Taliban Pakistan.*

As skirmishes between the military and the TNSM militants intensified in Swat by the end of July 2008, the Pakistan Army launched a full-fledged military operation. The government clamped down curfew on the whole Swat district initially to facilitate the military operations and prevent the movement and activities of the Fazlullah-led militants. There were some worrying aspects of the new round of violence in Swat. For the first time there were attacks by suspected militants on three girls' schools and on security checkpoints in Mingora, the twin town along with Saidu Sharif that served as headquarters of Swat district as well as the Malakand division. The attacks alarmed residents of the relatively peaceful Mingora-Saidu Sharif towns and prompted hundreds of families to start migrate to safer places away from Swat.

On 6 August 2008, Baitullah Mehsud threatened to launch countrywide suicide attacks if the government did not stop the military operation in the Swat valley. A few weeks later, on 12

October 2008, the ANP government began negotiations with Sufi Mohammad with regard to the enforcement of the *Shariah* regulations for the Malakand division, as per the May 2008 peace deal. The very next day, on 13 October 2008, Fazlullah announced a unilateral ceasefire after meeting with Sufi Mohammad at an undisclosed location in the valley. The same day, Sufi offered his services to bring back peace to Swat, saying if the government announced *Shariah* regulations for Malakand on his terms, he would bring a halt to the Fazlullah-led ongoing militancy in the valley.

However, in reality, the Fazlullah-led militants never stopped their violent actions and kept extending their tentacles in Swat and its adjoining areas. By that time, Swat had already witnessed eight suicide attacks in less than 10 months (between January to October 2008), killing 77 people, mostly security personnel, prompting the national media to start describing Swat as a lost valley. Hence a January 2008 news report published by daily *Dawn* titled "Desperate moves on to secure Swat – the lost valley" stated: "The second phase of the military operation *Rah-e-Haq* that was launched to regain control of Swat appears to have made little headway. After a year of military operations in Swat, the territory controlled by the terrorists has reportedly increased from 25 percent to 75 percent. The state writ has shrunk from 5337square kilometer area of Swat to the limits of its regional headquarters – Mingora – a city of 36 square kilometers".

The Dawn news report filed by Ismail Khan added: "Known for its green meadows, gushing river and snow-capped mountains, the Swat valley has unfortunately come to relive its historic name, Suvastu – the white serpent. The heavenly valley has gone really bad, and its image distorted beyond recognition. Pakistan's most popular tourist destination is now haunted by death and fear. Militants routinely carry out patrolling in Mingora, where its central square, the Green Chowk, came to be known as '*Chowk Zebahkhana*' (slaughter square). Almost 800 policemen – half of the sanctioned strength of police in Swat have either deserted or proceeded on long leave on one pretext or the other. Only one of the 600 police recruits trained by the military, volunteered to go and serve, while the others plainly refused to head to what is now being called the 'valley of death'."

As the NWFP government and Sufi Mohammad were still busy

in peace talks, the Swat chapter of the *Tehrik-e-Taliban Pakistan*, led by Fazlullah, issued a list of 47 'wanted persons' [on 26 January 2009] including former and serving federal and provincial ministers, incumbent members of the National and provincial assemblies and other prominent political figures, asking them to appear before the Taliban court or face the consequences. "The decision was taken at a *Shura* meeting with Maulana Fazlullah in the chair. Around 50 members of the *Shura* participated in the meeting and there was consensus on the names of 47 people declared as 'wanted' for opposing the Taliban. All of them will have to appear before the Taliban court, or will face action," said a Swat TTP spokesman.

Hardly 48 hours later, Pakistani Army Chief General Ashfaq Kayani went to Swat [on 28 January 2009] to express solidarity with his troops. Saying that the entire Pakistani nation was dedicated to rout the evil of terrorism, Kayani added that the military leadership has the will and resolve to defeat terrorists, restore peace and establish the writ of the state in violence-hit areas. He was actually putting the stamp of his authority on the third phase of *Operation Rah-e-Haq* against the Taliban led by warlord Fazlullah. The message to the troops was no doubt also intended for the rest of the country and for the world community that had become less and less sure about Pakistan's 'will and resolve' after the first two phases of the Swat operation were seen as failures.

As the Pakistani troops accelerated their anti-TNSM operation with a new vigour, Sufi Mohammad unveiled [on 24 February 2009] a nine-point plan for restoration of peace in Swat, asking both the militants as well as the government to fulfil their responsibility by taking steps to bring back calm to the valley. He also asked the Presidency to announce enforcement of *Shariah* for Swat and Malakand to overcome the present state of lawlessness in Swat. He reminded President Zardari that his assurance for peace in the troubled areas of NWFP was conditional with the setting up of an Islamic appellate court named *Darul Qaza* that could ensure speedy justice. Sufi's nine points plan for restoration of peace called for shifting of the Army from schools, houses, mosques, hospitals and other places to safer locations. The plan also urged people from all walks of life to help the TNSM in restoring peace and implementing the *Nizam-e-Adl* (system of justice).

On 2 March 2009, Maulana Sufi Mohammad addressed a press conference in Mingora, demanding the appointment of *qazis* as well as the release of the Taliban prisoners by 15 March 2009. Fresh talks were subsequently held on 5 March 2009 between the provincial government and the TNSM leadership, mainly to salvage the Swat peace accord agreed to a 17-point plan to bring back peace to the violence-hit valley. Besides the formation of a three-member committee to oversee the implementation of the accord, the security forces were made to vacate the Mamdherai headquarters of Fazlullah. However, the control of the headquarters was given to Maulana Sufi Mohammad.

On 7 March 2009, thousands of TNSM supporters offered Friday prayers at Mamdherai headquarters following the withdrawal of the Army after one and a half years. Ten days later, on 17 March 2009, the courts in the Swat valley stopped functioning. Sufi Mohammad said they were against *Shariah* and their functioning was a violation of the agreement signed by the provincial government. On 24 March 2009 Sufi threatened to wind up his peace camp in Mingora if the government failed to enforce the *Nizam-e-Adl* Regulation immediately. At a press conference in Saidu Sharif, Sufi said that he was dissatisfied over slow pace of implementation of the Swat peace accord.

The End of the Love Affair

Two weeks later, on 10 April 2009, Sufi Mohammad finally announced his decision to pull out of the peace deal, saying the government side was not serious about the implementation of *Shariah* in the trouble-stricken region. That was a major development because he was the individual responsible for getting his son-in-law and the commander of the Taliban in the area, to agree to the peace deal. He said that he was left with no other option but to pull himself out of the deal because President Ali Zardari had failed to enforce Islamic law in the valley.

Sufi Mohammad, who had brokered a peace deal between the NWFP government and the Taliban in February 2009, accused the Pakistani President of creating hurdles in the enforcement of *Shariah* in Malakand Division and said he would be held responsible for any resurgence of violence. Yet his son in law, Maulana Fazlullah vowed on 12 April 2009 to stick to the peace agreement despite his father-in-law's announcement, but only if President Asif Zardari signed the *Nizam-e-Adl* Regulation.

On 13 April 2009, the Pakistani media reported that Washington has asked Pakistan to scrap the February 2008 peace deal with the TNSM on the ground that it provides an opportunity for local militants to strengthen themselves and regroup. The reports said that two visiting senior US government officials, Richard Holbrooke, the special envoy to Pakistan and Afghanistan and Michael Mullen, chairman of the Joint Chiefs of Staff, made this demand during their meetings with Prime Minister Yousaf Raza Gilani and Army Chief General Ashfaq Pervez Kyani.

However, on 15 April 2009, the government announced that the *Shariah* courts have formally started functioning in Swat district. But the powers of these courts were limited owing to delay in signing of the *Nizam-e-Adl* Regulation by the president. However, the provincial government of the NWFP announced that after approval of the regulation by the president, these courts would have full powers. Welcoming the setting up of the *Shariah* courts, Maulana Fazlullah said the government has won the hearts of the people of the Malakand division and the Taliban and they would extend their full cooperation to the government.

Giving his reaction, Sufi Mohammad described the Pakistan Army the defender of the country and the nation and asked the militants to lay down their arms after ratification of the *Nizam-e-Adl* Regulation 2009 by the president. However, a few days later, on 19 April 2009 Maulana Sufi Mohammad declared that the Supreme Court and High Courts were '*Ghair Sharaee*' (un-Islamic) institutions and, therefore, it would be '*Haram*' (forbidden) to approach them to file appeals. Addressing a mammoth public meeting at Grassy Ground, he asked the government to abolish regular courts; sack judges, set up *Darul Qaza* for appeal and appoint *Qazis* at all *Shariah* courts by 23 April 2009 throughout the Malakand division as promised in the February 2009 accord.

The TNSM chief said: "We are custodians of Pakistan and its

Constitution, while the judges of the Supreme Court and High Courts, the politicians as well as the feudal lords are their enemies. I refused to be released on bail because the bail under the century-old British law was un-Islamic to me." He then warned the federal government to wind up its judicial system within four days and establish the appellate court of *Darul Qaza* for the Malakand division, or he would re-launch his anti-government protest campaign.

But things came to a head when the TNSM militants resorted to strong-arm tactics in Lower Dir and in Buner districts of Malakand. People had to flee to escape the wrath of vandalizing militants. No amount of pleadings by the ANP leaders made any impact on Sufi Mohammad and his son-in-law. Playing of a video tape on private television channels of a girl being flogged in Swat coupled with uncanny statements by Maulana Sufi, intensification of propaganda campaign and threatening statements by US leaders brought matters to a boil.

On 28 April 2009, the TNSM leadership suspended talks with the NWFP government, making it conditional with the stopping of the military action in some parts of Malakand. The TNSM spokesman Ameer Izzat Khan said no further talks would be held with the NWFP government until and unless the military operations are stopped in Buner and Dir areas. Declining an offer from NWFP Information Minister Iftikhar Hussain for a meeting with TNSM leaders, the TNSM spokesman accused the provincial government of violating the peace agreement besides holding it responsible for any adverse consequence.

Exactly two weeks later [on 3 May 2009], the NWFP government finally announced the establishment of *Darul Qaza* in the Malakand division as President Zardari signed the *Nizam-e-Adl* Regulation at last. However, in a surprised move, Muslim Khan, the spokesman for the Swat chapter of the *Tehrik-e-Taliban* and a close aide of Sufi, rejected the Islamic courts on 4 May 2009, saying the government did not consult either the Taliban or the TNSM on the establishment of *Darul Qaza*, or the senior Islamic appellate court, for Malakand Division.

Muslim Khan said that the *Darul Qaza* has literally been imposed by the government under the shadows of jets bombing and shelling.

We wanted *Darul Qaza* to be so powerful that it could even summon the president, prime minister, Sufi Mohammad and even Maulana Fazlullah to appear before it. "The militants in Swat, Matta, Kabal and Sangla and their commanders have asked for permission to fight everywhere. Since the security forces are attacking us in the neighbouring districts of Dir and Buner, our fighters would now attack security forces and the government figures everywhere. We will also act in other cities of Pakistan but will not target the general public", Muslim Khan added.

Three days later, on 8 May 2009, Prime Minister Syed Yousuf Raza Gilani ordered to launch a military operation against the militants and terrorists so as to flush them out completely from Swat and Malakand in order to ensure security, restore honour and dignity of the homeland and for the protection of the people. "The government will not bow before the militants and terrorists but will force them to lay down their weapons and will not compromise with them. The time had come to show unity in our ranks and stand up against those who wanted to make Jinnah's hostage on gunpoint", the prime minister said during his televised address to the nation.

The same day, Chief of Army Staff (COAS) General Ashfaq Kayani presided over the 118th Corps Commanders' Conference at the General Headquarters in Rawalpindi and said Pakistan was a sovereign state and the people under a democratic dispensation, being supported by the Army, were capable of handling the present crisis in their own national interest. The COAS said the present security situation required that all the elements of national power should work in close harmony to fight the menace of terrorism and extremism. "The Army is fully aware of the gravity of the internal threat and it will employ all requisite resources to ensure a decisive ascendancy over the Taliban militants", he added.

The same day (8 May 2009), President Zardari said the military operations against extremists would last until normalcy returns to the troubled Swat. Addressing a joint press conference along with Afghan President Hamid Karzai and US senators John Kerry and Richard Lugar, Zardari said the world is now fully aware that terrorism is not confined to Tora Bora in Afghanistan or the mountains of Pakhtoonkhwa. There is a realisation in the world that we have to cooperate more to defeat the enemy that we all jointly face".

Immediately after the Swat military operation was formally launched, the Pakistani security forces killed a son of Sufi Mohammad during a clash with the Taliban militants in Lower Dir. It was not clear whether he was the intended target. An Inter Services Public Relations (ISPR) press release stated that during an exchange of fire in Lower Dir, 10 Taliban, including Kifayatullah – son of Sufi Mohammad – were killed. "The operation was launched in an attempt to eliminate and flush out Taliban from the area. During exchange of fire, ten Taliban were killed including Kifayatullah, son of Sufi Mohammad", the ISPR hand out said. However, the TNSM spokesman Amir Izzat Khan said the 43-year-old was killed in helicopter gunship firing in Maidan area.

On 12 May 2009, the military operation entered a crucial stage in Swat when the commando units of the Special Services Group (SSG) of Pakistan Army were dropped by helicopters on the mountains around the Taliban headquarters in Peochar, said to be the hideout of the chieftain of militants in the region, Fazlullah. On 24 May, the Pakistani Army announced that it had retaken large parts of Mingora. The ISPR spokesman Major General Athar Abbas announced: "We want to eliminate the entire leadership of the Taliban".

On 28 May 2009, the government announced a cash reward of five million rupees ($134,000) for the arrest of Fazlullah, declaring him the architect of a Taliban-led uprising in the Swat valley. But the bounty for Fazlullah was revised the very next day [on 29 May] from five million to 50 million rupees in order to speed up efforts for his arrest. On 30 May, the Pakistani military announced that it had regained control of all of Mingora, though small pockets of resistance still remained in the city's outskirts. After retaking the town of Mingora the military moved on to Malam Jabba and Qambar Bazar taking those towns and killing the TNSM leaders of those towns.

On 5 June 2009, Interior Minister Rehman Malik said that Maulana Fazlullah may have been killed in the ongoing military operation in Swat. The very next day, on 6 June, an NWFP government spokesman said that Sufi had been arrested along with his deputy chief Maulana Mohammad Alam as well as his spokesman Amir Izzat Khan, during a raid on Bilal Mosque in Amandara area and have already been shifted to Malakand Fort. But some private television channels quoted the provincial government spokesman as saying Sufi Mohammad had been arrested along with his two sons Rizwanullah and Zia ullah. But the military authorities denied making any such arrests.

The next day, on 7 June 2009, two close aides of Sufi Mohammad were killed in an ambush when they were being transported in the custody of the security forces. "A prisoners' van was carrying the TNSM deputy chief Maulana Mohammad Alam and the group spokesman Amir Izzat from Malakand to Peshawar when an improvised explosive device exploded," the military spokesman Major General Athar Abbas told newsmen at a media briefing. He said the van was attacked by the Taliban militants at 5:10 am with an improvised explosive device in Sakhakot followed by intense firing by the terrorists, killing the TNSM leaders and a junior commissioned officer of the Pakistan army while leaving five security personnel injured.

On 9 June 2009, the Pakistani troops destroyed Fazlullah's headquarters in Mamdherai by blowing up the adjacent *madrassa* building, the mosque and the hostel with explosives. Built near the Swat River, the TNSM headquarters in Mamdherai were described by the security forces as the center of its militant training activities.

On 23 June 2009, Interior Minister Rehman Malik said Fazlullah has been encircled by the Pakistan security forces. Talking to reporters, the minister said Fazlullah had been spotted and there was no question of his escape. "By and large, we know the location where he is hiding. He may be dead, but nothing confirmed can be said at this stage without seeing his dead body". Nevertheless, the military spokesman said the same day at a news conference that he had no information about Fazlullah.

On 6 July 2009, the Pakistani media reported that Sufi Mohammad had been released from the Chakwal district of the Punjab province and had reached Peshawar, the capital of the NWFP. The media reports said Sufi, his wife and other family members were released after nearly two months of detention by a Pakistani security agency. "Maulana Sufi Mohammad was reportedly taken them into protective custody from the Mirpur area of the Pakistani-administered part of Kashmir almost two months ago", stated English daily *Dawn* on 7 July 2007, adding that the TNSM chief was reported missing at the onset of the fighting in Swat.

Sufi Mohammad finally arrested

On 28 July 2009, the Pakistani media reported that Sufi Mohammad has finally been arrested by the security forces along with two sons from his residence in Peshawar. The Maulana was subsequently shifted to the Peshawar Central Prison. A sedition case was subsequently registered against him and his nine colleagues at the Saidu Sharif police station in Swat. The action was taken only a week after the information minister of the NWFP had claimed that "Maulana Sufi Mohammad was history now and the government does not want to make him a hero by laying a hand on him."

On 10 July 2009, the *BBC* reported that Maulana Fazlullah is critically wounded and was close to death. The information, gathered by the *BBC* from interviews carried out in his NWFP heartland said Fazlullah was actually hit in two air strikes, and is critically wounded. However, on 12 July 2009, the TTP refuted reports that Fazlullah was injured during military operation in Swat. Maulvi Omar, a self-styled spokesman for the *Tehrik-e-Taliban Pakistan*, told a journalist on phone that the top leadership in Malakand had gone underground under a plan. "Maulana Fazlullah is safe and the military claims about his being hit having been were totally baseless, he told local journalists on phone from an undisclosed place."

On 13 July 2009, people displaced by fighting in Swat began returning to their homes under a government repatriation programme. Fazalullah subsequently broke his silence on 15 July 2009 after many months and vowed to continue his mission for imposition of Islamic *Shariah* in the Malakand division. In a video message received by a private TV channel, Fazlullah also strongly criticised the Pakistan government for launching a military offensive against them in Swat. On 18 July 2009, Fazlullah addressed the residents of Swat via his illegal FM radio station, the first such broadcast since reports emerged that the Taliban leader was injured during the military operation.

Almost four months later, on 17 November 2009, Maulana Fazlullah told *BBC* that he has escaped to Afghanistan and was planning new attacks on Pakistani forces. "I have reached Afghanistan safely. We are soon going to launch full-fledged punitive raids against the army in Swat". The *BBC* reporter in Peshawar who spoke to the Taliban leader said that the voice was recognisably Fazlullah's – he has a very distinct way of pronouncing words. "I have spoken to him on several occasions and met him twice. Fazlullah was calling from an Afghan number and sounded in good spirits when he called".

From Fazle Hayat to Mullah Radio to Maulvi Fazlullah

Popularly known as Maulana Radio for the illegal FM radio stations he used to run to instigate people for taking part in jehad, Maulana Fazlullah became a house hold name in the Swat valley due to the fierce resistance his privately raised army gave to the Pakistan army when it had first launched the military operation in the picturesque valley on 22 October 2007 to rout the TNSM/TTP militants and dismantle their jehadi infrastructure.

The Pakistani intelligence circles believe that Maulana Fazlullah, whose private army gave a tough resistance to the security forces in Swat under his command, has growing links with Taliban and *Al-Qaeda* operatives, thereby turning the NWFP and the FATA regions of Pakistan into havens of extremist elements. It was on 13 July 2007, hardly two days after the *Lal Masjid* operation came to an end, that General Musharraf approved a plan for immediate deployment of the paramilitary forces in Swat to crush the growing militancy. On 24 October, over 3,000 Pakistani troops were sent to Swat to confront Taliban forces that were massing in the district in a bid to impose *Shariah* law in the valley. The Pakistani troops were deployed to the hill-tops of the rugged terrain.

However, the Fazlullah's forces, being backed by the TTP militants, soon proved to be the nemesis of the Pakistan Army, with many of its *jawans* either beheaded publicly or killed in suicide attacks within a short span of two weeks after the operation was launched. On 25 October, barely two days after the operation began, 33 army soldiers were killed and 22 others injured in the Mingora town of the Swat district as two suicide bombers rammed their explosive-laden car into a truck carrying the paramilitary Frontier Constabulary personnel. The attack was carried out by a TNSM suicide bomber following a warning by Fazlullah against the deployment of the forces in the area.

The Maulana told his followers on his FM radio as soon as the security forces entered the area that the troops had been deployed to kill innocent people in a ruthless military operation and thus the military should be resisted with full might. This led to an intense series of gun battle between the well-armed TNSM/TTP militants led by Fazlullah and the Pakistani security forces in four subdivisions of Swat – Matta, Kabal, Charbagh and Khwaza Khela. The fighting spread to the hills almost immediately, with the militants attacking the military posts and the troops targeting their hideouts.

The situation took an ominous turn when Fazlullah joined hands with the *Tehrik-e-Taliban Pakistan,* led by Baitullah Mehsud, in a bid to provide an umbrella to all insurgent movements operating in several tribal agencies and settled areas of NWFP. Maulana Fazlullah was thus made the *ameer* of the Swat chapter of the TTP. Fazlullah, therefore, announced that he and his followers would now be toeing the TTP chief, Baitullah Mehsud's line, whether they are signing a peace pact with the government or dumping a ceasefire agreement.

The gun battle between the military and the militants in Swat that started with the launching of the military operation lasted for next six months, before the new government assumed power in Islamabad as a result of the 2008 general elections and signed a peace deal with Maulana Fazlullah on 21 May 2008. It took the coalition government comprising the secular Awami National Party and the Pakistan People's Party and the Fazlullah-led militants hardly three rounds of talks spreading over 13 days to reach the peace accord. The 16-point handwritten accord in Urdu was described by analysts as a comprehensive document of give-and-take by the two sides.

A Roller-Coaster Ride

Maulana Fazlullah's ascend to prominence has been like a roller-coaster ride. He is a resident of the Mamdheray area in Swat who was born on 1 March 1975 at the house of Biladar Khan, a Pukhtun of Babukarkhel clan of the Yusufzai tribe of the Swat district. He passed his secondary school certificate from the village school and then took admission at Government Degree College Saidu Sharif, Swat from where he passed his intermediate exam. Till then, he was known as Fazle Hayat who finally became a daily wage earner – an operator of a manual chairlift on the famous River Swat. Having worked there for a few years, Fazle Hayat left Swat and he went to Maidan town in Lower Dir district to join *Jamia Mazahir-ul-Uloom* – a religious seminary run by Sufi Mohammad.

It was Sufi Mohammad who had renamed his student from Fazle Hayat to Maulvi Fazlullah, and then chose him to be his son-in-law. He returned to Mamdheray after completing his religious education and began imparting religious education at a mosque-cum-*madrassa*. Fazlullah has, however, admitted he was not a *mufti* (Islamic scholar), has no *madrassa* certificate and has only received early religious education from his father-in-law. While tracking his rise to prominence, one comes to know that like thousands of others TNSM activists, Fazlullah too went to Afghanistan in November 2001 along with his father-in-law, Sufi Mohammad, to fight alongside the Taliban there.

Upon their return home, Fazlullah was taken into custody by the Pakistani security forces along with Sufi Mohammad and few of his comrades and sent to the central prison in the Dera Ismail Khan district of the NWFP. While Sufi was sentenced for ten years, Maulvi Fazlullah was luckier – he was released after 17 months in prison, on charges of inciting youngsters to illegally cross the Pak-Afghan border to wage jehad against the Allied Forces. In the absence of Sufi Mohammad, Maulvi Fazlullah came forward and emerged as a popular *Wahabi* militant leader through his activities, mainly using his clout as the son-in-law of Sufi Mohammad.

While his father in law was behind bars, Fazlullah made his native village Mamdheray the TNSM headquarters and got it shifted from

Kumbar, Dir to Mamdheray, Swat. The next step was the reorganisation of the TNSM. Fazlullah appointed two *shuras* or councils to assist him in the decision-making process. One was the *Ulema Shura* with several senior Swati clerics who used to advise him about the religious policies of the group. Another *shura*, called the executive body, was the highest policy making organ of the TNSM, having many ex-servicemen, including retired commissioned officers of the army, as its members. He further created his private army and named it as Shaheen Commando Force which was meant to establish his authority in Swat and which had established a parallel administration in the valley by dispensing summary justice besides regulating traffic and patrolling villages and towns.

Fazlullah then decided to enforce his own version of Islam in the valley by using his FM Radio, commonly known as 'Mullah Radio' in a big way. Being a fiery orator, Maulana Fazlullah attracted local people through his sermons and reportedly earned the support of women who urged their men folk to grow beards and donate money to his seminary. The essence of his sizzling speeches had been none other than the TNSM motto: "*Shariah ya Shahadat* (Islamic laws or martyrdom)". He used to warn parents through his FM channel against sending their girls to schools unless they observe full *purdah*. Barbers in the area were under standing instructions not to shave beards, while shops were proscribed from selling CDs and music cassettes. He had also ordered his followers not to administer polio drops to their children. Reason: the polio drop was part of an US-Zionist plot to render them sterile.

For Friday prayers, a vast strip of land had been leveled near the TNSM's Mamdheray headquarters to accommodate a large number of people from almost all villages of Swat. After the Friday prayers, Fazlullah, who was fond of riding a black steed, used to make a riding show (with himself on a black horse) in the same ground, so that the people could have a glimpse of him. His rantings were typical of those subscribing to the intellectual tradition of the Taliban. Before the start of the military operation in Swat, Fazlullah had a fighting strength of 5000, with an added 1000-member Shaheen Commando Force that used to patrol the streets with guns placed on their vehicles.

Mullah Radio had first turned against the Pakistani security forces in the aftermath of the July 2007 *Lal Masjid* operation in the heart of Islamabad. As soon as the Operation Silence was concluded, Maulana Fazlullah came into action against the security forces to avenge the military operation. A large number of people armed with rifles, Kalashnikovs and small arms started gathering at his *madrassa* [while the operation was still in progress] after he had announced that it was time to go to war. His announcement that thousands of the TNSM militants were ready to avenge the *Lal Masjid* 'attack' was followed by a series of suicide attacks in the NWFP, targeting the Pakistani security forces.

With the dawn of 2007, Fazlullah had announced plans to construct a TNSM headquarters, a *madrassa* and a mosque at Mamdheray in Swat and appealed to the people through his FM Radio station to generously fund the project. The people in Swat and its surrounding localities subsequently donated over Rs 38,00,000 within the first 24 hours of the appeal (as per his own claims). Constructed over 10 kanals of land on the bank of River Swat, Maulana Fazlullah received a huge donation of Rs 35 million from the TNSM followers till October 2007 when the army decided to launch an operation there and take over the under-construction TNSM headquarters, which were eventually blown up after the start of a fresh military operation in the Swat valley in May 2009.

In July 2009, the Pakistani security forces claimed they had achieved their main objective in Swat by recapturing its administrative seat of Mingora which had been seized by the TNSM and TTP militants, led by Maulana Fazlullah. The armed forces' victory claim was crucial from the point of view of a larger front which *Al-Qaeda* and Taliban linked militants had been trying to create in the Switzerland of Pakistan – Swat, which is just 160 kilometers from the federal capital – Islamabad. However, the Army's victory claim suffered a major blow in the third week of February 2010 when a suicide bomber riding a car targeted a military convoy in Mingora, the capital of Swat, and killed 10 people.

A subsequent editorial by *Daily Times* on 24 February 2010 stated: The attack on a military convoy in Mingora should be enough to open our eyes to the threat that still persists in the areas declared as 'cleared' by the military. That innocent civilians are being killed in these bombings does not seem to bother the attackers, as long as their goal of terrorising the populace and taking the security forces by surprise is served. The military maintained that the main areas had been cleared and it was doing mop-up operations on the fringes. What it did not take into account while declaring its victory was that, by its very nature, guerilla struggle is a protracted war. The guerillas move away when they are under pressure and live to fight another day. It was inevitable that they would not regain the kind of foothold they had in Swat earlier, which was achieved through a mixture of intimidation and terrorisation of the local population through force of arms and promises of a better system of governance and quick and cheap justice. But once the momentum of the military offensive slowed, it was the ideal time for them to strike again. And that is what they did, shattering the calm of the area. It is necessary to prepare the public to fight a long war. Conceded that the force of the militants in Swat has been eroded considerably, and the writ of the government has been re-established, but the militants have gone back to subversion tactics, which fritter away the resolve of the fighting force as well as the people. Hence, premature claims of victory and the triumphalism of the army were premature. Make no mistake: the Taliban are here to stay for a long time and we had better not let our guard down.

Therefore, many security experts argue that counter-insurgency operations cannot be a one-time action, and it would be wrong to conclude that the Swat militants, after suffering setbacks in the valley, will give up their fight altogether. Analysts say the 'shape and clear' phase of the Swat military operation is almost complete. The intense kinetic mission is over but military action is still underway against sporadic pockets of resistance. The 'hold and build' stage of the operation is now unfolding. Definite judgments can only be given once the stabilisation efforts make more headway. At the same time, however, a decisive action to uproot the enormous infrastructure of the Pakistan-based jehadi organisations active in India and Afghanistan is the only viable option to rehabilitate the writ of the state and regain the trust of the masses in the ability and determination of their elected government as well as the military leadership to seize the growing *Talibanisation* of Pakistan.

REFERENCES

1. Ismail Khan, Desperate moves on to secure Swat – the lost valley, *Dawn*, January 2008.
2. Report, *BBC*, 10 July 2009.
3. Maulana Fazlullah, *BBC*, 17 January 2009.
4. Maulana Fazlullah, Video Message, 15 July 2009.
5. Maulana Fazlullah, FM Radio Speech, 18 July 2009.
6. Maulana Fazlullah, *BBC* Talk, 17 November 2009.
7. Editorial, *Daily Times*, 24 February 2010.

Index